DYLAN HAD A DREAM
THAT TOOK AMERICA BY STORM

After years as a recluse, Bob Dylan went back to his roots. He hit the road with the most glittering rock circus ever assembled. Joan Baez, Ronee Blakley, Robbie Robertson, Mohammed Ali, Rubin "Hurricane" Carter, Joni Mitchell, Gordon Lightfoot, Kinky Friedman, Ramblin' Jack Elliot, Arlo Guthrie, Albert Grossman, Bobbie Neuwirth —plus an assorted cast of groupies, hookers, pickers, crazies, criminals and saints—made the Rolling Thunder Revue a cosmic experience. And this is how it really was out there . . .

ON THE ROAD WITH BOB DYLAN
By Larry Sloman

Including 16 pages of
on-the-spot photos

On the Road With Bob Dylan

~~~~~~~~~

Rolling With the Thunder

~~~~~~~~~

By Larry Sloman

BANTAM BOOKS

TORONTO · NEW YORK · LONDON

ON THE ROAD WITH BOB DYLAN
A Bantam Book | June 1978

Cover photograph of Bob Dylan by Mary Alfieri

ACKNOWLEDGMENTS

Quotations from In Search of the Miraculous *by P.D. Ouspensky, copyright 1949 by Harcourt Brace Jovanovich, Inc., renewed 1977 by Tatiana Nagro, are reprinted by permission of the publisher. The lyrics to "Ride 'Em Jewboy" and "Asshole From El Paso" by Kinky Friedman, both copyright © 1973 by Glaser Publications, Inc., are reprinted by permission of the author. An excerpt from "A Voice Still Blowin' In The Wind" by Neil Hickey, copyright © 1976 by Triangle Publications, Inc., Radnor, PA, is used by permission of TV Guide. The poem, "Sunrise Ceremony Verse Improvised With Australian Aborigine Song-Sticks at Request of Medicine-Man Rolling Thunder, November 5, 1975" by Allen Ginsberg, copyright © 1977 by Allen Ginsberg, is reprinted by permission of the author. The lyrics to "On the Rolling Thunder Revue" are reprinted by permission of Roger Cowen. "The Singer" by Tom Pacheco, copyright © 1976 by Chappell & Co., Inc., and Huckleberry Creek Music, is used by permission of the publishers. A quotation from "Is Dylan Interested in Money? Small Clubs Give Way to Arenas" by Mike Madden is reprinted from* Variety, *November 12, 1975, by permission of the publisher. The lyrics to "Shadows and Light," copyright © 1975 by Crazy Crow Music (BMI), and "Coyote," copyright © 1976 by Crazy Crow Music (BMI), both by Joni Mitchell, are reprinted by permission of the publisher. The lyrics to three untitled songs by Leonard Cohen are reprinted with his permission. In addition, portions of this book were originally published as "Bob Dylan and Friends on the Bus: Like A Rolling Thunder" by Larry Sloman in* Rolling Stone, *Issue #201, December 4, 1975, and as "Dylan Tour Snowballs: It's Not a Nightclub Show" by the editors in* Rolling Stone, *Issue #202, December 18, 1975, both copyright © 1975 by Straight Arrow Publishers, and are reprinted here by permission of* Rolling Stone.

ISBN 0-553-11641-X

Published simultaneously in the United States and Canada

Bantam Books are published by Bantam Books, Inc. Its trademark, consisting of the words "Bantam Books" and the portrayal of a bantam, is registered in the United States Patent Office and in other countries. Marca Registrada. Bantam Books, Inc., 666 Fifth Avenue, New York, New York 10019.

PRINTED IN THE UNITED STATES OF AMERICA

Dedicated to

my parents
Lynn
and the memory of Phil Ochs

Acknowledgments

Literally hundreds of people helped with this book but a few must be singled out. George Lois, the Greek Godfather of this effort, can't be thanked enough. David Blue helped to kick it off, as did Abe Peck. George Barkin made the early going less tedious. Lynn came out of nowhere. Lola Cohen did some invaluable legwork. Debbie Weiner put me up in Boston. Keefe Laundry gave me Ex-Lax when I was upset. The film crew kept me alive. Hope Antman accepted the charges. Ron Delsener offered us shelter for the storm. St. Robin fed me for three months while I was writing. Dr. David Leibling added the salt. Crazy Benny furnished me with tape. Naomi and Mildred kept the lines open. Rocky Singer, Marie Brown, Rona Wyeth, and Ciel Reisner transcribed the garbled tapes and typed the massive manuscript. John Brockman, superagent, sold it. Tobi Sanders bought it and whipped Ratso into shape. Jim Cusimano and Lou Gorfain read it through, carefully and critically. All those I left out did their bits wonderfully. You shoulda been there . . .

I once asked Gurdjieff about the ballet which had been mentioned in the papers and referred to in the story "Glimpses of Truth" and whether this ballet would have the nature of a 'mystery play.'

"My ballet is not a 'mystery,'" said G. "The object I had in view was to produce an interesting and beautiful spectacle. Of course, there is a certain meaning hidden beneath the outward form, but I have not pursued the aim of exposing and emphasizing this meaning . . ."

I understood from what he said subsequently that this would not be a ballet in the strict meaning of the word, but a series of dramatic and mimic scenes held together by a common plot, accompanied by music and intermixed with songs and dances. The most appropriate name for these scenes would be "revue," but without any comic element. The "ballet" or "revue" was to be called "The Struggle of the Magicians." The important scenes represented the schools of a "Black Magician" and a "White Magician," with exercises by pupils of both schools and a struggle between the two schools. The action was to take place against the background of the life of an Eastern city, intermixed with sacred dances, Dervish dances, and various national Eastern dances, all this interwoven with a love story which itself would have an allegorical meaning.

—P. D. Ouspensky
In Search of the Miraculous

Preface

Minsky was my first hero. Minsky was a Jewish hood who wore a black leather motorcycle jacket, carried a greasy black comb in his back pocket, hung round the benches in Forest Park in Queens, occasionally spitting or cursing at homos or stealing weaklings' basketballs. He was always flicking his burned-down cigarette at least fifteen feet in a marvelous blazing arc, all of which in 1958 was grounds for pariahhood.

But I loved Minsky, I loved his mountain slope of a pompadour and his perfect Elvis sneer and the incredible knack he had of holding a can of beer in one hand and fielding a grounder with the other, dropping his glove, picking up the ball, and throwing the runner out at first with a behind-the-back fastball. And Minsky was my hero because he was going out with Kathy Muldoon, a beautiful Irish redhead who lived in my building and who escorted me home from the park every afternoon, riding me up the elevator to my floor, then giving me a sweet, mischievous smile as I gaped at her boobs.

But then we moved to Bayside, leaving Minsky and Kathy Muldoon and Forest Park light-years behind. And I started going to high school and I cultivated a new hero, Andy Bathgate of the Rangers. But it wasn't the same. Then, I wandered into a music store on Bell Boulevard in June of 1965 and picked up the latest Top 100 list and noticed a strange name at Number 43. The entry read "Like a Rolling Stone—B. Dylan."

I got furious, steaming to myself about this Dylan character trying to rip off the Stones name, riding to fame on their boot heels. In anger, I bought the single. It changed my life.

Oh, that sound! That rapturous organ and that searing guitar and that mocking piano. And that voice, that half-sneer, half-lullabyic razor of a voice. The next day I took my father's car for the first time since I had finished Driver's Ed and I drove into Flushing where Gertz had a sale on Dylan's *Highway 61* LP. $1.88 in mono.

And the album finished me off. Those incredible songs, "Tombstone Blues," "Ballad of a Thin Man," "Highway 61 Revisited," "Desolation Row." There I was, a nice Jewish boy, almost in the suburbs, with an after-school job reconciling bank statements for the accountant down the hall, ready to start Queens College and pick a nice, safe, respectable career, like accounting.

After *Highway 61,* I rushed back to Flushing and, one by one, I picked up all the other albums. And listened, really listened. Then I started going to the Village, to the Paul Sergeant store that was mentioned in the liner notes to *Highway 61,* then to MacDougal Street, finally to the Players Theatre, where the Fugs were setting new standards for perversity and honesty.

So when I spotted a small ad for a Bob Dylan concert in February of 1966, in White Plains, I immediately wrote for two tickets, one for me and one for my friend Fiegelberg, who had a long leg cast as a result of a skiing accident.

The night of the concert I was on pins and needles, enthralled at the prospect of seeing Dylan live, in the flesh! My parents drove us out there, then left to take in a local movie. I walked and Fiegelberg hobbled to our seats, in the rear but at least on the floor. And, after an hour's wait, Dylan strode onstage.

He did a stunning solo set, the classic folk ballads, some of the middle-period love-hate songs, then the new, intense stuff, like "Freeze-Out" (later to be released as "Visions of Johanna") and "Desolation Row." A quick bow and he was off.

After the intermission, the lights dimmed and five strange-looking figures wandered out onstage and plugged into amplifiers. And then Dylan was back, in an olive box-checkered suit. And I heard the most incredible rock music of my life. But all too fast, it was over, Dylan taking a final half-bow, then pausing to wave to someone in the audience. I stumbled into the lobby in a haze.

My parents met us and we walked to the car, Fiegelberg and me climbing into the back seat. After a few minutes, my father half turned to us.

"So how did you like it?" he asked.

"It was incredible. I loved it!" I managed to answer over the din of all those songs still running through my head.

"It's funny," my father shouted, alternately turning to us, then checking the road ahead, "when we came to pick you guys up, we got there early and two people were leaving so I got their stubs and went in to look for you. I walked right up the aisle, right up to the front. That noise!" He held his head in one hand and shook it.

"You what!" I shouted. "You walked by us? I didn't see you. Which aisle? How far up did you go?"

"Right up to the front. The first row. I looked up and saw Dylan from about ten feet away." My father chuckled.

"What! You saw him that close. What did he look like? What was he wearing? Suede boots? What kinda shirt was that? Did he see you? What did he look like?" I was starting to repeat myself.

My father just shrugged and looked back at the road. "What are you getting so excited about?" he shouted, one hand on the wheel, the other punctuating the air. "He didn't seem like anything special. The songs seemed nice, loud but nice. But he didn't look so hot. What are you making such a fuss over? He was a small, ordinary guy. He looked like a shipping clerk," the old man said with finality. With that, I slumped back down into the seat and rode the rest of the way home in silence.

The next day I ran into someone from Kew Gardens who told me that Minsky had been busted.

On the Road With Bob Dylan

1

To begin at the beginning, you'd have to go back to the old folkie days of the Village or maybe just the set of *Pat Garrett and Billy the Kid* or maybe even the old auditorium of Hibbing High. Who knows where Dylan first got the idea, really decided that he wanted to go out again and do what it was that he does so well. Namely, tell the tribe the news of the hour. Depending on who you speak to, you'll get a hundred different versions of how the Rolling Thunder Revue idea was crystallized. Some say it was Bobby Neuwirth's pet project, a guerrilla attack on the hamlets of Middle America. Others credit Ramblin' Jack Elliott with the original idea. Still others believe it was Bob's all along, that he was only waiting for the right time and people. No matter, it happened. With a vengeance. Guitar sounds filled the air, Scarlett's haunting gypsy violin presiding over the clatter in hot, musky gyms and clean, stainless-steel auditoriums. The Rolling Thunder Revue was a caravan of gypsies, hoboes, trapeze artists, lonesome guitar stranglers, and spiritual green berets who came into your town for your daughters and left with your minds. They took to the road in the fall of '75, a weird karass, Dylan, Baez, Mitchell, Elliott, Neuwirth, McGuinn, Ronson, Blakley, Ginsberg, it went on and on, and you'll meet them all here, sooner or later. And they barnstormed for six weeks, shaking up the great Northeast, making a quick foray over the border into the land of snow. Then, with a bang at Madison Square Garden, playing to twenty thousand in a benefit for Rubin "Hurricane" Carter, it was over. At least, until Dylan decides to round up the troops, pack up the guitars, and head your way again.

But to begin at the beginning of this story, we might as

well flash back to a lazy Indian-summery Sunday night in October 1975.

I remembered that Sammy Walker was playing at Gerdes Folk City on Third Street, so I walked in. Typical Gerdes night: Allyn (she's a girl) was tending bar, owner Mike Porco was tending Allyn with a hawk's eye. A few patrons at the bar. Inside, in the music room, Walker was onstage singing about Patty Hearst and her scorpions. My eyes scanned the room and stopped short at center rear. Ensconced at the table near the men's room was none other than old friend Roger McGuinn and party.

McGuinn is one of the rock 'n roll hall-of-famers. With Chris Hillman and David Crosby, he founded America's greatest rock band, the Byrds. And long after Crosby departed for the greener pastures of CSNY and Hillman founded the Burrito Brothers, McGuinn was still plugging away as a Byrd. Then around 1970, he started anew, first fronting a small combo, then going out solo and doing the folkie harmonica neck-rack bit. And it was hard years for the man who gave us "Eight Miles High," and the definitive hard-rock version of "Tambourine Man." The solo Byrd never really got off the ground, so Roger went back to a combo idea and re-formed the Roger McGuinn Band. And here at Gerdes up from a date in Philly, were Roger, his guitarist, Richard Bowden, and his road manager, Al Hirsh.

I joined Roger and his party and Porco came by and bought us all a round of drinks. Porco, of course, is best known in the music biz as one of the first discoverers of Bob Dylan. Dylan's first professional appearance was at Mike's original club on Fourth Street, and in those days, Porco was like a father to Bob, making sure that he had his cabaret cards, and generally looking after the ragamuffin minstrel.

Porco has fathered many a rising star over the years; among the headliners who first got their careers moving at Gerdes are Simon and Garfunkel, Judy Collins, and Phil Ochs. And that night, in that same folk tradition, Sammy Walker, a teenager from Norcross, Georgia, was onstage singing a selection of songs from his first album on the small folk label, Folkways Records. And among those songs was "Ragamuffin Minstrel Boy," a tribute to Dylan, whom Walker resembled both musically and physically. McGuinn was listening intently, enjoying the new-comer, and at one point, after I egged him on a bit, he agreed to do a guest number with Sammy—only McGuinn did it in his own inimitable fashion. Since Roger's an electronics freak, he carries around two two-way walkie-talkies wherever he goes, so Hirsh was dispatched to the stage where he whipped out his gadget, and held it up to the mike.

"There's some that's born in New York town," an eerie, disembodied voice floated over Hirsh's walkie-talkie into the microphone, and McGuinn became the first guest star to sit in from his seat. But after the cackly sea chanty, "Heave Away," the audience screamed for more, so Roger vaulted up to the stage, borrowed Sammy's guitar, and broke into "Chestnut Mare," the compelling saga of a boy and his horse that Roger cowrote with Off-Broadway director, Jacques Levy.

Apparently the singing had built up Roger's appetite, so we all headed down to Chinatown for a late dinner. And over martinis, the talk turned to Dylan. "I've been hanging out a lot with Bob in Malibu," Roger told us, "playing basketball, and stuff. One day, he was sitting on my couch and we were trying to write a song together and I asked him if he had anything and he said he had one that he started but he was probably gonna use it him-self and he started playing 'Never Say Goodbye.' He hadn't written all the verses yet, but he had the tune. I liked it, but it was his.

"He's really brilliant, but sometimes he acts naive, like there are gaps in his perception and if you fill in the spots for him, he really freaks out.

"We once were talking about the airplane Bob used to have and I asked him if he would charter it out when he wasn't using it and he said no. And I said, 'Well, that's what people do who have those airplanes, you gotta char-ter it out in order to pay the maintenance because they're too expensive to keep otherwise. Even everybody who's really rich charters them out and stuff.' And Bob said, real wide-eyed, 'Nobody ever told me that before.' What a great line."

It was getting on to 2 A.M. and McGuinn was set to pack it in and go back to his room at the Gramercy, but I suggested we stop for a nightcap at the Other End. Roger demurred. "C'mon, Roger, I hear Dylan just got into town and even if he's not there I'm sure Levy'll be there." So we took a cab over to LaGuardia Place, jumped out, and rang Jacques' bell. No answer. Roger led the way around the corner to the Other End. Bleecker Street was unusually quiet, almost eerie with a moist mist floating in. Something was in the air. I led the way into the club and immediately saw owner Paul Colby, who, at the sight of us, frantically summoned us to a side table. We turned the corner, and hidden in the first niche were two tables that had been pushed together. I scanned the tables and saw singer David Blue, Off-Broadway director, and McGuinn song collaborator Jacques Levy, assorted other nondescript friends, and, hidden in the center of this motley crew, a black-jacketed Bob Dylan. "Roger!" Dylan screamed out, and lunged to hug McGuinn, spilling most of the drinks in the process. "Where you been, man, we been waiting for you all night."

By then a large crowd was observing and Levy suggested we go someplace a bit quieter. "Let's go to Menachem's," Bob interjected. So we trudged out of the Other End, Dylan and McGuinn in the lead, the others slowly following. "Hey Roger, we're going to go out on tour, wanna come with us?" Dylan was cajoling McGuinn, who seemed to be still recovering from the greeting. We hit the sidewalk outside the club and Dylan turned to me. I introduced myself. "Oh, *you're* Larry Sloman. I heard you were doing an article on Hurricane Carter. Did ya see him, how is he?" I began to answer but got cut off when a nervous teenager squeezed between us and asked Dylan if she could shake his hand. Dylan peered at her quickly, then broke into a smile. "Sure." She grabbed his hand and began a monologue about how much Dylan had changed her life. Bob began to look a bit uncomfortable and we got rescued by Lou Kemp, Dylan's friend, who steered our party to Bob's car: a cherry-red Eldorado. Jacques, his friend Muffin, Kemp, and I piled into the back seat, and Dylan, McGuinn, and Bob's friend Mike jumped in the front. Dylan careened around the Village, made an incredible left onto MacDougal, and pulled up in front of the Olive Tree. But Menachem had already called it a night, so we trudged across the street, to the Kettle of Fish, an old hangout for the folkies in the early '60s. As we crossed the street, Dylan picked up on our conversation about Hurricane Carter, the boxer who's spent ten years in jail in New Jersey for a crime he never committed. "You're doing a story, good, he needs that, that'll be a big help. So will the song I did. We got to get that out, get it out right away. Maybe you could put some pressure on Columbia, Larry. You can lean on them, you got some pull there."

Inside the Kettle we took two tables, Dylan, Eric Frandsen, a folksinger friend, Muffin, and me at one; Kemp, McGuinn, Levy and Mike at the other. Dylan and Frandsen were talking about obscure songs and movies, and Dylan seemed really animated. He reached for his Remy and it tipped over. "Oh, I must really be drunk," Bob moaned. Kemp ordered another one, and Dylan started to talk about his new album. I told him about Jake and the Family Jewels, a great Village band ripe for a big breakout. "Have you heard my new band?" Bob interrupted. "They're great. That Rob (Stoner), he's got such a pretty voice." "Did you ever see his Elvis collection?" I asked Dylan. "He's got this incredible Elvis scrapbook, with really rare articles." "Hey listen, Larry," Dylan leaned in, "you wanna go on the road with us and cover the tour?" "Sure," I pondered, "I could probably cover it for *Rolling Stone*." "Hey Louie," Bob screamed back at Kemp, "Larry's going to go out with us; sign him up. It might as well be him, I'd rather have him do it than anyone else." Dylan swung back and leaned across the table at me, preoccupied with Hurricane again. "We're gonna get him out in ninety days." "Did ya hear what Ali said at Trenton the other day?" I asked Dylan. "He predicted that Hurricane would be free in three days." Dylan didn't blink, "We're gonna get him out in ninety days, that's our slogan, ninety days or we fight." "You mean ninety days after the single's released," I corrected. Dylan smiled. "Yeah, after release."

Bob seemed restless and his hungry eyes scanned the room. "See that painting up there." He pointed to a canvas over the bar. "I remember coming in here in the '60s and always seeing that painting." The talk then turned to old friends, songwriters Phil Ochs and Kinky Friedman.

"Keenky," Bob mimicked, "who's Keenky?"

"C'mon, you know Kinky. You love him."

"Well, Kinky's all right, but he's too sensitive. You know what Kinky's problem is, he came just a little bit too late."

It was 4 A.M. and Kemp made his move. "C'mon Bob, let's get out of here, we got a lot to do tomorrow."

Dylan looked hurt. "Aw, c'mon, lemme finish this drink, then we'll split." I mentioned that Thursday night there was going to be a surprise birthday party for Folk City owner Mike Porco and Dylan's eyes lit up. "Hey Lou, you got that man, a surprise party for Porco Thursday night, what time man?" I gave him the details and he got up and said good-bye to me and Roger. Dylan and his entourage filed out of the Kettle leaving me, McGuinn, and Levy and a bevy of astonished patrons.

McGuinn still looked stunned. "And you didn't want to go to the Other End. You schmuck," I laughed. Roger managed a nod, and we shook hands, and stepped out into the MacDougal Street morning. It was raining hard now so McGuinn hailed a cab as I walked home to the sound of thunder. Rolling thunder.

2

It was a different Village that Dylan returned to in the summer of '75. On MacDougal Street, instead of the Gaslight Cafe, where Kerouac had read his jazz-backed poetry, Lord Buckley had spun his moralistic word-weavings, Hugh Romney (later to be Wavy Gravy of Hog Farm fame) had done stand-up comedy routines, and countless folksingers, Dylan included, had sung and strummed for whatever the basket that circulated in the audience could reap, instead there now was a Middle Eastern boutique with a special on strawberry incense. Across the street at the Cafe Wha?, which once boasted the sounds of Jimmy James, later to be known as Hendrix, was a months-old marquee and a shuttered door. Further up the block at the historic junction of Bleecker and Mac-Dougal, the Figaro, the archetypical Beat-era coffeehouse, had been closed for years. And the Blimpie Base that seemed a harbinger of the decay of the early '70s—even that had gone out of business. The Cafe Au go go, where Tim Hardin, Odetta, and Frank Zappa and the Mothers first tried out their acts in New York, was long gone too.

In their wake, the sleaze merchants had scurried in, with armful after armful of schlock Indian garments, head-shop paraphernalia, falafel stands and T-shirt emporiums. The music was gone, with the hard rockers heading east for the grime of the Bowery and the new bars that dotted the derelict strip. For the sophisticates the chic venues were the gay-dominated discos and nightclubs, places like Reno Sweeneys and Les Jardins, all further uptown. The only club that was still thriving in the Village was the Bottom Line, and to get a booking there you usually had to have a record contract and support from the label.

But in June, the old Bitter End, long a folkies hangout

7

and closed for a year or so, reopened as the Other End, featuring a bar and restaurant next door to a few-hundred-seat cabaret. The Village music scene quickly coalesced around Paul Colby's place, so it was no surprise that Dylan was drawn to the club. But it was quite a shock to see Dylan actually hanging out, munching on a hamburger, talking to strangers, shuffling across the saw-dust-strewn floor over to the cabaret section to soak in some music. The reclusive icon, he who retreated her-metic-style to Woodstock after a much-publicized motor-cycle crash, who holed up in the upstate mountains, only coming down every few years to release an album, who swooped out to the West Coast to play an enigmatic role in a movie his friend Kristofferson was shooting, and then settled by the beach in Malibu, still the recluse, who relished his privacy and was never known to make a fool-ish move, what was he doing hanging out, soaking up the streetvibe, haunting the old haunts? Something was, as they say, blowing in the wind.

Dylan was about to create. After all, it had been al-most a year since the sessions that produced *Blood on the Tracks,* an album that many had felt was a triumphant comeback for Dylan. And the *Basement Tapes* which Columbia had released that summer were, as everybody knew, a compilation of years-old demo tapes that Bob and the Band had recorded the year he was recuperating from the accident. And when you're carrying a muse like Dylan's, sometimes you have to pick up the guitar, pack up the suitcase, and let the road bring you back to the starting point.

So Dylan was back, walking down the same streets, drinking in the same old bars, meeting some of the same old people. And as the word spread, some of Dylan's friends began to seek him out. One of them was Sheena, a raven-haired itinerant singer-songwriter, who had known Dylan for a few years, once even writing a song with him about Krishna consciousness called "Come to Krish-na," a song that Bob gave her. Sheena started peppering Dylan's studio with notes that read, "Please contact me," and she left offerings and incense. Then early one after-noon in June the phone rang in her Lower East Side pad.

"Sheena?" a male voice.

"Yeah," Sheena replied, fighting off sleep.

"This is Bob."

"Bob who?" Sheena questioned.

"The real one," Dylan replied.

And what a surprise, since a moment earlier she had actually been dreaming about him, so she went right into a discussion of her new band, and told Dylan about this dynamite black female bass player she found. "Wow, that's just what I'm looking for," Dylan bubbled and they made plans to meet for coffee and talk.

"Bob said he wanted to check out my band," Sheena related, "so we went up to my friend's loft on Seventh Avenue and it was a heavy trip, they didn't know Bob was coming, so we just strolled in. And he was wearing this black leather jacket that he was so excited about, he kept saying, 'How do you like my new leather jacket.' It was from 1968 or something from his first motorcycle or maybe the accident, someone had sent it back to him. So this guitarist in the band who is really an uptight envious jerk walks over to Bob and says, 'You look like what's-his-name, Bob Dylan. I can't stand that guy's music, I think he stinks.' And Bob was just looking at him so I said, 'It's time to go.' But I'll tell you something about Dylan, whatever situation he's in, he is completely there. He gets completely wherever he is at the moment. I mean there is no other moment. So already he was buying a loft like the one I brought him to.

"So anyway we decided to leave the place, and we were riding around and I said, 'Where do you wanna go now?' and he said, 'Well, I would really like to go visit my friend, how'd you like to go to Paterson, New Jersey, with me? I got this book from this guy who's in jail, his name is Rubin Carter.' But we decided it wouldn't be the best thing to do to take a woman to jail so now we were gonna go to Harlem to hear some music. Like he was literally searching for musicians. I took him to see the bass player I was playing with but she was real big and fat and he took one look and said, 'Uh uh, she's not the bass player I was thinking about.' "

So they hopped back into the car, Dylan behind the wheel and Sheena peering out the window, talking animatedly now about her band. They drove aimlessly now, down Second Avenue, heading toward the East Village, when Dylan spotted this woman with hair down to her waist, carrying a violin. "I know what you need for your band, you need a violinist," he enthused. "Should we stop?"

Sheena assented and rolled the window down, as Dylan screeched to a stop.

"I asked her where she was going and she said she was going to a rehearsal uptown and I asked her if she could play that violin and she said yeah," Sheena remembered, "and I asked her if she needed a ride, it was almost as if I was seducing her in a roundabout way, 'cause Bob was so shy, he didn't say a peep and I've got a big mouth. She told me later that she thought I was a prostitute and Bob was my pimp and we were trying to get her into the ring. But she got into the car and we told her my name was Sheena and his name was Danny and we had just come back from Europe and we were from Hungary and we were so hungry. Bob and I were both laughing, talking about how hungry we were, really piling it on her."

Once in the car, the threesome headed over to the Village, to Dylan's studio, and once there, the violinist, who told them her name was Scarlett Rivera, took out her instrument and started playing. Dylan picked up a guitar and started into "One More Cup of Coffee," a new song as yet unrecorded, and Scarlett joined in. "Hey man," Dylan nudged Sheena, "she ain't bad, she's good, she's real good." By now Scarlett had recognized "Danny's" voice, having grown up on his songs, and she was a bit dazed, jamming with Dylan being a far cry from her current gig making twenty dollars a night playing in a Latin band. A friend of Bob's dropped by and the foursome headed uptown to a jazz club, but first they stopped by the Other End where Dylan eagerly introduced Scarlett around—"She's in my band, she's gonna be in my band," he boasted.

Dylan was a familiar sight that summer in the Village, walking down MacDougal Street, sometimes with guitar in hand, usually with a notebook. And he began to make all the music scenes, catching Muddy Waters, Buddy Guy, and, one night at the Other End, the rage of punk rockdom, a twenty-eight-year-old rock poet Patti Smith. Patti, a gamine Keith Richards look-alike, had always dreamed of meeting Dylan, and when she heard Dylan was in her audience she began playing the set to him, throwing him lines like, "Don't you go near my parking meter, Jack." And afterward, Dylan headed backstage to meet the New Guard. "He just sat there and didn't say a word the whole show," Faris Bouhafa, a Columbia Records employee, remembered, "and afterward, he went backstage, opened the door, and Patti was sitting there by herself. And a couple of photographers. It was weird because as soon as he walked in, she looked up, they were introduced, and suddenly this weird ballet started taking place. The participants were the two photographers, Dylan, and Patti. They were just circling, almost like slow motion. Nobody was saying, 'Hey I want you to take my picture,' they were all trying to avoid the cameras. And the photographers were trying to line them up, and they were all sort of dancing around the room, with a shy kind of smile, almost bashful. Finally Patti said, 'Fuck it, Bob, let's take a picture,' and she grabbed his shoulder and that broke the ice, they started talking. They didn't seem to have that much to say to each other. She was happy and he was smashed so it all worked out very well."

One of the people that Dylan bumped into that summer was Jacques Levy, an affable, fortyish, off-off Broadway director, who gave up a promising career as a clinical psychologist to direct avant-garde plays like, *Oh! Calcutta!* But in his music circles, Levy gained recognition as Roger McGuinn's lyricist, penning numerous songs over the years with the ex-Byrd. And as Dylan and Levy renewed their friendship at the Other End, a collaboration was discussed. So the two trekked over to Levy's loft, just around the corner from the club, and Dylan began performing some of the songs he was working on. "We were just sitting, just talking, then he sang something and then he went to the piano, sat down, and he started to play 'Isis,' " Levy recalled later. "But it was a very different style of 'Isis' than you hear now, it was almost a dirge, slow, unlike anything I'd ever heard before, slow, obviously setting you up for a long story. So the two of us started working on that together. I started writing words, then he would say, 'Well, no, how about this, what about that,' a totally cooperative venture. It was just extraordinary, the two of us started to get hot together. And we began to work on this thing and we just kept going with it, and we'd stop and we didn't know where the story was gonna go next."

"It's impossible to remember now who did what, it's like we'd push each other in the sense that he'll have an idea, then I'll have an idea, then he'll have an idea until finally we get to a point where we both recognize what the right idea is and what the right words are and whether it comes from him or from me it doesn't make a difference. I knew I had found it amazing, he found it amazing. Well, he has written a few songs with other people before, but I don't think it's been this kind of way. This was really a thing of both of us trying to find the right word."

"Whose songs were whose?" I asked Levy.

"Well, it's hard to know, it varied with every song, honestly, there are some songs that started out because Bob has a tune. Like 'Durango' . . ."

"Wasn't 'Durango' written during *Pat Garrett?*"

"The story has nothing to do with that. What happened with 'Durango' was that he had a kind of Mexican melody and we were talking about 'Durango' but the first thing that came was an image I had from a postcard that was once sent to me by Jack Gelber, the playwright. He sent me a postcard with a picture of a Mexican hacienda or something, some Mexican shack not a hacienda, a shack with a bunch of chili peppers on the roof in the sun. So the first line was 'Hot chili peppers in the sun,' and I remember saying, 'No, *blistering* sun,' so we got the first line. And then there was this escape."

"You know what Dylan told me? He told me he was eating chili peppers every morning," I laughed.

"He was eating chili peppers, that was when we were staying out in East Hampton, but I should go back to the story I was telling you before about how we started to write. What happened was that we finished Isis that one night, up all night till the next morning, not the final version, we redid some stuff, but the basic story was there and I would write this stuff down and then type it up and we would go over the stuff. And we went down to the Other End and Bob read the lyrics to a bunch of people sitting around the bar, just read them, and everybody responded to the thing because everyone gets hooked in that story, apparently. The two of us didn't know that at that time, I mean we were getting hooked."

"You know what I thought, I read a story by D. H. Lawrence called 'The Man Who Died,' the story about Christ meeting Isis . . ."

"It doesn't have anything to do with that, it doesn't have anything to do with the Egyptian goddess either. The only thing it has to do with the Egyptian goddess is that at some point we threw in the pyramids instead of the Grand Teton Mountains which is probably really what it's about. Going up into the hills somewhere in Wyoming or something."

"Where does the story come from?"

"I don't know the story of that. I don't know how that story came about and Bob doesn't either. It came about through the two of us, just a kind of unconscious connection we were making."

"Who wrote 'One More Cup of Coffee'?"

"Bob had written that before we got together in the summer. He had written a couple of songs. . . ."

" 'Sara'?"

"No, he had not written 'Sara.' Bob wrote that during the time that we were out in East Hampton. You see what happened is that we finished 'Isis' then we wrote a couple of other songs, but what was happening was that we were going out and hanging out late at night and we were getting together the next afternoon and there were lots and lots of distractions. So we said, 'Let's get out of here,' and suddenly it became serious that we were really going to do some serious work together, so we went out to a place out in the Hamptons. Nobody was around, and the two of us were just there for like three weeks together, that summer. We had already written a couple of songs so there was a feeling of confidence that we both had that we could really do it. Some of the songs that we've been doing, one of the things about them that's so wonderful is that they give him a chance to do some acting. Some of the things that happened with us over that period in the summertime was that feeling that Bob had is that he was really open, ready to come out, ready to express how he felt about things, and as far as I was concerned I couldn't have been happier. I know I was spurring him and he was spurring me."

"That's what he needed, I think."

"He was doing all right without me," Jacques chuckled.

"That's true, *Blood on the Tracks* was a great album. Did you ever hear the original takes? They're chilling, really down to the bone . . ."

"I'll tell ya, I had never listened to *Blood on the Tracks*. I had heard of *Jack of Hearts* on the radio and Bob sang a couple of love songs from the album to me because I'd never heard them before. He played 'Idiot Wind' and

'Simple Twist of Fate' and I thought they could be better than they were and he's gone ahead now and changed 'Simple Twist,' he's gotten more into the plot, there's much more of a plot now. Well, I love stories and plots, I think they're just great, there's nothing like 'em. They may be window dressing, you know, because they're really not what's really important, but even—"

"Even 'Sara,' a song about his wife, has a plot. Like a fucking movie, with flashbacks."

"You know, that takes place because Bob was in East Hampton at the time. And he was writing all during the time that we were working on these other songs. And he was out on the beach and the place out there was a place that he and Sara had stayed at. But calling it 'Sara' isn't that amazing. He's been fooling around with that idea for years, he told me."

"So what was it like out in the Hamptons? Were you just woodshedding, writing the whole thing . . ."

"Yeah, right, we were doing that, going out at night shooting eight-ball once in a while, but not too much."

"Any people visit?"

"No, nobody at all. We went out a couple of nights, one night we went to a bar and Bob sang a couple of the songs and we hung out with some people that night just to get away from things. The pressure was tremendous and intense on both of us, and we'd stop in the middle of a song and go shoot a game of eight-ball."

They returned to the city in late July and Dylan immediately began preparing to record the tunes that he and Levy had just crafted. And by the night of the first session, Monday, July 28, Dylan had assembled a cast of musicians that was Felliniesque in its scope. Crammed into Columbia's studio that night were superstar guitarist Eric Clapton, his backup vocalist Yvonne Elliman, Kokomo—an eight-member English rhythm-and-blues funk band, Emmy Lou Harris, a country-rock singer, studio musicians like Hugh McCracken and Vinnie Bell. Then there were the Village stalwarts, people like bassist Rob Stoner, who was currently backing long-time Dylan pal Bobby Neuwirth, Eric Frandsen, who'd been picking his folk guitar around the Village for years, and even Sugar Blue, whose regular gig was blowing harp out on Eighth Street for spare change. And thrown in for good measure, Scarlett and Sheena. It was like a total madhouse, musicians wandering around in the studio, with no charts to aid them, only the very haphazard directions from Dylan, who also didn't seem to know what he really wanted in terms of a sound. "No one in that room had heard the material and I'm pretty sure Bob didn't know what he was gonna do," one observer recalled, "so everybody was improvising and you could tell that on the tapes. Sometimes it sounds too slick, because all these musicians were used to doing studio work, and sometimes it sounds like two different songs recorded at the same time."

They ran through about seven tunes that first night, a take of "Durango" with Eric Clapton on guitar that ultimately was used on the LP; two songs, "Wiretappin' " ("Wire tapping, it can happen") and "Money Blues," that never were released; "Catfish," Dylan and Levy's ode to Catfish Hunter; "Mozambique," and "Oh Sister." But there was no focus, and Dylan was unhappy with the results. "That was amazing," Clapton later told a *Rolling Stone* interviewer. "He was trying to find a situation, you see, where he could make music with new people. He was just driving around, picking musicians up and bringing them back to the sessions. It ended up with something like twenty-four musicians in the studio, all playing these incredibly incongruous instruments. Accordion, violin—and it didn't really work. He was after a large sound but the songs were so personal that he wasn't comfortable with all the people around. He even wrote on the spot. All in one night. It was very hard to keep up with him. He wasn't sure what he wanted. He was really looking, racing from song to song. I had to get out in the fresh air 'cause it was just madness in there."

Mad enough to cut a long, nearly *disco* version of "Hurricane," Bob's song about boxer Rubin Carter, complete with backup singers chanting, "Hurricane, Hurricane." And Tuesday wasn't much better. Clapton and his entourage had gone but the elements were still too disparate and the session petered out to an early end. Afterward, Stoner, who as bassist had become the de facto bandleader by watching Dylan's fingers and communicating the changes to the rest of the musicians, met with Dylan and DeVito and they decided to try to record with a smaller group. Since Kokomo was departing, a drummer was needed and frantic calls were put in to Jim Gordon

and Kenny Buttrey, two studio musicians who had previously worked with Dylan. No luck. Then Stoner suggested his drummer, Howie Wyeth, and on Wednesday
night, it was a skeletal crew that tromped into the studios.

Emmy Lou Harris was still around to sing backup,
Stoner and Wyeth would function as the rhythm section,
Scarlett would play the lead instrument, violin, and Sheena could kick in on whatever percussive instrument she
could fathom. Dylan himself alternated between piano and
guitar. And it worked. By now Stoner and Scarlett were
semifamiliar with the chord changes, Wyeth fit right in,
and the atmosphere was no longer like a rock 'n roll circus.
Dylan started by warming up with some Little Richard
tunes, then Emmy Lou got loose with some country standards. Then Dylan went straight into a slow version of
"Isis" and the magic began.

Sheena remembered that day: "Wednesday night, that
was the album. I thought it was very special, like when
those who were really chosen to come will be there to
make the candle shine. Dylan had called me that afternoon and he told me that he couldn't sleep much because
the energy was so high, so intense, all this commotion,
and magic, and trying to do this art form. Like you get all
these vibrations. But it all sifted out. By Wednesday, he
felt very comfortable and very relaxed, it was three wom-
en, and three men, that was number six, a good number. It
was very balanced."

For journeyman bassist Stoner the explanation was a
bit less mystical: "Right away that version of 'Isis' was a
take because it was a small group, there was no confusion,
and the first time that Bob got through a tune, it was a
take, it was right there. That's the way he likes it and
that's the way the whole album ended up. Right after we
finished 'Isis' Bob came over to me and said, 'Your drummer's great, it sounds great,' and we all felt great because
it was intimate. It had the sound that you can hear on
Desire, just a bunch of people playing in a room with no
overdubs, all live, happening right before your ears, and
we could get that first-take spontaneity because we didn't
have to keep going over and over things to show them to
all these musicians who were faking it. Because nobody
was faking it, except Scarlett and myself who were good
at that sort of thing.

"So after we listened to that take of 'Isis,' we just went back into the studio and started running through tunes, bam, bam, bam, just getting every complete take, every complete tune was a take. If we got through it all the way, it was a record. Just like that. We were so hot we did 'Rita Mae,' which wasn't on the record, 'One More Cup of Coffee,' 'Joey,' 'Mozambique,' 'Hurricane,' 'Oh Sister,' 'Black Diamond Bay,' we did them all that night. We were just going bam, bam, bam. I think we were still doing takes as late as 5 and 6 A.M. that morning, and we hung out listening to the playbacks until we had to go out to the street to move our cars at 8 so they wouldn't get towed away. Otherwise, we might have stayed there for another twelve hours."

The atmosphere was electric that morning, everyone high on the knowledge that the bulk of the album had been completed, after so many false starts. And already Dylan's mind was racing as he drove back to the Village, dropping off the band. "He felt that he had succeeded, from the playbacks, from the vibrations," Sheena recollects, "and he immediately started talking about a tour. He said, 'Oh man, I would really like to take this band out on the road, I'd really like to go on the road with everybody.' That was what was on his mind. For the road. One more cup of coffee. For the road. For the road. Everything was like getting ready to hit the road. Like he was very enthusiastic, turned on, alive, he became youthful again. It was a whole new phase in his life and like big stars, you get bored, man, you need inspiration. And Dylan who is such an entertainer in his own right, just loves being entertained himself."

But the planning for a tour would have to wait because Dylan was due in court that morning to testify as a character witness on behalf of Clive Davis, former president of Columbia Records, who was under indictment for income-tax evasion. So it was a weary troubador who showed up for the Thursday night session, accompanied by his wife Sara, who had the perfect cynical attitude toward the rock world, an almost weary detachment that was evidenced when Sheena bounced over to her and bubbled: "Isn't this exciting? I'm so excited and I feel so good. How do you like this?" "Well," Sara shrugged, "it's just another one."

It was a quiet session, a lot of listening to playbacks, a stab at a new song, "Love Copy" that would not make the album. But then, Dylan suddenly turned to his wife and said "This is for you," and broke into the compelling song he had written for her that summer in the Hamptons. No one had heard it before, but Stoner and Scarlett and Wyeth picked up the tempo, Scarlett playing some exquisite fills, underlining the melancholy of the lyrics. They ran through it in one take, and everyone seemed stunned, there was dead silence. People eyed Sara for a reaction but she seemed impassive. And then Dylan came into the control room and a friend of Sheena's broke the spell, asking him the name of the song. "Sara," Dylan shot back, annoyed, "Part One."

The next night, Friday, was devoted to a listening party. Neuwirth dropped by, the tequila was flowing, the major work was behind. For each song, they had three basic tracks to choose from, one take of Dylan on guitar, one take on piano, and one take from the big-band sessions of Monday and Tuesday. And as they played back, Dylan was constantly badgering Neuwirth, asking how that one sounded, how this other one felt, how a third one might go over. It was as if Dylan trusted Neuwirth more than himself.

But the atmosphere was light, a solid album was under their belts, and a few of the participants decided to reconvene at producer DeVito's West Side apartment to continue the party and talk about the possibility of a tour. So they left the studio around 6 A.M. and headed uptown, DeVito and his date leading the way in his little sportscar, Dylan, Sara, Neuwirth, and Levy following in their giant rented Buick, and Stoner and Brouhafa picking up the rear. It was Saturday morning, the traffic was light, and Dylan was mischievously feisty, so when DeVito stopped at the first red light, Dylan just came right onto his rear and started pushing DeVito across the intersection. And soon it became clear to DeVito that there wasn't going to be any such thing as a red light that morning, from 52nd and Madison all the way to 79th and Riverside Drive, through the park, across Central Park West, Columbus, Amsterdam, every time DeVito slowed down, Dylan was on his ass, crashing the sportscar through every light. They finally got to Broadway and 72nd and hit traffic so DeVito relaxed, braked, and stopped at the light, knowing well that Dylan would never . . . thud. The Buick careened into DeVito's rear, knocking off the license plate and slowly inching the hapless producer across Broadway.

Once at DeVito's, the talk turned to the possibility of taking the new group out on the road. "Dylan started explaining how he wanted the tour," Brouhafa recollected. "He was really getting indignant. He said, 'You know that play *The Fantastiks?* It's been running for ten years Off-Broadway, man, how come they won't let us do that. They'd never let us get something together that would last ten years.' He seemed to be feeling real paranoid. And he said that what he really wanted was the kind of tour that would last forever. He would start it off and then he would be able to go home and two months later, if he was bored, he could call up and find out where it was and take a plane and join it. Just join the tour for a couple of weeks and then leave. And all the other artists in the country would do the same thing. He mentioned Crosby Stills Nash and Young, McGuinn, Patti Smith, all those people, wherever they were in the country, whenever they had time off, they would always know that there was this show. It was very important to him that everybody know that there was this show going on, on an ongoing basis around the country, and all you had to do was call a number to find out where it was.

"Everyone thought that it was a great idea and someone asked what we should call the tour and Dylan said he wanted to call it the 'Montezuma Revue.' And then he had this idea that it should be self-contained. Our own sound system, our own crew, buses, and we would be able to call up a school on two or three days' notice and just say 'Hey, do you have a stage available.' All they have to do is provide a stage and we would come in with a sound system, lights, everything, and announce the show the day of the show on the radio station or something, pass the word, sell out, and go on to the next place. Totally unannounced. We were even thinking of having our own tickets so that no school or promoter or concert hall would have to worry about anything. We would just call up and ask if they had an empty stage. Wherever there was an empty stage, we could perform, sell our own tickets, pay for expenses, be all self-contained. Nobody had to be hassled. Just three or four buses traveling around the Northeast. Haphazardly."

So the only problem that remained was getting the initial financing for the somewhat Utopian venture. De-Vito and Brouhafa felt that Columbia would provide the backing and Brouhafa left the meeting and began to draw up a proposal to submit to his supervisors at the record company. Meanwhile, Dylan and his wife left New York for a stay in Minnesota, and the musicians returned home to await word.

That Monday, Brouhafa submitted a four-page memo to some of the CBS brass. It was a comprehensive syn-thesis of the early discussions translated into corporate bureaucratese, outlining the premises of the tour. It was a heady proposal, brash, confident, yet careful to point out the potential gains to the corporation. And it really wasn't such an unreasonable idea now; in a mass society fragmented by big business and big government, certainly there should be room for that spark of individual en-trepreneurship, that return to the intimacy and warmth of the extended family. Certainly Dylan could once again be in the artistic vanguard, packing up his family and friends, jumping on the bus, and rolling out to deliver his visions in the simplest, most unfettered way.

Brouhafa received Columbia's reaction to the proposal a few days later, a simple, direct, one-word response, penciled in along the top left of the first page. It was "Bullshit!"

But that had been months before, and near the end of October, Dylan was seriously enacting the pipe dream of the summer. Independently and without assistance from giant corporations like Columbia, Dylan was surround-ing himself with his own people, people like Louie Kemp, hardly your typical rock entrepreneur. An old camp buddy of Dylan's, Louie owns three huge fish-processing plants, but Kemp's first splash into the world of rock was on Dylan's last outing, the 1974 tour with the Band, where Louie played companion and protector. And, after that, it was back to the salmon, until he got a call from Bob in early September.

One of the first things Kemp did was to contact Barry Imhoff, a rotund rock impresario who looks a little like a Jewish Nero. Imhoff cut his teeth in the music business apprenticing for rock's premier producer, Bill Graham. He left Graham, under somewhat strained circumstances during 1975, and headed east to New York where he formed Zebra Productions with the financial backing of Steve Greenberg, who had made a fortune publishing a tip sheet for the Wall Street crowd. Kemp, who had met Imhoff during the Dylan/Band tour that Graham's organization had handled, knew little about the technical aspects of touring, so Imhoff would coordinate the sound, lighting, and security, leaving Louie free to keep a wary eye on Dylan.

And that's exactly what Kemp was doing the night of the surprise birthday party for Gerdes Folk City owner, Mike Porco. The rumors were all over the Village that Dylan would show up at the club. So by 9 P.M. the usually sparsely populated room filled to the rafters. Mel Howard, the tour film's producer, was hanging around outside the club, and inside the film crew was setting up, using the cover that they're working for NET doing a documentary on the Village scene. The place was packed with celebrities, hangers-on, and the simply curious. Phil Ochs, who'd been battling his own private demons of late, was downing one Tequila Sunrise after another. Then Tom Waits wandered in, in shabby sport coat and floppy cap, looking like he walked straight out of a Kerouac novel. David Blue was talking with Eric Anderson, and in walked Dave Van Ronk, who gave them both a big bear-hug greeting. There was a strange feeling of being in a time warp, with the Old Guard joined tonight by the new, Village stalwarts like Patti Smith and singer-songwriter Tom Pacheco. Even rockabilly stars Commander Cody and his Lost Planet Airmen limoed down from their uptown gig to check out the scene.

Outside, the sidewalk was littered with the human refuse of the Village streets, winos, ambulatory schizophrenics, smack heads, all panhandling or hassling pedestrians or just fighting among themselves. Inside, the festivities started, with local folksinger Jack Hardy doing a tepid set to the half-attentive audience who kept eying the entrance to see when the Stars would arrive. Rosie, a short, pudgy, brassy woman who wears scarves around her head and regularly serves as the M.C. for the Tuesday night hoots, decided it was time for the cake and she dragged Mike up to the stage for the presentation, only to drop the cake just as she handed it to him.

Finally, the call came, and Mel Howard reported that Dylan and company would be down at 1:30. By that time, McGuinn, who was never one to arrive too soon and had been hanging out outside in a limo, decided to mingle inside. Finally, the cherry-red Cadillac swooped up. Kemp jumped out, followed by Neuwirth, and a wary Bob Dylan, followed by a youthful-looking Joan Baez. They zoomed in, and rushed right over to the bowled-over Porco to offer birthday greetings. Mrs. Porco grabbed Dylan as he walked by. "Hey Bobby, remember me?" "It's Mike's wife," he cracked into a smile. "Hey Neuwirth, remember Mrs. Porco?" They retreated to a booth in the far rear of the club, but Rosie had already seized the opportunity. "Ladies and gentlemen, we have a lot of surprises for you tonight," she gushed into the mike. "Here's the greatest star of all, Bob Dylan." Dylan got up from the table and grabbed Baez and they made their way onstage, joined by Rob Stoner on acoustic bass. "We're happy to be here tonight," Dylan announced. "Happy birthday, Mike, and many more," Joan added and they broke into a slightly off-key rendition of "Happy Birthday." The crowd seemed stunned, not believing Dylan and Baez were actually up there in front of that tacky Spanish mural.

Dylan leaned over to Joan, conferred a minute, and then they began "One Too Many Mornings," Dylan on acoustic, Baez harmonizing along with her arm on Dylan's shoulder. But suddenly, Stoner snapped the bridge right off his bass and Dylan seized the moment to escape, obviously tired from a day-long rehearsal and the previous night's activities. "Let's turn the stage over to Ramblin' Jack Elliot," he grinned. But Rosie had other plans. She was entreating Eric Anderson, who had joined Dylan onstage for the last aborted attempt at "One Too Many Mornings," to remain. "What a beautiful hunk of a man," Rosie blurted into the mike. "Don't cover up baby, we want to see all of you Eric."

But Jack had already moseyed up to the stage and he soon started into "San Francisco Bay Blues," a Jessie Fuller song that was popularized by Richie Havens. Meanwhile, back at Dylan's table, someone introduced Tom

Waits to Dylan. "How ya doing, man?" Waits growled in that unmistakable gravel-lined voice of his. Dylan broke into a wide grin. "OK man, how are you?" he growled back. They chatted on a bit, Dylan responding to each of Waits' statements with a letter-perfect imitation.

Meanwhile, Jack finished his song. He leapt over a few tables like a cowboy Errol Flynn, and made his way back to the entourage. And Bette Midler, who had arrived a bit earlier with Atlantic Records President Ahmet Ertegun, vaulted onstage, dragging along guitarist Buzzy Linhardt. She belted out a creditable version of the oldie, "When Will I Be Loved?" Not one to be outdone, Rosie regained the stage and cracked, "Let's hear it for the wonderful Betty Miller." Back at Dylan's table, Neuwirth shook his head in amazement. "I can't believe it, she's like the Borscht belt."

But the crowd called Bette back for more, and she sang with Buzzy on the song he wrote that became her theme of sorts, "Friends." And it seemed like there was no end to this surreal hoot night, with star after star inheriting the stage. Eric Anderson and Patti Smith got up to duet on "Sweet Surprise," and as the song concluded, Eric gave a humble bow in Dylan's direction. Meanwhile, Neuwirth was wearing Dylan's gaucho hat and a black mask, and with his thin moustache he resembled a '30s Cuban porno star. Jack Hardy led the crowd into yet another rendition of "Happy Birthday" to "the father of folk music in New York, and the greatest man in New York City." The crowd screamed for a speech and Porco was reluctantly pulled onstage.

"I gotta no words, really," Porco stuttered, obviously moved. "Thank God we here and we hope to be here in the future."

T-Bone Burnette, a lanky stringbean of a Texan, ambled onstage to join Neuwirth and they did a quick song. "It's getting hard to work in this room," Neuwirth cracked as Rosie jumped onstage trying to regain the mike, "it's like working in Momma's kitchen. How much you go for, Momma?" Rosie rolled her eyes and shot back, "You can't afford me, baby." The crowd was getting a bit restless and a few people called out for Phil Ochs, who'd been on the periphery of the scene all night just downing drink after drink.

"You can sing along on this one for someone who

ain't here," Neuwirth said, and went into a slow, stirring
version of "Mercedes-Benz," the song that Janis Joplin
made famous. "Try singing it once, you turkeys," Neuwirth shouted, as Ochs made his way up front. Neuwirth
exited and the calls for Ochs increased and despite some
reluctance, since it was already 4:20, Phil lurched onstage. He was disheveled, and somehow he managed to
grab Dylan's hat and with his sunglasses and shirt hanging
out, this folksinger who had always seemed to be in Dylan's shadow, looked all the more pathetic.

He tried to tune up and made a few false starts on some
songs, lapsing into mumbled apologies after each. "Roll it,
Phil," David Blue screamed encouragingly from the back,
but apparently a drunk in the second row had a knife
and Ochs glared at him, "You better use it or I will."
"C'mon, Phil," Neuwirth shouted out, "we're not making a
snuff film."

So with a strained voice, Ochs started into a medley
of old folk songs, seemingly afraid to sing the material
that he himself had penned. But the songs were beautiful
and the performance was stunning and sensitive, as Phil
poignantly sang his way through "Jimmy Brown the
Newsboy," "There You Go," "Too Many Parties," and "I'll
Be a Bachelor Till I Die." Moved by Phil's incredible
courage and spirit, everyone in the Dylan entourage was
standing. "Oh man," Dylan whistled to himself, "I haven't
heard these songs for such a long time."

Phil went on with his trip down folkdom memory
lane, singing "The Blue and the Gray" and Marty Rob-
bins' "Big Iron," but Dylan began to worry about his hat
and Kemp, Dylan, and Blue plotted out a strategy, covering the exits, setting up an ambush to waylay Ochs and
regain the hat. Dylan started off to the bar, where Neuwirth was posted, and Ochs called out feebly, "Where you
going, Bobby, c'mon onstage and sing this with me." "I'm
just going to the bar," Dylan reassured him, and molli-
fied, Phil said, "Well, here's a song of yours I've always
wanted to do." He broke into a dirgelike "Lay Down Your
Weary Tune" and then stumbled offstage into the waiting
arms of David Blue, who rescued the hat and returned it
to Dylan. Kemp then moved into action, rounding up the
performers, hustling them out of the bar and escorting
them to the proper cars for the ride back uptown. Within

minutes, they vanished, leaving only the gapers, the usual Gerdes regulars, a slew of empty beer bottles to clear up, tables to wipe down, chairs to be turned over, and one more magical memory for Mike Porco.

3

If the Village and the old hangouts like Gerdes and the Kettle provided a vehicle for some sort of musical re-enactment of Dylan's past, it was Hurricane Carter who provided the fuel that propelled this band of minstrels on their whirlwind tour. For in Hurricane Carter, the troupe found a cause that conjured up the old days of Dylan and Baez and civil rights rallies down in Mississippi. Once again, a black man was getting fucked.

Carter was a dynamic boxer, probably one of the most exciting fighters of the '60s, with his Fu Manchu moustache-goatee and his stone-shaved head. Dylan sings "Rubin could take a man out with just one punch," and that's really no exaggeration. He's a stocky man, 5'8" and 155 pounds of solid rock. He won 27 of his 39 professional bouts, 21 of them KO's, but unlike most of his black counterparts in the ring, Rubin was no Mr. Nice Guy outside the canvas. He had a "problem childhood," namely early tastes of poor environment, gang cohorts, police run-ins, reform school crime educational courses, the whole rags-to-rags story. But then, what the social workers call his "antisocial behavior" was channeled into prizefighting and Rubin did well enough to drive around in a mono-grammed black Eldorado.

But Carter also developed a nascent racial conscious-ness, and he began speaking out on social and racial is-sues, something that boxers just didn't do in the pre–Ali/Floyd Patterson era. And when Carter had the balls to offhandedly tell a reporter during the Harlem Fruit Riots of 1964 that blacks should protect their communities from invasion by occupying police, even if it meant fighting to the death for self-protection, Rubin became a marked man in the eyes of the New Jersey justice machine.

So it was no coincidence that Rubin and companion John Artis were hauled in by the Paterson, New Jersey police the night of June 17, 1966, on suspicion of murdering three whites in a tavern shootout. From the start, anyone familiar with the facts could smell a frame. As described by two wounded victims, the suspected killer was a light-skinned black, about six feet tall, with a pencil-thin moustache. Hardly Hurricane. In fact, police were forced to release Rubin and Artis that night, and it wasn't until four months later that the pair were arrested for the murders, due to the testimony of two habitual criminals who "positively identified" Carter in return for lighter sentences for their own misdeeds, which in one case included robbing the cash register of the freshly shot-up tavern. At any rate, the case got more and more Byzantine and it is fully documented in Carter's book, *The Sixteenth Round*.

So on June 29, 1967, Carter and Artis went to jail. And waited. And waited. The luster of Hurricane's fame began to wear off, and soon he was a forgotten man, rotting in Rahway State Prison. And it wasn't until eight long years later that some support for Rubin was generated. Some reporters in New Jersey and New York began digging for the facts. A defense committee was put together by a young independent screenwriter, Richard Solomon. Hopefully sympathetic celebrities were contacted. Two of those men were George Lois and Bob Dylan.

Lois is one crazy motherfucker. A Greek florist's son who cajoled, screamed, ranted, and generally loudly displayed his amazing creative talents and pushed his way into the Madison Avenue Advertising Pantheon. He had just finished reading Rubin's book when Solomon chanced up to his office one day. It seems that Rubin was convinced that the only people who could promote his innocence were admen, a shrewd decision in a consumer society. Repackage this nigger, sell him to the suburbs, and get his ass out of stir. So Solomon began making the rounds of advertising agencies. Fat chance. The liberals of Madison Avenue didn't want to know from a nigger with a shaved head who beat the shit out of white boys in the ring and allegedly shot the shit out of white adults in the bars. Hardly the stuff that would go over big in Scarsdale. They all turned Solomon down, but they all agreed on one thing. George Lois was the only lunatic that would take on a cause like that.

So Solomon approached George that day. "Mr. Lois, I'm here to ask you to support Rubin 'Hurricane' Carter, a boxer—" Lois, having just finished the book, almost jumped for joy. "Sure, kid, listen, well . . ." And he began plotting out a campaign. "But Mr. Lois, you may scare off some of your advertisers by supporting Rubin," Solomon was so amazed that he was actually hedging, warning Lois, based on his experience with the other admen. Lois laughed, "Hey schmuck, you working for or against this nigger? I'll do it." And a few days later, Lois went out to visit Rubin, armed with a full campaign that included a large celebrity drive (which ultimately netted people like Muhammed Ali, who chaired the committee, Walt Frazier, Billy Friedkin, Dyan Cannon, Johnny Cash, etc.), fund-raising activity, and a "The Only Innocent Hurricane" T-shirt. The ball was rolling.

And then it rolled out to California. Solomon sent Dylan a copy of Rubin's book, Dylan began it and couldn't put it down. He decided that as soon as he came east, he'd go out and meet the man. And he did.

One of the first things that Dylan did when he arrived in New York that summer was to take a ride with Richard out to Trenton State Prison, Rubin's latest home. I went out there too, a few months later, and talked with Hurricane. We spent about three hours together that day, holed up in the back of the prison library, Rubin nattily dressed in brown boots, pressed slacks, and turtleneck, sipping coffee from a plastic container. Carter had been rotting in this shithole, refusing to eat convict food, refusing to dress in convict garb, refusing to be fucked in his convict asshole. Just obsessed with one thing, devoting all his energies for his freedom, not maniacally, but with a calm, fervent devotion. It was like being in the eye of a hurricane.

And Rubin spoke about Dylan. "I sent Bob a book some time ago. I was thinking about getting people with a high visibility, that means celebrities, and Bob Dylan was one of the people that Richard suggested to send a book to. So we sent a book to him and we never heard anything from him, and then one day Richard got a call from him and he said he wanted to come down here after he read the book.

"So when he came down here, of course I didn't know much about Bob Dylan. I've listened to some of his records when I was free on the street and he had a lot of truth in what he was saying and this was his particular medium upon which to do his thing, but I really didn't know him as a man. So when he comes here, I'm sitting here, now two of us meeting for the first time ever, and he knows more about me than I do him at this time 'cause he had the book, so I'm sitting here talking to this man, and it wasn't but a second that I'm sitting here talking to him and I see that here's a man, here's a man that not only is this a man that knows what he's looking at, but he sees what he's looking at and by seeing what he's looking at he's understanding what he's seeing, and understanding what he's looking at, and I'm saying, 'Wow, he's from the Midwest and I know that they don't have the problems that the urban places have with the black-white thing.' I'm sitting there listening to this man, he don't talk too much, he do a lot of listening, I'm sitting here talking to this man and I say, 'My God, two men always can meet no matter what their backgrounds are, no matter what their colors are, no matter what their philosophy might be or persuasions of any kind,' and then I realized that that's why Muhammed had to go to the mountain because two mountains never meet but two men can always do this and I just felt good after talking to him for four, five hours."

I asked Rubin what they talked about.

"We sat right here where we're sitting right now. We talked about some of everything, religion, God, society, people, that's what it all boiled down to—life, living, instead of death and dying. It seems like this society . . . this is one of the main things that we covered, in this society that has become contrary to all nature, we have become people who are wasting the water, the air, the soil, the fields. The only thing that we seem to be promoting in this country is concrete. We talked about growing, a part of life, at any rate, when Bob left he said, 'I want to come back,' I mean knowing that this man is almost a recluse, almost a hermit, and just the fact that he come down here and he was straight home from France and he was telling me that he had to go to France to get away from people because people suck his soul, just suck his soul, just suck him dry. I mean, here's a man that's

trying to get the public to, er, give the people some
truth here and the people don't even understand what
he's saying. He's so far ahead of his time."

"Did he talk about that?"

"Yeah, his reaction was . . . well, I don't know what
his reaction to it was, I can only give you my opinion of
what I feel his reaction was, 'cause I don't want to put no
words in his mouth, so anything I say here is not straight
out of his mouth, it's paraphrasing. I might be saying
more than he said or I might not have gotten his message at all, but he was saying that he was seeing things
that it seemed to him that other people just couldn't see
and he couldn't understand why they couldn't see it and
the only thing that he could do was to put it to music
because, as I said, he don't like to talk much and I understand that because at one time I couldn't talk so
therefore I could relate so closely to this man because of
his desire to be alone, because of his not wanting to talk,
because of his thoughts, I could relate so closely with him
and I said, 'Damn, here come a man from a totally different background and yet so similar so I think that there
are two things about all human beings that are true, that
we all are the same and yet we're all different and upon
those two facts all human wisdom is founded. So the man
was just simply fantastic, there's no doubt about that, I
mean when he walked in here I liked him, when he
walked away from here, I loved him because he was real.
There's no phoniness about him and when he says that he
was gonna write a song about me . . ."

"Right after the first visit?"

"Well, he never really told me, he didn't say he was
gonna write anything, but as I am sitting here talking to
him, he was jotting little things down. . . ."

"Almost like interviewing you?"

"No, no, but he was looking at me as if to say, 'Who
are you, man?' I mean that's what he was saying. 'What
are you? Tell me who you are? Are you what I see?' But
he wouldn't put those questions in words, but that was
what he was saying. . . ."

"Did you tell him who you were?"

"I tried to. I tried to tell him who I was, but he knew
who I was, he knew who I was. Like I said, two men can
always meet, he knew who I was, you see, and he just
wanted to know if I knew who I was." Rubin explodes

with a hearty laugh. "Later on, I called him up because he gave me his telephone number and he told me he was gonna write a song. This was June, July, something like that, time here means nothing to me. I don't know about the time, I just go day by day by day because yesterday is only a dream while tomorrow is only a vision and I believe that the day well lived, the day well planned, the day well thought out makes every yesterday a dream of happiness and every tomorrow a vision of hope so I don't go by time, time don't mean anything to me. The only thing means anything to me is that I don't have my freedom. At any rate, when he told me that he was thinking about putting something together, it didn't mean anything to me one way or the other but it made me feel good that indeed this man really understood what I was talking about, that if you're gonna do something for me or I'm gonna do something for you let me do it *now!* Let me not hesitate or neglect. I'm trying to get this down right. Tomorrow's not promised to us. There's been many many songs and monuments written and erected for people after they were dead but the fact that this man, a man of his magnitude, not only of his celebrity, if that's a word, but a man of his understanding, for him to do this to me when I'm alive, where I can enjoy it, where I know that somebody feels about me the way that he feels about me, I mean that just makes me feel proud, man. That makes me proud, that makes me feel good. Dylan's willing to help anybody that's willing to help himself and that's beautiful as far as I'm concerned."

We started talking about "The Hurricane" and I asked Rubin what he thought about the song in comparison with other socially relevant tunes Dylan had written, like "George Jackson" and "Hattie Carroll." Rubin frowned.

"I don't know, man, because I'm not too much into his songs and things like that, not here, not here, 'cause all that soothing music, this ain't no place to be soothed. This is a place, man, to be very very angry. Angry intelligently. You're being brutalized and killed here, this is not a place to sit and listen to music. No time for music, man, this is a place to be serious. No no no man. I read, I must continue to grow because everything around me is dying."

"But Rubin, some of Dylan's stuff is revolutionary in the sense that it's tremendously aware of the absurdity of the system. Take an album like *Highway 61*, that's not escapist music. . . ."

"He got one song that I really like that I do listen to constantly. 'It's All Right Mama, I'm Only Bleeding.' I like that, man. I don't talk to many people in here but when he sent me that album, I called some young guys to my cell and I told them, 'Listen!' See we have a lot of people in here that are misinformed in their mind, their thinking is incorrect, they love their enemies and hate their friends. They hate each other, and I said, 'Listen to this. Now this is a white man talking here, listen to what he's saying about you. He know more about you than you know about yourself.'

"So even when Bob was here I was telling him, 'My Lord, you are a sixteen-cylinder man operating on four cylinders,' because black people don't even know who he is and that is a sin. They'd rather listen to somebody talk than listen to the truth. If this man could get to all people, if people would be educated to this man, whew— if he could travel on sixteen cylinders, whew. I told Bob he was a sixteen-cylinder man operating on four cylinders and he laughed, he laughed, but it's true. If his audience included blue, black, green people, because his songs are about people, and there's no division in his songs, in his messages, that's why I dug him coming from where he's coming from."

"What was your reaction to Bob's song about you?"

"I ain't got no reaction. I never react to anything, that's negative. A reaction is like when all these people are shooting at the President, then everybody steps up and says we need stricter gun control, that's a reaction because it's not there to solve the problem, just to give a cosmetic solution to a very serious problem. An action would be why are these people so frustrated that they got to shoot at the President. It's because of the economic and political system that's forcing people to become powerless. These aren't paid assassins, they're little housewives, little mixed-up children, feeling helpless. That's the most predominant social emotion out in society today. Everybody feels so powerless to influence anybody to change anybody, to direct their own lives and destinies. So when you look at powerlessness by its more personal names, helplessness and weakness, that brings that sense of powerlessness all the more down on people.

"But I feel good about the song. Bob sent me a demo of it and I sat down and listened to it first and—eeehhh, it was a song to me, but the more I sat there and listened to it and really understood what he was saying, I said, 'Wow man, this cat's a genius, this guy is a genius.' It was just totally fantastic. So the more I listened to it the more incredulous I became. It's more inspiring to me to know that Rubin, man, keep on pushing, 'cause you got to be doing something right you got all these good people coming to try and help you."

Rubin's plight became of such paramount importance to Dylan that at first it seemed that Bob was having difficulty writing the song about Hurricane because he was too emotionally involved in the situation. Jacques Levy, who cowrote most of the *Desire* LP, told me about Dylan's difficulty:

"When the Hurricane thing started, Bob wasn't sure that he could write a song at that point. He was just filled with all these feelings about Hurricane. He couldn't make the first step. I think the first step was putting the song in a total storytelling mode. I don't remember whose idea it was to do that. But really, the beginning of the song is like stage directions, like what you would read in a script, 'Pistol shots ring out in the barroom night/Enter Patty Valentine from the outer hall/She sees the bartender in a pool of blood/Cries out My God they killed them all/Here comes the story of the Hurricane/' Boom, titles. You know, Bob loves movies, and he can write these movies that take place in eight-to-ten minutes yet seem as full or fuller than regular movies."

"Hurricane" was certainly full, eleven one-two punch stanzas to the body of New Jersey Injustice. Perhaps too full. Because the original lyrics Dylan and Levy wrote contained one major factual mistake; they confused Alfred Bradley with Albert Bello and placed Bradley in the bar at the scene of the crime. So on Friday, October 24, a series of harried phone calls were made by George Lois to Dylan at the Gramercy Park Hotel.

Lois was standing in his cavernous, immaculate Fifth Avenue office, the model of advertising chic, in his army-surplus safari jacket and kelly-green sneakers, running over the lyrics to Hurricane with Dylan on the other end. "Yeah, yeah, they say it's potentially libelous the way it stands now. It was Bello who was in the bar, not Bradley. Yeah, yeah, now in stanza seven it should be Bello that says, 'I'm really not sure!' " A puzzled look crossed Lois' face. "Wait a minute, no, I'm sorry, that is Bradley saying that, yeah, yeah, I'm mixed up now." And Lois handed me back the phone, with a by now thoroughly confused Dylan hanging on. "Tell Lois we'll get right on it and re-write it and call ya back," Dylan decided and hung up. About two hours later the phone rang, and this time Jacques Levy was on the line, ready to read the new lyrics. Lois grabbed a pen and started the corrections. "And another man named Bello, right, moving kinda mysteriously, that's great, that's a great image, you can just see him prowling around, great correction, yeah, yeah."

And so around 10:30 that night, Dylan strode briskly into Columbia Studio I, where a Janis Ian mixing session had been preempted, followed by Kemp, Levy, producer Don DeVito, Howie Wyeth, Scarlett, Stoner, Soles, Blakley, and percussionist Luther Rix. Dylan was wearing the same shirt he had on at Gerdes and was nervously pacing and strumming his Martin as Wyeth set up the drum kit. The engineers were setting up the soundproof baffles that absorb sound leakage between players. Scarlett, resplendent in a sleeveless *Creem* magazine T-shirt, was isolated in a booth at the left, with Wyeth and Rix set up behind her, Soles and Blakley, who were to sing backup vocals, near the center of the studio, Dylan at a stool at the right, and Stoner about five feet to Dylan's left. As warm-up, Dylan broke into "Jimmy Brown the Newsboy," the beautiful song that Ochs performed the night before. Then they started into "Sitting On Top of the World," followed by the Arthur Crudup song, "It's All Right Mama." At 11:15, the studio lights were dimmed.

But there were still some technical problems, so Dylan moseyed over to the piano and started jamming with Blakley. He tired of that, picked up his guitar and started a familiar strum. "We're gonna send this out to Larry, he's out there somewhere," and Dylan broke into a spirited version of Kinky Friedman's "Ride 'Em Jewboy." But by midnight all the technical problems had been resolved and DeVito called out for a first take. Bob kicked the song off with a bit of acoustic guitar and Scarlett's haunting violin jumped in, but then Dylan's harmonica slipped from his neck. "Hold it, my harp rack fell." After that false start they started in again, but it wasn't really cooking, and everyone felt that. During the playback Dylan came into the studio and consulted some of us. I told him it sounded muffled and he reported this to DeVito. "We all blew the phrasing," Stoner added. "Hey Howie, can you play just as good on the next one as that one?" Scarlett seemed perturbed. "The arrangement's not right," she whispered to me. "It's not the same feel we had the first time we recorded it."

They went back into the studio and set up for another take. "Let's get the old-time mikes," Dylan quipped. "Hey Don, where's the tequila." A second take was attempted but the tempo slacked off and it was stopped. They started in again, and hit an uptempo groove. DeVito's head started nodding, and he was shouting to no one in particular, "Not that slow waltz, that's it, that's it! All right!" There was a pause between takes and Dylan and Stoner broke into some old country tunes like "I'm Dreaming Tonight of My Blues Eyes." "Let's sing this one for Johnny," Dylan announced. "Send it out to everyone who loves Johnny Cash," and they broke into "I Still Miss Someone." Take three began at 1:25, slow at first, then building up in intensity, until the tempo fell off. DeVito clicked on his mike and announced into the studio, "Hold that tempo, Bob, that was starting to smoke." On the next take, everything jelled; Wyeth did some ethereal drumming, and Dylan seemed satisfied. Kemp leaned over to DeVito and smiled. "He knows it's good."

They began take five, Blakley doing some sort of pagan dance, waving her hands in the air, and at the end, Dylan blew some harp, weaving it in with Scarlett's violin, a weird interplay. They faded out slowly, and DeVito announced, "A good rehearsal." It was clear that Dylan was getting restless. "Hey Don, it's past rehearsal time," he moaned. "What was the matter with that one besides fucking up the lyrics?" DeVito ordered another take and Dylan kids, "But Don, we all got dates tonight." DeVito pointed to Lou Waxman, the middle-aged engineer. "Keep 'em here with Lou, they don't call him Lou the Tongue for nothing."

The sixth take was incredible, the band really smoked, and Dylan rode that energy, straining, punching out the words as Blakley did some cheerleader moves, and Bob screamed, "But one time he coulda been the champion of the woorrlllldddd." DeVito nonchalantly called them in for the playback. "I think we got it covered, let's do just one more for insurance." It was close to 2 A.M. and Dylan lit up a cigarette and took a long drag. He obviously needed prodding. Levy took up the battle: "I think the next one might be great." But Dylan was stubborn: "C'mon, we want to get this out, time is of the essence, Don. Maybe you ought to decide which take by a roll of the dice. I mean, we can always do it better. What does everybody think, let's vote." So a straw poll was taken with Dylan polling the band. "Scarlett says no," DeVito looks at Steve and Howie who seem dissatisfied, "Steve and Howie vote yes," DeVito added. "They do?" Bob blurted, "OK, let's do just one more. I might just fade away. I mean we can do it seventy-five times but I just want to get it out on the streets."

Everyone went back into the studio, but Dylan lingered in the control room. Some cheese and wine had been brought in and I was nibbling on the Brie. "Hey Larry, did you hear the song I dedicated to you before." I nodded, "Yeah, it was great, you even got some of the words right; I'll tell Kinky."

Dylan smiled. "Hey, Kinky doesn't understand me. He's been in Texas too long. I told him that he ought to live with Allen Ginsberg for a year, that'll straighten him out." Stoner joined us and started discussing the takes with Dylan. "We can do it better, we're pros." Dylan looked at me. "We got either pros or cons on this tour and you can quote me." We drifted back into the studio and Dylan pulled me over to the piano.

"Hey, I rewrote 'Simple Twist of Fate.' Wanna hear it?" And he began a stunning solo recitation. The lyrics were changed a bit, to give the song a more cohesive narrative, and by the third verse, Stoner and Wyeth joined in, kicking the piano along with some fine rhythm. Jacques came into the room and called for some order, and Dylan dutifully returned to his setup. "Hey, I also rewrote 'If You See Her Say Hello,'" he shouted as I turned to head back to the control room. "It goes, 'If you see her say hello/she might be in Babylon/she left here last early spring/it took me a long time to learn that she was gone.'"

Dylan then signaled DeVito. "Hey Don, do we have to

use the Dolbys?" DeVito went through a patient explanation of the sound leakage and tape hiss using sixteen-track tape but Dylan was in a playful mood.

"How about cutting it in mono, man, or 78? When was Dolby invented anyway?"

"We worked on it all last week," DeVito explained, straight-faced.

"Let's do it un-Dolbied," Bob decided.

Take seven was called and Blakley kicked it off with some exotic, almost Middle Eastern chanting, but Dylan came in sloppily, like a drunken chorus. DeVito and Levy weren't pleased.

"We ain't gonna do it anymore," Dylan said. "We're gonna go."

"C'mon, just do it once more with just Bob singing," Levy suggested. "You're getting too far away from it."

Stoner came in in defense of Levy, reminding everyone that in Chicago at the PBS-TV taping Dylan sang it solo.

Dylan, pressured back into the studio, slowly pulled his guitar on. "How about doing 'Who Killed Davey Moore,'" he quipped. "I need Albert Grossman. Send for Albert immediately, he'll straighten this out. He's a bulldozer. I want Ronee to sing again. Everybody wants Bob Dylan alone." He frowned. He started up take eight, but midway, he blew the lines, singing the old version.

"Shit," Dylan cursed, "I'm used to singing it that way. I like 'bodies' much better than 'registers.'"

"Yeah," DeVito cautioned, "but bodies are libelous, registers aren't."

The ninth take is called for and Blakley, dancing like a dervish, was in front of Bob as he worked into the cut, but there was no magic, and Dylan even forgot to do a harp break. Everyone looked wasted as they trudged into the control room for the playbacks. "In my humble opinion, this is nowhere, man," Stoner groaned and sank onto the couch. Levy and DeVito were conferring over the tapes. "Don't play back the one where she goes crazy," Levy whispered to DeVito, and DeVito went right to take six, the most dynamic version. "We got to mix this song and press it tomorrow," Dylan said. Levy asked Stoner for an opinion. "I don't know, it's too late," Stoner moaned again. "I can't tell. But I can't hear the famous magic of the August take." Dylan, meanwhile, was small-talking about his diet. "I always eat hot peppers the first thing when I wake up," he smiled at Ronee, "it sets my day off, it's fantastic."

"Yeah," DeVito chuckled, "Ol' Red Eyes is back."

It was 4 A.M. and DeVito cued up the sixth take again. "I like this one," Bob said, "but I like the intro to seven better. Where's John Hammond? He'd know." Levy meanwhile was still pressing for one more take. Dylan demurred. "But we promised the record would go right out. What's with these guys," he moaned to Louie, "one more, one more. I feel like Robert Johnson. But if it's a test to see who can outlast who, we'll stay till the end."

The talk turned to food, a favorite topic in the encapsulated world of recording studios. "Hey, did ya hear about the time T-Bone went down to Umberto's?" Dylan asked. "He was just sitting there when he felt something strange about his seat, and it turned out to be a bullet hole. They sat him at the chair where Joey got shot."

"Did you know his bodyguard, Pete the Greek, got shot in the ass?" Levy added. "They found twelve hundred dollars in cash in the Greek's pocket, too." Kemp jumped in then and told a story about a cop who shot someone up the rectum. "C'mon," Levy nudged Bob, "go to work before you pass out."

So, for the last time, Dylan walked back into the studio. Luther had already left, everyone else looked wiped. It was 4:20 when the tenth take started, and everything was fine until Dylan hit the line about robbing the "bodies." The music came to an abrupt halt.

"Let 'em sue," Bob cursed. "CBS'll drown him. Hey, my vision is going, I'm seeing double."

But they prodded him into one last take, not a bad one at that, only one slight mistake in the last verse.

"Shit," Dylan grinned, "they can splice that in. Hey, let's go home. Don, pick a good one." And with a cavalier grin after five hours in the studio, Dylan and entourage departed, leaving DeVito with eleven takes from which to construct the story of the Hurricane.

4

Dylan's re-emergence into the Village scene seemed a certain indication that he was looser, much more accessible. It had been years since he had actually hung out in the Village, and here he was making the music scene regularly, doing such uncharacteristic things as allowing himself to be photographed with Patti Smith, and, for the first time since 1969, consenting to do a TV show.

It was a one-day affair, Dylan, Stoner, Wyeth, and Scarlett flying out to Chicago to tape a PBS Soundstage Tribute to John Hammond, the music biz giant who had signed Dylan as a rosy-cheeked minor to his first Columbia Records contract.

The show itself was magic, Dylan appearing as some sort of psychedelic shaman, in '60s surplus black-and-white-striped pants, ruffled white tuxedo shirt, open at the neck, and the inevitable black leather jacket. But the most compelling thing about him was those eyes, burning with passion and fire, flaming out even through the television screen, a luminous presence. It was Dylan as street punk again, the hair ragged and shockingly wild, the pose gruff and determined, the enthusiasm starkly evident.

And the enthusiasm spread like wildfire when they got back to New York, with the talk of a tour hot on the tip of every trendmaker's tongue. Everyone in the Village music scene was ready to pack, everyone but Stoner.

"I've been in the music business so long," the twenty-eight-year-old bassist sighed, "and been through so many scenes where like people seem enthusiastic and it doesn't come off, because like I had seen it so many times before, great enthusiasm leading to nothing. Like I don't get excited about nothing until I see my airplane ticket. Until my

39

fucking airplane ticket is in my hand, man, I don't start to count on a gig."

Well, Stoner got his plane ticket to fly back to New York after that Soundstage gig and here it was six weeks later and he found himself rehearsing every night up at Studio Instrument Rentals, with sound men conferring behind their console, equipment needs being catalogued, gofers providing a steady stream of hero sandwiches and beers. In fact, the only thing missing to convince the cynical Mr. Stoner that this wild-eyed scheme hatched over the last few weeks was actually going to happen was that prepaid TWA plane ticket in his hand. But that he'd never see. This tour would be going by bus.

But not before one more party. A pure setup, arranged to get still more footage for the documentary of the tour. The Ginsberg and Porco affairs were fortuitous bonuses, but this Saturday night bash had been planned for days. The host was MacDougal Mike, a friend of Dylan's who once ran a camera shop opposite Bob's MacDougal Street townhouse. Mike is sort of the Pearl Mesta of the Village folk scene, getting together a party whenever the latest lyrical luminary hits town. And his place is an ideal setting for a party scene, a duplex with lush thick shag carpeting downstairs, a vast array of tall tropical plants, soft velvet couches, and a bedroom upstairs that overlooks the scene below from a balcony.

All the regulars were there quite early, Eric Anderson, Ginsberg, Blue, Neuwirth, Patti Smith, Ochs, Ian Hunter (of Mott the Hoople fame), and Ronee Blakley. Dylan was hiding out in the bathroom upstairs with Ramblin' Jack, as the rest of the scenemakers scurried up Eighth Street, talked their way past the uniformed rent-a-guard Mike had employed for the evening, and made their entrances. After a half-hour or so, Dylan tentatively peeked out of the bathroom and tried to brave the throngs hanging out but was immediately besieged by Allen Ginsberg and Eric Anderson and looked around for a way out. He spotted me slouched on the bed and scurried over.

"Hey Larry, you'll never guess what happened to me. I was over taking a break from rehearsal the other night and we went to the Cosell show and Cosell came over to where we were sitting during a break and wanted me to do a song." His eyes widened with mock amazement. "But

I didn't have my guitar with me and so he goes into this long rap about how he's helping Rubin and how he's gonna get him out of jail single-handedly." We both scoffed at Cosell's rhetoric, especially since I knew that the sportscaster had done nothing to aid Rubin outside of showing up at a fund-raising party a few months earlier after George Lois virtually twisted his arm off in an attempt to gain his support. But it was clear Dylan was just biding time, idle chatting in an attempt to escape the succession of partygoers who had one reason or another to hit on him.

But, there was a film to be made, so Dylan got up from the bed and warily made his way downstairs. Ginsberg immediately suggested a shot. He'd go out across the street and hang out in front of the Orange Julius stand on Eighth Street so the camera could pan slowly over the lush apartment, over to the window, then zoom in on Allen, standing there like some aging hawk, doing the street scene. "Sure, Allen," Dylan answered with a preoccupied glaze across his eyes. "We can try that."

But then Bob was distracted by this curvaceous platinum blonde, an uptown-looking ingénue decked out in satin pants and a clinging silk shirt, open one or two buttons and exposing the top of a magnificent chest. She was coming on to him and Dylan cued the camera crew and they rushed over as he began to engage her in a long dialogue about marriage, centering on a concept he tells her he's been toying with, mental marriage. But after a few minutes, he seemed restless and Phil Ochs buttonholed him and began an inebriated rap about a Charles Bronson detective movie he'd just seen, describing detail after detail. Again, Dylan cued the camera crew and turned to Eric Frandsen who'd been sitting on the bed, strumming an acoustic guitar. "Play some slow slide stuff," Bob whispered, and suddenly the encounter was turned into another possible scene for the movie.

The party dragged on and Dylan seemed bored, having exhausted all the possibilities for good footage. He couldn't move without getting hit on, from friends, strangers, and even a reporter from *People* magazine, who was relentlessly stalking his prey, the subject of *People*'s next cover.

Just then the *People* magazine reporter sidled up, attempting to catch Dylan's ear. He mumbled a few phrases, and Dylan listened politely, but at the first opportunity the singer scooted away. "I'm getting bummed out, man," he said, "I can't believe that guy from *People*. He keeps asking me all these questions. I mean, I gave him an hour, isn't that enough?" Then Eric Anderson pushed his way up past the reporter to present Dylan with a sketch of the songwriter that Eric had just done at the party. It's labeled "The Hurricane" and signed at the bottom. Dylan awkwardly grabbed it and turned to me. "Here, take this." "Don't you want it?" "Naw, you keep it." He seemed edgy and was looking for a way out, so I spirited him away from the crowd over to the door, grabbed the elevator, pushed him in, and closed the iron cage doors. A great party exit.

Later on, I bumped into Blue near the kitchen and he began to reminisce about Dylan, trying to make sense out of the impending tour. "He's just an ordinary fucking guy," Blue growled. "Great songwriter. He got swept up in the fame thing and he knew how to control it, he rode with it. He's real shrewd. He's paying everyone back now, you know, it's like a family thing." And Blue was right, just a quick glance around the room could confirm that. Besides Blue, there was Neuwirth, Dylan's old road manager and confidant, shepherding T-Bone Burnette, a lanky Texan discovery of Neuwirth's, through the crowded room. Not unusual, except T-Bone had a bag of golf clubs on his back, a driver in his hands, and Neuwirth was screaming, "Playing through, playing through." Then there was Eric Anderson, another of the original Villageites, and Phil Ochs, sprawled across a couch. Ramblin' Jack was roaming around, the one who hung out with both the fathers and the sons, the real link to the Guthrie folk scene and the folk-rock set that Dylan spawned. Even Bard Ginsberg was around to offer his benediction. And the magnet luring this scene together? He had escaped hours before, riding his fame down the elevator and back onto the street.

5

The next night, Sunday, was the last rehearsal before they hit the road, so there was a sense of expectancy in the air circulating through Studio A at Studio Instrument Rentals in midtown Manhattan. The studio itself was bare and dark, a lone sofa and some chairs at the rear of the room behind an old coffee table saddled with soft drinks and beers. Imhoff had made some alterations, bringing in an electric tennis game machine to forestall the inevitable boredom. As I walked in, Ramblin' Jack was on the makeshift stage, romping through "Me and the Devil," an old Grateful Dead tune, with Stoner thumping along on bass. Patti Smith was wandering around the rear, directing the music with grandiose sweeps of her arms.

Dylan walked in and quickly surveyed the room, then slumped into a soft chair, the toll of the week's activities clearly etched into his face. Onstage, Jack was improvising a song, "I'm tired, and I'm wired, I tried to wire you, I tried all I could do, on the telephone." He chuckled and blurted out to no one in particular, "I ought to write that down, I like that." Jack has not written a song in years, since he never does get around to writing them down.

I sat down next to Dylan and reminded him about the interview we had discussed previously. He looked wary, as if he were thinking of ways to put it off some more. Finally, he got up, sighed, and turned to me. "OK, let's do it, but I ain't gonna talk much."

He led the way out through the dingy hall and into a small, poorly lit office. Mel Howard was sitting at a desk near the rear of the room talking on a phone. I was steered to a desk on the opposite side of the office, and began setting up the tape recorder as Bob flopped down

43

into a chair. He was edgy at first, but it soon became clear that he was actually nervous. That helped to put me at ease.

Dylan looked at his watch. "I can give you a half-hour, that's all now."

I started by asking about Rubin, someone we both could relate to.

"How'd you find out about Rubin, Bob?"

He thought a bit while pounding his nails against the table, and suddenly answered, with a rush of words.

"OK, from Richard. Exactly like it was in the transcript of the interview with Rubin you showed me. I got the book. I read it. I made a mental note that if I was east, I would visit him. And then I did it."

"You drove out there. What was it like?"

"I mean, er, what was it like? What's Trenton like? Uh . . ." he repeated quizzically.

"You drove out there, got to those red brick walls . . ."

Dylan picked it up: ". . . got to the brick walls. There was no problem getting in because Richard had the keys to get in. We met in the library and we were there for most of the day as far as I can remember. We got there in the morning and left when it was dark."

"What happened in between?"

"In between what?"

"The morning and the darkness."

"Rubin has this poem, I don't know if he recited it for you, ask him next time you see him. A poem about a bird on the wall or a bird out the window, watching a bird on the window. I can't quote it, I don't remember it too well anyway, but what happened—well, we talked, different people kept passing by, we sat in the back, we weren't interrupted at all. And I left with Richard. What did we talk about? We talked about a lot of things. I hadn't talked with anybody for a long time and actually talking . . ."

"You had just come back from France, Rubin told me."

"Yeah, I had come back from overseas and I hadn't talked with anybody for a long time. Actually it was the first time that I had talked with anybody, really talked. One thing that he left on me was the fact that, you know, they really bummed him out with this eye trip (Rubin lost the vision in one eye during his incarceration) and so when they took him to the hospital, the nurse there asked him his name and number and all this and he just responded like he would normally respond, like he was responding how he was conditioned to respond, and he told me he felt that it was too heavy to respond that way, so he started to rethink his attitude toward people and I think at that moment—at least he conveyed to me that he was gonna try and reach people instead of retreating and not giving a shit. And so after that he expressed himself instead of keeping it all in and that made an impression on me to see this man, who—well, I have a different idea about him. I think this guy's a natural-born leader. I mean, I'll tell you something very strange, I went out there and I think it's gonna happen, I saw a billboard sign on the way to the prison and the billboard sign said, 'Wallace and Carter.' " Dylan chuckled. "I said to myself. 'Oh yeah, that might be the next ticket.' "

"He is incredibly charismatic."

"Not only that, but he's got the energy and the willpower and the concern, and I'm not saying that he would like to do it, I wouldn't want to do that, to think for him or nothing, but he has got the ability for sure to run things."

"He's running his whole fucking defense, for the most part."

Dylan leaned in and stopped tapping his nails. "The first time I saw him, I left knowing one thing. That this man—and I got a lot out of the book too but after meeting him I realized that the man's philosophy and my philosophy were running on the same road, and you don't meet too many people like that, you know, kinda that are on the same path mentally, you know."

"But he was behind bars . . ."

"And the difference was that he was behind bars but shit, man, there are more people walking around outside of them bars that are more of a prisoner than he is inside of the bars."

"So you came back . . ."

"I went back to see him the next time that I had a chance. I went back to see him because I considered him a friend and this time I felt like going back because I wanted to see him, you know, I would go back right now. I would just like to go see him, wherever he was."

"Rubin tells me you took notes . . ."

"I took notes because I wasn't aware of all the facts and I thought that maybe sometime I could put it, condense it down and put it into a song."

"Did you believe him all along?" I asked, playing the devil's advocate.

"Oh I always believed him, sure," Dylan flashed, a bit miffed. "I never doubted him for a moment. He's just not that kind of man. You're talking about a different type of a person. I mean he's not gonna walk into a bar . . . he's not the guy. It's just like the guy who was there in the hospital when they asked him, 'Is this the guy?' and the guy said, 'No,' and he only had one eye to see. You never thought he was guilty. I don't know how anybody in their right mind is gonna think he was guilty of something like that."

"People who read the newspapers might think he was guilty."

"Ah," a look of disgust crawls across Bob's face, "the newspapers railroaded him too."

"How'd the song come about? You got back and had the germ of an idea to do the song. Why?"

"Well, I was just in town, you know, and saw Jacques on the street. We ran into each other and we had seen each other off and on throughout the years, so we wound up just over at his place sitting around and I had a few songs. I certainly wasn't thinking of making a record album but I had bits and pieces of some songs I was working on and I played them for him on the piano, and asked him if they meant anything to him, and he took it someplace else, and then I took it someplace else, then he went further, then I went further, and it wound up that we had this song which was out there, you know. Was I doing my bit for Rubin? I wrote that song because it was tops in my mind, it had priority in my mind at the time to get that song done. Richard came up to the studio and I gave him a cassette."

"What do you think the reaction to the song's gonna be, in terms of people thinking of it as a return to protest. Sort of Hattie Carroll Revisited or something."

Dylan rocked back in his chair, reflecting for a moment. "Look, there's an injustice that has been done, and you know Rubin's gonna get out,* there's no doubt about it, but the fact is that it can happen to anybody. We have to be confronted with that. People from up on top to the

---

*Hurricane Carter was released on bail pending a new trial on March 20, 1976. He was tried and found guilty in December of that year.

bottom, they should be very aware that it can happen to anybody at any time."

"It's the system. It transcends the one-to-one relationship, really. I mean, you wrote this song about a cat that personally touched you, Rubin the man. But the song goes way beyond that. Lines like that 'pig circus' shit . . .'"

"Well, it can always go beyond that. The intention was just to keep the facts straight, which didn't happen, as you know. I wasn't aware of all those facts, they just told me there were other cats there, yeah right, the wrong people . . ."

It's about twenty minutes into the interview and it's clear that this isn't the most pleasurable task in the world for Dylan. He keeps glancing over at the clock, moving around in his seat, snapping his fingers in the air, like the j.d.s in *West Side Story*. I decided to change the topic.

"Why tour?"

The question took him by surprise.

"Why tour? 'Cause, uh, I think that's what I have to do. It's in my bood."

"And your blood is on the tracks?"

"Yeah, hah, my blood is on the tracks. Well, somebody's blood is on the tracks."

"Why small halls?"

"Why small halls? Because the atmosphere in small halls is more conducive to what we do. We're gonna play big halls too, but there's no pattern for it. We got a big show so we're gonna have to, you know, we got expenses to meet. So we're gonna have to play some big halls; I think the biggest one is maybe twelve thousand. Where? I really don't know."

"The strongest handle that I have on this whole thing right now, is it's like a family thing, really. I was talking to David Blue the other night and we were saying about how you rode your fame to the fullest, then it was like you were recycling some of it. . . ."

"These are all the people that have meaning in my life, they're all involved in the show. I wouldn't do it otherwise."

"And the film?"

"Well, I'll tell ya about the film. That's a whole other story. The film is . . . We're just getting all set up into position right now. What does the film have to do with it? I'll tell you what the film has to do with it. Howard Alk, ten years ago, we made this other movie."

"*Eat the Document,* right. But that was never released."

"No, the film wasn't released, the film didn't have much to do with anybody. That film was a project which we did to rescue a bunch of garbage footage that was shot on one of our tours. The whole thing fell through, but Howard and I, we got together and decided if we ever get the chance again to shoot good footage before we get to the editing room, some things that we can connect, we can make a fantastic movie on the screen. There's so much here already and we ain't even left town yet. We haven't even gotten into what we're gonna get into. We'll probably end up making four or five movies with the footage we got. The public can definitely be into this one."

"Let's talk for a minute about the resurgence of the Village scene. It's like there's all this energy being generated now, a real sense that it's happening again, and you're sort of like a catalyst, like a flashlight. It seems like you're coming back and hanging out again, really . . ."

"I don't know. I'm only aware of where I am at a certain time. I'm not aware of what it's like after I'm gone or what it's like before I get there."

"Where are you at?"

Dylan smiled, looked around at the decrepit room, then fired back:

"Right now. I'm right here, speaking with you in this, what is it, a toilet. I don't know, it's some kind of backstage somewhere in somebody's house."

"Just driving around the Village with you the other night, though, it was like a weird feeling, like an outtake from some movie. What's it like for you?"

"For me? It's the same. You mean driving that car that night? Uhhh. I don't know, man, this is my life. I'd be doing it one way or the other."

"But you're doing it on the same streets."

"Oh, you mean being back on the same streets. Right. I feel it, I can feel it. When I'm in New York I can feel that buzz from fifteen, twenty years ago. I can feel it from the '30s. I can feel it from the '20s in New York. Certain parts of New York I can imagine what it was like in the 1800s. New York does that to me."

"You did research for this album?"

"No, that's not right. You mean you want to know how the song 'Joey' came about. You know who turned us on to that. I was with Jacques. I was leaving town and Jacques says he was going up to some place to have supper and I was invited to come if I felt like it and I was hungry so I went with him and it was up to Marty and Jerry Orbach's place and as soon as I walked in the door, Marty was talking about Joey. She was a good friend of Joey's. They were real tight. I just listened for a few hours, they were talking about this guy, and I remember Joey. At that time, I wasn't involved in anything that he was involved in, but he left a certain impression on me. I never considered him a gangster, I always thought of him as some kind of a hero in some kind of a way. An underdog fighting against the elements. He retained a certain amount of his freedom and he went out the way he had to. But she laid all these facts out and it was like listening to a story about Billy the Kid so we went ahead and wrote that up in one night. I was living around Little Italy so I was always walking around there and I spent a couple of days down there but, uh, Little Italy, I don't know the difference between Little Italy and Chinatown really."

"Canal Street?"

"Yeah, hah, I think we might recut 'Joey' and put it on the next album."

"You're sort of like back on the streets now. I mean I don't know where you were. *Planet Waves* certainly wasn't like the stuff you're doing now. That seemed to me to be about reconciling everyday domesticity with bizarre artistic vision. I thought *Planet Waves* was a great fucking album, though."

"You told me. You were one of the few cats that ever told me that."

"I told Leonard Cohen that you got slaughtered on that album and he said it was because most critics are like children, they can't comprehend songs that deal with the complexities of lasting relationships. How'd you feel about the critical reception *Planet Waves* got?"

"I didn't feel any way about it."

"You didn't. You musta . . ."

"When it got slaughtered? No, I was on the road at the time and I didn't read any of that. Who slaughtered it?"

"I don't remember names. I just read reviews. They all jumped on the fucking *Blood on the Tracks* express, though. How'd you feel when they attacked the *Pat Garrett* LP?"

"Oh, Landau [Jon, reviewer for *Rolling Stone* magazine], man. He's got his head up his ass. He wrote that article from a very inexperienced and immature position because he had no reason to say that about it. He wasn't connecting it to the film. He's into rock 'n roll, man, the way it was in the '50s."

"Did the attacks spur you on?"

"No, Landau I had already crossed off as someone who just didn't understand. Those attacks don't do nothing to me. I'll tell ya why. It doesn't do nothing to my art or me because for me it's always going by, it's . . . I'm gonna be busy doing the next thing. They're concerned with that thing and they can be concerned with that thing, that's their trip, that's not my trip."

"But your trip is communication . . ."

"I'm involved with communication but not with . . . I'm only involved in communication when it's live. If the people dig it, it's enough. Take something like Rubin's book, though. There aren't too many people who can do that to ya. Who can write and come across."

"So you make records and come across . . ."

"Well, I didn't come across in the right way for those people. They expected something else. They expected *Blonde on Blonde* ten years later, they're still expecting *Blonde on Blonde*. I mean these people, they're still looking in the same mirror. They look in the mirror and they don't realize that they're seeing somebody different than they saw ten years ago. Photographs have meaning for them."

"So an album like *Self Portrait* . . ."

"Did you like that one too?"

"Sure did."

"Well, that means more to me than all the fucking critics who say that it was a bad album."

"At any rate, it seems that the criticisms of *Self Portrait*, especially that piece in *Rolling Stone*, spurred you to do *New Morning* two months later because you were doing a fucking album every ten years at that point."

"No, that's wrong. We had a few of the tracks for *New Morning* before that *Self Portrait* LP came out. I didn't say, 'Oh my God, they don't like this let me do another one.' It wasn't like that. It just happened coincidentally that one came out and then the other one did as soon as it did. The *Self Portrait* LP laid around for I think a year. We were working on *New Morning* when the *Self Portrait* album got put together. Some of that stuff was left over from *Nashville Skyline*."

A few questions back, Lou Kemp had come into the room and by this time was hovering over us, clearly trying to remind Bob about the rehearsal.

"Is it time to rehearse, Louie?" Bob asked.

"They're all waiting for you," Kemp replied.

"OK man," Dylan nodded, "see ya later," and the songwriter picked himself up, straightened his sleeves, and moved on to the next thing.

The next thing being a quick rehearsal with Joan Baez. Baez had just arrived the previous Thursday, literally rushing to Porco's birthday party straight from the airport, so she'd had less of a chance to rehearse with the ensemble. And the first strains of their harmonizing on "Oh Sister" showed that roughness. Baez looked composed though, almost serene in a *Paris Match* T-shirt and corded dungarees while Dylan, always the outlaw, stalked the stage in denim pants and black leather jacket.

They started into an uptempo tune and Bob yelled out to Levy, who was directing with a clipboard in his hand at the rear of the hall. "What are we doing?" Dylan queried, "running over the songs we did before?" Levy nodded and Dylan moved back to the mike he was sharing with Baez. Ken Regan, the tour photographer, was about five feet in front of center stage, shooting flash from a chair. T-Bone was sprawled across the couch, fast asleep.

Next was a Johnny Ace song, "Never Let me Go," Baez sloping her arm around Dylan's shoulder, a weird flashback to '63, when she first introduced the ragamuffin poet to her own concert audiences. Stoner and Wyeth picked up the beat and Mick Ronson and David Mansfield picked up guitars and they all broke into fragments of a few songs, ending up riffing on a fast, almost countryish version of "Tangled Up in Blue." "We need McGuinn's banjo here," Baez commented, then sat on a chair onstage, leafing through a lyric book.

An audience was forming in the hall, as Ramblin' Jack strolled in to look over some Polaroids, Scarlett was wandering around in black fedora, T-shirt, and black vest, and Allen Ginsberg and Anne Waldman, a New York poet, took seats near the side. Dylan and Baez were dueting on "Tears of Rage," Baez with the lyric book open in her lap, but even that didn't help as Dylan playfully changed the lyrics. Baez looked askance at him. "Don't worry," Dylan chuckled, "I'll tell ya later," and he went on, Baez holding back, then leering at Regan who was shooting her holding her nose. "Print that one, huh, Ken." Neuwirth and Blakley walked in, Neuwirth looking collegiate in vest sweater and tennis shoes, while Blakley was L.A. bohemian in a multicolored smock, loose black pants, and beret.

Meanwhile, Dylan continued his improvisation, "I want you to know just before you go running off for something that was done to you, I myself thought it was the only thing for you to do," and Baez chimed in on the chorus. But the song just petered out and Joan looked perturbed. "Do you wanna figure out an ending or is that it?" she asked Dylan. Dylan frowned. "Aw, let someone else figure it out, I'll just forget it." He was desperate for a smoke and within seconds a cigarette was rushed up, just as, earlier, some juice instantly appeared when he pointed toward the container.

While the songwriter took a breather, Baez was busy leafing through the Dylan songbook. She looked up brightly. "'Times they are changing,' we should do that one, give the people their money's worth." So Dylan and she broke into the old protest classic, but Baez, frolicsome, played with the words and delivered a mock sermonette, "Beware the water that runs into the sea, accept it or soon you'll be just like me." Dylan looked at her a bit incredulously, and they tentatively started into "Tomorrow is a Long Time," another old Dylan ballad. But they weren't clicking, Baez awkwardly trying to follow Dylan's erratic phrasing, looking more and more frustrated.

"You don't want to smoke that," Baez frowned maternally, and plucked the cigarette out of Dylan's lips and crushed it on the floor. She returned to leafing through the songbook, throwing out suggestion after suggestion. "How about 'If Not For You'?" No response from Dylan. "I wanna try 'Wheels on Fire,'" Dylan blurted out and started strumming, while Baez continued to peruse the book. Stoner started into a rockabilly tune, and Peter

Orlovsky began bouncing behind Ginsberg, his long pony-tail flailing in the air like a pennant. Dylan joined in on the rocker and Stoner screamed to him, "We don't have too many rockers."

Baez meanwhile found it. "Let's do 'Hattie Carroll.'" Dylan's eyes lit up. "Sure, yeah, that one," and he started a slow strum. All activity stopped in the room. Even the roadies stopped to listen as Baez punctuated Dylan's emotional singing with some funereal scat singing and a few blasts of hand trumpet.

Dylan immediately broke into a new version of "If You See Her Say Hello," and Ronson, who was sitting on the lip of the stage, looking like a lost sheepdog with his blond shag hairdo, grabbed a guitar. Mansfield, who had played mandolin on "Hattie Carroll," switched over to steel guitar, as Dylan spat out the new words, "If she passes through this way most likely I'd be gone, But if I'm not don't tell her so, just let her pass on," turning the mournful lost-love ballad into a revenge song.

The song spurted to an end, and Dylan seemed pleased. Imhoff, who had been watching from the corner, scurried over to me at the break. "Don't you know the worst thing you can do is write while an artist is performing?" he chided. Ginsberg meanwhile was screaming up at Dylan from his seat. "Do the princess and the prince discuss," a reference to "Gates of Eden." Dylan looked gently down at him, "We can't do everything, Allen!"

"Isis" came off impressively and then Wyeth got a phone call and a break was called. Dylan took advantage of it by jumping off the stage and striding to the back of the room. He couldn't sit still, though. In a few minutes, Wyeth returned and they started into "When I Paint My Masterpiece," Neuwirth and Dylan sharing the lead vocal, bouncing the song along with an infectious good-timey beat. Everyone in the audience was hopping around, Ginsberg and Orlovsky, like little kids, pulled their chairs closer to the stage, eyes glued to the performers.

"They just did it!" Ginsberg yelled back at me. "That sounds so good, I've never heard Dylan sing so powerful before. He sounds like an emperor of sound." Ginsberg turned back to the stage, then swiftly leaned to me again. "He had the authority of an emperor of sound."

The band churned on, plowing into a speeded-up version of "She Belongs to Me." Onstage, Neuwirth was cutting up, giving Dylan a sly look on the line, "salute her when her birthday comes," then suggesting that "For Christmas, buy her a whip." Ginsberg was enthralled, amazed at how Dylan had managed to breathe new life into these old standards. "He can't remember them, it's like they were somebody else's songs," he told me incredulously, "he's completely egoless." We turned back to watch Dylan and Neuwirth cavorting together on the stage. "Look at them sharing humor and playfulness," Ginsberg pointed out professionally. "It's great, both Dylan and Neuwirth seem to understand the music in a marvelously sympathetic way, like a bunch of genius kids playing someone else's songs. It's amazing, the precision of his rhythm and the precision of the way he pronounces the syllables."

Allen rushed up and took a front-row seat, his eyes scanning the assemblage onstage. "Look at Mansfield," he pointed to the cherubic multitalented player, "he has the face of a Botticelli angel, a Florentine princeling." Onstage, they rolled into "Hard Rain," rocking new life into the once-somber folksong. Ginsberg was almost beside himself, singing along, stamping his foot, slapping his thighs. "It's more like he's actually pronouncing the words," Ginsberg shouted. "The electric-made rhythm is exact to actual American speech with no romantic distortion. It syncopates even more." Dylan was boogying, bouncing around on one foot, as Allen moved his chair even closer, almost to the lip of the stage. "The song has become a dance of joy!" he screamed over the din.

They ground to an end and an emissary from Kemp came over to me. "Louie wants to see you," he whispered and we moved out to the hall. Kemp was standing there, looking like a model of parental authority. "You've had enough; you'll OD. Go home and write your story." I protested, but to no avail.

Later that night, I wandered over to the Gramercy Hotel to see McGuinn and walked in on an impromptu party for Steve Soles in the bar. It was Soles' twenty-fifth birthday, and Thunderers Blakley, Elliot, and Ronson were sitting around a table, swapping stories. A crew-cutted Lou Reed walked by, accompanied by a dark androgynous companion named Rachel. Reed, who had worked with Ronson on his *Transformer* LP, joined the table and began talking about gore photos. Jack Elliot started to pick out a lazy country tune. "I want to learn the electric geetar," he drawled. "I'm tired of Jerry Garcia picking circles around me 'cause he's got twelve million dollars." Jack got interrupted by a call, then moseyed back to the crowd. "Telephone and eating food," he mused, shaking his head, "two dirty New York habits."

Reed, clearly out of his element among these folkies, tried to cajole Ronson into splitting for a loft around the corner. But Ronson was too settled and after a few more entreaties Reed gave up, a look of disgust crossing his world-weary face. "C'mon," he signaled to Rachel, "let's split, this is slumming." By now, some more tour members had filtered into the now-closed bar, and were frantically devising a way to break the lock off the liquor cabinet. Dylan walked in and we struck up a conversation, a conversation that lasted about a minute, until Kemp spotted us. Louie charged over, motioning me away. "C'mon, give him room, man." I retreated to the company of those that don't need protection.

By now, someone had located the owner's son, and he authorized the impending destruction of the liquor cabinet's lock. Bowden, McGuinn's bear of a guitar player, vaulted the bar and hunched over the cabinet like an expert safe man. The lock was maddeningly resistant so Bowden simply ripped the entire cabinet door off its hinges and the thirsty crowd cheered. Chesley Milliken, Ramblin' Jack's road manager, and the scion of the Gramercy, served as impromptu bartenders, and Dylan ordered five Remys. "That'll be ten dollars for the five brandies," the owner's son said straight-faced. "He's charging for these fucking drinks," Ronson muttered, but the scion stood firm: "Look, that's not bar prices, it's a substantial discount." It's clear the Gramercy will be in good hands.

Dylan retreated to a far corner of the bar, loosening up with the Remys, the omnipresent Kemp never more than one or two bodies away. Chesley, who had been serving up those brandies, leaned over toward Dylan. "Why'd you call this thing 'Rolling Thunder,' man?" he queried. Dylan focused in on him, thought for a minute, then leaned conspiratorially over the bar. "I was just sitting outside my house one day," he finally replied, "thinking about a name for this tour, when all of a sudden, I looked into the sky and I heard a *boom!*" Dylan's black-leather-jacketed arm sprung into the air, delivering synchronized punches to his narrative. "Then, *boom, boom, boom, boom*, rolling from west to east. So I figured that that should be the name." He leaned back, with a sly grin on his face. "You know what Rolling Thunder means to the Indians?" questioned Chesley, something of an authority on Indian lore. "No. What?" Dylan snapped back. "Speaking truth," Chesley smiled. Silence. Dylan shifted his hat and rocked back on his barstool. "Well, well. I'm glad to hear that man, I'm real glad to hear that."

6

The buses took off promptly the next morning with their bleary-eyed passengers. But the camper was long gone, Dylan so excited about the tour that he had pulled out from the Gramercy before dawn. Up in Massachusetts, the troupe sequestered itself at the Sea Crest Motel, a lush, rambling resort in North Falmouth, about a half-hour's drive from the first gigs in Plymouth. For the musicians, it was a chance to lounge a few days and get some additional rehearsal in, in a relaxed setting. The tennis courts were converted to an outdoor rehearsal hall and the only distractions were some nice Jewish mommas lodged at the Sea Crest for their annual Mah-Jongg convention.

It was such a relaxed setting that one night, Bob and Joan decided to hang out with those old ladies, dropping in on one of their meetings and doing a short set, a couple of nice acoustic ballads. Of course, they brought the film crew with them.

I hadn't planned to leave the city until Wednesday night in order to have a chance to straighten out final domestic details, rent a car, get a letter of authorization from *Rolling Stone,* and pack. And to call Kinky Friedman down in Rio Duckworth, Texas, and get the lyrics to "Ride 'Em Jewboy" for Dylan.

Kinky is the original Texas Jewboy, the first member of his religious persuasion to opt for country music stardom, if you don't count Stringbean who was a closet Jew. Actually he's sort of the Groucho Marx of music, sporting a Menorah-emblazoned silk cowboy shirt, a cross between a ten-gallon cowboy hat and a Jewish-old-man fedora riding snugly atop his mossy hair, and those long ceegars dangling unlit from his lower lip. He sports chaps onstage and his guitar has a long fuzzy aqua fur strap. The sound is

57

distinctly country, the patter decidedly crude, punctuated by burps and frequent ethnic slurs ("We've been about as busy as a set of jumper cables at a nigger funeral.") But the songs are brilliant, sensitive, and finely crafted jewels. Perhaps the most stunning is "Ride 'Em Jewboy," the only rock song written about the Holocaust, a touching treatment that belies the sensationalistic title.

It was about noon, Texas time, when I called Kinky and after a few rings a fuzzy sleep-edged voice blurted out, "Hello, what be thy name?" I identified myself and Kinky jarred himself awake. "Hey hoss," he chuckled, "how you doing in your New York area, boychick." We exchanged a few amenities and I mentioned the business at hand, the lyrics to "Ride 'Em Jewboy."

"OK, it starts with 'Ride' . . ." Kinky began.

"No, start with the recitation you'd do."

"I never do that anymore."

"I don't care, that was the most moving part."

"OK, it went, 'Father,' it was huh?, 'Father, let our blessing touch us and remain, guiding all our actions, till we meet again. Unto all thy children here and everywhere, Father give us comfort of thy loving care.' Then I go into the yodel, eeehhheeeiiii, just yodeling, OK, then into Ridddddeee . . . ride 'em jewboy ride 'em all around the old corral

I'm I'm with you boy if I got to ride six million miles

Now the smokes from camps arising
See the helpless creatures on their way
Hey old pal, ain't it surprising
How far you can go before you stay

And don't you let the morning blind you
When on your sleeve you wore the yeller star
Old memories still live behind ya
Can't you see by your outfits who you are

How long will you be driven relentless around the world
The blood in the rhythm of the soul . . .

I jumped into Kinky's recitation here. "The blood in the rhythm? I always thought it was 'river.' "

Kinky paused. "No, 'rhythm,' the 'blood in the rhythm of the soul.' But 'river' would be OK too. So would 'rivet.' Just about anything." He moved back into his performance.

"Then we do this yodel about three times, go completely bonkers, and lately I've been taking up, you know, these little plastic zingers that kids swing around. I been using that at the end, all the music stops, and I'm doing this little zinger thing close to the mike, then suddenly all the music comes back in with the yodels and everything like that. It's really a strong effect. Then I do my Jimmy Durante exit."

"Listen, Kinky . . ."

"I'll eat your dick if Dylan records the fucker or does it on the tour."

"You got any message for Dylan, Kink?"

"I don't know. Uh, uh," Kinky stammered, "tell him shalom, shalom. I mean, what should I tell him?"

"He told me that he doesn't think you understand him. I think he really likes you."

"Tell him shalom, then. I mean tell him, 'Are you new in town sailor?' He is a good old boy now. Hey, keep me posted on this tour shit, niggerlips."

"OK, I think Dylan'll do the song."

"I hope he does, man."

"He said he would."

"Well, if he does," Kinky brightened, "then tell him I like him. Be good now boychick. Bye-bye."

By Wednesday I was on the road to Plymouth, with a red Hertz Granada and my friend George, an inveterate Dylan fan, along to help with the driving. It was a pleasant ride, aided by a steady stream of Dylan cassettes and an animated conversation with George about the influence Dylan had had on both our lives. "I got too jammed up on Dylan," George moaned, "he began to influence my writing too much. I had to outgrow him in a sense. But he's had such a weird effect on other people. I once knew a girl, she was pretty schizoid. One night she had me on the phone about four hours till sunrise, translating *Blonde on Blonde* for me. It wasn't that she was just interpreting the words, when she ran out of words she started fucking translating the music on that album into words. A lot of people get weird behind Dylan."

In our excitement we missed the cutoff for North Falmouth, and it wasn't till we hit Boston that we realized we'd driven about an hour out of our way. So at 4 A.M.

we finally staggered into the Sea Crest and got a room. A room that we were forced to vacate about twelve hours later.

It all started at breakfast late Thursday morning, the beginning of the whole incredible morass.

There was a 2 P.M. soundcheck at the Armory in Plymouth so by noon all the musicians had fallen into the dining room to catch a late breakfast. David Blue and Ronson were pissed off because Stoner had been making some last-minute cuts in the songs. A bleary-eyed Bob Neuwirth joined us at the table, sharing concern over the cuts in the program. Just then, Chris O'Dell, a thin blonde, who has worked as tour coordinator for everyone from the Beatles to the Rolling Stones, beckoned me out of the dining room. "You can't hang out in there with the musicians," she gently chided. "Louie's freaking out. No press are allowed in the hotel. Listen, keep a low profile for the first few days and I'm sure you'll work something out." We walked along the hall until we got to an office that had a makeshift hand-lettered sign on the door reading *Zebra Productions*. Inside, Kemp was talking on the phone. He signaled that I should wait outside.

A few minutes later he stormed into the hall. "What are you doing here? You can't stay at the same hotel as us." I was flabbergasted and managed only a few hesitant stammers before Kemp was off into another tirade. "You better check out right now. There's no press allowed to stay where we are. Those are just the rules that you've got to follow. If you want any cooperation from us, then you're just gonna have to play along." I protested a bit, but realizing that it was a futile effort, I went over to the front desk to check out. On the way I saw Stoner. "Hey, how's it going Larry," he smiled. "Shit," I growled, "they're treating me like a nigger." Stoner rolled his eyes. "I know what you mean. I'm on the show and I'm a nigger."

At the desk I rang up George and told him to pack the bags. He came out a few minutes later, livid and weighed down with luggage. "What is this shit?" he screamed.

"It's the road," I sighed. "In New York it was my turf, like I was turning them on to parties and things. But here it's Camp Kemp. And we just flunked inspection."

"Fuck him," George bellowed, "you can talk to anyone you want. Write Dylan a letter, see if he knows about this." "And what," I fumed, "address it 'Bob Dylan—Rolling Thunder Road?' Or should I put it in a box and have a UPS guy deliver it to his Holiday Inn door? Look, you can throw the old rulebook right out the window. What happened in the past or future don't mean shit. It's all happening now. Forget about Dylan digging something I said at the party in New York or Baez smiling at you at the rehearsal, or Kemp letting me stay at that late-night jam. Right now, they are the Rolling Thunder Revue. And we're nothing."

And with that, we poured into the Granada and stormed down the road to another motel.

Plymouth is a quaint little town, with one main strip leading down to the water, a few decent-looking seafood restaurants, gas stations, a few banks. On the way to the first concert we stopped at the Walgreen's and passed an older man in a lumber jacket poring over the soft-core porn books on the rack, stuff like *Biff Bam Thank You 'Mam*.

There was a certain humility and reverence mixed with a pinch of arrogance in choosing this place to kick off the tour. This was one of the first settlements of the New World after all, the first place the Pilgrims touched down and started the great experiment that more than two hundred years later was still alive if somewhat shaky. And for Dylan and company, it was the perfect place to make their new beginning, to kick off their caravan, to bring to the people in as direct and unimpeded a manner as possible the messages that sustained and fed our culture through the '60s and which power the sounds of the '70s. It was to be Plymouth Rock for the bicentennial. The symbolic significance aside, a town with a population under twenty thousand ain't a bad place to break in the act before you hit Boston and Montreal.

Down the road from Walgreen's is the Plymouth Memorial Auditorium. An old imposing building, lots of nice woodwork, seating about 1,800 at most, including the sea of folding chairs that have been set up on the basketball court floor. The place had been rented the previous week by Barry Imhoff's advance men, Jerry Seltzer and Jacob Van Cleef, for the staggering sum of $250 a night. At first, they told the Plymouth authorities it was to be a Joan Baez concert, but then word was leaked on some local radio stations and Seltzer and Van Cleef started distributing handbills, which featured ornate Wild West show logos and photos of Dylan, Neuwirth, Elliot, and Baez under the Rolling Thunder Revue banner. And the tickets started getting snapped up in this predominantly working-class town, even at $7.50 a shot. So as we pull up to the auditorium a good hour before showtime the handwritten sign on the red brick edifice spells it out: BAEZ-DYLAN CONCERTS BOTH PERFORMANCES SOLD OUT.

At the three doors leading into the lobby, the early-arriving ticketholders undergo a skin search, with cameras, tape recorders, and booze the taboo possessions. Kemp and Imhoff are off to one side, supervising the opening-night proceedings in the lobby. A ticket booth has been set up and Ava Megna has the complimentary list. I ask for my two tickets. "Two tickets? I only have you down for one, Larry." Incredible, another indignity. The sacred canon of *two* comps shamelessly violated by the brash fish merchant. I make a beeline for Kemp, followed closely by one of the camera crews. The kleigs light up the hall. "What the fuck's going on here," I shout, ever mindful of the camera angle. "First you kick me out of the hotel, then you give me only one ticket." "What, do you have a date?" Kemp caustically replies. "Fuck," I motion toward George, the cameras panning in the direction of my outstretched hand, "how's my driver going to see it. He's a big Dylan freak." Louie seems taken aback. "Driver?" He peers in George's direction. "Shit, I didn't even know you had a car." After a bit more hassle, Kemp promises to scrape up a ticket for George and I sidle over to Imhoff, complaining about the press arrangements. "Look, you can't talk to the band," Imhoff lectures. He points a beefy finger toward the incoming hordes. "Interview these people. Do it on these people, they're the real story."

The crowd keeps pouring in, incredibly vibrant, not as young as I had anticipated. During a lull, I walk over to Dave Meyers, who, in his denims and beat-up black cowboy hat, looks like he's shooting a Peckinpah film. "What does Dylan mean to you?" I say solemnly, pressing a pen into his face. "That's easy, one word," Meyers shouts back: "Money."

At about 8:20 the band rambles onstage to no introduction, and Neuwirth grabs center stage on an easygoing uptempo countryish tune, "Good Love Is Hard To Find."

And what a motley crew at that, Neuwirth in his Joe College tweed sport coat, Soles and Stoner in basic rockabilly denims and cowboy shirts, Ronson in butch black T-shirt and blue jeans.

T-Bone Burnette, the Fort Worth flash, follows with one of his Dadaistic originals, then Rockin' Rob Stoner takes the spotlight, slowing the pace down with a tragic tale of the bottle and love's disappointment, "This Situation's Too Good To Be Wasted, But I'm Too Wasted To Be Any Good." Neuwirth is emceeing, introducing each soloist, and his spirit is infectious, a real revue, in fact, and Neuwirth is not far off the mark when he says at one point, "Welcome to your living room." Stevie Soles, of the L.A. Sensitive School of Songwriting, rocks surprisingly hard with "Don't Blame Me," and David Mansfield, who was the musical glue of Quacky Duck, amazes everyone with his virtuosity on everything from guitar to pedal steel to violin.

Then Ronson charges into a Bowiesque "Is There Life On Mars" and all of a sudden the band is English glitter rock. "I can't believe them," George is screaming, nudging me with his elbow, "this fucking band's like silly putty. They can play everything." Ronee Blakley walks on, in stunning white suit complete with flowers in her hair, and backs Neuwirth on a shitkicking-good version of "They Say Hank Williams is Dead." "This band's been together eight days," Neuwirth exults, and yields the stage to Blakley for a solo spot. She seems a little nervous, moving a bit woodenly, but leaves to polite applause. "She'll be back, everybody'll be back," Neuwirth teases. "It's hot but it gets even better."

There's a great warmth emanating from that stage, a folksy down-home ambience that is usually missing in rock concerts. So when Ramblin' Jack rambles onstage during a song Neuwirth was singing about him, it doesn't seem coy or melodramatic. Jack's the archetypical Brooklyn beat-cowboy, his sad puppy-dog face framed by wire-rim glasses and the ever-present ten-gallon hat. He hoots and howls his way through four numbers, joined by an unintroduced Roger McGuinn on banjo. And the audience loves this old master, chuckling at his wry introductions ("Here's a song Deroll Adams sang at my first wedding ever"), lapping up his lost-boy preambulations. He finishes with an old Carter family song, and Neuwirth leaps on in his best Ed Sullivan, calling him back with "Take a bow, man."

A lull, and then a short, wiry figure emerges from the backstage darkness. And before anyone realizes it, Dylan strides onstage, strumming an acoustic, wearing the same black leather jacket, the cherished hat, and a vest. "Here's another old friend," and it isn't until Neuwirth and Dylan romp into "When I Paint My Masterpiece" that the audience recognizes Dylan and emits a long, sustained cheer. Dylan seems edgy, unsure at first, singing harmony to Neuwirth's lead, watching his former road manager, and only midway through the song sneaking a glance at the audience. But as the song progresses, he seems to loosen up, even allowing an incredulous bug-eyed gesture at the line "big police." And by the time they grind the song to a conclusion, the troupe has transformed Dylan's ironic song about the limitations on artistic achievement into a heraldic triumph. Not only is Dylan about to paint that masterpiece, he'll gladly do it in front of you.

And he proceeds. A short huddle with Neuwirth, then Ronson kicks off a bouncy, almost *bossa nova* version of "It Ain't Me Babe." Dylan takes the mike alone for the first time, singing more melodically than ever, smiling for the first time as the audience cheers the familiar chorus of "No, No, No." The bitterness, the recrimination of the song is gone, and the crowd goes wild when he pulls off his guitar and leans into the mike to blow some harmonica for the first time. They rock to an end, sending most of the crowd of 1,800 to its feet in delight. Neuwirth smiles and leaps into the mike, gesturing toward his famous friend. "Bob Dylan," he shouts.

The tempo gets picked up with a searing version of "Hard Rain," Dylan punching out the words, Stoner strutting across the stage behind him, emitting some guttural bass. Ronson gets a chance to get looser on guitar here and he pulls out all the stops, winding up by playing a figure from "I'm a Man." Another standing ovation. Dylan steps back from the mike, rolls up his sleeves, nervously tugs at his hair, and coughs. "We'll play a new song for ya, this is Scarlett Rivera." And Scarlett makes her entrance, a figure in black, looking almost like a female Peter Wolf with dark shades, and black vest and pants. They start into "Durango," a new song, Dylan's El Paso, and he plays the role of the fated gunslinger perfectly.

Then without pause, he slips off his guitar, sips some coffee, and grabs the mike as the band rips into "Isis," another haunting narrative written with Levy. This is naked Dylan, no guitar, no props. Just the poet, sweating from the brilliant spots, gesturing with one hand, now two, feet constantly tapping, eyes burning intensely as he tells the story of love and collaboration. The music kicks him on, Wyeth knocking out the beat with some solid drums, Scarlett flailing at the melody with her violin. Dylan's much more confident now, playing with the narrative, delivering the punch lines flawlessly to hearty cheers from the audience. The song ends with a flourish, Dylan wailing on his harp, then a quick wave and the curtain slowly tumbles down, ending the first half of the show.

In the lobby I spot Ginsberg and Orlovsky and they seem charged by Dylan's performance. "It's the vision of the '60s becoming real," Ginsberg exults. "His diction is real clear, I'm impressed by the way he lifts his lip in what seems to be a sneer but is really an attempt to pronounce the consonants clearly. He's showing an elastic, rhythmic precision, singing much more like he speaks." I ask Allen about the songs themselves. " 'Isis' seems sphinxlike, it's into all sorts of stuff, the pyramid references. But I haven't seen the texts yet."

"There was a good driving rhythmic force," Peter adds, "full of energy with long single-minded songs about one subject." Allen listens and then leans over to me, smiling. "I've been crying," he confides.

The lights flicker, signaling the second half and we scatter back to our seats. And with the curtain still down, a familiar sound rings through the hall. Two iconographic voices, one low and guttural, the other vibrant and soaring, combining perfectly, to issue a warning about the inevitability of social change. The curtain slowly lifts to reveal an amazing sight, Dylan and Baez, together again, sharing a mike, singing "The Times They Are A-Changing." Close your eyes and it could have been Newport in 1963, when Baez, who was a star in her own right, began introducing her ragamuffin friend during her own concert appearances. But tonight, they share the stage as equals at least.

And Dylan is even loose enough to actually announce the songs, almost bantering with the audience at times.

"This was written by Johnny Ace," he notes, "everyone remembers Johnny Ace, right?" as they break into the haunting "Never Let Me Go." They end with Dylan staring right at Baez with a fiery intensity as Joan picks up her drink and toasts Dylan. But he continues to strum his guitar relentlessly, waiting till she's ready, then starting into a slow, compelling version of "Hattie Carroll." But there's a discordant element in it, somehow the song doesn't move with the drive it possesses. "Shit," George whispers to me, "she's holding Dylan back. He's like a robot on a leash."

But with "I Shall Be Released," the momentum is back, Baez discarding her guitar and sidling up to Dylan, throwing a maternal arm around his shoulder and raising her other arm in some weird Kate Smith gesture. Ronson plays a blistering solo, the song comes to a triumphant end, and the crowd jumps to its feet as Dylan chuckles, affectionately pats Baez on the hair, and yields the stage to his former patron.

"That kid is talented," Baez shakes her head in wonder, but then a heckler screams out something derogatory. "Your neck is red, honey, but you're still green," she comes back then marches into the beautiful "Diamonds and Rust," a bittersweet, almost ominous remembrance of her love affair with Dylan. Suddenly, she moves into an *a cappella* version of "Swing Low, Sweet Chariot" that mesmerizes the audience until the final line "coming to carry me, you, us, on home" prompts a huge ovation. Baez is pulling out all the stops, doing spirituals, political songs, ("Joe Hill" introduced with "I guess this had to be my political statement, I hope the city fathers will forgive me"), even a slick cover of the top-forty hit, "Please Come to Boston." But when Baez swings into the gospel hit, "Oh Happy Day," George begins mumbling to himself. "She sucks," he sneers, "she's soul-less." He casts a baleful eye at the audience, happily clapping along. "These fucking Yankee dogs," he sneers, "goddamn pilgrims."

"We have more goodies coming," Baez promises. "Here's a gentleman who's been lurking around in the back," and Roger McGuinn takes center stage and leads the band into a blistering hard-rock version of "Chestnut Mare," featuring four-part harmony. It's the first real chance for the band to work out and it's clear that this is the kind of music they've been aching to play. McGuinn gets a nice hand and Baez returns to finish her set with "The Night They Drove Old Dixie Down," a nice tight version, highlighted by some hot piano from Howie Wyeth.

Baez and the band depart to a thunderous ovation that swells when the wiry, small figure ambles onstage alone. Dylan starts right into "Mr. Tambourine Man," and suddenly it's 1966. Now the delivery is less manic, more mature, yet it's just as powerful. After the one solo song, Stoner, Wyeth, and Scarlett come on for the haunting, spiritual "Oh Sister." Then a screen is slowly lowered and Rubin Carter's face appears above the performers. "This is a song about Rubin Carter," Dylan mumbles, and the band rips through "Hurricane." Dylan seems uneasy still, nervously strumming his guitar between tunes. He starts into the ominous, murky "One More Cup of Coffee," which reminds me of a mature "Maggie's Farm." Someone yells out for the unreleased song about Joey Gallo and Dylan seems surprised. "Where'd you hear that?" he queries. And then, after a false start in which his harmonica holder slips from his mouth, Dylan breaks into "Sara," a beautiful bittersweet lament to his wife.

Now the rest of the band is filtering on for a moving "Just Like A Woman" with Ronee Blakley singing close harmonies. Then it's hoot time, and everyone plows into "This Land is Your Land," Neuwirth, Ramblin' Jack, Baez, and Dylan each taking a verse, with David Blue and Allen Ginsberg joining the crowd onstage for extra karma. And by 11:30, some three hours after showtime, Dylan leads the group off. But the audience won't stop, wave after wave of cheers cascade around this beautiful hall. The ovation lasts for a full eight minutes, an amazing outpouring of warmth and affection. Then slowly, in clusters, the pilgrimage begins filtering out. They had come looking for the new world in music and it seemed evident that they had found it. They were the first to see Plymouth Rock.

In the lobby, Kemp is holding court, receiving well-wishers and smiling for the first time now, the premier concert under his belt. I pull him aside and ask how he got involved in the whole thing. "The germ started in the Other End," Kemp recalls, "Bob decided he wanted to do it, but he didn't have anyone to help. I came back from Alaska three weeks later. He told me about his summer, asked me about mine. I hired Imhoff, I called him up and asked him if he would be in charge of the technical aspects. The whole tour was Bob's idea, he told me what he wanted and I put it together." Kemp pauses, and his eyes grow wide. "I didn't do so bad for a fish peddler from Duluth, did I?"

Back at the seats, George is talking to a familiar-looking girl. She looks young, real sad-eyed, with a large feathered hat topping off her post-hippie garb. Her name is Lisa; she had been at MacDougal Mike's party the previous Saturday, and she had driven here in her old black Chevy Impala, hung out around the Auditorium, hoping to hit on someone who could give her a ticket. And the waiting paid off. "I saw Bob and he remembered me because I had once given him a painting and he had shown me his house on MacDougal Street," Lisa gushes. "It was weird, real dark with all these papers and stuff on the floor. But he recognized me and told Barry to give me tickets to the concert."

We drive back to North Falmouth and meet Lisa at Johnnie's all-night diner. And her story sounds familiar: middle class Jewish family, grew up in Westchester, struggled through high school, then did the counterculture route, psychedelics, mysticism, currently working as a waitress at a health-food restaurant in Vermont. But that wasn't the whole story. It seems it wasn't that easy to get to the Sea Crest rehearsal, especially when the whole tour was shrouded in an aura of mystery. So Lisa had to pay dearly for the little tidbits of information, like what hotel they were staying at, where the hall was, which was Dylan's camper. "I fucked four guys to get to Dylan." She shrugs a bit too casually. "But then I blew it." I inquire why. Lisa looks up, real sad-eyed and just stares vacantly for a while. She glances down at the table and mumbles, "Bob is gonna be really mad at me. He's really pissed." I ask why. Lisa looks up, with a slight mischievous smile. "When I saw him at the rehearsal, after he gave me the tickets, I leaned over to him and whispered, 'I want to have your baby.' He just stood there and got real tense and then screamed, 'Ah, go back to school, man.' I think he's pissed at me."

The next day I wake up early and call over to the Sea Crest to arrange to meet Baez for an interview. We decide to meet in the dining room and I last there about four minutes when Imhoff signals to a huge black security guard who politely escorts me to a room and then proceeds to lock me in. "These are Barry's orders," he shrugs, "you're not to leave the room, if you do, you'll have to leave the grounds. We'll bring anyone who agrees to speak to you here."

"Jesus Christ, this is a fucking house arrest," I fume to myself, but then I begin to assess the situation. It's a cheery room, the bed is huge, much softer than the one at the dive where I'm staying. And that view of the water is breathtaking. The reverie is interrupted when a black-jacketed figure comes in off the sand and climbs onto the terrace, rapping at the sliding glass doors.

I open the terrace and let Joan Baez in. We exchange greetings and she plops into a chair, revealing a two-piece bathing suit under the black leather. She looks tanned and vigorous, and maybe a trifle uneasy. I set up the tape recorder and start the interview.

"How'd you find out about the tour? How were you contacted?"

"Bob called me and asked me what I was doing for the month of November. I had a tour we were working on and . . . you know."

"In other words, you had bookings already?"

"Yeah, the first contracts were going to be signed and sealed in the next few days. Usually, I'm not working with a dollar sign in front of my face. But I was and I had to give it considerable thought."

"Yeah, I read about the pressure they were putting on you at the record company. They felt you weren't being commercial enough."

"Oh, I wouldn't say it that way." Baez frowned. "I put my own pressure on. I decided I had a certain lifestyle and I'd like to keep it. You know, financially things were falling out beneath me, so I went to work.

"I just thought it was very exciting, kind of nerve-racking. I didn't trust a lot of it. I said, 'What if Ramblin' Jack decides he wants to leave on a freight train for two months and Bobby Neuwirth decides to throw himself in the ocean.' I mean, what's that leave? 'Cause I've known these guys for a long time, and I love them dearly, but everybody's a little unstable.'"

"Well, it certainly turned out OK. The balance was

there last night. I mean they certainly seemed to resolve the tension between Stoner's slick professionalism and Neuwirth's drunken good-timey camaraderie."

"I thought the show was very beautiful." Joan smiles. "I think the audience simply didn't believe what was happening for a long time . . ."

"I'll tell you, the thing that knocked me out the most was the second half of the show, when the curtain went up and you two were singing."

"I was really honored to be given that position in the show. I couldn't have been handed a nicer gift in that sense. I know for the audience that was really exciting. That can be the '60s, it can be now, it can be anything."

"How did you feel working with Dylan?"

"It was delightful. He's a constant challenge, he's relatively impossible to follow, so that's a challenge, but I need that. I'm bored if I don't have some kind of challenge. I remember most of the songs and what I don't remember I lip-read, and that's what we were doing last night and I thought 1,800 people wouldn't mind lip-reading."

"Yeah, I could see Bob saying to you, 'One more chorus, one more.' "

"We rehearsed it, but then we did it completely different than how we rehearsed it. I knew that would happen, so I had my guitar unplugged. It's on what I call the Marcus Welby, and so I'm half playing and half not so that if he changes keys or tunes I follow."

"I remember at the rehearsals you were going through the Dylan songbook with him on stage."

Joan smiles and slumps down into her chair. "That was very funny, him saying 'Did I write all this shit?' "

"It was interesting, I remember that at the first concerts you sang together, it was like you were his patron or something, you used to introduce him to your audiences. What's it like for you now, this much more egalitarian thing, like two artists meeting . . ."

Baez pauses and measures her words carefully. "It's very pleasant . . . Uh, I can't get away from the feeling that it was an honor to have been invited on a thing like this. I'd also like to establish myself, which is hard to do because I can't tell why the people are there. You see, I'm used to giving Joan Baez concerts for fifteen years or so.

I'm used to knowing why the people are there. It's my own little problem choosing what they would like to hear, what they relate to. I'm just trying it out to see what they like to hear."

"What was your reaction last night?"

"Myself? It was all right. I couldn't see the audience. I couldn't see if they were sixteen or twenty or thirty. I guess they were twenty to thirty."

"They were a tremendous audience, I'd say about twenty-five."

"Neuwirth and I have known each other for sixteen years and Neuwirth wanted me to go back and do 'Mary Hamilton.' Some of the New England places remind me of the beginning and I'm really tempted to do stuff that I wouldn't expect people to remember. Like some guy last night shouted out 'Hey Club 47,' which is where I started out when I was seventeen or eighteen years old, and I'm tempted to do that but then I think young kids out there don't know it from a hole in the ground. I thought last night was OK, though. It would be boring to go through a critique. I'm going to change some stuff and not change others, ya know?"

"You do a lot of new stuff from *Diamonds and Rust*."

"Yeah, I did some."

"What was Dylan's reaction to some of the songs written for him?"

"You'd have to ask him that," Baez answers curtly. She looks out the window, out over the sand to the ocean. "It's beautiful here," she sighs.

"This is a great place to start a tour."

"It's out of the way, it's a place where we can make as many mistakes as we have to while we get this thing together. And it's a tiny hall."

"Yeah, but the spirit, it's amazing. It wasn't a media event like Bangladesh, it was an event!"

Joan smiles. "It was the size of the hall. That's the massive part of it, that determined quite a bit. That determined that it would be an old-timey feeling instead of a star show. Family versus star."

"You know who deserves a hell of a lot of credit?" I ask.

"Neuwirth," Baez anticipates correctly.

"He just set the stage. Totally egoless!"

"None of us is egoless," Joan corrects. "But he did a

great job of m.c.ing and holding it together and keeping the ego thing for all of us. That's pretty hard because anyone who walks on the stage has an ego larger than the average person who doesn't go onstage. So you're dealing with a bunch of fucking freight trains and when they're going like this and like that on the same track together everybody has a little squabble here and a squabble there. It's a basic theme. It's hard to keep it cool, ya know, and people have made an effort to do it and I think it's good training, it's a good lesson."

"I think it was so great to see Neuwirth and Dylan on the same stage."

"It wasn't great," Joan gently chides, "it was lovely."

"It was amazing."

"It wasn't amazing, it was just lovely."

"To me it was amazing," I stand firm.

"The show was relatively electrifying. I don't go to too many shows so I don't know what to compare it to. I don't know very much about music. I don't go very many places. I'm a mother; I stay at home. I put the guitar away between tours. I don't play it again until the next tour. The first night I walked into rehearsal my fingers were made out of rubber. I hadn't touched it in two months. See, basically, I'm not your intense musician."

"But you're writing more now."

"I haven't written for a while, yeah, but I did start writing five or six years ago then I recorded everything I've written—that period. I never wrote up till then. It's not easy."

"That first song is nice."

"The 'Diamonds and Rust' thing?" Joan allows a warm smile. "Yeah, I would like to just get back into writing music, but, there are too many parts of my life, you know. I've temporarily dropped the campaigns on the streetcorners because I wanted to be a good mother in the important years of my son's life. It's important enough to me that he's gonna join us toward the end of the tour because a month in a five-year-old's life is more like a year. So I called this morning at school to wish him a Happy Halloween, and he's going to be the Road Runner tonight."

"He's going to join the tour?"

"Yeah, 'cause that will have been four weeks away

from him and beyond that it ain't good for him. . . . He'll be fine, another person will be with him and as long as I'm there he'll have a good time. He sleeps a lot, it wears the shit out of him. I remember him through the *Diamonds and Rust* tour last summer, he'd come and sit on the amp during the last songs 'cause he'd be standing there and it was the part where I was at the end and I was loud enough for him to come out and he'd come and sit on the amp and he'd say 'Yeah, yeah, only one more now, Momma.' To him it's 'I wish she'd be with me.' He loves the drums, he loves the guys, he'll have fun, maybe there'll be another kid around. Where most musicians are into being a musician sixteen hours a day, I'm into being a mother and a woman and doing a lot with the house, lately, and I've been trying to write a book. I have two songbooks to do that I've been putting off. I've given politics a rest. It has to, it's not fair to my music, my kid. But it's still there. I'm a rabid pacifist. I'm a nutcake radical-pacifist. I've been assured one couldn't make statements like this because people change but I've been a nonviolent soldier since I can remember, since I could verbalize it, at sixteen. . . . But the concept of moving in another direction from that doesn't exist in my mind. I've felt these things since I was ten."

"Were you a red-diaper baby?"

"What's that?"

"Did you come from an old Communist Party family?"

"No, my parents were Quakers. They became Quakers when I was five. To them I owe the fact that I have no country. For that I'm eternally grateful. 'Cause what I think has fucked most of our heads around is the fact that we can think of ourselves as Americans. It's an accident that I'm an American. So that gives you a little bit of humility."

" 'A Simple Twist of Fate,' huh? Are you going to do that song, by the way?"

"I thought about it. He doesn't want to do it. He has mixed feelings about me mimicking him. But I love doing it. I love to tease him."

At that, Joan smiles, asks if I have some sense of what she's about, and when I nod, she gets up, says good-bye, walks over to the terrace, vaults out onto the sand again. The interview concluded, I lay out on the terrace for a few minutes, soaking up the Massachusetts sun, then call Gene. He lumbers up, escorts me to my car, and I leave the Sea Crest and all its secrets behind.

That night there are some empty seats in the auditorium, about 150, as Guam, the newly named backup band, starts into their warmup set. And in honor of Halloween Neuwirth and then Jack Elliot come out in masks. After Jack's set, Dylan bounds on, in black leather jacket, long Indian scarf, and a grotesque, transparent plastic-sequined life mask. He seems totally relaxed tonight, clowning with Neuwirth during "Masterpiece," then almost crooning the new arrangement of "It Ain't Me Babe." He's so intense that he forgets one small detail as he starts into the harmonica break: it's hard to blow harp through a mask. A quick swirl, the mask goes, and the audience explodes at the sight of the familiar face.

The performers are much looser tonight, Dylan bantering more with the audience, dedicating a song to David Crosby, "who's out there somewhere." Baez, who seems more comfortable following Dylan's often impetuous leads in their duet segment, does a wonderful imitation of Lily Tomlin, sings an old old folkie standard, "Mary Hamilton," then undercuts the preciousness with a newer song, "Love Song to a Stranger," written "after I had cast my Madonna image to the winds." The band is burning, everyone seems on, yet strangely enough, tonight's audience is much more reserved. In fact, after the finale, the cheers go on for a minute or two and then quickly peter out. I turn to Jacques Levy, who's had the responsibility of stage-directing the show. "What a reserved audience. They don't seem to have any enthusiasm," I note ruefully. Jacques smiles. "It's better, everyone's exhausted on stage. It's better." He looks out at those who continue to applaud. "Stop applauding," Jacques laughs. "Go home and fuck."

7

Saturday and we sleep late. I roll out of bed around noon but George is up already, so we drive over to Johnnie's for breakfast, and run into Lisa again. She's been working the hotel, trying to get to someone close enough to the tour to know the next few days' itinerary. So during breakfast, she's pumping us for info, confirming where that night's concert is, double-checking on where the tour's staying, jotting down driving directions. I ask for some change for the jukebox. "You cheap Jew," she fumes, "you're just like Dylan. He's cheap too. When I saw him in the Village, he asked me for fifty cents for smokes."

We decide to get an early start and arrive early for the night's gig in North Dartmouth. This is going to be an important concert, the first date on a college campus, before an exclusively student audience. After an hour and a half's ride, we pull into Southern Massachusetts University, a sprawling modernesque campus. The concert will be in the gym, and already, two hours before showtime, a line has formed, snaking its way around the building.

At 6:30 the sound check starts, but in the lobby the odd pair of tickets are still being sold. Jerry Seltzer, a nice middle-aged Jewish man who's in charge of ticket sales and advance work for the tour, is chatting with Ava Megna, a diminutive, attractive blonde, whose job is to run the box office at each venue. The talk turns to tonight's audience. "These aren't Dylan's generation," Seltzer tells me, "this is a college crowd. I'll be interested in seeing their reaction. The first two shows when Dylan walked on, many people in the audience had no idea who he was.

"You should have been here last Sunday, though," he continues. "We went around the campus awakening the kids. Went to every room and gave out handbills announcing the concert. And we had the film crew with us."

Is this a way to run a tour? Run around like meshuganas a week before the concert, passing out handbills as if for the hottest massage parlor in town? Wake up kids, stick a leaflet in their hands, and film it? "Wait a minute," I buttonhole Seltzer, "just what is the philosophy of this tour anyway?"

Seltzer just smiles. "I don't discuss that, that's not my major."

At 7:05 the doors open and the kids scramble past us, fighting for spots on the floor close to the stage. About four thousand kids will cram their way into this gym, filling the open areas on the floor, the seats, the bleachers on the side, even watching from the overhanging balconies behind the stage. I'm about to start for a seat when a reporter for the local college paper whose been eying us gets up enough nerve to ask what we do. Seltzer and I explain our functions but then the journalist, who's named Jerry, launches into a critique of the first shows.

"Look, I didn't like those first shows, I thought they were decidedly mediocre. Number one, Bob Dylan can't sing duets with anyone. He's got a distinct style and a voice and no one can match it. Number two, they try to feature each artist and it doesn't come off too well, it's too disjointed. Ramblin' Jack, for example, was on too long. Number three, Roger McGuinn's solo spot was excellent, he should do more. Number four, all the backup musicians are good, but they should stay in the back. Maybe the whole spirit is wrong, I can explain it in different ways but I still don't like it. I didn't think Dylan's performance was inspired."

That pronouncement over, I lunge into a counterattack, but Jerry interrupts.

"Dylan's stagnant. He selects this state to start running around in because it was the only state for McGovern. He sounds like the Beach Boys to me. He doesn't change his music at all. He doesn't change his political consciousness at all either; he never talks about anything. He's not political anymore; I think he's just a joker. And that 'Hurricane' song. That's bandwagon, he's just jumping on Hurricane's bandwagon. Who was there before Dylan? Ali, Jessie Jackson, *People* magazine, a long time ago. Dylan's like better late than never. It's too bad.

I wasn't into early Dylan, but I really dug *Blonde on Blonde*. All that speed and acid shit."

It's too late to hope to find a seat so George and I walk back to the sound booth, and stand next to Louie Kemp. And two days into this tour, it's clear that Kemp will be the press' main adversary. Already the media have had problems in getting tickets, getting an itinerary, getting access to the performers, in short, in performing their functions. The hotels, as I found out, are off limits, the penalty being a charming afternoon locked up in a vacant RTR room with two burly security guards at your door and no phone contact to the outside world. At least that's what happened to one particularly obnoxious *Village Voice* reporter at the Sea Crest.

Kemp found that incident so amusing that he can't keep from telling it to everyone he sees and he begins to regale George and me with the data and with the tragic footnote that the *Voice* reporter was so hungry for a piece of the Thunder pie that he wrote Louie a note telling him that he understands the whole thing and by the end of his miserable missive was actually thanking the fishman for locking him up and keeping him straight.

Louie laughs heartily and I notice his plastic ID badge, the standard tour identification. Only there's one thing strange about this one. In the picture, Kemp is smiling sardonically, and giving the camera the finger.

This is the first large hall and the band is really pumping out a full sound, especially Ronson whose style is much more suited to amphitheaters. Stoner, too, is pulling out all the stops, playing Dylan's unrecorded song about Catfish Hunter, doing a neat bass solo between verses. "Fuck," George nudges me, "Stoner was born to be a rock 'n roll star." By this time a fairly large crowd had gathered in the sound booth, Chris O'Dell, Jacques Levy, Ronee Blakley, all cheering the proceedings.

And when Dylan walks on, the audience erupts, giving him a standing ovation before the first notes of "Masterpiece" ring out. During "It Ain't Me Babe," Jerry the journalist finds us. "Who arranged this," he gushes breathlessly, "I really like it." Dylan plows through the same set as at Plymouth, but with tremendous assurance. I move down to stage left and from that angle Dylan looks like a caged animal, stalking the stage, punching out the words to "Isis." At one point he turns his back and gestures, arms outstretched, and he looks like the IWW symbol, breaking chains like they were made of paper. He finishes "Isis" and exits to a standing ovation, and a waiting Barry Imhoff, who towels him off and walks him to the dressing room.

I watch the second half from a balcony behind the stage as Dylan roars through "I Don't Believe You," his foot keeping desperate time with the lyrics of betrayal. The band comes back and they sound like a machine, so tight and precise, especially Wyeth who's hitting his vast array of drums with the regularity of a drill press. The sweat is pouring off Dylan's face now, as he croons "Just Like a Woman," with stiletto-sharp phrasing. "But you break just like a little girrrlll . . ." he sings, and at once, the lights fly on as McGuinn, Neuwirth, Baez, Blakley, Ginsberg, and David Blue race on for the finale. By 11:05, it's over, the performers already hurtling toward the Sea Crest in their buses, the crowd slowly filtering out, and Jerry Seltzer, running through the kids like a banshee, shrilling that tickets are still on sale for next week's concert in Providence.

George slides behind the wheel and we start back. "That really pisses me off," I fume. "Kemp let that guy from *People* magazine backstage, then had the balls to tell me no press was allowed back there. And when I called him on it, he just said 'I run my show the way I want it.'"

"Kemp is so straight," George sputters, "fucking Dylan should hang out with us. Kemp's like the kid you went to school with who always laughed at you while you were creatively insane. He was laughing but he still got good grades, he'd goad you on but never jeopardize his position, just suck your soul."

We pull into Johnnie's for a late-night snack. Johnnie, a rotund, garrulous thirty-five-year-old, is behind the counter, his wife is in the kitchen, and their daughter is waitressing. I call Kinky in Texas and he's fine, doing some gigs locally. Again I try to cajole Kinky into joining the tour. "Goddamn it, I'd do it, but how am I gonna make money off this thing. And how are you going to? But you don't care about that, all you care about is your art. You're crazy, boychick," Kinky screams from Texas. I put Johnnie on to talk to the Kinky man, and I go back to my omelette.

Johnnie joins us in the booth, shaking his head. "What a nut that Kinky is," he laughs. "He kept saying 'Thank you for being an American.'" Johnnie leans back and relaxes. "I gotta get ready for the rush. I caught two hundred pounds of fish yesterday and I'm going out again this morning at 6."

"Shit, we oughta get Dylan here to film in this diner," I moan.

"We oughta take Dylan fishing," Johnnie beams; "that'd drive him nuts." He laughs heartily. "Tell Dylan I'll take him fishing, we'll go out there and catch a bass, he'll get so crazy he won't know what hit him. I'll inspire him to write a fish song. He could, you know; that'd be a good idea for him, you know, the people of the United States are getting screwed by the Russians, no kidding, right here. We haven't got that two hundred-mile limit passed yet. I ain't putting you on, the Russians, the Germans, all of them. It's almost fished out. Maybe he could come up with a fish song."

I run to the phone and call Mel Howard, begging him to bring the crew to shoot in Johnnie's. "It's too late," Mel draws sleepily, "we already shot some scenes in another diner. Dylan played an alchemist and Ginsberg was an emperor presiding over a bankrupt empire. And Dylan did this alchemy number with crackers, ketchup, pie, milk, coffee, all the stuff at the diner. It was great. But keep on calling with these tips, I'm sure we'll be able to use them. And I got a tip for you, don't say I told you, but I think we're staying overnight in Lowell in the Holiday Inn." I thank Mel and rush back to the table. It was almost 2 A.M. and we have a long drive to Lowell tomorrow, so George and I pay the checks and go back into the kitchen to say good-bye to Johnnie.

"Take care of yourselves," he shouts, wiping his hands on his apron, "and anytime you're around, bring Dylan. We'll go out fishing, that'll kill him."

Back at our motel, we settle in for a few hours of restless sleep. And at ten, as we go to load the car, I discover the reason for our apprehension. The Granada had been broken into while we slept, and the ignition had been snapped off. "Jesus Christ," George snarls, "it must have been a Kemp-Imhoff job. It looks like sabotage." "I'm not so sure," I moan, "it could have been those local greasers we met the other night. I told them I'm writing for *Rolling Stone* and to them that must mean we're fucking pinkos."

At any rate, it looked hopeless. Here it was Sunday morning, no service stations would be open, the car was totally inoperable, and there was a concert that night in Lowell, over a hundred miles away. But we borrow some tools from the motel owners, hack at the ignition till the key fits into the serrated opening, and inside of an hour, we're on the road again.

Howard had told me that the film crew would be shooting that afternoon in Nicky's, a bar in Lowell that was owned by Jack Kerouac's brother-in-law. So before we even check into the Holiday Inn, we pull off the highway onto Gorham Street and park in front of Nicky's. Lowell is a gray, grim industrial town and Nicky's is the workingman's favorite watering hole. It's splendidly seedy, with a smattering of old winos, young toughs, and today, a host of local labor leaders, precinct captains, and a secretary or two, celebrating the campaign of a local politician. Standing by the front door, Allen Ginsberg and Peter Orlovsky look a little out of place, a bit like Buddhists at a bar mitzvah. But in a second, Nicky himself is out to greet them.

"Hey Allen, how you doing," Nicky bellows lustily as his big beefy hands corral one of Ginsberg's, threatening to pulverize it into poet-pulp. Nicky's genuinely happy to see Kerouac's old college chum and introductions are made all around.

But Dylan, who was supposed to do some filming here at Nicky's, hasn't shown up yet, and after sampling some of the cold cuts and spread, we all head back to the Holiday Inn to prepare for the night's show.

At the Lowell College gym, the promoters have decided on "festival seating," a euphemism that means they try to cram as many sweaty bodies as possible onto every available square inch of hardwood floor. Only this floor has been covered by a pale green tarp that is emitting one of the most pungent odors known to man—the smell of jocksweat. George and I wend our way over the bodies and finally find a niche near the makeshift stage-door entrance, two curtains pinned together. Ronee Blakley pops her head out of the curtain and surveys the crowd with a slight look of fear. "Where are we?" Ronee queries. "Is this a college?"

The crowd-buzz heightens in intensity and George's face begins to twitch. "I've got sick vibes," he whispers, "this place lends itself to chaos." But suddenly Neuwirth & Co. take the stage. "Here's an on-the-road song for ya," Neuwirth appropriately notes and I scamper to a balcony overhanging the side of the stage. Dylan is bouncing backstage in time to the music, his hat on, and his face swathed in whiteface makeup. Throughout the opening acts, Dylan is constantly on the prowl, watching the proceedings, playing with a basketball, tapping nervously on a tabletop, getting a cup of coffee, hugging Scarlett, smoking a cigarette, continually pacing. During the wait, he must have washed and towel-dried his hands ten times.

Somehow, Lisa has found her way to the gym and she's sitting like a pigeon, legs thrust through the railing, just staring woefully at Dylan.

They're filming tonight, and David Meyers' crew is following Dylan, recording his preparations. On stage, Jack Elliot is about to finish so Bob grabs his guitar and starts to strum nervously. Then Ramblin' Jack is through, jogging down the stage stairs, and it's time. "Let's go," exults Ginsberg as Dylan hops the stairs two at a time and walks unannounced onto the stage. It takes a while, a few seconds, but then the reaction sweeps over the crowd, the roar bouncing like so many basketballs through this musky arena, a crescendo of arousal directed at that little guy with the funny hat.

During the set I see Lola Cohen, a close friend and an actress in the tour film. "Do me a favor, give this note to Bob," I whisper. She agrees and I toss down a piece of paper to her. A few songs later, she scurries back. "What is this shit? Why don't you write something more important? What's 'We can't go on meeting like this' supposed to mean?"

Perhaps it's the camera crews, filming from about the fourth row, perhaps it's just the relief to be in an honest, unpretentious, down-home working-class environment—at any rate, everyone seems to be really on tonight. Dylan is hamming it up during the dramatic "Isis," and Baez compliments him by putting on her own whiteface for their duet, Neuwirth keeps dedicating songs to Kerouac, the band is smoking. In fact, Dylan seems feisty enough to segue from "Just Like A Woman" to a slow, haunting version of "Knocking on Heaven's Door" for the first time. And it's incredibly moving, Dylan so intense, knees bent as if he's ready to lunge, making up new verses on the spot. "Oh wipe that blood away from my face, I can't see through it anymore," he moans, "I need to get down to a new hiding place, believe I'll knock on heaven's door." Then McGuinn steps up and adds his own verse, followed by a stunning solo from Ronson. The obligatory "This Land" finale follows, climaxed by the usual pandemonium. And the thunder rolls on.

On to Newport, Rhode Island, that night, except for, as Mel Howard had alerted me, the film crew, Ginsberg, and the elusive Mr. D. A golden opportunity to try to corral the songster and get a bit more access to the tour participants. And sure enough, the desk clerk at our Holiday Inn confirms that Mr. Dylan had indeed checked in that afternoon. In fact, just as I'm inquiring, who should walk in the door but our favorite fish peddler, Mr. Kemp.

Louie's face turns sour, as if he's seen a shipload of spoiled salmon. I turn to him cheerily. "This hotel ain't big enough for the two of us, Kemp."

"Get out," Louie scowls, without a trace of irony.

"Wait a minute," I protest, "I was here first."

Kemp frowns, sensing defeat. "Then go to your room," he sputters. "Don't bug us. I don't want to see you around here." With that, he checks his messages and departs.

We eat down the road and repair to the hotel, but by now the tour is beginning to get to us. The beige Holiday Inn walls are starting to vibrate, there's nothing to read, no radio, and after twenty minutes, George is getting bored staring at the test pattern of Lowell's last TV station. A gleam slowly surfaces in his eyes. "Let's go looking for whores!" he beams.

Five minutes later, I swing the Granada past the Greyhound Station in downtown Lowell. It's 3:30 A.M. and the streets are deserted.

"Where are all the whores?" George grunts, scanning the silent alleys. "How much do you think they are here, anyway? How much for a blow job?"

We cruise slowly down the streets, obsessed with the idea of finding some action, anything.

The silence is punctuated by George's bloodcurdling yelp. "Stop! There's somebody walking right up ahead." I slow down and pull up alongside a young kid, in his teens, wearing work clothes, construction boots, a real working-class hero. George rolls down the window. "Hey, is there any action in this town?" he yells; "any action, you know, street action?"

The kid walks up to the car. "You mean fights and shit?" he says in a strange accent, one part Boston and one part Bowery Boy.

"No, no, whores," George corrects.

"You gotta go to Chanelsford to find whores," the kid asserts, "it's pretty fahr."

"Are there any funky places where like junkies hang out?" I chime in.

"Yeah," the kid's face brightens, "the Owl Diner. I'm going there, want me to show you where it is?" George unlocks the door and the kid scampers into the back seat. His name is Bob, a local, Lowell's version of a greaser. Seventeen and ready to kick ass. Or get kicked.

"What's Lowell like?" I shout to the back seat.

"It sucks," Bob blurts succinctly.

"Is it an industrial town?" George questions.

"Nah," Bob answers, "it's not an industrial town, it's a town for junkies and fucked-up people. But I'm no junkie, I never took dope. I don't hang around the Owl, I just go there for coffee. It's a tough place, though. If you fuck around there you get killed. It's run by the Mafia."

We drive in silence for a minute then George asks Bob if he plans to leave Lowell. "Yeah," the kid replies spiritedly, "I'm going to Arizona in two weeks. Shit, the Owl's closed. Keep going straight, we can go to the Club Diner, they got a lot of fucking assholes there too. There's no action on the street now, you'll find it all in the restaurants at this time."

George is brooding now, his vision of whore-chasing fading into the reality of hash browns and coffee. We pull up to the Club and get out.

"Where you guys from?" Bob inquires.

"New York," George mumbles.

"Are there a lot of movie stars out there?" the kid questions.

"Lots of junkies," George spits.

"Did you know this was Jack Kerouac's home town?" I change the subject.

"Who? Oh, Kerouac, yeah, I read about him. You better lock your door around here." Bob wheels and stares at George. "You ain't that guy that played in that fucking film *Shampoo*, are ya?"

George shakes his head no.

"I met him in Vegas," Bob continues on blithely, "he's a fucked-up guy."

We sit down at a booth. Bob turns to me. "You look like George Hamilton." He shakes his head in wonder.

"What do you do for excitement?" George probes.

"Fuck around, get high." Bob smiles impishly.

"Go to the concert?" I ask.

"Nah," Bob shrugs. "I like Dylan and Baez though. He's real talented."

"What do you do on the weekends around here?" George asks.

"Go to see the strippers in Liverty."

Suddenly Bob's eyes light up and the words begin spewing from his mouth like coins from a slot machine. "I put two kids in the hospital last night. One of them hit my mother. There was a little commotion going on on the street and they blamed my mother for it and the kid came over and hit my mother. They said my mother finked on them for smoking pot, so one of them come up and swinged, hit my mother and knocked her down. So man, I come down the stairs with a baseball bat and I says 'You, come here,' and I hit him right in the side of the head. He went down and I took the bat and kept hitting him." Bobby pauses for effect, then lifts his hand and smashes it onto the diner table. "Boom, boom, boom, maybe ten times on the head. He's on the critical list. I don't got to worry about it 'cause it was self-defense, they can't hang me for killing someone."

I ponder his strange notion of self-defense, but George is already lost in the menu. "Does this place have good food?" he wonders. "I'm hungry again."

But Bobby seems lost in his reverie. "The other one was just a small kid. I just grabbed him and went boom, boom, boom, just the face. Broke his jaw, broke his nose. One of them got me back though, I got a lump on the side of my head."

"How's your mother," I inquire politely.

"She's all right. Sore but she's OK. When the prick comes out of the hospital, I think he'll kill me but that's all right. I'll be gone in two weeks and he'll still be in there. I hope he's in for a year. I hope the prick dies."

George stirs from his menu. "What did your mother think of you bashing the guy's head in?"

Bobby smiles. "She shook my hand. Said 'Thank you.' Then my older brother, stepbrother, he's a good friend, calls my mother 'Ma' and shit, he said he wanted to go rip the prick out of bed and hit him some more.

"We went down to Washington, D.C., once, my partner and me. We get off the plane, just going into the what's-it-called, the terminal, right, and two black kids come over and say, 'Motherfucker, I want some money.' I says, 'Screw you, you black prick,' so he says, 'I'm gonna pop you' and I say, 'I'm gonna pop you back, but harder, boy.' Anyway, he swung at me, the stupidest thing he did 'cause I grab my suitcase. Whung! I hit him in the face, and he started bleeding all over the place. About fifty of them started coming down in motorcycles, and I look outside and I see a Lincoln Continental out there so I say, 'Let's get the fuck out of here.' And they started chasing us, we get on the plane screaming, 'Fuck you, niggers! We're leaving.' " Bobby's eyes turn cold. "This town sucks, I gotta get out of here." His face lights up. "I'm gonna go to Vegas. I love Vegas, I gambled there for two days. I saw Warren Beatty standing on the streetcorner. I knew it was him, I walked right up to him and said, 'Didn't you play in the picture *Shampoo?*' and he said, 'Yeah I was the star of the movie,' and I goes, 'Oh wow, how's it going?' and he said, 'Not too bad, kid' and the fucking cops go by and he sticks his middle finger up and goes, 'That's for you.' He was smoking a joint, he don't care."

Bobby hunches forward ready to tell us another insane lie, the once-savored sandwich now getting cold. "You should have seen the car he drives, know the thing he drove in the movie, the Honda motorcycle? That's what he was driving that day. 'Seventy-one chopper. I met the Fifth Dimension, too. And one of the Osmonds, Marie. What a talented, beautiful girl she is. But you can't touch her, you can't go near her. I tried just touching her face but she's got these big fucking bodyguards there with silencers."

The waitress brings the check and I pick it up, impressing Bob. "Does Dylan pay all your expenses?" I nod no. We start toward the car.

"Anyone else famous from this town, other than Kerouac?" George asks, suppressing a yawn.

"Yeah, President Ford," Bobby replies.

"Get out of here," we scream simultaneously.

Bobby explains, "He is. He's not from Lowell but he's known good in Lowell. He came to the auditorium, this is how good he is in Lowell. He came out of the auditorium and this guy had a double-barreled shotgun to his head, said, 'I'll blow your fucking brains out,' that's when his fucking bodyguards grabbed the guy, threw him in the wagon."

George and I exchange glances. "OK," Bob waves, "I'll see you guys. If I go through New York, I'll check you out." He starts to turn and walk home but first he stares at George, his eyes narrowing.

"Are you sure you weren't in *Shampoo?*"

The next day I wake up at noon. George is still sleeping so I walk over to the office to get a paper. And sure enough, there about five stalls down from our room is the bright shiny red Cadillac. Andy and Mooney, two of Dylan's driver-bodyguards, are poring over some brochures. I investigate.

"These are just different Cadillacs. Bob was so knocked out by this car that he's thinking of buying another like it," Andy relates cheerfully.

I keep sneaking glances over my shoulder at the camper, trying to buy time, small-talking with Andy and Mooney. And it pays off, for in two minutes Dylan strides out the Executive's door. And Kemp is nowhere to be seen.

I move in for the kill. "Hey Larry, how ya doin'," Dylan asks wearily. He's wearing the same clothes as he does onstage, the hat, the leather jacket, the dungarees. We start walking toward the office.

"You read my article yet, the first one for *Rolling Stone?*"

"Yeah, it was all right but you didn't say how you felt. You didn't write how the show made you feel."

I frown. "That shit just gets edited right out of your copy. They're bureaucrats there, they don't give a shit about feeling."

"That's important," Dylan stresses, "how the show made ya feel."

"Well, I want to write a book about the tour. Something I'd control. Sort of like a diary. Is that all right?"

Dylan hesitates before going into the office. "Sure, you can do anything you want, Larry."

"So how come Kemp keeps hassling me," I protest. "I can't talk to my friends, I can't get any backstage color, I can't stay at the same hotels. I don't think Louie likes me."

"Oh, come on," Bob smiles, "Louie's just doing his job. He's my friend."

We pass the front desk and continue toward the restaurant. I can see Ginsberg and Orlovsky and a few others already seated.

"So I can do a book, it's all right with you?" I reaffirm.

"You can do anything you want, Larry. Just tell me what you need."

At that, we enter the room and waiting there for Dylan is Mr. Kemp. He gives me a smoldering stare and I beat a hasty retreat.

"I hear they're filming something at Kerouac's grave," I tell George as we eat breakfast later.

"Let's go out there, I really want to see Jack's grave," George gushes, "that would mean a lot to me."

So we get the car, get directions at a gas station, and start toward the outskirts of town. It's a beautiful autumn day, the leaves have turned, and the air is crisp as we pull into the cemetery. George takes a left and heads down a narrow dirt road. And fifty feet ahead walking toward us with a huge wood stick as a cane is Dylan, followed by two bodyguards, Ginsberg, Kemp, and Orlovsky. We drive on and spot the film crew packing up. Suddenly, Larry Johnson and Dave Meyers start running up to our car, with their cameras rolling. I start to get out.

"What's going on? Did they film any—" I feel a huge arm propel me back into the car and the door slams.

Johnson's face appears at the window, smiling broadly. "We just wanted to get some footage of you getting kicked out. You're the reporter that gets shit on in the film, you know."

I seek out Mel to get a report on the shooting. "We did a beautiful scene," he relates, "just Dylan and Ginsberg improvising over Kerouac's grave. We couldn't hear much because for discretion we used long lenses and radial mikes but it seemed to be very effective." Bit by bit, I piece together the scene. First Ginsberg read a selection from *Mexico City Blues,* then both Dylan and he sat on the grave and Bob squeezed a tune on harmonium. Then he picked up his guitar and started a blues and Ginsberg improvised in an exalted manner, a poem with an image of Kerouac's skull looking down over them. Dylan stopped playing to pick up an autumn leaf and Ginsberg went merrily on in *a cappella* style. In all, a very moving scene.

George, meanwhile, has wandered away in search for the tombstone. After a few minutes, he comes across it, gives a yelp, and I rush over. The headstone is simple, just a small Indian eagle insignia and the stark lettering: JOHN KEROUAC MARCH 11, 1922 TO OCTOBER 21, 1969. HE HONORED LIFE. And there's a provision for Stella, his wife.

After a few silent moments, we head back for the car. "Fucking Kerouac means so much to me," George mumbles. "How I dug *The Dharma Bums,* you should read that. That really psyched me up, I'd lay in bed at night and I'd just fucking hoot and howl, I'd go whoooo, whoooo. I'd always start doing weird things after I read it, really up, manic, popping my fingers all the time." George pauses to pick up a leaf.

"Kerouac means more to me than Dylan," he continues. "No, I don't know. Shakespeare means more to me than Dylan, Keats, man, even though I wasn't around when they were creating."

On the way back to the Holiday Inn, we stop off at Nicky's. Nicky gives me a big greeting, based I guess on the premise that any friend of Ginsberg's, who was a friend of Kerouac's, who was his brother-in-law and best friend, is a friend of his. We sit down at a table near the bar.

"Hey, Nicky, we just got back from the cemetery," I report. "Did you ever make it to the concert last night?"

"I went but I walked out on it," Nicky relates in his heavy accent, sounding a bit like a Greek Archie Bunker. "I had to sit down in the gym so I said I'll just let it go, ya know what I mean. Hey youse guys want a drink?"

Nicky takes our order, barks it over to the bartender,

and hollers to have the jukebox turned down. He settles down with the authority that only bar owners possess.

"How'd you like that food yesterday? I made it myself. I could have opened an Italian restaurant after the army. Jack used to call me the quartermaster sergeant in a couple of his books."

The mere mention of Kerouac's name has set Nicky into a slight reverie and I take the opportunity to scan the bar. It's afternoon and there are about fifteen locals, working-class kids playing pinball and drinking beer from the bottle. Plaques, trophies, and photos hang on the walls. The smells of sweat and urine waft in the air. Kerouac must have loved this joint.

"How'd you feel about seeing Jack's friends?" George breaks the silence.

"Jack's mother and stuff, she never liked Ginsberg and that crowd," Nicky recalls. "She didn't like Ginsberg for smoking pot and all that. Know what I mean? But he didn't want to leave Lowell, you know that, when Jack got to Florida we got this friend of mine with a beach wagon to drive it down 'cause she was in a stretcher like, when he got into Florida he says, 'Here, here's your Florida.'" Nicky pauses, careening off on his tangent. "I tell you the God's truth, right before he passed away he sent me a penny postcard telling me to look around for another house for him. He was gonna move back here. He always used to send me dese penny postcards, I got them up at the house you know. I got one a week before he passed away. And you know where he used to hang around. Here lemme show you . . ."

And suddenly Nicky springs to his feet, grabbing one of us with each hand, leading us to a small table in the rear. Releasing us, he slaps the formica like a newborn. "He used to sit right here. He used to play all the old-time music. This is a dance area here." One of the kids who's been playing cards at a circular table in the rear asks Nicky if he wants someone to finish his hand.

"Yeah, go ahead finish it," Nicky growls impatiently. He continues the narrative: "You know she made a remark, what the hell was her name? The one that wrote *Kerouac*, Ann Charters, yeah. What did I think of the book? It was bullshit. Lemme tell you why, I gotta show you one very important point." And again George and I get scooped up out of our seats and herded back over to the bar. Nicky scurries behind the counter and grabs a bottle of wine.

"Not that I'm trying to be a wise guy," Nicky complains, "but look at this, the cheapest wine I got. Mavrodaffi. You don't see no bar wine or nothing. This is a high-class wine, Mavrodaffi. Jack never drank wine and she says in her book I used cheap wine in my place of business." Nick's getting expansive now, the pride just oozing out of him like sweat. He gestures up and down the myriad bottles behind him. "Show me one cheap wine there that I ever carried. Ask anybody. I can tell you what Jack used to drink. Johnny Walker Red or Black with a glass of beer."

"Was it on the house?" George asks.

"No, he used to have a tab and every month he would send me a check. I'll show you one of the letters I got."

But Nicky is still mulling over Charters' slur and he grabs an old-timer sitting placidly at the bar.

"Did I ever carry any cheap wine in my place?" he badgers the barfly; "I'm talking about cheap wine, the bar wine and all that." The old-timer manages a nod. "No, right," Nicky fumes, "always carried the Mavro-daffi, right, and that's not a cheap wine and that's the God's truth, I don't like someone who writes what's not."

We return to Jack's booth and Nicky gets called away to answer the phone. George is animated and he grabs my ear. He shouts over the din of the jukebox, "Fucking Kerouac was organic. He's like a fucking Faulkner or a fucking Melville. Part of the tradition, man. The fucking American myth stopped with Kerouac, all that expansion west. He was crazy when he got there, driving around crazy looking for new frontiers. He was desperate, man."

George is getting impatient with Nicky's small talk, he wants more Kerouac data. "Would Jack just sit by him-self or would he mingle with people? Did he talk?" George asks when the bar owner comes back.

"He wouldn't mingle with the people. This was '67, '68. Billy, keep it down a little, we're trying to have a con-versation."

"What kind of shape was he in?" George asks.

"He was good," Nicky remembers, "that surprised me, you know. I tried to get him to stop his drinking but he wouldn't stop his drinking. He used to get up in the morning, you know, lay on his head you know doing exercise. Stand on his head. He said that helped his legs."

George looks like he's about to burst a blood vessel. "Did you ever see him do it?"

Nicky smiles. "Yeah, sure, I seen him do it, you know. Where was he living at the time? He was living in the Jewish ghetto of Lowell. One of the high-class places in Lowell. He bought a nice beautiful home and he was living with my sister Stella and with his mother-in-law. They used to call me up to go up there for coffee. His mother was sick. He had bought that house and he was pressed for money and that book *Visions of Duluoz*, he rushed that book. He used to call me up and he used to have the long typewriter and he used to type and all that and he said, 'I gotta do this book in three weeks.' That was the only book that he was really rushed on but he really didn't want to do that book so fast."

George jumps in with, "How did he feel all of a sudden when he started getting real famous at the end and they ignored him when he was real young writing all that great stuff? Was he bitter about it, did he feel sick about it?"

"No, never!" Nicky notes emphatically. "To him he was the same guy."

"How much time did he spend here?" I ask.

"He used to be here every day," Nicky recollects. "When he moved here from the Cape I hadn't seen him for about fifteen years. I was in the army and he walks in one day, he was still living at the Cape and he had one of them long hats and boots and he says, 'Who are you?' and I said, 'Who are you?' but I loved him, you know. What he used to do, he had a funny thing about him I'll tell ya. Let's say there was a wino or something, drinking a draft beer or something, 'cause you know this is a poor town not a rich man's town and the guy'll be drinking a draft beer, like this kid Chris, an old alcoholic. Jack would send him across the street for a fifteen-cent cigar and give him a five-dollar bill and he would come back and Jack would be gone. That would probably be Jack's last five dollars in his pocket, know what I mean. And this guy who wrote *Visions of Kerouac*, this guy Jarvis, he wasn't as close to Jack as people think he was. You talk to people in Lowell High School, they'll tell you the same thing, personal friends of Jack, they all want to know who is he? I mean what the hell, the guy's feeling good, he's drunk, you don't show the bad, you show the good side of him. He would always help the poor guy, in his way, like a secret. Like the guy did him an errand and he wanted to give him the five dollars so he smoked the cigar.

"One thing about Jack, when he was feeling good he'd sit here and talk to me and he could recite poetry that was out of this world."

"Did he make it up spontaneously, on the spot or was it poems . . . ?" George interrogates.

"I don't know," Nicky interrupts, "he used to recite it and then if we were having an argument or something he'd say, 'Look, Nick, let me tell you something, the pen is mightier than the sword.' When we went to Spain it was a funny thing, my first cousin passed away, and we went to the wake, and after the wake Jack called me on the phone to tell me that my cousin had passed away, and to me my first cousin was like my brother, so I was stunned and I flipped my lid a little. Anyway, after the wake we all decided to go to Spain, so we all went, Jack, my brother, my other cousin, and this other friend of mine. So before we all decided to go to Spain, I went to the little bank for some money and the banker was French Canadian and he says to me that Jack can have anything he wants.

"We started from here drinking, went to Boston, we were pretty high, and we got on a DC 8 to Madrid, but first we stopped in Lisbon. It's a funny thing, when we stopped in Lisbon, he'd go off by himself. He used to hit the dives by the waterfront and he hit the same dives, the Texas Tavern or something, that was the same one that the guy that shot Martin Luther King was in, it was the same cafe he was hiding in, and we were in the hotel, all staying at the same hotel and I get a loud knock on my door, boom, boom, boom, who the hell would it be but Jack?

"I used to hold his money for him, I used to give him one hundred dollars, he would spend it all. Honest to God, the same night he would come back again, boom, boom, boom, I'd give him another hundred dollars. We stayed there for two days and all he drank was Scotch, where the hell he spent his money, I don't know but he must have gone through six hundred dollars in two days in Portugal.

To him life was a big ball, that's all it was, just a big ball. He didn't care about nothing. Funny thing is, the man was so important, people used to come in here looking for him, they used to come in from all over the country. You never knew who the hell was gonna walk in. For him, it was just another day. One day, I seen him all dressed up, he had a shirt and stuff on, and I said, 'Where the hell you been?' and he said, 'Some millionaire from out west, some friend of mine sent a limo over for me, he wanted me to speak to his son.' His son was going to Fawkes Academy, Landover, Mass., and Jack had to speak to the kid about life."

Nicky pauses for a breath, obviously moved by the flood of memories we've tapped. He leans over across the table to us. "What does Bobby think of Jack?" he wonders.

"Bobby doesn't have much time right now because he's in the middle of the tour," I assert, "but he scheduled a day off so they could spend a day here in Lowell. He told Ginsberg that he was really influenced by reading *Mexico City Blues* back in Minnesota when he was a kid. They dedicated songs to Jack a couple of times last night and the audience went wild."

"Guys like Bobby, they learnt from Jack," George adds. "Allen, all them, that's where they get all their stuff from."

"Even this kid we were talking to last night, this tough working-class teenager, he says his mother reads Jack's books all the time," I add.

Nicky turns away for a second and when he turns back, a chill runs down my spine. Huge tears are rolling down his ruddy cheeks. He makes a couple of ineffectual stabs at them with his beefy hands then allows himself the expression of his grief.

"I still get broken up," he stammers, his huge body racked by sobs, "he had his happiest years when he stayed here in Lowell. The last year and a half, that was his happiest year he told me. He really enjoyed it, he didn't want to go to Florida no way. His mother insisted on going to Florida."

Nicky wipes away a final tear and bangs the table for emphasis. "But he loved his mother so much, that was the whole thing. I think that's what killed him. He was drinking but he could control it, but I guess when he went down there he really wanted to come back to Lowell. He really wanted to come back bad, believe me, he wouldn't have died if he was here."

With that Nicky gets up and walks us around the bar, showing us pictures of Jack in the club, in Spain, in Monticello, in Germany.

"OK guys, I'll catch you," Nicky is saying good-bye at the door. "And Larry, if you can ask Bobby for a picture and get it autographed for me. Tell him to put down 'To Big Nick' or something." Nicky wipes his eyes one last time. "Take care of yourselves," he waves.

We walk to the car and I start to head back up Gorham Street toward the Holiday Inn. "Wait," George yells, "let's check out the peep shows," pointing at a porno store up the block.

"We have no time, we have to get on the road to Newport," I lecture.

George smolders. "See, this is what Kerouac'd do," he spits. "He'd skunk around and look around the waterfronts like I like to do. You're nowhere."

We get into Newport early that evening and I pull right up to check into the Sheraton, where the tour was staying. And just as I pocket the receipt, Kemp strolls into the lobby.

He rushes up, beside himself with rage. "What the fuck are you doing here? Didn't we go through this in Falmouth?" he rants.

"But Lou, Dylan said it was OK to write a book and offered anything I needed. So I just assumed if it was OK to do that, it was OK to stay at the hotel." I smile.

"Well, you assumed wrong," Kemp glares, "you're just a *chozzer*, you want more and more. You're like Weberman."

"Bullshit," I retort, "I ain't going through garbage or stuff like that, I'm just trying to do my job. This means a lot to me."

"Well," Kemp seems to soften, "you were presumptuous. Keep cool and you'll come out OK; don't keep cool and you'll have me on your throat."

I nod and rejoin George and once again we drive down the road, searching for the nearest motel.

The next day, I wake up and George is already dressed, and all his clothes are packed. "I'm splitting, I can't take this shit," he barks. "You're fucking losing your soul in this rock 'n roll bullshit. You're becoming totally manic, totally insensitive, if you keep it up and get a little more outrageous, I'm sure they'll let you on the tour. But I can't take it anymore. Just call me a few times and let me know how the music's going."

We talk a bit but he's adamant, he doesn't even want to stick around for tonight's concert in Providence, the first in a large convention center. On the way to the bus station, George spies a young woman with a child, carrying laundry. She's got close-cropped brownish hair, wears homemade clothing. "Ask her," George points, "I'm sure she'll want to see Dylan." We pull over and stop to talk. The woman is Priscilla, a Newport local, and yes, she'd be ecstatic. She wanted to see the concert but had no money.

A few hours later, Priscilla and her daughter meet me in the lobby of the motel. Jenny, a cute little four-year-old, jumps in the back seat and Priscilla slides in the front for the drive to Providence.

The opening segment has already begun as Priscilla, Jenny, and I trudge to our seats. Ronson has just been introduced by Neuwirth as "the man who invented David Bowie" and as we settle into our fourteenth-row seats, I see the band is all wearing T-shirts with the name "Guam" embossed across the front.

The sound has been boosted for this big hall and by the time Dylan enters to a standing ovation, the band is primed. Dylan's in his standard getup, same boots, jeans, black leather, and hat, only it seems that he's taken an affinity to the whiteface that he wore for the filming in Lowell. In fact, with the hat adorned with fresh flowers, courtesy of Lola, and the clown makeup, he resembles a Pierrot figure, and in this large arena "Masterpiece" is more appropriate than ever, recalling the hours he's spent "inside the Coliseum, dodging lions and wasting time." Neuwirth is smiling, singing along, wearing a black T-shirt that says, "Bob Who?"

Dylan seems in control by now, picking up more assurance with each concert. "Durango" is less static, and "Hard Rain" threatens to melt the hockey ice beneath the wood floorboards, prompting one kid in the second row to exult, "Rock 'n roll!" By now Dylan is as manically relaxed as Sinatra, he's leaping into the air, stalking around like a grave robber, trotting back to the mike, and when he cups his hands around the lips to deliver the dramatic ending to "Isis," it's not Dylan up there, it's a fucking rock 'n roll Jolson. "See ya in fifteen minutes," he screams and runs off as the house lights come up for intermission.

The light gives me an opportunity to check out the three Indians in full Cherokee regalia who are sitting to our left. I introduce myself. "We're from Nevada," the older man replies, "My name is Rolling Thunder and this is my wife Spotted Fawn." Rolling Thunder is a medicine man of some note who was flown in by Dylan when the coincidence in names was brought to his attention. And it might be a working vacation too, Rolling Thunder hints.

Just then, Larry Johnson of the film crew stops by to chat. The film crew seem to be my most faithful allies at this point, being outsiders in a sense themselves. They have to rely on Imhoff for the itinerary and even that's kept secret from them and the performers until a day or so before the next stop. "What you been doing?" Johnson asks. "You got any interesting stuff?" I nod toward Priscilla. "How about a native of Newport who saw Dylan at the early Festivals, and is real articulate." Johnson smiles. "Great, bring her backstage between shows, I'll meet you at the side of the stage."

Dylan and Baez march through their set and Joan seems in particularly high spirits tonight. The audience goes wild for her pure-white "Swing Low" then someone screams out " 'Newport!' "

"Yes, I remember Newport," Baez lectures, hand on hip. "It wasn't such a short time ago, dearies. I was the world's Madonna. But that's all changed, what a bore!"

Dylan comes on next for his solo spot. Tonight he plows into an incredibly moving "God On Our Side," the audience cheering every stanza, and when he reaches the line about learning to hate the Russians, he updates it in light of recent anticommunist developments, shouting the new list North Korea, Cuba, China, Vietnam, like it were some State Department litany. Then suddenly, a young woman advances to the lip of the stage, proferring a young baby to Bob, as if following some weird ritual. Dylan seems taken aback, then his expression of amazement turns to bemusement. He refuses the child and leans into the mike. "I'm not a politician," he laughs.

In fact, over the years, Dylan had studiously avoided becoming involved in electoral politics, unlike many of his musical colleagues. Simon and Garfunkel played fund-raising benefits for Eugene McCarthy in 1968. In 1972, the McGovern forces who succeeded in reuniting Simon and Garfunkel, and Peter, Paul and Mary for a gala concert failed to woo Dylan. In 1976, Jerry Brown corralled the Eagles and Linda Ronstadt and Jackson Browne but Carter countered with the Allman Bros., a connection that would prove embarrassing after the cocaine trial of Gregg Allman's road manager.

In fact, there was much speculation that Carter had vainly attempted to enlist Dylan in his camp. Their relationship goes back to 1974 when Carter invited Dylan and the Band to a post-concert party during Dylan's Tour 1974. And on January 21, 1974, Dylan and party limoed to the Georgia governor's mansion and joined Carter and his family (including son Chip who once journeyed all the way to Woodstock to shake Dylan's hand; obviously he's the real Dylan fanatic in the family), and Georgia rock-scene luminaries such as Phil Walden and Frank Fenner of Capricorn Records for a down-home buffet of ham, eggs, grits, and vegetables in cheese sauce.

Speculation was rife that Dylan was impressed by Carter's interest in Israel (the governor had toured the Holy Land in 1972). However, Carter told reporters, "When I mentioned Israel, Dylan changed the subject and said he and his wife had recently been to Mexico and had enjoyed that country, too." He felt Dylan was reticent but warm. "He never initiates conversation, but he'll answer a question if you ask him," Carter reported. In all, the evening seemed to be pleasant, Carter escorting Dylan on a tour of the mansion, then the two slipping outside for a secluded walk around the grounds. "I asked him if he wanted a drink," Carter would observe the next morning, "but he only wanted orange juice and would only eat the vegetables."

Apparently, Dylan made a strong impression on the Georgia governor, at least politically. In May of that year, in a Law Day speech at the university in Athens, Georgia (a speech which mesmerized Hunter Thompson into the Carter camp), Carter would tell his audience of attorneys and judges, "But I read and I listen a lot. One of the sources for my understanding about the proper application of criminal justice and the system of equities is from Reinhold Niebuhr. The other source of my understanding about what's right and wrong in this society is from a friend of mine, a poet named Bob Dylan. Listening to his records about 'The Lonesome Death of Hattie Carroll' and 'Like a Rolling Stone' and 'The Times They Are A Changin',' I've learned to appreciate the dynamism of change in a modern society."

For his part, Dylan seemed amused by Carter's endorsement of his ideas. "I don't know what to think about that," he told *TV Guide*. "People have told me there was a man running for President quoting me. I don't know if that's good or bad," he laughed, "but he's just another guy running for President. I sometimes dream of running the country and putting all my friends in office. That's the way it works now, anyway. I'd like to see Thomas Jefferson, Benjamin Franklin, and a few of those other guys come back. If they did I'd go out and vote. They knew what was happening." Perhaps a sneak glimpse of a Dylan Administration was provided in a 1966 *Playboy* interview when Dylan hinted that he would replace "The Star-Spangled Banner" as national anthem if elected. His choice? "Desolation Row."

The set continues without incident until the last number, "Knocking on Heaven's Door!" when Dylan cuts his hand on a guitar string. His face becomes a scowl and he turns his back on the audience, licking the cut, but wheeling back just in time to deliver his line about "wiping the blood off my face." Ginsberg and Blue, who today is looking like a '30s gangster, hop on for the finale, and it's clear the hand hurts Dylan. The house lights are up, the entire ten thousand plus audience standing, cheering along. "We don't know any more songs," Baez screams out over the din of the instruments, "so there'll be no encore. You've been a beautiful audience, thank you, thank you, thank you." And then she just soars into the last note of "This Land is Your Land" as Dylan beats a hasty retreat offstage.

Next to me Priscilla is glowing. "Incredible," she shakes her head, "what an up." We make our way to the side of the stage and meet Johnson, who takes us backstage. In the hall, Meyers comes up with a camera and they shoot Priscilla and Jenny, leaning against the wall, reminiscing about Dylan, who himself is about twenty yards down the hall, talking animatedly with Chief Rolling Thunder. Kemp stands next to Dylan keeping a watchful eye on me. After the interview, I say good-bye to Priscilla, who's taking a bus back to Newport. Meyers comes rushing up with, "Sloman, that was a great scene, she was the most articulate person we've interviewed so far. Don't worry, we'll tell Dylan what you're bringing in." I smile, as Meyers leaves to join the others who are eating a catered supper between shows, a supper that Chris O'Dell has warned me not to try to attend.

The second show is fairly routine until the finale. The old chief had made his way to the front of the stage, cutting a striking figure in his Indian boots, rolled-up white pants, striped Cherokee shirt, and fedora-style hat, but he looked natural up there as he coolly surveyed the scene, glancing from the stage out to the vast audience, mysteriously stroking a long feather, exuding that Don Juanish prairie power, seeming to know that more than anyone else onstage or out in that sea of faces, this land was his land.

Back in Newport later, I was restless and made the rounds of some of the bars. I had called Stoner to see if he wanted to check out the local action but he declined, preferring to stay in the hospitality suite set up next to Chris O'Dell's room. The hospitality suite, an institution borrowed from the world of corporate socializing, functions on a rock tour as a means to program the performers into a self-contained world. In one of the rooms rented by the entourage, liquor and food are provided (until a reasonable hour, then suddenly strategically withdrawn), a context is provided so performers can let off steam (short of destroying furniture which went out with Led Zeppelin and Alice Cooper tours), and security is provided in the form of several imposing-looking ex-football players who screen the outside inputs. Attractive women usually pass through this filter. Ragged journalists don't.

"C'mon, Stoner," I rant over the phone from my motel down the road, "let's go out barhopping, I found some great places. You gonna just be a zombie, letting them load you on the bus to the gig, load you back, throw you into a hotel room, get you shit-faced, then safely take you to bed? That's a real antitour, huh, really getting out and meeting the people. You wouldn't even know if there was Rolling Thunder, you're always indoors."

To no avail. So I make the rounds and by four I drift over to the troupe's hotel. And surprisingly enough, there seems to be a flurry of activity in the lobby. Rolling Thunder and Spotted Fawn and their brave friend are in one corner. Mel Howard is running around frantically. Ginsberg and Orlovsky and Denise Mercedes, hard-rock guitarist and Peter's girlfriend, are milling about. "Stick around," Mel shouts to me as he scurries by, "we may be doing a scene with Rolling Thunder. I think Bob wants to do a sunrise ceremony." As the time passes, more and more people filter into the lobby, McGuinn, then Blakley, Neuwirth, Blue, Jack Elliot, a few girlfriends, even a female correspondent from *Newsweek*, who's just flown in to do a story and hasn't succeeded in getting near Dylan yet.

In the lobby, I run into my friend Mary, a photographer from the Village, who gets permission from Rolling Thunder to photograph the ceremony. By now about twenty people have amassed, and Spotted Fawn has pulled all the females in one corner for a huddle, making sure that no one was currently in the midst of her period (Tampax is taboo at these affairs). It's almost light by now, and finally Dylan steps off the elevator and we fill three cars and follow Bob's camper to the grounds of someone's friend, who lives in an old restored mansion off Rhode Island Sound.

It turns out to be an old stone building, currently an artist's co-op. We trudge through the grounds to a beautiful isolated spot on the edge of the sound. The sky is beginning to lighten so Rolling Thunder and the brave set out at once to build a campfire. That done, Rolling Thunder has us form a huge circle around the fire and I find myself between Roger McGuinn and Lola. The brave passes around a tobacco pouch from which each of us is instructed to take a pinch of tobacco to be thrown into the fire as we make our own individual prayers. Then Rolling Thunder sternly warns us of the seriousness and sanctity of the ceremony and he bans all cameras and tape recorders.

Rolling Thunder begins the ceremony by explaining the meaning that sunrise has to the Indians, the affirmation, the renewal, the generosity of the Great Spirit. When he concludes his talk, he asks us to make our own prayers starting clockwise. Peter Orlovsky steps to the fire with, "I pray that we should all eat well and stop smoking cigarettes that are bad for us." "May the spirit of this tour extend to everyone we meet along the road," Ramblin' Jack notes poignantly. Then all eyes shift to Dylan, who's been standing with his head shyly burrowed into his chest, his Tibetan scarf flowing in the wind. He rocks back and forth on his boot heels, nervously kneading the tobacco in his fist. "I pray that man will soon realize that we are all of one soul," he says gently, then strides to the fire and tosses the tobacco into the flames. Ronee Blakley shyly monotones a message that nobody can really hear and then Roger McGuinn vaults to the fire. "I pray that we'll realize that everything's gonna be all right," he enthuses. It's my turn. I step to the fire, "For life . . . and love."

After the circle is completed, Rolling Thunder invites Allen Ginsberg to recite a poem. Ginsberg, in jean jacket, scarf, and red bandanna tied around his balding pate, pulls some Australian aborigine song sticks from his shoulder bag and begins to improvise a poem-chant to the accompaniment of the sticks.

> When Music was needed Music sounded
> When a Ceremony was needed a Teacher appeared
> When Students were needed Telephones rang
> When Cars were needed Wheels rolled in
> When a Place was needed a Mansion appeared
> When a Fire was needed Wood appeared
> When an Ocean was needed Waters rippled waves
> When Shore was needed Shore met ocean
> When Sun was needed the Sun rose east
> When People were needed People arrived
> When a circle was needed a Circle was formed.

The recitation over, Rolling Thunder addressed the circle again: "There was a girl who wanted to take photographs. It is permissible now." Mary whips out her Nikon, and starts to circle the circle, trying to line up Dylan, who begins a cat-and-mouse game with her. She darts discreetly behind McGuinn and snaps just as Dylan notices something interesting on his shoe. She retreats and peeks around Blakley; Dylan suddenly has an impulse to stare at the tree behind him. The game goes on as Neuwirth helps the brave to put out the fire.

The rest of us huddle together, warding off the cold, as the sun rises magnificently over the Sound. Everybody seems a little dewy-eyed, moved by the experience. We start back to the mansion, our host promising us a glimpse at some of the art work there.

I'm walking with Mary when someone calls to us from the rear. We look back and it's Rolling Thunder, deftly hopping over the rocks, scampering toward us. He pulls alongside and begins to talk to Mary about photography and mentions the book that was written about him. "Listen," he smiles, "do you think you could send me a copy of your contact sheets?" And as I walk on toward the house, the medicine man is scribbling his post-office-box address on a piece of paper.

8

We march single file into the house, proceed up a narrow flight of stairs, and are led down a long corridor, peeking into room after room filled with oil paintings, watercolors, and some sculpture. I linger in one room, presently joined by David Blue, Mary, and a few others. Suddenly Dylan storms in. He stops about three feet from Mary and casts a penetrating glare. "Who are you?" he spits out. Mary blanches and finally manages to stammer her name. "Well, what are you doing here? Who invited you?" Dylan snarls, rocking back and forth on his heels. Mary looks like she's about to faint and finally she weakly points to me and David Blue. "I know them," she whispers.

Dylan rolls his eyes. "Oh great, Larry. She's your photographer, huh," he snaps, then turns back to her. "I bet you got some great pictures." Mary smiles faintly. "Well, I'd like to see 'em," he adds. With the change in tone Mary blurts out, "Where can I get in touch with you?" Dylan smiles sarcastically: "Ask Larry, he seems to know where we are." With that, he turns on his heel and walks out of the room.

After a few more minutes of house-seeing, we file back down to the cars. Dylan, Neuwirth, and McGuinn pile into the singer's camper, which leads the caravan back to the hotel. It's almost 10 A.M. now, time for breakfast, so a few of us grab seats in the coffee shop. Blakley, Soles, McGuinn, Blue, and I cram into a booth as Ramblin' Jack just sort of wanders around. Roger, an electronics freak, has brought his walkie-talkies with him and hands one to Jack and they start a conversation across the room. Blue relieves Elliot and starts to wander outside, broadcasting his whereabouts every few seconds in a fuzzy garbled tone.

Blakley cracks up. "I never saw two kids with a couple of tin cans crazier than you guys are." Roger just smiles and goes back to his unit. "Come back, David," he screams into the walkie-talkie, "where are you going? Over and out." After a few more minutes of this the food arrives, signaling a suspension of communications.

McGuinn and I begin to discuss our present relationships with women, both of us being in the throes of some difficult times. "My old lady's upset about me being on the road," Roger notes somberly, "about balling other women, and all that. I told her to go out and get laid, it wouldn't bother me. I could've brought her on the road but I didn't want to, even though the newsletter said it was all right."

I commiserate. "My problem is that my girlfriend makes me feel like I'm a sexual monster, that I'm totally over-sexed if I want to get laid once a night."

"Once a night, that's not unreasonable," McGuinn sympathizes with a smile.

Suddenly Blakley looks up from stirring her coffee. She leans over toward us and smiles conspiratorially. "I'd like to get laid at least three times a day," she leers, pausing for effect. She leans back, nonchalantly, then chuckles, "Depending on how long each one is."

After breakfast, I return to my motel, partake of some artificial stimulation, and begin to pack for the trip to Stockbridge, Massachusetts, our next stop. Finally, an hour or so later, I pull out in the Granada, feeling grubby, weary, and glum at the prospect of driving alone for hours, but incredibly enough, there right ahead of me are the two tour buses. Aha, a convoy, I smile to myself, as I scoot in line and guard the rear.

We drive on for ten minutes, winding through magnificently scenic streets of Newport until the buses pull into a parking lot on a narrow tree-lined road. Everyone's filing off the buses and crossing the street where Chris O'Dell is standing in front of the archway to a cobblestoned road that leads to an incredible mansion. It's like a scene out of summer camp, O'Dell standing there with clipboard, checking off each body, then reciting their name out loud. I sneak into line behind the film crew and blithely smile as I scurry under the archway. O'Dell shrugs.

We assemble at the foot of the stairs leading to the

house, and since we're too numerous to go through at one time, O'Dell divides us into groups. I'm thrust with Ginsberg, Orlovsky, Levy, McGuinn, Stoner, Elliot, and Kemp, who's doing a slow burn staring at me. "Good afternoon, I'm Mrs. Welch," a matronly red-jacketed woman announces. "Welcome to the Breakers, the Vanderbilt mansion." We step in to a massive lobby, replete with antiques, portraits, and exquisite fixtures. "This is nice," Mel Howard scans the room, "but it's nothing like our place." "This is the Old Commodore, Cornelius Vanderbilt," our guide points to a portrait, "and this is his grandson. This is the countess." They all look rich. Kemp keeps asking Mrs. Welch financial questions, how much the mansion's worth, how much the upkeep is. Ginsberg plops into a chair. "This is where you had to wait around if they didn't want to see you," he gleefully reports.

"The house is 250 feet long, and 150 feet wide," Welch drones on in her sweet rehearsed monotone, "made of Indiana limestone." Ronee Blakley walks in, along with a three-man film crew. "There's an open courtyard," Welch reports, then spies the cameras. "There are no pictures allowed in the house," smiling her saccharine smile. "Right on," Jack Elliot mutters. "Great," Levy laughs out loud, "the film crew is getting kicked out again." Stoner leans over to me. "I bet we're the rudest tourists yet," he snickers.

"These are pillars of Italian marble," Welch continues. "I say gaudy," Levy twinkles. "I say expensive," Kemp counters. Our guide frowns. We start up the stairs. "Send a security guard up here," McGuinn shrieks into his walkie-talkie. Upstairs, there's a bedroom and surrounding the bed is a cage. "That was to protect the chick who lived up here," McGuinn cracks. Welch seems a bit shaken and Kemp frowns at Roger. "McGuinn was misbehaving," Stoner taunts. Kemp eases the tension by asking about the taxes on the mansion.

We pass several other rooms. "Don't rich people shit?" I inquire. "They hide it behind the door," Stoner snaps. Finally, at the end of the hall, we reach the bathroom. It's vast, L-shaped, and Stoner seems truly awed. "I can't believe it," he gasps, "it's bigger than my pad." "There are no closets," Mrs. Welch demonstrates, "they're built into the paneling." Peter Orlovsky wanders over to the bathtub, a huge porcelain monster, complete with four faucets. Mrs. Welch smiles. "Salt water flows in," she cheerily tells Peter. "Look at those faucets, Allen," Peter marvels ingenuously, "you can wash your cock, pussy, and asshole in the same tub." Mrs. Welch turns a little green. Peter, though, is enthralled and twists a faucet, resulting in a spew of water cascading into the tub. "Oh, I'm sorry," Peter sincerely apologizes. "Dock him," Stoner sneers. "He can't go to the canteen tonight," I snicker.

We troop downstairs. By now Mrs. Welch has her composure back. "This is the largest fireplace ever built," she notes, "and this library wall has been carved to look like books." Rambling Jack peers at the wall. "I'd hate to be straight in this house," he drawls. We're in the library alcove now, the sun streaming in, as Mrs. Welch starts a detailed history of the family's fortunes. Allen takes out a pad and starts taking notes.

As we pass through the immense kitchen, the other group is starting their tour. "Dig the egg cups," Ginsberg laughs, as McGuinn examines an intercom system that has fifty-four stations throughout the house so the butlers know exactly where the caller was. I linger over the cutting table, examining the utensils. Baez leans her head in. "Move along, Ratso," she screams at me, "we're waiting for you guys to finish." In the corridor, Steve Soles joins our group. "Let's go to the gentlemen's waiting room and have an orgy," he leers. There are no takers.

Outside, Stoner and I are posing in front of the house. "Get Ken Regan," Stoner instructs. "Have him take a picture. It'll be my next album cover, 'Rob Stoner at Home!' " "Great, maybe I can use the photo in the book," I think and corral Regan, the official tour photographer. He mumbles that he's out of film then lowers his eyes. "I can't take any pictures for your book. Haven't you heard? Kemp's giving the book to someone else." I fume and go searching for Kemp, but he's already gone, so I stalk to the Granada, hit the ignition, and burn down the road to Stockbridge.

In the lazy Berkshire town of Stockbridge, the tour is staying at the Red Lion Lodge, a quaintly beautiful inn. But I'm still in a miserable mood as I stomp up to the desk clerk and ask to speak to Mr. Kemp. No answer, so I prowl the halls, walk through the old dining rooms, finally coming upon a few people from the tour. Chris O'Dell jumps up from her plate. "What are you doing here?" She stares at me incredulously.

"Looking for Louis."

"You can't come into the hotels. Don't you understand?" she lectures. "You've been pretty pushy the last few days. I'll just have to get security to deal with you," and as if on cue, two burly lumberjack types waddle into the room and grab an arm each. They escort me to the lobby where I go limp onto a sofa. "I'm not splitting. This is a public lobby," I sputter in my best oppressed voice. They confer and one leaves, the other discreetly standing guard a few yards away.

After a few minutes, Sam Shepard walks by. Shepard is a well-known Off-Broadway playwright, and he's been hired to help write the screenplay of the movie. Only it seems that he's been given a bit of a runaround and is seriously considering returning to his California ranch.

"I'm pissed off," the lean, angular writer snarls, "I've been lied to."

"You're pissed off," I sputter, "I get invited on this tour by Dylan, the minute we get out of New York I'm the nigger. I can't even talk to my friends."

"I'm ready to quit," Shepard sneers, "go home. They made some assurances to me in terms of money that they didn't follow through on. There's like this reverse Dylan generosity syndrome here. They say that because Bob is so generous and this tour is making a sort of antimoney, antiestablishment position in terms of money and large halls, therefore they can rip you off and it's all right 'cause it's an antimaterialist thing."

We commiserate a bit more and Shepard returns to his room. I burrow deeper into the couch, under the watchful eye of security. Apparently the other guard had left to get somebody to mediate because a few minutes later, Bobby Neuwirth bounces into the lobby. Neuwirth has been a quasi-legendary figure on the music scene for some time now. He's sort of the Truman Capote of the musical counterculture, knows everybody from Kristofferson to Nicholson to Kinky Friedman. And this is his first real exposure, playing onstage with the guy that he road-managed in the mid-'60s.

Neuwirth lopes over to an easy chair and plops down.

"What do you want, Larry, what do you want?" he rasps in his machine-gun-rapid style. "I got a million things to do, man. I got three crises. I just had to fire Cindy Bullens, man, my best friend. I fired her because she made a professional error when she decided to go with the Elton John tour. She came back here and it was too late, so I had to fire her. I couldn't even say good-bye to her, we would have broken into tears. I also got problems with the rehearsals. The band needs more rehearsal, this tour is still in a fucking rehearsal stage."

I manage to slip in my complaint about access. Neuwirth frowns.

"Shit," he growls. "You got more access than anyone so far. Maureen Orth from *Newsweek*, she couldn't even get past the breakfast table. Listen, you oughta go out and write, write. You're a creator. Create. You don't have to be here." Neuwirth pauses and his eyes turn softer. He hunches over closer and his voice turns gentle: "We're dumping people. You may go. I want you to be able to handle that. There's a question of ego versus intellect. So far a lot of people have been getting on ego trips instead of letting their intellects take precedence over their ego." He gets even closer and stares at me in his best Southern California sensitivity-session style. "Look me in the eye. Say you'll survive, you'll make it, you won't be upset. Shit, man, it's fifteen years later and we all survived. Tell me you won't be upset."

"Hey, all I want to do is do my job and do this book."

Neuwirth scowls. "Fuck, man, who needs another book on Bob Dylan? What are you gonna write about, what Bob Dylan eats for breakfast? Go out and write, man. There are a lot of things happening in the world, why don't you go and write about it? Just tell me you'll survive."

"I'll make it," I shrug and we shake hands. Neuwirth turns and heads back to his room.

I head for my car but outside on the porch, I bump into Gary Shafner, Bob's factotem.

"Just cool it for a while," Gary counsels, "Bob likes you. You don't want tension between yourself and Louie. Lay low. Deal with me and Chris. Jesus, when you came in the hotel this evening, in one minute we had heard you were around. Keep a low profile."

I thank him for the advice and drive back to my dumpy

hotel in nearby Lee. The phone doesn't work, the TV refuses to acknowledge any other program but Johnny Carson, and the stimulants are beginning to wear off, so I climb into the lumpy mattress and dream about the opulence of the Red Lion Lodge.

But the next day, at the Springfield concert, good news comes in the form of Howard Alk. Alk is a bear of a man, huge, with a tremendous beard that covers virtually every inch of his round, warm face, and an old shopping-bag-man fedora precariously balanced on his head. He's worked with Dylan before, editing the now legendary *Eat the Document*, footage of Dylan's 1967 tour that has never been released, except for a short run at the Whitney Museum in New York. But now Howard is hard at work on Bob's latest project, the massive film of the tour. And it's eighteen-hour-a-day work, shooting in the morning at a moment's notice, sometimes shooting the concert, and then viewing the daily rushes. Alk seems like he's beginning to drag.

"Listen, we saw the rushes of the scene you did at the party and it was fabulous," Howard tells me. "It was one of the classic interviews in documentary film. Bob loved it. You got nothing to worry about, you're in." On that cryptic note, he lumbered off.

I spot Allen Ginsberg and Peter Orlovsky up in the stands and I join them for the second half of the show, sliding in next to Peter just as Dylan and Baez start into "Never Let Me Go," and seconds later, Allen and Peter are harmonizing along.

"What do you think of this segment?" I lean over Peter and shout at Allen.

"It's just beautiful to watch them relating," he responds.

"Joanie told me it's very hard to follow Bob," I report.

"Well," Allen muses, "he's being playful all the time and changing things. It keeps people on their toes. Like here when they say 'in summer or in dream time,' he usually might stretch it. He keeps it awake and alert and alive."

Down below, the two small figures start into "Any Day Now" and Allen hums along then leans toward me. "Dylan's teaching her how to sing those songs. By over and over again looking into each other's eyes. Now the words are giving her the timing, giving her the way of doing this accurately. He had to teach her."

Allen gets bored with this vantage point and suggests

we move around, so we trundle all the way to the rear of the arena and stand in an entryway. From here, the performers look like ants but the sound system reaches us more than adequately. Allen and Peter start swaying to the music, prompting a young, slightly tipsy kid to do a triple take. Finally he sidles up to Ginsberg.

"That's Allen Ginsberg, huh," he asserts to no one in particular, pointing at the bearded poet.

"No," Ginsberg replies calmly, "he's dead."

"You're Allen Ginsberg," the kid is getting more brazen, "you wrote 'Howl.' Can you recite 'Howl'?"

"Not while Joan Baez is singing," Ginsberg fumes.

"She's singing," he notes with wonder, then turns back to the poet. "You're Allen Ginsberg," he shouts with finality.

Ginsberg throws his hands in the air in a fit of exasperation. "I'm me," he shouts almost at the top of his lungs.

"You're you," the youth admits, "but who are you?"

Ginsberg is relishing this cat-and-mouse exercise. "Nobody but me," he responds.

The kid lets it sink in, then raises the ante. "What is your identity?" he nonchalantly rolls back, "who is your nobody?" A smug look crosses his face. Heavy.

"There's no such thing as identity," Ginsberg back. A pause. Then, "I'm as empty as you are. The ultimate identity." The ultimate response. Game set, match point. The kid admits defeat just as Baez breaks into the line, "Here comes your ghost again." He draws nearer to Ginsberg and with a note of humility asks, "Can I talk to you. Is that possible in the future?"

"I don't know the future," Ginsberg counters.

"When I'm in a sober condition," the kid pleads. "It's a rare occasion."

Ginsberg relents and they move to the side and engage in a discussion about poetry. After a few minutes, Ginsberg edges toward me. "What's your favorite songs?" he asks.

I cite "Isis," "One More Cup," and "Sara."

" 'One More Cup of Coffee' is to me the high point," Allen asserts. "It's sacred and the mode of music is Hindu-Arabic. He uses cantillation. That's the ohohohoh-ohohoh, the wavering note. 'Sara' is very beautiful, it's personal."

The kid lurches toward us again. "He doesn't have to be singing though," Allen notes, "he can get it across just by reading it, and maybe get it across much faster. . . ."

"Look what happened to Nietzsche," the kid interrupts, "he went insane for eleven and a half years."

"That didn't have anything to do with him not singing, I'm sure," Ginsberg retorts.

"All of Hesse though is taken from Nietzsche, it appears to me," the kid goes blithely on.

Ginsberg smiles. "They're both about singing, so they should have just sang," he pronounces with impeccable logic.

Down below, Dylan mounts the stage for his solo spot. "Looks just like the old days with the black leather jacket. Remember *Don't Look Back*, Allen?" I inquire.

"I was in it," he stresses.

"He's got so much to say with his music," the kid chimes in.

"He's a good singer," Allen agrees.

"He's a poet," the kid shoots back.

"He's a great poet," Ginsberg corrects, as Dylan plows into "I Don't Believe You."

"He said in that *People* interview that he considers himself more of an artist than a musician," the kid adds.

"He paints, he's serious about it," Allen notes.

"Think they're any good?" I jump in.

Ginsberg frowns. "I don't think in those terms. Good and bad are irrelevant. The great mindfulness and mysteriousness is what's interesting. I viewed them with great interest and curiosity." Ginsberg turns back toward Dylan, watching the small figure below pumping his body to the beat and pushing the song along with his mournful harmonica. Ginsberg peers at the stage, then turns back to me.

"One thing that's really interesting is that he plays music with his whole body, foot tapping to knee to thigh to his hip, as well as his right arm and neck," Ginsberg lectures, as his hand scans Dylan's anatomy. "He's like a conductor for this . . ."

"Energy," I interrupt.

"If you say so, that's your word," Ginsberg allows.

"It's like waves, like orgone energy flowing through him," I elaborate.

"His movements are very simple and basic," Ginsberg

argues, "his physical involvement with the music. I think when you talk about orgones and cosmic forces it gets it away from the actual body, the stomping of the foot." Allen smiles. "It's just a simple foot-stomping but it's real."

"You've all heard of Hurricane Carter," Dylan announces from the stage.

"Free him," I scream.

"Hum, Hum, Hum," Peter issues the Buddhist cheer.

Ginsberg leans over to me. "What did he say?" I repeat the introduction as the band kicks into "Hurricane" with a vengeance. "It's just like the old protest songs, simple street language, accessible to the masses, no mystification about it, just a clear journalistic account," I tell Allen.

"I don't know if it's street language but it's more direct language," the poet responds. "The shit in 'George Jackson' and here 'what kind of shit is coming down,' he's using it in a way that's rhythmically very interesting."

"Such economy in that line about the judge making all of Rubin's witnesses drunkards from the slums, that sums up the whole trial," I add.

Ginsberg leans over Peter, "He's written the kind of song that the last rebels of the late '60s were demanding that he write."

"But he's doing it on his own terms," I add, "I think the demands have slackened off, now he's doing it 'cause he feels it. It isn't a simple knee-jerk Skinnerian response."

"I didn't mean that he was doing it 'cause they asked him to, or he was doing what they thought they wanted him to do. He'd been doing it all along actually," Allen adds.

We begin our way back because Allen has to go onstage for the encore, but directly stage left Peter finds three empty seats. We're high up, but we have a good vantage point as Dylan moves to the mike. "This song is straight out of the underground," he breathes, and the familiar murky strains of "One More Cup of Coffee" fill the civic center. Ginsberg is rocking in his seat, shout-singing along, "One more cup of coffee before I go down to the valley below!"

"Which valley?" I joke.

"Death!" Ginsberg notes with finality. "Or life; anything," then adds: "The valley below. The Biblical valley. The shadow of the valley . . ."

"This song is so mysterious and murky," I whisper, "it reminds me of a mature 'Maggie's Farm.' That gypsy violin is incredible."

"Well it's Moorish, gypsy, Arabic, semitic," Ginsberg points out. "It's a rabbinical, cantotorial thing he hasn't done before. It's just like a real Jewish melody. 'Sara' is also. Yiddish. This one's Hebraic, though. I'm just hearing the words as they come through."

"It's almost a put-down of hedonism with that line 'your pleasure knows no limits,' a put-down of excess," I say.

Dylan finishes the song. "Hum, Hum, Hum," Ginsberg screams, causing a sea of faces in our section to investigate the source of the strange warble. "For the moment that's my favorite song," he bubbles, "definitely a great song. 'Isis' and 'Hurricane,' I'm in sympathy with them in historical terms but this is sort of an archetypal song and the voicing of it is the most open we have in the Hebrew, that sort of ahhh . . . Wait, here comes 'Sara,' see 'Sara oh Sara' that's the Yiddish part, the refrain, 'Sara oh Sara.' He reminds me of some rabbi, some negun. He looks like a negun. Write that down you can use that."

We both watch Dylan in silence for a minute. "What'd he just say," I ask Ginsberg, " 'Arabian jewel'?"

"I think 'radiant jewel,' 'mystical wife,' " he corrects.

"What an amazing song, listen to the chronology," I yell. "After the beach scene, he talks about Woodstock, then living in the Chelsea Hotel. I wonder what she feels when she hears this?" We both start singing the chorus.

Dylan starts up the last stanza, "Now the beach is deserted except for some kelp . . ." Ginsberg leans over, "A sort of wave of consciousness goes through the audience when he goes through that stanza, a sudden realization of what he's doing. Back to the beach now."

"This is like 'Shelter from the Storm,' " I note, "but it's better, closer to the bone."

Ginsberg smiles. "He revealed his heart," he gestures with one finger in the air; "for Dylan to reveal his heart completely is for me a great historical event. For any man to reveal his heart completely is a great historical event. It gives other people permission to reveal their hearts. Look at the way he's bouncing now. He's very relaxed." Allen leans forward, devouring the scene. "Hum,

Hum, Hum," he shouts with his hands cupped to his mouth.

"What does that 'Hum' mean," I inquire.

"It's a mantra for intellectual penetration," Ginsberg explains, with his eyes fixed to the stage. "It's from the heart." Dylan swings into "Just Like a Woman," eliciting a roar from the audience.

"It's brilliant to go from that complete announcement of his totally open heart to some ancient open heart song," Allen admires, "completely transformed for them now. Everybody has thought about Dylan endlessly for ten years and now he's taken all those thoughts and summarized them and he's putting out the definitive statements about what we thought. All the fantasies people had about his children and his wife, he's out there doing them." He returns to the song. Dylan is hunched over the mike, his face temporarily hidden by the hat with the fresh flowers. "Queen Mary she's my friend," Dylan confides, "yes I believe I'll go see her again."

"He's right out there now," Ginsberg points, "giving. He's completely in his body, completely in the song, completely at one with his universe."

"I just don't fit," Dylan howls, as Allen hurries down to make his cue. And a few minutes later, the poet is behind a mike in the rear, beating on his finger cymbals to the Woody Guthrie classic, staring at the back of the little guy with the open heart.

There's another concert tonight, so I file outside with the ecstatic audience and look for a place to eat. Outside, I spot Bob Gruen, a freelance rock photographer, and Chris Charlesworth, a New York correspondent for *Melody Maker* magazine. They're hungry too and we settle on the Red Rose Cafe, a funky pizza parlor.

The jukebox is blaring "George Jackson" as we enter and grab a booth.

"What a scene," Gruen moans. "I had to smuggle my cameras in. After the shit Pulin went through in Plymouth, man, they confiscated his cameras and he didn't get them for hours. You should have seen 'em tonight, I had lenses in the hood of my coat, cameras in my boots." Our lasagnas come, and the waitress politely asks for $2.35 each upfront. She mumbles something about lots of walkouts.

Suddenly, I hear a familiar sound wafting through the room. It's the concert; "Oh Sister" is playing on someone's cassette. Bootleggers in Springfield! I investigate. Across the room, they're sitting around a booth, three of them, one lean, Italian-looking; one larger, ruddy-faced; one a petite brunette, real wired. I join the table and tell them I'm covering the tour for *Rolling Stone*. Instant assault.

"What's the tour like? Is Sara with him?" the skinny one asks.

"Is he at ease on this tour?" the burly one demands simultaneously. They laugh and we all introduce ourselves. There's Sal, the thin ascetic-looking one, Sheila, who seems about to pop her gourd, and Ken. They're all around thirty and all teach in New Jersey high schools. All stone Dylan fanatics.

"We all went to see him several times on the last tour with the Band," Ken says, "and the audience was so nice like everyone was dying to stand up and just scream but instead everybody like took it easy because they didn't want to scare him away. Do you think that has anything to do with him coming back here now? Like, he's so free and easy onstage now."

"I think seeing Rubin in jail affected him strongly, Rubin trying to reach out and touch people after years of being reclusive and antisocial," I suggest.

"I've never seen him like this," Ken marvels, playing with the remains of his spaghetti, "he looks like he did in 1966, like in *Eat the Document!*"

Sal lights up. "Yeah, we saw that at the Whitney Museum when it played. Went ten times, every day. By the way, do you know what ever happened to *Don't Look Back?*"

"He sued," I offer, "took it out of circulation."

"In *Eat the Document*, though, he seems as tight as a wire," Ken shakes his head, "but right now, we were right behind the stage and he turned around and he looked just like Buddha. He just smiled, he was so relaxed."

Sal is leaning over the table now, just waiting for a chance to jump in. "I saw both shows in Providence," he blurts, "and what really blew my mind was the way he was emoting. He was acting, it was like a play. He was just there. Besides the makeup, the expressions on his face were like *Eat the Document*."

"Why do you think he's wearing makeup?" I throw out. The three of them pause in their tracks, then Sal addresses the class. "I don't know," he muses, "I think it's because he wanted to create a Pierrot figure on the stage. You hand in your money and you go watch the geek and there he is onstage and he's doing that, in other words, he's saying, Don't take me too seriously, I'm one of the clowns in my songs."

"He always said he was a trapeze artist," I counter with a smile.

"What I really liked too was the reconciliation with Joanie," Sal adds. "Like for so many years she's been in such pain, every time I've seen her in concert she's talked about him and sung to him. The last time I saw her was at the Felt Forum and she said, 'Everybody tells me to leave Bobby alone, that there's nothing he cherishes more than his privacy, but I'll do anything I can to get him back onstage.' "

Ken suddenly snaps out of a reverie and looks at us with urgency. "You know, Sal said earlier that when you see Dylan at so much peace it's almost like he's going back and I asked him how we can explain Dylan going back to his roots. It's like if he's going back, if you read the Scaduto book, he's a real fuck, he burns everybody. Yet here he is sending bridges." His voice trails off quizzically, and he scans us for a response.

Sal scowls. "We met Scaduto," he smirks, "he's an asshole. We were interpreting songs, asking him what things meant and he didn't even know. At Brentano's, it was an autograph thing. We had to answer all the questions for him. How can anyone write a book about Dylan and give one paragraph to *Blonde on Blonde* and mention the *Basement Tapes* in one sentence." Sal shakes his head in disgust.

"It could have been Guy Lombardo he was writing about," Ken moans. "All it was, was police reporting."

"He couldn't penetrate Dylan's circle," I suggest. "After all, the people that he interviewed all had lost contact with Bob."

Sal stabs at the leftovers of his veal. "He interviewed people like the dish-cleaning woman at the Cafe Wha?, Beattie Zimmerman's next-door neighbor, shit like that. Where were the interviews with Robbie Robertson, and Mike Bloomfield?"

The table falls quiet, Sal and Ken lost in some private Dylan reverie; Sheila, who's stayed silent, seems to be biding her time till the second show starts. Ken breaks the silence: "What do you think about that *People* interview, like when he said he can't elude the Dylan myth any longer, it's what God wants?"

"He's doing God's work," Sal flatly states.

"I think he believes that," I say softly.

"Do you think it's a sign that on this tour he isn't doing any stuff from *Planet Waves* or *Blood on the Tracks?*" Sal inquires.

"I tried to teach McGuinn to do 'Never Say Goodbye,' " I laugh, "but he never had time to learn it. What do you think of *Planet Waves* anyway?"

Ken laughs, "After waiting so long for something . . ."

"After waiting all those years, of course we were ecstatic," Sal lectures, "but looking at it in perspective, last night we were playing the tape over and over again and listening to his new material we taped at the concert, it seems to me that since he's made the decision to come back, he's been trying to gain his ground. He did the *Planet Waves* LP, he did the tour with the Band, but he looked nervous, uptight. He didn't seem to be partying through most of that. Then came *Blood on the Tracks,* which was a gigantic step in the right direction, but I still don't think he was capturing the sound that he wanted to. But with this new material it seems that he's getting back to what he really wants to do."

"But what about the songs in that period?" I ask.

"A lot I didn't think were effective," Sal shrugs.

"*Blood on the Tracks* was," Ken asserts.

Sal grabs his fork and starts puncturing the air with it. "It seemed to me that Dylan reached a peak that no one else had managed to get near in *Blonde on Blonde, Highway 61,* that whole madness period, just pre-bike accident, and then he had the accident and went through all these heavy changes. He withdrew, tried withdrawal, it didn't work, he wanted to get back, he was itching. Made a number of abortive attempts to get back. Withdrew from those. Finally decided to take a lunge, did *Planet Waves. Planet Waves,* to me, relates more to *New Morning* than it does to *Blonde on Blonde* but this new material relates more to *Blonde on Blonde.*"

"He said to me the problem was that everyone expects another *Blonde on Blonde,*" I note.

Sal sighs, "But the intensity, the perfection of that record."

"*Planet Waves* is a precise LP," I interrupt, "a tremendous statement about the balancing of domesticity with the concerns of a mystical artist. It seems from that LP that he had to make a choice and now he made the decision."

"The choice we wanted him to make," Sal acknowledges with a smile.

"I asked him why he tours and he told me 'It's in my blood,' " I add.

"Look," Sal bangs the table, "it's like in 'Going, Going, Gone,' you could just see the changes he seemed to be going through there. He wasn't sure, living on the edge, playing it straight, but I gotta get back before it gets too late. See, he decided to go back to the edge again." Sal smiles smugly.

"If you perceived all this from the LP," Ken counters, "then the album was successful. That's what Larry's trying to say."

Sal grimaces. "I'm just playing devil's advocate here. I love everything he's done."

"That's why you asked me before why do I care about knowing about Sara." Sal is staring at me. "It's 'cause Dylan reveals pieces of his life, like a mosaic, on his records. You're intensely interested in what's going on in his life, of course, you see yourself in it, but everything about him, everything he does, you want to know."

It's time to leave for the Civic Center, but first the New Jerseyites are having an instant lottery. They have three tickets, one in the second row, one in the fourth, and one in the tenth. Sal carefully shuffles and places them face down on the table. They take turns picking. "I got it, I got it. The second row!" Sheila screams at the top of her lungs, jumping up and down. She hugs Sal.

We walk the few blocks to the arena discussing Dylan, of course. Sal is just about to explain his analogy between Springsteen and Donovan in *Don't Look Back,* when we come up to a kid singing in the mall right outside the hall. But this isn't just another panhandler. I stop.

"This song is dedicated to Bob Dylan," this kid is singing.

He's weird-looking, small, skinny, looking something like a cross between Paul Simon and Woody Allen. With a voice like a Lily Tomlin character. "My name is Roger Cowen," he's talk-singing. "I'm from around here. I was born and raised right here in Springfield, Mass., and I'm proud to be here. I came in from New York City just to play the Rolling Thunder Revue before this concert in my hometown. Yeah."

With his exaggerated jerkiness and perfect atonality this kid's a natural for the film, I thought to myself. I interrupt the recitation and ask him if he wants to be in a movie. He leans over toward me and continues strumming. "Do I want to be in a film?" he whispers. "Sure, I want to be in a film." Then he suddenly slams down on his strings, stomps his foot, and begins to howl, "It's all part of the Rolling Thunder Revue!"

The second show is incredible. Everyone's really loose, T-Bone going so far as to dress up like the Red Baron, with goggles, long scarf, and aviator cap. And midway through the opening set, a black-leather-pantsed Arlo Guthrie ambles on and picks out two new numbers aided by McGuinn on harp. Then Dylan bounds on, and he's singing incredibly, leaning sensually into the mike, then turning to the band half in authority and half in awe, then back to the mike, even gesturing gently to the sky on the line "make me a rainbow." The film crew is shooting tonight so everybody's a bit hotter than usual. In fact, Dylan's almost verbose with his introductions. "This is a tune from south of the border," he cracks before "Durango." "Remember now, raw lust does not hold a candle to true love. We're doing this tonight for Sam Peckinpah. Glad you could make it, Sam."

At intermission, I walk back to the bar for a drink. And right by the entrance with her long feathered hat and sad-eyed stare is Lisa. We walk in and sit on stools as a waitress out of the '50's takes our orders, a martini for me, a beer for Lisa.

"I gave a feather to Dylan," Lisa whispers, "Denise gave it to him for me. She gave it to him and he asked her what kind of feather it was and she told him to ask me." Lisa smiles. It seems she had to drive back up to Vermont, pay her rent, tell her boss she had a sick relative, load up the old Chevy with fresh blank cassettes and her beat-up old guitar, and then head straight back for the caravan. She found out about Stockbridge, hung out all afternoon on the street outside the hotel, and lucked into seeing Baez who took pity on her.

"I was standing there," Lisa relates, "and Joan came over and shook my hand. She said, 'What are you doing, just standing there and watching the confusion.' Then she told her road manager to give me a ticket. She said I'll be her guest, that I wasn't annoying anyone. I saw Bob too, he was alone, looking at windows of the shops. I asked him about the feather and he told me it was in good hands."

Lisa swigs from her draft and tries to pump me for information on my last few meetings with Dylan. "I told him it really gets tough sometimes," she sighs, "and he just said that I'll survive. I said, 'I'll never find the rainbow at the end of the highway,' and he said, 'It's all within, man.'" Lisa sighs again. It's almost time to go back to our seats. I down the martini and get up to leave. "Remember the song Bob dedicated to Herman Melville?" Lisa suddenly asks. "Who is Herman Melville?" I just roll my eyes and laugh. "Ah," I growl, "go back to school, man!"

The pace is just as torrid in the second half of the concert. Dylan and Baez open it with flawless duets then Baez keeps up the tempo with a set that evokes a standing ovation from drummer Wyeth. Then Dylan scampers on, looking funky with a few days' growth of stubble spotting his face. "We heard that Rubin is getting a new trial," he exults before doing "Hurricane," "and we also learned that Massachusetts was the only state that didn't vote for Nixon." A pause, then a chuckle. "We didn't vote for him, either," he slyly adds. "Hurricane" is great but the rumor is unfounded. And he still seems to be thinking of Nixon when they break into "Knocking on Heaven's Door." "Take these bugs out of my ears," Dylan ad-libs, "I can't hear through them anymore." The finale is wonderful, Arlo back on to do a chorus of his father's song and getting the loudest ovation of the night.

As soon as they head offstage, I bolt for the door and rush out to meet Roger Cowen. He's standing there with his beat-up guitar and his tall friend, Dan, and we battle the crowd back into the arena. Larry Johnson is waiting for us, and escorts us out to the floor.

All around us, chairs are being folded up, the stage is

being broken down, and the echoes of these activities eerily reverberate around the empty hall. Meyers has arrived with his camera strapped to his shoulder, and he's directing Roger to stand at a spot somewhere in the middle of the floor. Roger looks nervous, this scruffy, five-foot gnome with the beat-up guitar. His friend Dan towers behind him.

Meyers signals he's ready. "OK, Roger," I direct, "why don't you do that song you did outside the hall, then I'll ask you some questions." Cowen nods, as Meyers rolls it. Roger takes a deep breath and then he closes his eyes and leans his head back, as if he were entering some sort of self-induced trance state. Suddenly he rocks forward, slamming down on his guitar strings and shrieks in a high-pitched warble:

> May you earn your blessings
> From the work you do
> Your wealth will be judged
> By the work you do
> On the Rolling Thunder Revue
> Rolling Thunder Revue
> Rolling Thunder Revue
> How about you?

It's amazing, there's something absolutely compelling about this duo, the brash, gutsy little songwriter and his shy, lean vocal partner. It's the rawness, the edge of mania in their faces, the desperation in their voices. They look like a schizoid version of Simon and Garfunkel. Cowen is slapping the side of his guitar during the refrain, and now he assaults the strings again:

> Every man has the will to serve the Lord
> Love and knowledge are the test
> So won't you come aboard
> On the Rolling Thunder Revue
> Rolling Thunder Revue
> Rolling Thunder Revue
> Eyahhhhhhhhh. . . .

He's moaning now, rolling his eyes, and then he goes into this talking section, the voice cracking every so often. "This is my home town, and I traveled here from New York City to play for Bob Dylan right in my home town and may this be dedicated to him, God Bless You all on the Rolling Thunder Revue, Rolling Thunder Revue, Rolling Thunder Revue, how about you?"

> We are all instruments
> And love is our song
> Everybody has a part to play
> So won't you sing along
> On the Rolling Thunder Revue
> Rolling Thunder Revue
> Rolling Thunder Revue

When he reaches this last chorus Meyers begins to fade back, widening the frame, showing this little folksinger lost in the ever-increasing vastness of empty space around him. Meyers is propelling himself backward, shooting all the time, until he's about fifty feet from the kid. In the background you can hear the muffled sounds of the destruction of the stage. But life doesn't always acquiesce to art. Cowen'll have none of this poetic *cinéma-vérité* slow fade to tactfulness. This is real life! He's got a goddamn message to get across. This Rolling Thunder Revue, it's serious stuff, it's fucking spiritual. And this is the big break, this is what made those fourteen-, fifteen-hour days of hacking a cab around Manhattan worth anything.

Roger finishes the chorus, pauses after the last "Rolling Thunder Revue" and then suddenly, puts down his head, then lifts up an accusatory finger, aiming it right at Meyers' fat lens, and makes a headlong charge across the bare wood floor. "How about youuuuuuuu," this little bull is screaming at the top of his lungs, charging straight into Meyers' lens. He gets to within a foot of the camera, stops, leers at it and moans, "You."

Meyers turns to us, and rolls his eyes. "In-fucking-credible," smiling. But Johnson wants more dialogue so Meyers starts the camera again and Roger breaks into his singsong voice: "I was sitting in my apartment in New York City, picked up a copy of the *New York Times,* saw a picture of Bob Dylan and the Rolling Thunder Revue on the cover. Oh Lord, you know my heart started to beat so fast, I started breathing heavy, the Rolling Thunder Revue, I couldn't describe my feelings, so I traveled home to my home town which is Springfield, Massachusetts, the first time I heard a Bob Dylan record was here, oh Lord. Now I just came here to see my folks, I'd been reading about the Rolling Thunder Revue but I didn't know if he was actually gonna be playing here and when I got here I found he was playing here and I dedicate this song to him and I thank God and bless him and everyone else who's on the Rolling Thunder Revue. On the Rolling Thunder Thunder Revue."

Dan joins in now, both of them chanting the chorus "Rolling Thunder Revue" until Roger stops playing, looks at the mike and moans, "How about you? Bob?"

"OK, we got it," Meyers exults and winks at us. "Another score, Larry." I walk with him and Johnson to load the equipment in their van.

"You're in now," Johnson tells me, "you don't have to worry. We've been putting in good words for you to Dylan. We had a meeting to view the rushes the other night and Dylan asked if we really needed you and Meyers gave a five-minute speech on your behalf. He said that you were a better straight man than Kemp and that you brought in our best interview so far, that girl Priscilla in Newport."

"What did Dylan say?" I ask.

"Nothing. He never says anything," Johnson chuckles, "he just takes it all in."

After getting a bite at a bizarre all-night deli that serves as the watering hole for Springfield's drag queens and general underlife, I drive through a heavy fog back to Lenox, and get to bed around 6. Only to be awakened at 9 A.M. by the jangling phone.

"Eiiiiiiii," a familiar voice is screaming, "how you doin', boychick. It's Kinky." I fill him in on the latest developments, my running disputes with Kemp, Dylan's vague authorization to do a book, Kemp's counterploy in planning to give the official book to another writer, Meyers' defense of me. Kinky advises me to bide my time. "What should I do," he wonders, "do you think it would be profitable to come up?"

"Sure, you definitely should come up, even if you don't perform," I urge. "I broached the idea to Dylan the other day and he acted real coy. He said to me, 'Do we have room for Kinky?' and I said, 'Listen, man, if Kinky can't come why the fuck don't you sing "Ride 'Em Jewboy"?' and he says, 'You gave me the words to that didn't you?

I got the words to that,' and I said, 'Why the fuck don't you sing it?' So he thought for a second, then said, 'I'll tell ya what, I'll sing one of Kinky's songs if he sings one of mine.' "

"Fuck, I'll sing anything," Kinky burps.

"Look, the worst thing that can happen if you came out for a few days, is you'll get in the movie. The fucking film crew is primed for you. I got them so excited they can't wait."

"Yeah, but Dylan might edit it out," Kinky worries.

"No, man," I reassure, "he likes you. You're Jewish."

After the call, I grab a quick bite to eat and drive around Lenox for a few hours before starting off for Vermont. It's a beautiful Indian-summer day, almost in the 70s, as I slowly drive through Pittsfield. And right in front of me is Phydeaux. Phydeaux is a specially built Greyhound, owned by Frank Zappa who lent it to Barry Imhoff at the last minute for this tour. It's got a drawing of a slightly anemic dog, barking "ARF" in a comic balloon, two fangs protruding from its jaws, and a Band-Aid on its ass. The bus is customized for rockstar travel, the windows all tinted so gawkers can't see in, and the interior arranged complete with bunk beds, comfortable lounge seats, and TV and stereo systems.

There's an informal caste system developing, with the "stars," the musicians, getting to ride on Phydeaux, and the "lesser lights," Ginsberg, Orlovsky, Denise (who help out with the baggage), Raven, Chris O'Dell, Jacques Levy, Sam Shepard, the guests, and the occasional security man riding on the backup bus, an old Delmonico. They've named the second bus too. Ghetteaux.

It's a long ride to Vermont, and it's late afternoon by the time the buses pull up to the Shelbourne Inn, where the tour is staying. I drive on a few miles further to Burlington and check into the Holiday Inn, just about peaking on the excitement and the drugs of the last few days as I sit down in front of the typewriter, feed in a sheet of South Burlington Holiday Inn stationery, and start a letter to Phil Bender, Dylan's *nom de registration.*

Dear Mr. Bender,
This letter comes to you from a state of confusion, ennui, and overbearing mania. I was tremendously turned on by your warm response to my request to do a book about the

tour since my Rolling Stoned articles hardly do justice to
my personal feelings about the revue, namely that it's the
fucking musical event of the last 200 years, next to Kate
Smith's rendition of "God Bless America" at Flyer games.
However, in my rush of elation at your approval of my
plan, I forgot to mention the "practical" aspects as Allen
counseled me, to get down once and for all. I really appreciated your offer to help me in any way possible and I
guess this letter is my attempt to delineate the things I need
to do justice to this tour in book form.

But before we get into that, a real distressing thing happened to me on Wed. After being high on the book idea
since our Monday chance meeting (we really can't go on
meeting like that), Wednesday at the Breakers after a
great afternoon of hanging out and being foolish with
Stoner, McGuinn, and Elliot (for the first fucking time
since we left Manhattan I was able to relate to them as
the friends they are), I asked Regan to take a shot of
Stoner posed à la Elvis in front of the mansion for my
book. Regan first said he was out of film, then sheepishly
said he wouldn't be able to give me any pictures for my
book since "Lou and Bob decided on Tuesday to give the
official tour book" to a reporter from *People* magazine.
Needless to say, I was crestfallen, world of illusion suddenly at my feet. Then fucking Meyers and Johnson rush
over and start filming me at the height of my anguish.
However, I did manage some good lines. At any rate, I
felt double-crossed, that my book was being aborted, since
a book without pictures and access to the people on the
tour (most of whom I count as my friends) wouldn't stand
a chance against a book with fab pix.

I really don't understand why Louie seems to hate me,
he even had the gall to call me Weberman at one point.
[Lou's animosity seems to transcend our normal press/
manager adversary roles and the only explanation I have
is what McGuinn warned me about at the Gramercy, that
anyone new who Dylan seems to dig is fair game for the
wrath of some of your close friends.] I ain't trying to
compete with them, just write about some of the most exciting times I've had. So here's my book outline:

Tentative Title: THE MILLION DOLLAR BASH
On the Road with Bob Dylan and Friends

It'll be a diary form, relating the events on the road inter-
cut with profiles and interviews of each of the major participants, performers, Levy, Kemp, etc.

Also, it won't be limited to the tour party. I've been
sleeping about three hours a night and have been scout-

ing out the streetscene in each city we hit. So far I got real good shit in Lowell, a forty-five-minute interview with Nick, Kerouac's brother-in-law, at the end of which he breaks down in tears, moaning that Jack wouldn't have died if he stayed in Lowell. Also plan a complete chapter on the "Hurricane" session then a flashback to Rubin in jail and my interview with him. In other words, Dylan is just the searchlight, the catalyst for this book that'll touch on the people that Rolling Thunder comes in contact with.

OK, now as Allen says on to the practicalities. What I need for the book is:

1. Access to the performers—either in the form of back-stage passes, a tour badge, anything so I'm not hassled by the big po-leece of Barry Imhoff.

2. Photos—Regan has the monopoly and gave shit photos to Rolling Stoned and great ones to Peephole. All I want is equal access.

3. A chance to ride the bus. I want to maintain my financial independence and my own car, etc., but I'd like to get some color every once in a while and experience life from the bowels of Phydeaux and Ghetteaux. This is a minor point.

That's about it, I don't want to suck your soul, or hit on you unnecessarily, and I'm sorry this letter is so long but I want to impress on you the spirit in which I'm doing this shit. This is the stuff I was pointing toward all my fucking life. I was going to be a goddamn accountant until I heard Highway 61, then started hanging out in the Village at Paul Sargeant's, listening to the Fugs, reading EVO. I owe you a cultural debt, and I think I can pay some of it back via my coverage. Fuck the Johnny Come Latelys, you were always there, even when I was sitting in the administration building in Queens College and Nashville Skyline came out of nowhere.

Your criticism of my first Rolling Stone piece was that it wasn't personal enough. Naturally, since Stone is the People of the lumpens. Anyway, give me a chance to express my feelings about this surreal circus troupe. Let me write my song. And let me keep listening to yours.

Best,
Larry

The next morning the jarring phone shocks me out of slumber. It's my wake-up call, Saturday noon, time to throw on some clothes and meet Roger McGuinn for lunch. According to Kemp's ground rules, it's OK for me to drive up to their motel and wait in the car for whoever was foolish enough to want to leave their asylum and risk spending some time with a heathen like me. But, I thought to myself, maybe he was right. I sneak a look into the rearview mirror. Not quite natty. I haven't shaved since the tour began, haven't found a place to wash my clothes, even missed a shower or two. My vitamin C intake was down but was more than made up for by a surplus of vitamin M—Methedrine.

Lately, I had noticed myself doing strange things, like lecturing the Holiday Inn housekeepers about ethnomethodology as they made up the room, inviting strange secretaries on the street to view my famed collection of sea sponges, and on occasion watching *The Tonight Show*. The signs seem unmistakably the dread effects of Road Fever. I think about Kinky, one of the more tragic victims of this malady. A bright boy, a fine person, a credit to his religion. But after two years of touring with the Texas Jewboys, playing Godforsaken places, Kinky was just the shell of the man he used to be. I remember the last time I had seen him, he was staying at the Chelsea Hotel in New York and we went down to Chinatown about 2 A.M. Kinky was wearing his satin Menorah shirt, gaudy blue and yellow, and his alligator cowboy boots with steel toeguards. He had a red, white, and blue sport coat, a sequined cowboy hat, and a glittering silver mesh bandanna. And those strange chirping sounds he was making as the waiter brought the menu, the highpitched "Hi, hi, hi." And then when the beef chow fun finally came and it tasted as if it had been simmering for three weeks just waiting for us to arrive, and when everyone in the place was staring at us, with the same looks usually reserved for out-of-town zoos or female derelicts, a fusion of awe, compassion, and scorn, then Kinky leapt up, grabbed a handful of burnt noodles and hurled them to the floor, narrowly missing a horrified housewife from Forest Hills who was coming in, and then a strange low guttural sound issued from his lips, a slightly familiar sound, yes, it was unmistakably the sounds I once heard years ago at summer camp in the Catskills, the strange sound of a loud, long resonant belch that was somehow in perfectly comprehensible English, the burpwords drifting up past the startled diners and wafting into the kitchen loud and clear, scattering the three small cooks out into the room. "I DON'T LIKE IT HERE," Kinky burped, ground his cigar into his white rice, and vaulted up the stairs and out into the street.

I was still shaking my head, mourning Kinky's fate, when I pull up to the Shelbourne Inn to pick up McGuinn. Roger hops into the Granada and we start pulling out of the driveway but suddenly the car is surrounded. Meyers and Johnson and a few others from the film crew are lolling about, and directly in front of us, Baez and her road manager, Carlos, engage in horseplay.

Baez skips over to the car, and leaps up on the front hood. "It's Ratso," she laughs. And, of course, she was right. Meyers wipes the sweat off his brow. "Ratso, huh," he says, his eyes twinkling. "He is Ratso," Johnson shouts, leering at me. "Yeah, he is," Meyers agrees.

"Why do you call me Ratso, because I remind you of Dustin Hoffman?" I ask Baez.

"No," she leans her head into the car, "because you remind me of Ratso."

"Ha," McGuinn chuckles, "it's Ratso!"

I smile wanly, far too fragile at that point to argue with a rock star. And besides, there was little to argue about. I was Ratso, I realized, rolling with the punches, licking my wounds in auxilliary highway hotels, stuffing my frayed dreams into a tattered suitcase, limping along the highway in search of that warm sun that always follows the Thunder. And why not, if I couldn't cover the tour in the more prescribed fashion, why not become a sort of spiritual mascot, part fan, part scribe, part pharmacist, part jester? Ratso would be the perfect counterpoint to Kemp's Broderick Crawford, the victim of the overzealous trespasses of the highway patrol. It was an ideal role, one which didn't require a hell of a lot of Method preparation, and one that just might get me to that Miami sun after all. Ratso chuckled to himself at that.

"Where are you guys going?" Meyers peers in.

"I'm going to eat and get McGuinn some heroin," Ratso jokingly leers.

Baez starts bouncing up and down on the front fender. "Let's rock his car off," she shouts impishly. "Yeah," Carlos and Johnson join in, bouncing up and down until it feels like the inside of a boat. "Go ahead," McGuinn issues a challenge. "It's a Hertz, you can do anything you want to it." He turns to Ratso. "You have full coverage, don't you?"

They soon tire, and Baez walks over to the driver's window again. "You're gonna be lead weight forever, Ratso, unless you clean up that fucking hair," she warns, as she gingerly fingers a few strands of Ratso's mane.

"Get out of here," he slaps at her, then smiles sheepishly. "I gotta get some shaving cream."

"Wow, I'll get it for you," Baez quickly offers.

"Would you?" Ratso laughs.

"Honey," Baez rolls her eyes, "I would do anything." She pokes her hand in the car again. "Let me see," she narrows her eyes, her fingers groping for Ratso's hair again, "do you wash that?"

"I wash it every fucking day," Ratso lies indignantly, "I use Ogilvie."

Baez laughs. "I was wondering what you used, I thought it was toothpaste."

"Why, you got something better," Ratso pouts. "It's thin, that's all. You gonna make something of my genes?"

"No," Baez smiles maternally, "you're a good egg."

"I know it," Ratso softens. "Everybody knows it except Kemp. He thinks I'm a schmuck."

"Just clean up your act, Ratso." Baez starts off with Carlos.

"OK, Madonna," Ratso screams after her, as he screeches the Granada out into the highway.

"Whaddya want, breakfast or lunch? Want eggs?" Ratso asks McGuinn.

"I never eat eggs," McGuinn yawns, wiping the sleep out of his eyes, "I always eat lunch for breakfast." Roger moans and holds his stomach. "I got drunk again last night. I gotta watch that. I poured a bottle of vodka down the toilet today and—"

"And you drank it," Ratso laughs.

"No, I'm not gonna drink no more." Roger stares out the window. "You know, we were only a quarter of a mile from Alice's Restaurant but I didn't go there. I missed the filming too and the bus. It took off exactly on time. I didn't really want to go to the filming though, if I really wanted to go I would have made it. My attitude about it was I can always be in the film." McGuinn looks at Ratso for approval. "This thing's gonna keep shooting and shooting and like I'd rather be in the film by rolling into it as opposed to panting into it. I don't want to go 'huhuhuhuhuh,' " McGuinn pants, his tongue dangling down like a St. Bernard's.

"What do you think of the tour so far?"

"I'm in love with it, man," McGuinn bubbles like a hippie, "never done anything better in my life."

"Who you been hanging out with?"

"Everybody," McGuinn bubbles, "I've been hugging everybody and telling them that I love them and I mean it too, it's not bullshit."

"I hear the bus drivers are upset," Ratso interjects.

"They're cool. Well, they can't hang out with the musicians, they're not allowed to fraternize with us or something. That's too bad, but that's the way it is. It's that old thing of don't fraternize with the help."

"How does communication work?"

"They give us newsletters every day. I've even contributed to them."

Ratso swings the car into the parking lot of a small country-style restaurant. He and McGuinn enter and move to the back to a small sunlit patio. The hostess instantly comes over, with menus.

"Would you like a drink first," she asks, smiling.

"Conspiracy, conspiracy," McGuinn mumbles, pushing his longish dirty-blond hair out of his eyes as he peruses the menu.

"Have you been getting sick?" Ratso asks, concerned.

"No, not a bit," Roger smiles wanly. "I sweat it out. Literally."

A rosy-cheeked young waitress appears. "Hello," she bubbles, "would you like something to drink?"

McGuinn rolls his eyes. "You mean alcohol. No, no alcohol." He laughs. "We were just talking about the international conspiracy to get people to drink alcohol," he explains to the waitress.

"OK," she says cheerfully, "how about coffee?"

"There's an international conspiracy to get people to use caffeine too," Roger lectures. "It's a drug-oriented culture." He picks up his glass. "What's in this water? Seriously, I'd like a cheddarburger to drink. A liquid cheddarburger."

"I'll put it in the blender," the waitress shoots back, a bit annoyed.

Ratso orders cheesecake for breakfast and hands the

menu back to the girl. "There seems to be such a nice spirit, I mean Baez running around today like a meshugena."

"I'm so loose," Roger agrees, "now I feel like I can fly. I watched Dylan. I learned it from him. I watched him being constricted and tied down. I remember Eric Anderson saying Bob's making too many kids and being tied down and I noticed that and I said 'Uh huh,' and I have two kids by another marriage and I was tied down too. And I watched him blow out, get out of the thing with Sara, I mean he loves her. I love Linda. But I got my work cut out for me and I can't do it with her around. Linda's been doing silver and gold jewelry, going to UCLA, she's been constructive lately. She's a real smart girl and she was as tied down as I was, but she didn't realize it. She's twenty-five. She's got to have her shit together by that age."

McGuinn smiles at his last comment. "What am I saying, it took me that long. Where am I coming from? I'm thirty-three and I'm still a punk. I plan to stay one too. Peter Pan, you know. Never grow up, never grow up."

"But that song, 'Sara,' man, Levy told me how he wrote that," Ratso purrs, "being on the beach, remembering where they hung out. It's like a diary."

"Yeah, 'being at the Chelsea Hotel writing Sad Eyed Lady of the Lowlands for you.' I love that line so much."

"It's so personal, I can't believe he's singing that shit."

"To the world? Why not? That's what poets are for. He's one and he realizes it. I've never seen him more upfront, right. He's out there. It's great. This whole tour is amazing. Last night I had chateaubriand with Mick Ronson. Then I had a couple of martinis and that's the last thing I remember. So that's why I'm being good today."

"Your song . . ." Ratso starts.

"Oh, I know what I was gonna say," McGuinn blurts. "There have been some little girls following us around going 'Roger and Rono,' it's like the Ringo thing, like a campaign, they're pushing for that combination of Ronson and me."

The food finally arrives, and Roger bites into his cheddarburger with a vengeance.

Ratso begins to recount the anecdote in which Dylan had been concerned that Kinky didn't like him.

"But he does," Roger interrupts. "Bob asked me the

same thing. We brought Kinky over to the house in Malibu one night, and we all sat around and Bob made Kinky sing all of his songs. Then the next day Bob asked me if he had said anything wrong last night. Bob got drunk and didn't remember what he did so he asked me the next day. He said, 'I don't think Kinky likes me,' and I said, 'Kinky likes you, Kinky loves you man, do you remember singing go to sleep little Jewboys or Ride 'Em Jewboys or something,' and he said, 'No.' He didn't remember it but I told him that everything was fine and he conducted himself perfectly well."

"Then Dylan asked me what I thought about that guy, Bruce Springfield?" Ratso recalls. "You think he's jealous of Springsteen?"

McGuinn laughs. "It was like that scene in *Don't Look Back,*" Ratso continues, "with Donovan. Dylan going, 'Who's this Donovan guy?' But he wipes out Springsteen."

"Of course, he does," McGuinn shrugs.

"But he seems so insecure," Ratso wonders.

"Is anybody not insecure," Roger counsels. "Look, he's just a human being . . ."

"But he's the best," Ratso protests.

"He doesn't know that he's the best yet. That's the beautiful thing about him." McGuinn smiles. "If he finds out he's the best he might quit or something. Let's not tell him, let's tell him he sucks."

"That's Kinky's strategy," Ratso smirks. "Kinky shits on him every time he sees him."

"I do too," Roger boasts, "I treat him like he's one of the guys. Because if you look up to him, he doesn't like that, he won't respect you anymore. So I kick him around a little bit. But I'm a late bloomer. I'm going to be an overnight success, one of these days."

"You got too much too soon with the Byrds, Hillman told me that."

"We got indigestion, man," McGuinn plays with a half-eaten salad, "star lag. Now I'm recovering from it."

McGuinn orders another Sprite and Ratso remembers the period when Roger was playing solo, a few years back. It was mortifying, this giant in rock 'n roll history reduced to playing acoustic guitar in small holes in the wall. Ratso recalls seeing him in Good Karma, a hippie health-food restaurant in Madison, Wisconsin. The iconographic voice was still there but it was painful to watch;

McGuinn desperately namedropping between songs trying too hard to salvage a modicum of self-worth, introducing "Ballad of Easy Rider" by invoking the name of "Peter Fonda, who's a good friend of mine." Ratso had the feeling then that he was watching an acoustic dinosaur.

"How come you retired the Byrds?" Ratso breaks the silence.

"David Crosby got down on my case real heavy one day and he and I mutually decided that the original Byrds were the Byrds and let's not have any more bullshit about it."

"That's when you were doing that hyped reunion album," Ratso recollects. "I thought that sucked."

"I know, I know." McGuinn shakes his head sheepishly. "That's because Crosby overdid it, he didn't let me in on it. He intimidated me on purpose, he intimidated me and I couldn't do anything about it."

"What about Hillman?"

"He was just there, he thought it was all right. Hillman wants to do another one to save face for that last one and Crosby does too. He realizes his mistake, he does, he and I have talked about it."

"Well, you shouldn't let him produce it!" Ratso rails.

"No, we should get a professional producer," Roger agrees, then leans over conspiratorially toward Ratso, his hand shielding his mouth. "The thing is Crosby didn't produce that album," McGuinn whispers gleefully. "We all did, and we gave him the credit."

"And he thanked you no end, huh," Ratso laughs out loud.

"He did. He said, 'Wow, wow, thanks a lot you guys that's really great. Wow, I needed that.' We got away with something." Roger smiles impishly.

"That's brilliant. Boy, did that album suck."

"I know," Roger laughs.

"And that was almost as bad as *Byrdmaniax,* another all-time low."

McGuinn winces at the rattling of that old skeleton. "That was terrible. That was the all-time bottom-out. You gotta make a few bad ones."

"Even Dylan put out stuff like *Self Portait* and that blackmail Columbia LP, but you know, in retrospect I liked even them," Ratso marvels, "I like almost anything he sings."

"Yeah, me too," Roger enthuses. "He once came over to my house and looked through my record collection. You know, he'll look at your books first and then your records, checking you out. He found some of his records in my collection and he said, 'What do you listen to my records for?' I said, 'I like 'em, you know.' He said, 'Don't listen to my records, they're terrible'—he was pulling a number. So I said, 'OK,' and I actually did stop listening to his records for a while to prove to myself that I could do it. He said, 'I don't listen to your records, if I want to hear rock 'n roll I listen to B. B. King or somebody.'

"Wasn't that sunrise ceremony great," McGuinn suddenly veers off course. "Boy, that might have saved my life or something."

"You think so." Ratso seems skeptical.

"I don't know, I mean I've just felt spiritually OK ever since."

"I liked what everyone said."

"Everybody was real cool," Roger sips his Sprite, "except a couple of people who were a little stilted."

"Yeah, that chick from *Newsweek*."

"What she say?"

"I don't remember, something Newsweekese," Ratso hisses.

"Is that like Japanese? Dylan said something very nice. I sort of copied it. He said he hopes that everyone realizes that they are of the same spirit and I said I hope that everyone realizes that everything's gonna work out all right in the end."

"What did Neuwirth say?"

"I don't remember. I don't remember what a lot of people said. I don't even remember what Rolling Thunder said. I thought that was very cool, though, to be involved in an Indian ceremony of that magnitude, my first one. I mean a lot of my friends go out to the desert and hang out with the Hopis and take peyote and get enlightened and stuff like that. I can see where that's at now, I always thought it was kinda jive. You don't have to do that, you can just take peyote."

"Yeah, I mean Rolling Thunder was talking in English," Ratso injects, "and afterward he came over to my photographer friend and asked her for copies of her contact sheet."

"He lives in the real world," McGuinn smiles, "he's just a guy. He's a very enlightened guy."

"Dylan didn't know about him before the tour," Ratso reports. "It was just synchronicity."

"Oh, I thought the tour was named after him."

"No, Dylan told me he named it one day sitting in California listening to the thunder."

"If it was Malibu," Roger smiles slyly, "it was probably the Vanderburg Air Force Base. It's up the street."

"It was actually the air force, huh, not the rolling thunder?"

"It was probably sonic booms. The Sonic Boom Jet Revue. Not to be confused with Rolling Thunder."

McGuinn picks up his napkin and wipes his mouth, signaling Ratso into a frenzy over the large uneaten chunk of hamburger. "Why don't you eat the meat?" he shouts, pointing to the chunk of ground beef. "I got to take care of you, Roger!"

McGuinn picks up the hamburger and takes a tentative bite. "Thanks Ratso, you're right. I need the protein."

"I'm down to my last twenty dollars," Ratso moans, "I'd better call the *Rolling Stone* office."

"You know, this tour I haven't spent a penny yet," Roger marvels. "Everybody else is going around shopping and stuff but I haven't spent a penny on anything. I know what'll happen by the end of the tour. They'll have all these suitcases full of shit and they won't be able to walk around anymore. From experience, I don't do that anymore. I don't need it. I've got everything I need. I'm an artist and I don't look back."

They laugh.

"Neuwirth told me he's got no possessions," Ratso relates, "doesn't even have a home. Just his guitar."

"So what, that's his problem," McGuinn philosophizes. "He crashed at my house a lot. You gotta realize I like him a lot. He's my old buddy for years."

"He is like the glue to this thing," Ratso admits.

"Glue? Oh, like stick together," Roger comprehends. "You know what I think it is. Like, he's protecting Bob like a watchdog. But that's what it is and sometimes there's a little overkill in that. And that's what you're being subjected to. The reason I'm talking to you is that I understand the situation. If I felt you were a real threat to Bob or anything . . ." McGuinn trails off ominously.

"The reason Dylan talks to me is because he knows that—"

"You're not a real threat," Roger finishes.

We pay the bill and head out to the parking lot. "The letter should help," Ratso muses out loud. "I'm not going to hide under tables and pry."

"No," McGuinn climbs into the car, "you're cool." He puts his boot against the open door and turns to Ratso. "You know this trick, I learned this from Carlos." And he violently kicks the door almost off its moorings, quickly bringing his legs in, and calmly waits for the door to slam itself shut. "Not bad, huh." He smiles.

Ratso pulls into the Inn's driveway and McGuinn gets out. "Wanna see something neat," Roger asks. "We always used to do this with our rented cars." Stoner and Wyeth have drifted over and McGuinn has a small audience as he circles to the front of the car, takes a deep breath, and vaults onto the hood, jumps from the hood to the roof, alights onto the trunk and gracefully plops back down to earth. To Ratso inside the car, it sounds like thudding thunder.

Just then, Louie Kemp appears on the front porch of the Inn and beckons Ratso over. "C'mon," he grabs the writer, "I want to talk to you." He marches Ratso over to the far end of the porch.

"You've been out of line," he says.

"How?" Ratso shrugs innocently.

"Listen, shut up and listen. Then you can talk. All right, you were out of line first of all in going to the Indian thing. You were really out of line in having that chick come with the camera," Louie lectures.

"I didn't tell her to come," Ratso protests.

"She found out by herself, huh?"

"I didn't tell her to bring her equipment."

"You think she was there for her health," Kemp rails. "She took those pictures and she runs all around trying to sell them to everybody. She tried to. She tried *Time, Newsweek,* all those people. Anyway, if she wanted to take pictures she should have asked."

"She did. She asked Rolling Thunder." Ratso settles against the porch railing.

"Rolling Thunder has nothing to do with . . ." Kemp leaves the sentence unfinished. His eyes flare behind his dark glasses. "Then she should have just taken pictures of him, there's pictures of Bob in there. Look, we didn't want no photographers there. That film should have been taken out of her camera and given to me afterward. That's the way it should have been done. Instead she runs all over New York trying to sell it." Louie rolls his eyes.

"I screamed at her roommate over the phone," Ratso shows good faith, "I had a long conversation with my editor at *Rolling Stone* and I told him it was private land, a private ceremony and that the pictures weren't public domain. I told him it was a privilege for Mary to be there."

"For you too," Kemp shoots back acidly. "I don't know how she got there, but she's your fucking friend and you're gonna be responsible for her just like I'm responsible for my friends. And, we're not pleased with you following the bus and coming to the mansion," he adds.

"Shit," Ratso moans. "Why didn't you say something?"

"You were already in there, I didn't want to make a scene when you're in there. I didn't want to put you down," Kemp gets softer, "you gotta learn to control yourself and you don't seem capable of it. You can do it for a couple of hours and then your enthusiasm gets the best of you. I like you, but you're out of control."

"Have you seen me since the Breakers thing?" Ratso prods.

"No, I haven't."

"Well, I just had a talk with Gary . . ."

"Let me finish what I'm saying," Kemp interrupts. "I think your intentions are good but you're getting to be more work for me than you're worth. So just to let you know that I'm serious and I mean business, I'm not giving you tickets for tomorrow night's concert. And I'll pick it up again after that if you have your shit together but if you don't I'll just have to cut you off."

Ratso stays still, demonstrating to Louie that he's letting it sink in. He knows tomorrow night's concert is in New Hampshire, way up near the Maine border, a good eight-hour drive.

"Where's the concert tomorrow night?" he innocently asks Kemp.

"Find out for yourself. But there won't be tickets for you from me anyway. Because you just don't seem to understand . . ." Louie says sternly.

"Why are you punishing me?" Ratso whines.

"I just want to show you that if you keep on jerking round with me I'm not going to give you any cooperation."

"I'm not jerking around with you."

"I've given you more cooperation than with any other fucking journalist," Kemp seems to be getting mad again.

"What about the guy from *People*. You let him back-stage a few times," Ratso pouts.

"I want to state again your intentions are good—"

"Why did you call me Weberman then," Ratso interrupts.

"I think you're a good person," Louie calmly asserts, "but your problem is that you're overenthusiastic and it's getting in my way so the only way I can deal with that is that I got to take some action with you. It's just like a warning shot. You can go out and get tickets on your own."

"Can I buy them?" Ratso asks out of idle curiosity.

"You can buy them on the street."

"Can you at least tell me where it is?"

"It's in Durham."

"Is it far from here? Maybe I won't even go." Ratso looks wounded. "Can I go to tonight's concert?"

"I'm giving you tickets for tonight."

"OK," Ratso jumps off the railing and leans toward Kemp, "let's set up some boundaries. One, I'm not gonna come to the hotel. If I come it's only to call for somebody that I set up an appointment with like I did just now. I called to say I'm waiting in front . . ."

Kemp frowns. "But still there are the other people who are gonna walk in and out of that door and they're gonna see you and they're gonna say, 'Oh shit, here he is again.' "

"Who," Ratso screams like an owl.

"I'm gonna say it," Kemp shoots back.

"What should I do, wait across the street?"

"Something so the others don't have to feel that they're on. Minimize your presence off the concert-hall scene. In the concert hall you belong like anyone else."

"OK," Ratso starts to recapitulate, "so I set up appointments, obviously not stay in the same hotel, not hang around, and don't follow the bus. Is it OK if I try to buy a ticket to the next show?"

"Yeah, but don't ask anyone in the group for one," Lou

cautions. "If you can buy them on the street, that's fine."

"Well, let me write down the itinerary, I'm not going tomorrow," Ratso decides.

"Hey, I'm not telling you you can't go," Lou backpedals, "all I'm telling you is I'm not going to give you a ticket. I believe in free enterprise. I really do."

"I know you do," Ratso scowls.

"If I don't have any problems with you from now to Waterbury, there'll be a ticket for you at Waterbury. I'm just telling you straight, I just want you to know I'm serious. I got other things to do." Kemp starts to walk back to the door.

"Wait," Ratso screeches, "I'm not being greedy now, but I need two tickets to each show."

"You're getting one now, what do you need two tickets for?"

"I always take in a kid or something, I take notes."

"What does the kid do?" Louie asks sarcastically.

"I pick up somebody in that town who's a good person to interview."

"That's all bullshit." Kemp frowns. "Five thousand people in the town and you pick one person and he's in the book."

"You were the one who told me to talk to the people."

"Lots of people," Kemp screams, "not one person."

"But that one person in Newport I brought to the camera crew was the best interview they got."

"They told me that, too," Louie admits. "I acknowledge that."

"And another girl I brought in once, an eighteen-year-old tripping on acid, turned out to be the most articulate—"

"Look," Kemp interrupts, "I'm not doubting it. I just want you to understand where your place is and how to do it. I've helped you plenty of times."

"I know you have," Ratso admits.

"But when you get in my fucking way, then I'm gonna have to treat you accordingly."

"But the other night you thought I was sneaking behind your back when I asked Dylan if I could write a book," Ratso protests.

"Yeah, you were," Kemp snarls. "That's still not the protocol . . . you don't go up to Dylan and ask him to write a book. If you want to do that, you come to me, we'll go through channels and we'll get back to you with a legitimate answer. I won't make the decision myself, I'll discuss it with him."

"I have an outline. Should I give it to you?"

"I told you that two weeks ago," Kemp shakes his head.

"You didn't give him any of my other messages. I would feel much more at ease if I felt I wasn't being jerked off," Ratso screams.

"Jerked off, how are you being jerked off?"

"Bob invited me on this fucking tour. You were there."

"Bob's human too," Louie purrs, "Bob has a few drinks like anybody else and somebody comes up to him and asks—"

"Hey," Ratso yells, "I didn't ask him. He asked me!"

"Well, I wasn't there," Lou admits, "and I didn't hear. All I knew is he was looser those nights. He was drinking, he was enjoying himself. Listen, I think you're basically a good guy. OK. If I didn't think you were you wouldn't have gotten this far."

"Did you like my first piece for *Rolling Stone?*" Ratso inquires.

"Basically I liked it. There was a lot of what I would call *Rolling Stone*-type shit in there. Trivia, you know."

"That's *Rolling Stone*."

"That's *Rolling Stone*," Kemp agrees. "I don't dig that. How much of that is you and how much is you reacting to them I don't know."

"You should hear the shit I'm getting from them," Ratso moans.

"I don't doubt that, I think they're a bunch of assholes," Kemp spits, "I told you that at the beginning. Look, just don't make your article petty. I want meat there. I don't want a lot of stringbeans. Make it meat."

"Hey, there was more meat in my first article than any other one," Ratso protests, "the stuff with Rubin . . ."

"That part was good," Lou admits, "I'll go through the article and underline what I thought the shit was. I gotta go."

Kemp starts toward the Inn but again Ratso interrupts. "Hey Louie, one more thing, I got a friend that works for the *National Enquirer* and they want me to do an article on Bob." Kemp rolls his eyes, shakes his head, and walks into the lobby.

Ratso had promised McGuinn that he would take him to the Curio Lounge, a strange bar that he had discovered the previous night. They drive over and Ratso rushes into the bar, immediately asking the barmaid to see the owner. She goes into the kitchen and returns with a thin, bespectacled man around fifty, smoking a pipe and exuding amused, cynical detachment. Ratso flies into a breathless gush about what a great-weird place this is, perfect for the movie that we're shooting, the movie of the tour that we're in the middle of. And Ratso's right, the place is even more bizarre in the daytime than it was last night when he and Levy were here for a drink.

For one, there's these weird exhibits all over the walls, like the doll on the wall as you enter, a doll the legend underneath tells us was made by an armsmaker to royalty, who made the doll complete with a hidden gun, then gave it as a gift to his unfaithful amour, Katina, who as was her habit pressed this cherished gift to her bosom and blew her chest out. Our jealous suitor then proceeded to pick up the doll and blow his own brains out. Or take that display case in the rear of the front room, featuring what's purported to be the remains of a Civil War general, complete with a red, pulsating heart visible in the bony rib cage. This number was executed for the owner by a friend named Dr. Paul Dudley White, a heart surgeon who was Eisenhower's personal physician. And the sign below the skeleton reads, "We thank Dr. Paul Dudley White for his wizardry with the living heart. We toast Dr. Wally for his wizardry with the whimsical heart. Signed Amen."

"What do you think of that one?" Dr. Wally booms, as he sneaks behind Ratso who's still gaping at the skeleton. "It is the actual remains of a Civil War general. They think I'm a little nutty around here and a very interesting character," Wally boasts.

Just then Howard Alk arrives to scout the bar for the film crew and Ratso immediately takes him on a tour of the guns, skeletons, dragon heads, and other bizarre curios. "Oh my God," Alk gapes, "we could spend months shooting in here." Ratso rejoins McGuinn and Wally as Alk rushes to call a film crew down.

"You're a weird little guy," Wally tells Ratso.

"People like that don't live long," McGuinn cautions.

"Yeah, but when they do they really live." Wally smiles. "He surprised the hell out of me, smoking that cigar. He doesn't look like a cigar smoker, usually fat bombers smoke 'em." The three chat and Wally reveals that he's an opthamologist, still practicing, who has this obsession with guns and other strange memorabilia. And he built the bar to his own strange specifications, mainly so he could have a place to hang out.

Ratso and McGuinn sit down at a table as Wally goes to answer the phone. Not your conventional table, though, this one has a Ouija board for a top. Right above their heads is a plaster cast of Lucifer's head, complete with flames shooting out the nostrils. Wally rejoins them. "Did you see my Capone windows?" he asks, sipping on his ginger ale. He leaps up and drags them over to a display case near the bar. "I have all his guns." Wally gestures toward an array of handguns, shotguns, even a submachine gun all under glass. "There was a lot of good in that man. I can't move these guns you know, it's classified as a museum, if I want to move them the government charges me money. Yup, Capone was quite a guy."

Alk rejoins the trio as they stroll around the bar. "This place has a lot of nooks and crannies," Wally points out. "I do my own designing and thinking. Did you see 'The Chained Madonna'? It's one of the rarest paintings in the world, done by a famous artist at the turn of the century." Wally leads them to a painting of a beautiful young woman, wrapped in chains. "She looks happier with chains on." He smiles paternally. "Jesus," Alk mutters to himself, "this is primo." "And here's 'The Silent Woman.' " Wally beams in front of a painting of a woman, beheaded. "You oughta bring Dylan over," he smiles, "I think he'd enjoy this."

They walk back to the bar, passing a urinal sticking out of the wall, then a suit of armor. "We dress people up in that." Wally shrugs. "Last Halloween, we had him in front." It's almost five and a few early patrons are wandering into the bar. The film crew van pulls up and Larry Johnson and David Meyers tramp in, carrying box after box of equipment, and begin setting up in the rear. "Jesus," Johnson stares in awe, "he must be in big bucks to do this."

Just then, the camper pulls up, and Neuwirth hops out, followed by Dylan and Gary. Ratso rushes out to escort them. "You better split, man," Neuwirth barks at him, "it's a closed set." Ratso ignores him and collars Dylan. "Lou said it's a closed set," Dylan mumbles apologetically.

"I spoke to Lou," Ratso counters, "it's cool." Dylan shrugs and they both walk in. They stand in the hallway, just scanning the bizarre interior. Wally steps up. "You know the place, Ratso, show them around."

They walk around for a few minutes, then Alk collars Dylan, showing him the room he chose for the scene. "We can aim at the bar, then move to the tables to discuss important business." Dylan takes it in, stroking his chin, adjusting his dark glasses. Neuwirth interrupts and drags Dylan to a back room to show him a full-sized organ made out of guns.

They troop back to the room, Dylan pausing to sign a few autographs, and then the singer takes charge. "Who's here?" he muses out loud. "Oh there's Roger. Howie, why don't you play 'As Time Goes By.' " He directs Wyeth to an electric piano. "What can we tie this in with?" Dylan asks Neuwirth. "How about the alchemist scene?"

The film crew sets up as Neuwirth walks to the bar. "I want a tall ridiculous drink, make it a ginger ale. With a ten-inch straw." About fifteen people from the tour have filtered in, including Lola, an actress who's been in some of the earlier scenes. "Can we use Lola to bring some drinks in?" Dylan wonders. Neuwirth meanwhile is looking for a hat, to compliment his wardrobe of black T-shirt with 2025 across the front, jeans, and red aviator shades. Back at the table Dylan and playwright Sam Shepard are conferring, working out the scene.

"I got it," Shepard yelps, scribbling down an idea on his clipboard. "This is the object," he holds up what looks like a turkey carcass, "the secret bone. What you came for."

"And the answer's only a foot away." Dylan smiles.

"It's a mojo bone," Shepard adds.

"OK, well we don't need this." Dylan pulls a large bottle off the table then checks his watch. "We got an eight o'clock show," he reminds everyone.

In a few minutes they're ready, the spectators have been herded to the rear, Dylan is leaning against the bar, his back to the camera. "Order the green devil at the bar," Neuwirth shoots a last-minute instruction as Johnson screams for quiet. Wyeth goes to the piano and plays some soft cocktail-lounge doodlings. "Hey Howie," Dylan screams, "play some *Casablanca*-type music." "Do 'As Time Goes By' over and over again," Neuwirth shouts.

Finally the camera rolls.

Neuwirth snaps his fingers and Lola scurries over. "Waitress, ask him to join me please." He points in Dylan's direction, then takes a long drag on his cigarette. Dylan acts real coy and joins Neuwirth.

"Howdy," he smiles.

"Are you new in town?" Neuwirth leers in a heavy accent.

"Yeah," Dylan leans over the table.

"Looking for anything?" Neuwirth sips his drink.

"Yeah," Dylan enthuses, "Isis."

"I heard about her." Neuwirth nods.

"The same one?" Dylan marvels.

"Could be. Maybe I can help. I'm Ted," Neuwirth offers.

"I'm Jerry," Dylan replies.

"Ted the Head," Neuwirth corrects.

Dylan cracks up. "I started this place four years ago as a hot-dog stand," Neuwirth continues, "I understand you're looking for a truck stop."

Dylan nods. Neuwirth snaps for the waitress and Lola rushes to the table. "Take this back," Neuwirth throws a dish and Lola returns promptly with a plate with the lobster tail on it. "What's written on that lobster tail?" Neuwirth asks Dylan. "There's more here than I can see." Dylan grins. Neuwirth lights Dylan's dangling cigarette and picks up the bone. "The secrets are only a foot away. Take this with you, don't let anybody see you, carry it, show it to the man at the front desk. Just show it to him."

Dylan takes the carcass and fingers it gently. "You've been real helpful. We came thousands of miles."

"Take that," Neuwirth urges, and sends Dylan off. Lola comes in. "There's a gentleman named T-Bone waiting to see you," she tells Neuwirth. Neuwirth leans back, smiles, and snaps his fingers. "Play it again, Tony," he shouts.

"CUT," Johnson yells and Dylan, Neuwirth, and Shepard huddle, discussing the take.

"Good," Meyers shouts. "One more time?" Dylan wonders. "What was that, four minutes? Let's do it once more to cover it. Any suggestions, Sam?"

"Get heavy with each other," Larry Johnson suggests.

"We can do it once more," Neuwirth agrees.

The camera rolls again and Dylan sits down. "I'm looking for this heavyset dude, with an earring in his left ear and a scar."

"What do you want him for?" Neuwirth's accent is getting thicker by the minute.

"I know he can change water into wine," Dylan gushes. "I can make a trade. I got bread from North America, a couple of red blankets, and a buffalo skin."

"Where are you staying?"

"I'm staying at the edge of town. Route 52."

"Near the Howard Johnson's?"

"Yeah. I've seen it."

"Go to the Howard Johnson's, go to the kitchen. Ask for Lafcadio. Tell him what you want. If he says OK, call me here. If you're not the right person we won't see you again."

"That sounds fair to me." Dylan shakes hands and leaves.

Neuwirth summons Lola. "I want that gentleman followed." Then he gets up and rushes out of the room.

"OK," Shepard jots on his clipboard. "We can pick up the exterior with him falling down the street." They decide to shoot the last line again, so Neuwirth sits down and Lola enters. "I want that gentleman followed," Neuwirth growls.

"What was his name?" Lola ad-libs.

"I have no idea." Neuwirth shakes his head.

Dylan, standing on the side, grins.

The lights get doused, the crew starts breaking down, the clientele is buzzing about the stars and the movie, and Wally turns to Ratso. "The unrehearsed minute is the best," he smiles sagely. "You can't relive it."

The concert is due to start in about an hour so the performers group to ride back to the hotel. Dylan comes over to Wally to say good-bye. They shake hands and Wally sizes him up. "So you're Dylan." He smiles, peering into his face. "You look healthy enough. Pretty myopic, though."

Ratso sits down and joins some of the film crew, who since they're not shooting the concert have time for a leisurely dinner. He sits next to Johnson who seems to be pissed off. "That was shit," Johnson moans, "those parts were real pretentious. They were doing schtick."

"It was art," Ratso mocks.

Johnson rolls his eyes. "Great, let's see it, that's the

test. We did a great scene last night though, Joan on a bed with a picture of her kid. Joan's a great lady."

"Did you like this place?" Ratso modestly asks.

"Don't worry," Johnson semisneers, "I told Dylan you set this one up. Look Ratso, I don't personally care whether you live or die, you're great for the film, that's what's important. You're a caricature of *Rolling Stone,* you're where Ben Fong Wrong went right, a speed-freak fanatic, a man of the people. Look, Meyers and I have been together for eleven years, shot some of the best documentaries ever made, did Neil Young's film, Cocker's Mad Dogs tour. Meyers is sixty-four you know, and you brought us that kid in Springfield that sang that Rolling Thunder song and then charged right for the camera at the end. That made our top-ten list of greatest sequences we've ever shot. That's why I like you."

Around the table, Shepard, Alk, Meyers, and Howard are discussing the film. Shepard seems disturbed, claiming that making a movie isn't like writing a song, it needs more planning and more scripting. Alk shakes his head vigorously. "Look, Dylan is a film genius. Genius. We can let Bobby go anytime as long as we prep the other people." They continue on, discussing yesterday's Baez scene as Ratso wolfs down a steak and then drives over to the college.

The gym is packed to overflowing as Ratso walks in and begins to make his way to the front. There are bleachers ringing the gym on three sides, chairs in the center, and bodies where the aisles once were. Halfway to the stage, Allen Ginsberg sits with a group of Buddhists in rows, and Ratso waves, then fights his way to the backstage entrance and manages to pass the letter he wrote to Dylan to Lola, who promises swift delivery.

These are perhaps the worst conditions yet encountered on the tour, certainly rivaling Lowell's gym, and with the crowd rocketing the temperature to close to 100 degrees it's certainly no picnic up on stage. But onstage everybody's pouring their guts out, Dylan sweating so hard his pancake makeup is completely washed off by his fourth number.

Outside, a bottle war is raging, the disgruntled students and hangers-on who couldn't get in using the university police as targets for their Ripple and Thunderbird wine bottles. Ratso ventures out cautiously, hears a bottle whiz by his ear and smash up against the wall, splattering into a thousand glass fragments; he decides he likes the heat better.

A wise decision as he gets to see a compelling new version of "Simple Twist of Fate," a scorching "Oh Sister," a humid "Hurricane." By now, even Scarlett looks hot in this sauna and she ain't even human, Ratso marvels. "Bring on Roger," someone screams for McGuinn and Dylan chuckles. "Roger'll be right back," he announces, "he's gonna stay here all night." Then "Just Like a Woman," and a hush falls over the crowd, a hush as thick as the pea-soup atmosphere. Dylan's picking his guitar like a machine gun, ratatating the phrases out over the mesmerized audience, a good percentage of whom are singing the words right back to him. McGuinn runs on to cheers and they shift into "Knocking on Heaven's Door," the sweat pouring off Dylan now like a shower. Then everyone into the pool, the whole gang's on for "This Land is Your Land," Baez looking like some hippie beachcomber, barefoot, glitter T-shirted, and jeans rolled up, throwing Ratso a wink in the first row.

Then it's over and they stream off the stage, with Raven like some water boy, standing, handing out towels as they flow by and run directly to the warmed-up buses. Ratso walks around the gym a bit, checks out the now peaceful battle front, and then strolls back inside. The standing ovation is still pouring out, lasting at least ten minutes by now. Ratso walks to the backstage entrance where his car is parked.

By the stage door, Jacques Levy and his girlfriend Claudia are getting some well-deserved fresh air and Ratso stops to chat with them. Suddenly, a young kid tears around the building, stops, then stumbles the last few feet. He seems to be looking for something and lurches toward the trio.

"I can't believe it," he moans, "nothing, nothing."

He looks over toward Levy.

"They're not here, are they," he asks rhetorically, "they left, huh?"

Levy smiles and nods.

"I can't believe it," the kid keeps mumbling, scanning the desolate grass field. "They're gone." He kicks at the dirt. "Like some goddamn dream."

9

The tour left that night directly for Maine, but Ratso, true to his word to Louie, stayed behind and headed back to New York the next day for a breather before rejoining the troupe in Waterbury, Connecticut, on Tuesday night.

The reporter finds his way to the section stage left where guests and friends of the Revue are sitting and he plops into a seat as Neuwirth introduces a radiant Ronee Blakley, decked out in a long violet gown. Suddenly he looks up to see Ginsberg bearing down on him. "Bobby wants to see your article," Ginsberg motions toward the advance copy of *Rolling Stone* Ratso has on his lap, "but I want to get your permission first." Ratso shrugs and gives Allen the paper, settling back to watch Jack Elliot ramble through his set. Then Dylan strides on, without makeup tonight, but no doubt aware of the two cameras that are trained on his every gesture. He plows through his set, fairly unloquacious except for the inevitable dedication to Sam Peckinpah.

At intermission, Ratso buys some popcorn and settles down to dinner just as Lola comes out of the backstage door with Ginsberg. She looks concerned. "Listen, Bob is pissed. You shouldn't have bad-mouthed Ronee in the article," she sternly lectures.

"What the fuck are you talking about?" Ratso's amazed.

"Why'd you call her a neurotic?" Lola demands.

Suddenly it dawns on Ratso. In his article, he had described Blakley as the *Nashville Neurotic*, referring to her movie role as Barbara Jean. Dylan must have skimmed the article, seen the phrase, and blown up. It's nice he's so loyal to his performers, Ratso muses.

"Look, schmuck, it's in italics. I'm talking about the movie, not the city. She was a neurotic in the film, that was her role. I love Blakley, I'm listening to the tape of her new album every night, it's great. Tell Bob what I meant, show him the context." Lola agrees and scurries backstage before the Dylan-Baez segment.

Dylan and Baez start their set and Ratso settles back to listen. Until he feels this feather tickling his ear. He turns and looks at the seat next to his. Lisa again.

"Guess what?" she smiles her hapless smile, "I just got the itinerary this week and I haven't slept with anybody." Just then one of the security guards grabs Lisa and starts to dance with her in the aisle. After a few minutes, Lisa returns. "Barry Imhoff is hassling me to points of no end," she moans, " 'cause I'm all over. He saw me in the dressing room and really freaked out."

Ratso settles back again, watching Baez rip through a torrid set, culminating with her doing the frug to Mc-Guinn's "Eight Miles High," all captured by the omnipresent camera eye of filmmaker Meyers. Dylan returns to rip into "Hurricane," giving it a special urgency since Rubin had been transferred that day from Trenton State to a much lower-security facility. But one that still believed in locks on the doors. Dylan is wailing, then he shifts into "One More Cup of Coffee" and is bending the words like a pretzel maker, sending sideliner Ginsberg into fits of ecstasy. Just then, Lola comes out into the hall and catches Ratso's eye. She gives him the high sign then disappears mysteriously.

The band finishes "One More Cup" and Dylan turns his back on the audience, adjusting his guitar strap. He wheels back and leans into the mike. "We're gonna send this next one out to Larry. He's out there somewhere," he peers, "he's our favorite reporter." A clamor arises in the audience, coming from the section where some of Ratso's friends from New York are sitting. Weird little screams of "Larry, Larry" reminiscent of the days of Sinatra and the Beatles, issue out. Dylan smiles, then leans back into the mike. "He tells it like it is," he laughs, then starts into the beautiful "Sara."

Ratso is stunned. After a few chords the dedication sinks in and he walks back out to the lobby, moved. After a minute or so, he starts back and bumps into Perry, Stoner's girlfriend. "Good for you," she pats his head, "you got your just reward."

The next day, Ratso wakes early and works on his second *Rolling Stone* piece, due that Friday, and then gets a call from Tom Pacheco in New York. Pacheco is one of the new turks on the Village scene, a singer-songwriter who during the psychedelic years fronted a rock band named the Ragamuffins, and then discovered his folk and country roots, and is about to release his first solo album on RCA. It seems that Pacheco had just written a song about Dylan and he wanted Ratso to hear it. The reporter tells Pacheco to hold on, hooks up his tape recorder, and tapes the tribute, a rollicking rocker in the style of Dylan's first single, "Mixed Up Confusion."

That night, Ratso drives over to the tour hotel, article and tape in tow. In the lobby, Ginsberg and Orlovsky are sitting on a couch. "Wanna see my second article," Ratso asks Allen, and the poet adjusts his glasses and scans the first page. After a minute he begins fumbling in his shoulder bag for a pen. "You should say 'encompass' here, not 'engulf,'" Ginsberg notes, striking out the offending word like an English professor correcting an essay. "And 'it was poetic justice'—that's stronger. And change this description from 'particularly obnoxious' to 'confused.' He is confused, you don't want to say obnoxious, someone might lay that on your karma."

"Shit, Allen," Ratso protests, "do I change your poetry? You look like a fucking professor." "I am," Ginsberg smiles, "director of the Jack Kerouac School of Disembodied Poetics and a member of the Academy of Arts and Letters to boot." They move into the dining room and Ginsberg spots Neuwirth eating. So they stop to chat. Neuwirth starts to scan the article. "Shit, man," he glowers at Ratso, "don't print that fucking shit about the bus, man. They'll spot us everywhere we go." He reads on and grabs a pen from his shirt, and starts inking out a word. "I'm Bob, not Bobby," he frowns, carefully crossing out the "by." "Man," he shakes his head, "why do you have to put that shit about Dylan and Baez together again." "It's in my contract," Ratso says straight-faced, *"Rolling Stone* demands something in the lead about them together again." Neuwirth just shakes his head. He tosses the manuscript across the table to Ratso, giving him a high sign. "You're the only reporter who got Bob's quote right at that ceremony," Neuwirth observes, then goes back to his steak.

Ratso floats back to the lobby and bumps into Jack

Elliot. Elliot sees the article and asks to read it. He slowly scans the pages, silently, with no pen, then hands the article back. "How'd you like the way I ended the story with your quote at the ceremony?" Ratso asks. "I didn't put any words in your mouth, did I?" "No," Jack drawls, pushing his cowboy hat off his eyes, "you just translated what I said into English."

Just then Baez walks by and Ratso corrals her, and whips out his cassette player and the Pacheco tape. "What now, Ratso?" Joan sighs, and the reporter sits her and Jack down and plays the song. "That's nice," she smiles, "that is sweet."

McGuinn falls by and shortly after that, Dylan rounds the corner. He spots Ratso's machine. "Ratso, what's happening. What you got there?" Ratso grabs his arm. "Sit down, sit down, I gotta play you this song. My friend wrote it, it's about you, and he's gonna go into the studio this week and RCA might rush to release it as a single."

"Uhhh, I gotta go somewhere," Dylan protests.

"Sit down, it's only a couple of minutes long," Ratso urges.

Dylan consents, but remains standing, his hands in his jeans pockets, his booted foot nervously tapping the carpet. Ratso rewinds, and starts the tape. Pacheco's resonant booming voice blares out:

He blew into New York City on a bitter freezing day
And he drifted to the Village and sang in the cafes
Hanging out till sunrise sleep till the afternoon
The Kettle and the Gaslight and the Woody Guthrie tunes
Paxton, Ochs and Clayton, Dave Van Ronk and Ramblin' Jack
They marveled at this singer with the funny corduroy hat.
And the songs he started writing were songs that had never been
The word spread through the Village, his name was in the wind.
All across the country people heard him from Newport all the way to New Orleans
His songs were done by everyone in music
Blowing in the wind, made him the king.
And the records started coming, his fame began to grow,
This kid from Minnesota with the wise man in his soul.
The times were changin' quickly, and now Kennedy was gone
He stirred a nation's conscience that was sleeping much too long

Then he plugged into the cosmic and electric lyrics
    screamed
Always changing horses but never changing streams.
All across the country people heard him from Newport
    all the way to New Orleans
His songs were done by everyone in music
Like a Rolling Stone made him the king.
People called him Jesus while others put him down
And some misunderstood him and some went underground
And the madness and the fury almost tore apart his soul
His motorcycle saved him when it took him off the road
And his spirit healed in Woodstock as rumor filled the air
And he moved into the mystic and songs he wrote were
    prayers
Then drifting down to Nashville he sang of simple things
While the country shook with violence and Steppenwolf
    and Cream.
All across the country people heard him from Newport
    all the way to New Orleans
His songs were done by everyone in music
Lay Lady Lay made him the king.
And the turning of the decade brought a quiet to his life
He raised himself a family and he took long walks at night
But now he's back on the road again and back in the city
    lights
His vision and perception still a beacon in the night.
And I don't think that I'd be writing if it wasn't for what
    he did
So this song is for ya Bobby, 'cause you're still the best
    there is.

Dylan listens attentively throughout, tapping his foot,
suppressing a smile, even giggling at the line "took long
walks at night" and wondering out loud, "How'd he know
that?" When it was over, there was a second of embarrassed silence, then Dylan smiles. "Maybe Neuwirth ought
to sing this before I go on," he smiles at Jack, a reference
to Neuwirth's tribute song to Elliot. A second later,
Dylan is loping down the hall.

The next day, Thursday, the rain is teeming down as
Ratso pulls the Granada out of the driveway and scoots
off toward New Haven. It's to be another doubleheader,
two shows at the large Coliseum, a building that looks
like it was designed to serve as a set for *2001*. Ratso
parks in the nearby lot and joins the young crowd bustling for the entrance. This is the most cosmopolitan

date yet, New Haven, home of Yale, and the audience is the freakiest Ratso's encountered this tour.

The first show goes without a hitch, but the second brings out all the stars. Ratso notes Bruce Springsteen, Bill Graham, Patti Smith, even a silver-ponytailed Albert Grossman in the audience. But he's more concerned with finding his own guests, Tom Pacheco, who's coming up from the Village with a tape of the song for Dylan that Kemp requested, and George Lois, up to represent Rubin Carter and negotiate a possible benefit for the boxer's defense fund.

"Motherfucker!" a friendly voice booms out as Ratso wanders near the stage. It's Lois, sitting in the third row with Paul Sapounakis, the owner of the New York night-club the Blue Angel, and a member of the Hurricane Fund. Ratso sits down just as Ronee Blakley steps to the mike. "I'd like to bring on a special friend," she says huskily, and a radiant Joni Mitchell walks on to a thunderous standing ovation. She looks Parisian in a beret, black shirt, and violet pants, and they both share a piano stool for Blakley's "Dues." Joni then picks up an acoustic guitar and does two new ballads, both haunting and beautiful, and leaves to another standing ovation. Lois and Sapounakis talk through Elliot's set but fall quiet when Dylan struts on. But the tour is taking its toll on Dylan's voice, as it has on Neuwirth's and Blakley's. His stage presence is as great as ever but the songs seem to suffer a bit and he appears to be rushing through them.

At intermission Lois turns to Ratso, "You should see the *Newark Star Journal*. They printed all the fucking lyrics to 'Hurricane.'" They slap hands. "I was talking to Ali the other day, trying to get him to emcee the benefit," Lois enthuses, "and a few months ago I had mentioned that Dylan might play and Ali said, 'Who he? Who he?' but now after the single when I told him it looks like we got Dylan for the show, Ali says, 'Oh, you mean the big white singer.' I like that," Lois laughs, " 'big white singer.' "

The curtain rises to "Blowing in the Wind" and Ratso spies Albert Grossman in the third row center, munching on popcorn. "We're gonna do this next one for Gertrude Stein," Dylan announces. Lois spots Ginsberg walking to a seat. "What's he doing on the tour?" he asks Ratso. "Is he getting paid?"

Dylan leaves and Baez commands the stage, following "Diamonds and Rust" with the *a cappella* "Swing Low, Sweet Chariot," which has been getting a marvelous reception so far. Lois and Sapounakis are attentive, and when Baez breaks into "Joe Hill," Lois' face lights up. "I used to sing this in Music and Art when I was a commie." He nudges Ratso. "You ever hear Robeson sing it? It'll knock you on your ass."

After the song, Baez brings on Mimi Fariña, her younger sister, and they harmonize together beautifully. After a few numbers, Sapounakis leans over Lois to Ratso. "I don't understand something," he puzzles. "If they're sisters how come they have different last names?" Ratso looks incredulous and leans over to George. "That guy own a nightclub?" Just then, Patti Smith walks by and Ratso points out the new sensation to George. "Can you imagine living with that all your life?" Lois marvels.

"Please come to Boston," Baez is crooning the Kenny Loggins hit that Ratso loathes so much. "What do you think of this song?" he asks Lois. George listens to a bar or two, then turns back. "It sucks," he sneers, "it's like a McDonald's hamburger." "You been a lot of fun, thank you," Baez trills as she prepares to exit. "She doesn't know what fun is," the adman snorts, "she should put her head between my legs."

Dylan stalks on, trailing a long Tibetan scarf from his black leather jacket. The makeup is caked now, and his eyes are searingly intense, giving him the look of a maniacal character in a Fritz Lang movie. He sits down on the stool and plows right into "I Don't Believe You," a gem from the past. The band strolls on and "One More Cup" is next, with a completely new, slower arrangement than the one used when the tour opened. Dylan is on this show, his phrasing as precise and stunning as karate chops. Then they start into "Hurricane." "This is it." Lois jabs Paul and Ratso. "Do it good, Bobby," he screams toward the stage. They bounce along to the song, slapping hands every so often, jumping to a standing ovation at the conclusion. "All right, motherfucker," Lois exults.

After that, the rest of the set seems anticlimactic, and Ratso follows George and Paul to the stage door. Lois and Sapounakis enter, but Ratso gets stopped. "He's with us," Lois tells the security guard, "he works for Rubin."

Kemp hurries over. "Look George, it's fine for you to come backstage, but we can't let Ratso."

"But Lou, Ratso works for Rubin. He's on the defense committee."

"He's a reporter. We can't have reporters backstage," Kemp snaps.

"Look, I know I'm a guest of yours, but Ratso is a very important part of our committee. Rubin would be upset if he gets hassled."

"He's still a reporter," Kemp argues, "he might hear or see something he shouldn't."

Lois apologizes to the reporter-defender and goes back, as Ratso watches Patti Smith and her entourage, Grossman and his wife, Springsteen, his girlfriend, and about fifteen Columbia Records executives pass by and head backstage. Just then, Pacheco and his girlfriend Melissa walk up. Pacheco is wearing his standard Australian cowboy hat and he's carrying a beautiful hand-painted wine bottle, a gift for Dylan. Ratso knows he's too shy to push his way back, so he hollers for Kemp and introduces the folksinger to the manager. Kemp gets the tape and escorts Pacheco back.

But Ratso isn't really missing much. It's a mob scene backstage, almost fifty people, few of whom know each other, few of whom even have much in common, so little enclaves form, with the hurried glances and suspicious whispers that are so endemic to the rock 'n roll business.

Dylan is sitting in the corner of a small room, surrounded by a mob, makeup smeared by his sweat, fatigue etched into his face, absentmindedly playing with a rose. He gets introduced to Springsteen and they exchange a few taciturn sentences, Dylan shyly glancing to the floor, swinging the rose back and forth until suddenly the flower flies off, leaving him holding the stem. The awkward silence is broken by Springsteen's red-haired girlfriend Karen, who asks Dylan why he wears makeup. "I saw it once in a movie," he mumbles.

After a while Pacheco and Melissa come back out, bottle still in tow, and Ratso joins them as they head for the cars. "We couldn't get near Dylan, too many people." Pacheco sadly tucks the wine bottle under his arm. "I'll send it to him for Christmas." On the way to the garage, they pass a wiped-out Springsteen, in a dirty mechanic's

jumpsuit, draped around his girlfriend who's supporting
him on their way to the waiting limo. "Hey," Ratso
points, "he looked so fine at first and left looking just
like a ghost."

They arrive at Ratso's car only to find more sabotage.
The distributor cap has nearly been pulled out of the
engine and the car refuses to start. Ratso curses, hops
into Pacheco's car, and they go to search for an open
gas station.

Instead they find a diner and two hours later it's 5
A.M., Melissa is almost sleeping, Pacheco's got a long
drive back to the Village, so they head back to the Coliseum. The Hertz office opens around 7:30 and Ratso opts
to kill a couple of hours at the downtown Dunkin' Do-
nuts, so he parts company with his friends, walks over to
an all-night newsstand, snatches up a copy of *Hustler*
magazine, and settles into a rear stool at the donut shop.
Later, he walks over to the Hertz office, picks out a new
bright-red Monte Carlo, and slides in next to the Hertz
mechanic who's gonna go check out the Granada.

The old black man floors the car and they speed past the
lovely ivy-covered walls of Yale. "Fucking whorehouse,"
the mechanic spits, eyes scanning the virginal 7 A.M.
campus, "bunch of junkies go here." His bony finger
points toward Yale's green. "They always catch them
down there on the green with no pants on, fucking
chicks."

The Hertz man expertly wheels the car around a corner and heads up toward the Coliseum. "What do you
do?" he asks Ratso. The reporter explains about the tour,
Dylan, Baez, etc. The old man's eyes light up. "I used to
sing. I was in showbiz, still do it part-time. It's a dog,
though." They fall silent. The Hertz man shakes his head,
moans, "I'll tell ya, those fucking one-night stands kill
ya, most of us old-timers are getting out. We don't play
that shit for young folks. We work gigs for the fur-and-
diamond set." He swings the car up the long circular
ramp of the parking facility. "Where the fuck does this
thing end?" he wonders halfway up. "Where you from?
New York? Yeah, I wouldn't live in that motherfucker
for anything. I live here now. I've had it with the fucking
road. You know how most entertainers are, make it and
fuck it up. They think it'll last forever. Well I got a fucking house out of it. You want some advice?" The Hertz

man pauses and stares at Ratso. Ratso nods. "Save it."
He floors the Monte Carlo through the deserted parking
level.

"What's your name?" Ratso finally asks.

"Ray Reid."

"What group did you work with?"

"The Inkspots, joined in I forget the fucking year, but
I been with 'em for fourteen years. I'm sixty-two now.
It's a rough fucking life, man. Living out of a suitcase.
It's lots of fun now when we still do it. It's in our blood.
Just shuck it and fuck it. We had a chance to go on the
road and do one-nighters last winter but we said fuck it.
I don't want it no more. We were out with Andy Kirk
and the Clouds of Joy last time. Your parents heard of
him. We went out for ten weeks, one-nighters." He spots
the Granada and stops on a dime. "Yup, you've got a car
here." Ray hops out and quickly looks over the Granada
engine. "Shit, we gotta leave this motherfucker here and
get a tow truck."

On the way back, Ratso fills Ray in on some of his experiences with this tour. Ray's soaking in the road stories, his eyes wide, his cracked face breaking into a grin.
"Shit, when I get off if I want I go out on a gig," he
sighs, "but through the week I gotta go and make that
dollar shit. Why not? It's not a bad job. They may give
you shit about getting this Monte Carlo for that Granada
though."

"Fuck 'em," Ratso fumes expansively, "I'll tell 'em they
fucked me out of a four-thousand-dollar gig because the
car wouldn't start." Ratso smiles and pulls into the
Hertz garage. "All right my man, take care," Ray waves
to Ratso. "Hey Ray, if you can still sing what the fuck
are you doing working in a garage?" Ratso shouts. Ray
makes a face. "Fuck that shit. I'm through with these
one-nighters. I'm semi-retired." He turns to enter the office. "But if you get me with a group," he smiles, "I can
still swing a bit."

Ratso gets back to his hotel in Danbury around 9 A.M.
and settles down for a few hours of much-needed sleep.
But once again, the jarring phone interrupts at noon.
Rolling Stone this time. The urgent tones of his New
York editor jump out of the receiver and jolt the reporter
awake like tiny splashes of ice water. Flippo, the editor,
is enraged over the piece.

"It just is not a good piece," he flatly declares in his Southern twang. "It doesn't reflect two weeks of traveling. You seem like an adman, like you're too close to get some perspective. Details, you need details. How much are people making?"

"You want me to ask Baez to say how much she's making?" Ratso barks incredulously. "I wouldn't tell her how much I'm making. How much do you make?"

"You're not doing a story on me," Flippo says flippantly.

The conversation goes on a bit and Ratso promises to try to get some additional quotes and information on the business aspects of the tour. But first a trip to the Pathmark and some vitamin C, vitamin B-6, vitamin B-12, Expectorate, Robitussin, orange juice, grapefruit juice, and cough drops for the miserable cold he's been carrying around since Vermont. By the afternoon, the room looks like a hospital ward, the juices stored in an ice-filled garbage can, the medicines and vitamin bottles strewn around the various dresser- and tabletops. And the sick reporter lying in the middle of all this with the phone permanently attached to his left ear. He's been trying the Niagara Hilton all day, to no avail. Finally, around 6, he reaches Kemp's room.

"Louie, this is Ratso, I'm still in Connecticut. My fucking car was broken into last night and I got beat up."

"Who broke into it?"

"I don't know. Some hoods probably tried to steal it."

"Yeah, who beat you up?"

"The fucking bikers that work for the local promoter," Ratso moans.

"Why?"

"Because I didn't have a badge."

"Well, where were you that you weren't supposed to be that they beat you up?" Kemp sounds like a stern parent.

"I was in a seat that wasn't occupied. The guy says let me see your stub, and I said, 'I don't have a ticket for this seat,' and the guy says, 'Get up,' and he pulls me like I'm a kid trying to crash a seat and I said, 'Listen man, I'm with *Rolling Stone*,' and he says, 'Yeah, the fuck you are.' He was one of those biker types, Gestapo mentality, and he starts pulling me by—"

"Hey Larry," Kemp interrupts, "what can I do for you?"

"All right, what I need now is *Rolling Stone* called and they need fifteen hundred more words. I need some quotes by tonight."

"What do you mean you need quotes?"

"They want reactions to the tour so far."

"From who?" Kemp says suspiciously.

"Blakley, Elliot, Ronson," Ratso pauses, "and Dylan."

"Well you can get the first ones for sure," Kemp assures.

"Well, what about Dylan!" Ratso urges.

"I don't know."

"I'm not trying to sweat on you," the reporter screams, "you know that."

"Well," Kemp softens, "what's the question?"

"How the tour has been," Ratso improvises, "you know, his reaction to the tour so far, just the general kind of thing . . ."

"That's bullshit!" Kemp screams.

"I know it's bullshit but it's what they want. Do me a favor. Ask Dylan. I really need two paragraphs from him, you know, something like that saying why he's the loosest he's ever been. . . ."

"We'll see," Kemp says ominously. "Call me back later."

Ratso hangs up and paces the floor. He's got a deadline coming up in about twelve hours, he's hundreds of miles away from the people that he's got to interview, relying on that goddamn phone. As if by magic, it rings.

But it's only *Rolling Stone* again, this time Abe Peck, the San Francisco–based editor of the music section. Ratso and Peck are old friends, in fact, Ratso introduced Abe to the *Rolling Stone* people and in some way feels responsible for his getting him his present position. Of course, it was Abe that assigned Ratso to the Rubin Carter story.

"What you filed is kind of rambling, really," Peck pronounces. "It doesn't report on the evolution of the tour. If you read that piece you have no idea what the dates are. Look, here's the situation. We have a tour here that has turned from a tour where Dylan says, 'We're gonna play for the people,' only doing small halls, to a tour where they're knocking off $150,000 a night. The major unanswered question that has nothing to do with color or Rolling Thunder or a student that runs away from home like you have in your piece. You should be more factual.

The news of this tour is the change from what their story was—"

"Levy told me it was never intended to be small clubs," Ratso protests. "That was the rumor, from Columbia."

"Your job is to cut through the gossip. Why were Kemp and Imhoff being so reluctant, because of the mysterious nature of the tour or to create hype? Did you see the new *Variety?* There's an article here about the tour that seems to be the right question to ask. The headline says, 'Is Dylan Interested in Money? Small Clubs Give Way to Arenas.' "

"Read it," Ratso yells.

"OK." Peck plows in:

Providence, Nov. 11

Bob Dylan and the Rolling Thunder Revue drew 20,878 customers who paid $158,000 for two performances at the 12,500 seat Providence Civic Center last week but it was virtually a textbook example of how a show should not be promoted.

Center general manager Charles J. Toomey was telephoned October 6 by promoters Shelly Finkle and Barry Imhoff who wanted to book a "dynamic show" into the building. They said Dylan would come to town with a complement of singers and musicians, but Toomey was to tell no one, least of all the press.

They reportedly were acting on Dylan's dictates in all matters.

Toomey kept the information under his bonnet to the extent none of the Civic Center personnel had any inkling who the "mystery" performer would be. Rumors circulated it might be Barbra Streisand, Liza Minnelli, Neil Diamond or Elton John, but checks indicated these talents would be otherwise occupied Nov. 4.

Toomey admits some folks correctly guessed it would be Dylan but he remained mum. The promoters had threatened to yank the shows if the word was leaked.

Tickets went on sale Saturday morning Oct. 25, at 10 o'clock, and some 200 people were queued up outside. At the same time announcements were made over radio stations WRBU and WPRO.

The tickets said "Rolling Thunder Revue" but gave no suggestion as to what a Rolling Thunder Revue is. There were youngsters—tickets in hand—asking "Who is it? What is it?" They were visibly relieved when told it was Dylan and not perhaps a kettle drum recital or religious crusade.

Imhoff, meanwhile, said there would be no press accommodations because "We don't need any publicity." Promoters said they wanted to give "the people an equal chance to see Bob." One scribe noted this is referred to in business school as "maximizing profit."

"All right, stop, I'll get the article," Ratso yells.

"Look, someone created the hype, the illusion. Even *Variety* said they were gonna play small halls. The point is they're doubling up, playing two concerts a night, doing $100,000 nights. You're lacking hard info on the mechanics of the tour, on the success or failure of the original concept of this tour. The central theme of the piece should be, it seems to me, that two weeks into this tour it became clear that the concept had changed. Look, the first eleven shows of the tour in seven cities brought an estimated 75,000 customers between $7.50 and $8.50 so the grosses are almost $600,000. That's not intimate clubs. Why the change? Who changed? Who started the myth of small clubs? What does Dylan feel about the myth? That one theme.

"The other theme is the continuation of the music. Has the music changed? Was it good in the beginning? Are they growing as an aggregate? Rumors of superstars coming? How's Ginsberg? How did Joni get there? We have to be finished by Tuesday afternoon, starting inquiries at this point is very late. Then we need much more stuff from Dylan. You've been saying to me and Chet that you have great access. Then why the fuck doesn't he talk to you? What have you been doing for two weeks with Dylan?"

"I had great access in the city," Ratso rails, "we hung out nearly every night. But we got on the road and Kemp starts treating me like a nigger."

"So write about that if you can't get the interview."

"Kemp's job is to keep me away," Ratso's voice is a shrug.

"Who says it? All those good parts of your first piece are missing in this second one. I think right now is just a collection of anecdotes."

"I dug that second piece more than anything I've written."

"That's not my feeling. I'm not saying only to do a business piece. Look, these guys went out on tour and told

everyone, whoever, they told, blah, I love Rubin Carter,
I'm busting my ass to get this guy out of jail. Suddenly
they're playing two shows in big fucking halls. How's this
happen? Look we need about a thousand more words.
OK?"

Ratso assents, slams down the phone, and picks it right
back up. The phone in Kemp's room in Niagara Falls
rings twice.

"Hello," a soft feminine voice answers. It's Susan,
Louie's girlfriend from Minnesota. Ratso starts babbling
to her about the crisis, the deadline, the needed quotes,
the car being broken into, and his fight with security.

"Would you like to speak to Louie," she suggests, and
passes the phone.

"You got a problem out there, huh?" the familiar fish
peddler's voice booms across the miles.

"Louie, they just called me," Ratso tries to sound frantic,
"they said they don't like the piece. Doesn't have any
detail and they said that I told them I have access to him,
that I'm holding stuff back from them, read me a piece in
Variety putting down the way the tour's been promoted,
shit like that. They're really sweating on me."

"What do you want me to do?" Kemp finally responds.

"Help me out a little," Ratso squeaks.

"I helped you out plenty. You talked to all those other
people, you got quotes, use them."

"I didn't talk to anybody," Ratso whines. "Would you
give me a quote, at least?"

"No," Kemp thunders. "On what?"

"I'll ask you some questions," Ratso senses an opening.

"No, call those other entertainers."

"They can't help. They want to know why it was
changed from small halls to large arenas."

"That's all they're concerned about," Kemp says con-
temptuously.

"Yeah, isn't that stupid," Ratso laughs. "Who changed
it? How is Dylan responding to the changes?" Ratso
mocks the list of questions.

"They're not large arenas. They're medium-sized halls."

"Yeah, Lou, but if you do two shows a night in 12,000-
seat arenas that's 24,000 seats at $8.50 a seat. That's
money, not small clubs."

"So what's the question?" Lou sounds impatient.

"They said the original theme was to play for the people. I had a quote from Bob saying that small halls are more conducive to my kind of music so the question is, has the concept of the tour changed? Now Levy told me some shit about that."

"What he say?"

"He said we had a lot of expenses and you had to do large halls."

"That's it," Kemp jumps in. "In order to cover the large expenses of the entourage and the film we have to play some larger halls to meet expenses."

"So you have to pay for the film. How much does that cost?"

"I don't give out any figures," Kemp snaps back.

"But a lot, huh?" Ratso presses. "How many people are on the film crew?"

"That's it," Kemp seems anxious to go, "a large entourage."

"How many people?"

"We're carrying a total of about seventy people."

"And that's at twenty dollars per diem," Ratso adds helpfully.

"Well, there are a lot more expenses than that, a lot. They get room, board, transportation, and all supporting services. The musicians are on salary. They all get paid, everyone's getting paid but Bob, he's the only one who's not getting paid."

"No shit," Ratso whistles.

"Yeah, he hasn't asked for nothing. He's not looking for nothing. But all these other people are getting paid so lots of money gets paid in both salaries and expenses."

"Let's run this down," Ratso gets professional. "There are two film crews, support people in New York who all work for the film crew, so you're talking of a film crew of fifteen people."

"That's right."

"Nobody has this information," Ratso bursts, "you should tell the people this."

"I don't think it's anybody's business," Kemp argues.

"People are asking about that," Ratso screams. "This *Variety* piece starts by asking those nasty questions."

"That's the only reason. If it was up to us, we'd just play really small halls but we have to pay for the film and all those other people. If it was up to Bob, he ain't looking for nothing."

"If it was up to Bob, he'd play in the street," Ratso gets carried away.

"That's right," Louie agrees.

"Would you say that," Ratso smells the headline.

"Say what?"

"If it was up to Bob he'd play in the streets."

"You said that, I didn't say that," Kemp explodes.

"All right, I'll say that," Ratso concedes.

"I ain't gonna say that."

"Will you say something like that?" Ratso prods. Kemp seems to hesitate. "Ask Susan!" Ratso suggests.

"What can we say, you got that thing . . ." Kemp muses.

"Say something I can quote," the reporter eggs.

"OK, uh," Kemp pauses, searching for the phrase, "I'm the one that has to be concerned with the balancing of the budget so I'm the one that deems it necessary in order to cover expenses to play bigger halls so we can afford smaller ones. If it was up to Bob we'd play all small halls."

"Because it's more conducive to his music," Ratso parrots.

"That's right."

"What's his reaction to the large halls so far?"

"Sue says you should talk about the crowd and how they feel," Kemp changes the subject. "What was your question?"

"Bob's reaction so far to the tour and shit. Could you have him call me or could you get in the room with him and call me. . . ?"

"No, he don't want to be bothered," Louie decides.

"Ah, man, they're really sweating on me," Ratso says in disgust.

"I just gave you some good stuff."

"They want quotes from him, you know that."

"I know, I know," Louie concedes, "I ain't gonna bother him now with this shit. You should be able to whip this stuff in shape."

"I need quotes from him," Ratso whines, "you know that."

"Maybe tomorrow," Kemp softens. "We'll see how it goes."

"Tomorrow morning, my deadline is at noon."

"Ah, they always change those deadlines," Kemp says cavalierly.

"Let me ask you another thing. Who started this whole small-club thing?"

"It was small halls."

"They told me the first eleven shows, in seven cities, paying customers totaled $600,000 gross."

"What they know, they know," Kemp counters, "but Bob hasn't made a cent and isn't making any money on this thing. It's still in the red."

"Let me say that, let me say that," Ratso bubbles.

"Well, Bob isn't making a cent on this thing so far," Louie repeats, "and with all the expenses of the film crew and the large entourage, his prospects of making money are not good. He can make more money in one night if he wanted to than he will on this whole tour. All right, so that's a quote, use that quote, that sums it up. All the money's going to pay the expenses of the other entertainers, salaries, etcetera."

"Did you read the *Variety* piece yet?" Ratso asks. "The headline says 'Is Dylan Interested in Money?'"

"We don't give a shit if they're that fucked up," Kemp spits, "that's their problem."

"They also asked why the price went from $7.50 to $8.50," Ratso prods.

"Because we're not covering our expenses," Kemp answers impatiently. "We're having a hard time between the movie and the large amount of expenses related with all these people we take with it. Everybody's getting a salary except for Bob. And we felt that at $8.50 it was still a bargain compared to what other people were selling for more money."

Ratso's running out of questions and it's nearly eight and he still hasn't eaten but he can't resist one more stab. "Talk to Bob, Louie. Maybe you could get a quote from him. The question is, how is he? What's his feelings, given the fact that he said in the last—"

"I answered that question," Kemp interrupts.

"You can't answer for him," Ratso rails.

"Well, I'm answering it the way I see it."

"I'm asking for his view. Ask him how he sees it. And I want to get his reaction to the music so far. I know he loves Ronee's segment."

"I can't speak for him on that," Kemp hurries. "Call me back later."

Ratso walks to the restaurant and grabs a fast bite.

Back in the room, he grabs his copy of *Hustler* and starts to read when the phone rings again. Flippo this time.

"I just spoke to Kemp," Ratso reassures, "I got ten minutes on the phone with me asking questions and charges about the expenses and shit."

"Great."

"I also told him I need a quote from Dylan. My fucking phone bill's gonna be astronomical. There's no paging system in the Hilton, every time I have to get transferred I get disconnected. Kemp told me everyone on the tour is on salary. The film crew is fifteen people alone. One of the reasons they play large halls is to pay for the film that's getting made. They see daily rushes, big sessions where they all sit around. I play a *Rolling Stone* reporter in the movie."

"That's secondary," the editor snaps, "get the fucking story."

"I can't control it," Ratso shrugs, "they just come in, barge in, I was interviewing someone on the street and they come up and start filming the interview."

"Well, manipulate them, man. All I care about is the story, Larry. Dylan's the key. You got to have Dylan. Are you aware that Blakley's sleeping with Dylan?" Flippo says tongue-in-cheek.

"No," Ratso scoffs.

"That's a fact."

"What do you mean that's a fact."

"I know it from somebody on the tour. Now look, I'm not totally stupid, Larry."

"I hear she's a dyke," Ratso lies.

"I don't know about that now. I heard this from a fairly good authority. That's the only reason Bob took her along."

"That's not true," Ratso protests.

"She ain't the greatest singer in the world," Flippo smirks. "Got to admit that."

"I love her, I think she's a great songwriter."

"But she can't sing. She's a fair songwriter. No one can tell you she can sing. She's not an Emmy Lou Harris by any means. So what's her charm then. I'll tell you what her charm is. Round heels."

"What's that?" Ratso asks.

"That means she bends over backward. You touch her and she falls over backward, that's Southern. Dig it."

"That means she fucks?" Ratso plays dumb.

"Round heels," Flippo's screaming, "she can't stand up straight. She falls over."

"And what happens when she falls over?"

"What do you think happens when she falls over?" Flippo fumes. "Jesus Christ."

"You think I can fuck her?" Ratso asks innocently.

"Well if she has round heels . . ."

"Wouldn't that be a great story," Ratso gushes.

"Yeah, but you ain't Dylan, that's the problem."

"Yeah, too bad, just think I could wire myself for sound and get an interview in bed."

"Let's not worry about that now," Flippo cautions.

"What a good concept though," Ratso continues. "Somebody really told you that about her and Dylan, huh, somebody on the tour. A performer?"

"Let's not play twenty questions here."

"Give me a hint," Ratso begs.

"I can't tell you. . . . Well, have you seen any indications of that?"

"No," Ratso emphasizes, "I thought he was sleeping with Neuwirth."

"Look," Flippo gets serious, "the hours are creeping down. You had two fucking weeks. That story had a lot of holes."

Ratso yawns. "What's going on in the real world?"

"I want to know what's going on in the tour," Flippo yells. "He ain't playing small halls, he's grossed almost $600,000 in less than two weeks. . . ."

"He hasn't made any money," Ratso reports.

"C'mon."

"Look, there are seventy people on the road all being paid salary."

"How much?" Flippo snaps.

"They won't tell me that."

"Ask them. Ask Baez. She might tell you. It's worth the fucking chance, man."

"Well, seventy people on the road," Ratso calculates, "let's say the average salary is . . ."

"Two hundred a week," Flippo butts in.

"No, more than that. The fucking stagehands make more than $200 a week. They couldn't get anybody for $200 a week. Maybe $350 a week plus everyone gets $20 a day per diem."

"OK, seventy people at $300 a week, that's $21,000 a week. So how does $100,000 a night, c'mon, he's grossed about $600,000. Twenty grand a week, that's peanuts."

"Wait a minute. Staying at hotels costs at least $30 a night for rooms. That's $2,100 a night. Times seven. They have to pay every night even if they don't play. That's $14,700 a week for rooms," Ratso figures.

"And the gross so far is almost $600,000," Flippo reminds.

"Wait, we ain't done yet . . ."

"Look man, he ain't playing to save the whales, we know that. I mean this is not a benefit tour. How do you take $596,000 for two weeks and justify that for expenses. C'mon, really."

"I got $10,000 a week in per diems," Ratso's still figuring.

"Ain't much."

"Equipment, buses, and stuff costs."

"Not much, minimal."

"OK, what's he paying the musicians, we don't know that."

"OK, that's what we need to know," Flippo stresses, "where is this fucking money going. He's making it hand over fist, now why is he doubling up? In these big halls, man. Why is he playing for 25,000 a day?"

Ratso yawns.

"Man, you were too easy on Kemp in this story," Flippo continues. "You were apologizing for him. You were kind to him, said he was a valuable friend to Dylan. You back off when Dylan and Neuwirth both say, 'Well man, this is what Lou has to do.' That's bullshit, he doesn't have to do that. That's crap, there's no fucking excuse for doing what Kemp is doing to the press."

"Can I quote you?" Ratso asks.

"Kemp is just on a fucking ego ride, that's what it is. What else, if you're Dylan's right-hand man, what's going to happen to your mind. You get sucked into his orbit if he needs to deal with you by being halfway friendly here and there. It gets you in fairly close then he just kind of gets you to do what he wants to do, man. That's obvious, I've seen that for years."

"Who?" Ratso challenges.

"From Bill Graham to Imhoff. I don't have time to go into it now."

"I'm sleeping only three hours a night, man," Ratso boasts.

"What are you doing all that time that you're not reporting?"

"I'm trying, I'm getting beat up, my car's been broken into . . ."

"Who beat you up?"

"I wasn't beat up but I was roughly escorted out by the security guards at one concert."

"Put all this in the story," Flippo stresses. "Obviously Kemp and Imhoff are not your typical sterling Walt Disney characters and that needs to be brought out. What you filed here was not reporting."

"It was feature stuff."

"Yeah, feature material that is not long enough to sustain as a feature. But we have to think about this issue, like what cities have they played, that kind of crap. That should have been in the goddamn story. What I want is fucking news."

"Last time you said you wanted more color. You wanted what the buses looked like. I have that."

"You still have not said how many goddamn buses there are."

"There are two buses," Ratso screams, "I had that in the goddamn article."

"You had one, Phydeaux."

"I said a caravan of two buses and a mobile home."

"What kind of buses are they? Greyhound? Detail, detail."

"One is a regular fucking Delmonico bus, should I say that?" Ratso can't believe this.

"Details, yeah, this is the news section. Don't worry about the length, if it's good we can make it go as long as it needs to."

Ratso hangs up and starts pacing the room, stopping for a shot of Expectorate. Time is wasting, he thinks, I gotta get to Dylan. He picks up the phone again.

"What do you want to know? Have you written the article yet?" Kemp growls.

"I spoke to Flippo, they want a quote from Dylan."

"I gave you information. Yeah, well what they want and what they get may be two different things," Kemp growls.

"I'd like it too, personally."

"Saying what? What would you like the guy to say?" Kemp challenges.

"I don't want to put words in his mouth."

"Well, what is it you want to know from him?"

"I told you what I want to know. I want to know what he thinks about the tour so far, playing large halls—"

"I told you," Kemp interrupts.

"But that's not him."

"That's it, you know. The guy's not accessible to everyone that wants to talk to him. You know that, that's the facts of life."

"I know he's accessible to me."

"Not whenever you want to talk to him."

"Well, I've laid low for two weeks," Ratso points out.

"I don't want Bob bugged about these things. These are questions that fall in my area and I've answered them. I told you what he likes, what his preferences were and I told you what I was doing on the basis of what had to be done in order to—"

"What do you mean? Like, he likes to play small halls."

"He likes to play small halls," Louie repeats, "that's his preference."

"I'd like to ask him what he thinks about the show so far, if he thinks it's good, why he feels so comfortable."

"I think those are dumb questions, why does he feel so comfortable?"

"Why is he so animated?" Ratso rewords it.

"Those are bullshit questions," Lou scoffs.

"I don't think it's bullshit," Ratso raises his voice, "I've never seen him so comfortable on stage before."

"I don't think Bob should have to be subjected to questions like that."

"Hey, did you tell the *People* guy what questions to ask him?" Ratso wonders.

"If you had an interview you could ask what you feel but you don't have an interview so you'll just have to settle—"

"When can I have an interview?" Ratso interrupts shrilly.

"When can you have an interview? I'll put your name on the list."

"What list?"

"The list of the other ten thousand people that requested it before you. You're constantly badgering me for the same shtick."

"I'm just trying to do my job," Ratso repeats.

"Do it then, you can see the guy's loose, that's the important thing."

"You know as well as I do that I can say it but if he says the same thing it means more than if I say it."

"OK, well," Lou concedes, "but the facts are what they are."

"Do you think he'd feel I was intruding if I asked him questions like that?"

"I don't want to subject him to questions," Lou decides. "If he wants to do an interview with you, he'll call you, OK."

"Could you ask him," Ratso pleads. "I don't want an interview, give him the message. I just need about two paragraphs now, I don't need an hour."

"Another thing you haven't put in your articles that I think you should put in is the low-keyed way the tickets are being sold for the benefit of the people in the street. So it's a nonhype easygoing type of thing."

"Tell me the way it's done," Ratso reluctantly gets out a pen.

"Jerry Seltzer's the guy that runs ticket sales. He goes into a town approximately five, six days ahead of time, with the tickets already printed up. For example, Worcester went on sale today for a Tuesday show. We put them on sale with handbills, just handbills and follow it up on a couple of stations once in a while with a couple of short radio spots in outlying areas, where we want people to have a chance to get tickets also."

"Do you have to pay for the ads?"

"In some cases we have bought a few spots, but in most cases the radio stations pick it up off the handbills or word-of-mouth. We're not hyping anybody, we're putting the tickets out there and anybody wants to buy them they're welcome. If they don't this ain't no big rock 'n roll hype."

"The *Variety* article talked about the way you booked the Springfield date."

"Yeah, how'd we do that," Kemp says sarcastically.

"It said Imhoff called up and said we have name talent, wouldn't say who it was, and speculation ranged from Anne Murray to Elton John. I also talked to a kid promoter in Southeast Massachusetts, that was pissed off 'cause Imhoff bought all the T-shirts he had printed up with the Rolling Thunder logo. . . ."

Just then the phone buzzes, signaling another call coming into Kemp's line. "Go write your story," he chides the reporter. "Excuse me, sir," the operator's voice chimes in, "Carlos Santana is on the line waiting."

It's midnight and still no quotes and Ratso is restless. Danbury ain't exactly Marina Del Rey but there must be some hip bars, the reporter prays. He hops into the Monte Carlo, stops at the first gas station, and gets directions to a nearby music club. Five minutes later, Ratso locks the car, hops over some puddles, opens the door and gets bathed in the warm sounds of rock 'n roll. The band ain't bad, the beer is cold and cheap, and there's this one blonde that keeps eying him. They talk for a while, drink a few beers, and it's two, bartime. Ratso speeds back to the motel and parades the blonde past the awed young night clerk.

In the room, she settles gingerly down onto the bed, making some space between the sheafs of copy paper, the tape recorder, the strewn cassettes, the bottles of vitamins, the iced juice, and begins to leaf through *Hustler*. Ratso seizes the opportunity to size her up. Nice tits, bulging out at him from behind the cashmere sweater, but the rest of the body is on the pudgy side. And those tacky white platform shoes, and all that sleazy makeup, and those black patterned stockings, he'd only seen that shit on aging bohemians. Oh well, it'll have to do, Ratso thinks, after all this is Danbury. He moved onto the bed next to her. "Oh," she says coyly, "I forgot to tell you what happened after I broke up with my boyfriend. I had an operation last week." She pauses, dramatically, and looks at the ceiling. "An abortion." Ratso just moans and sinks back into the bed.

He finally gets to sleep close to four, his only companion the tape recorder lying on the other twin bed. And once again, after about a half hour of REM bliss, the jangling phone rips him back to reality. It's Jacques Levy in New York, returning his earlier call.

"*Rolling Stone* wants to know details," he mumbles. "What happened to the concept of small clubs, now it's big arenas."

"That's ridiculous," Levy scoffs. "What are they trying to do? Are they trying to bad-mouth it already? Why?"

"Did you see the *Variety* piece? The headline asked if Dylan was looking for money."

"Looking for money?" Levy sputters. "He's gonna go to the fucking toilet with this." He laughs heartily. "He's not gonna make any money off this."

"Yeah, and the *Rolling Stone* people read the *Variety* article and they told me to add——"

"Aw, don't let them do that. Anyway, you know it's only because Bob's Jewish," Levy cracks.

"I told Kemp the tack is to attack you on the big-arena angle."

"OK," Levy interrupts, "so what do you want? This is my nickel."

"I need a reaction to the charges that the spirit of the show has been altered by playing in large halls. By the way, I almost got beat up. I don't mind playing the role of a harassed reporter . . ."

"I can see you as Jimmy Stewart," Levy laughs.

"But it wasn't even filmed that night and——"

"Sloman, Sloman, don't tell me these stories, I know about your bad luck. What do you want from me? You want me to defend Bob from the attack that he's a commercial prick? Is that it? That as far as I know——"

"That as far as you know," Ratso picks it up, "the spirit of the thing hasn't been altered."

"Go on, keep going, Sloman," Levy roars.

"You say it," the reporter protests.

"No, no you say it. I'll give you a yes or no." Levy cracks up. "C'mon make up your own quote."

"As far as I know the spirit of the show has not been altered——"

"What is that?" Levy interrupts him. "The spirit of the show hasn't been altered. It's ridiculous this charge, why should you even pay attention to it?"

"I got editors," Ratso moans and pulls the blankets tighter, "you think I have a free hand? I get it from all sides, you think it's easy?"

They hang up and Ratso gets a few more hours sleep, then at 10 A.M. rings up Kemp. "Louie's bar and grill," Susan answers, and the reporter says hello.

"Would you like to speak to Mr. Kemp?" In the background, Ratso can hear the sound of Saturday morning TV. Louie's watching cartoons.

"Yeah," Kemp's jaded voice floats to Danbury.

"Louie Kemp was reached while watching his favorite program, *Crusader Duck*," Ratso goes into his best anchorman voice.

"Whaddya want?" Louie growls.

"Are you awake. You sober? I got two hours, Lou. I need a quote from Dylan," Ratso pleads. "You know that. *Rolling Stone* is paying $250 a week to keep me alive on the road and they'll be pissed off if they don't get two fucking paragraphs."

Louie pauses. "Well, he'll give you a quote," he says softly.

Ratso is speechless. "Great," he manages weakly.

"When he wakes up. I don't know what time that'll be, he stayed up late last night."

Ratso thanks Louie profusely and hangs up. He's got about an hour to kill so he makes a few personal calls, then reaches Baez's manager Bernie Gelb and sets up a phone interview for later that day. The last call is to Kinky, who's playing in Dallas.

"Keno," Ratso screams, "everybody's waiting on pins and needles for you to come, boy."

"I'm definitely coming now, Rats. Of course, this could be the biggest debacle you ever pulled off."

"My cock is the biggest debacle I ever pulled off."

"All right realll nice" Kinky purrs, "that's a good line. I'll see you up there somewhere between the twenty-second and the twenty-eighth."

Ratso hangs up and starts to work on the article. The phone rings.

"Larry, it's Louie. Have you started to write that yet?"

"I'm transcribing. Doing inserts," Ratso replies.

"OK, I just talked to Bob. He's up, you can call him directly and talk to him for a few minutes. Don't badger him," Kemp warns.

"I'm not badgering him."

"I'm just telling you. Listen, just ask him those few questions that you want and that's it. OK, he's in room 505."

Ratso immediately dials the room. The phone rings, rings again, rings a third time.

"Bob? This is Larry," Ratso blurts out when he hears the receiver picked up.

"Yeah Larry," a weary, obviously half-awake Dylan greets, "how you doing?"

"I'm in Connecticut. You got a minute? I gotta do a story in an hour and I need a couple of paragraphs from you. OK?"

"OK," Dylan sounds amiable.

"You up?"

"Yeah, sort of."

"You want me to call back later? I just spoke to Kinky."

"Yeah."

"He's in Dallas."

"Uh huh," Dylan sounds ready to nod out.

"He says hello."

"How's it going down there?" Bob manages to ask.

"All right, he's playing some clubs and shit, I was in the Holiday Inn in Burlington and he's looking for a piano player and there was this fifty-year-old woman, like a Belle Barth type, real ribald, doing raunchy material, telling dirty jokes and her name is Hurricane Hattie."

"Oh yeah," Dylan says with a modicum of interest.

"So I told Kinky to call her agent. She looks like Sophie Tucker. He's gonna try to get her into the Jewboys."

"Oh yeah, how does she sound?"

"She's funny. She'd be great with Kinky to work off him."

Dylan yawns audibly.

"OK," Ratso gets on with it, "the schmucks at *Rolling Stone* are such bureaucrats. Did you read my second story yet?"

"No," Dylan sounds truly apologetic, "I haven't had a chance to see it."

"Well, I dug it. I'm inspired by the whole tour and the ambience and they call up and they say that I don't have any details, I don't have how much money the tour made, all that bullshit. I said, why don't they get someone who went to business school to write the story if they want those details. I'm writing about the spirit. And there's this big article in *Variety* this week with the headline: IS DYLAN INTERESTED IN MONEY? SMALL CLUBS GIVE WAY TO ARENAS, and it's a real bitchy piece that talks about how much the tour is making now and how they're playing double dates in big halls."

"Oh yeah," Dylan sounds interested.

"So that's the new tack," Ratso breezes on, "people who are gonna attack you now are gonna go from the angle that it was announced as a tour of small clubs. In fact, that's exactly what they asked me at *Rolling Stone*, they said how come it was announced as small clubs originally—"

"Who announced that?" Dylan snaps.

"I don't know, Columbia? Levy told me it was never gonna be small clubs, it was gonna be small halls."

"Right," Dylan affirms."

"Jacques called me at four in the morning today and gave me a complete rundown so I got the info from him saying that it was never gonna be that. In fact, you even told me the first time we did that interview in the rehearsal studio that you'd do some big dates but mostly small halls."

"Yeah."

"So anyway, this is the new tack they're taking. *Rolling Stone* reads off the figures to me saying the first eleven shows pulled in 75,000 paying customers averaging $8 a ticket, that's $600,000 gross," Ratso recites.

"So what does Elton John charge?" Dylan sounds annoyed.

"I know that. This show is much better than anything else anyway. You get four hours of solid entertainment to begin with, so the questions that these bureaucrats are asking are questions like 'Why has there been a change?' They took that quote you gave me that small halls are more conducive to what you do and said that if Dylan's feeling that way why is he playing large halls now. The whole thing is because of the original misconception that it was gonna be small clubs like the Other End, that set a framework for these people to say that ten thousand seats is a large fucking stadium."

"Yeah," Dylan says disgustedly.

"Anyway," Ratso is running out of steam, "what do you think?"

"Nothing," Dylan says cavalierly, "it don't concern me what those people say."

"Lou gave me a quote, he said that everybody's on salary but Dylan, that you're not making a cent so far."

"Hey look, we got seventy people going around, you know. I don't know what to tell ya, we just—"

"What do you want to talk about?" Ratso tries to change the subject. "Why don't you just talk about the music?"

"Well, what do you want to know?"

"I've never seen you so loose on stage. I've never seen you so comfortable. How come?"

"Uhh," Dylan hesitates, "it's just the element I work best in."

"Which is the element you work best in?" Ratso presses.

"This, uh, this, uh, Jesus Christ you really got me early in the morning, man," Dylan moans, "I can't even think. Well, you know, we're gonna play anyplace that's gonna have us. We're gonna go anyplace we can. But we also have a lot of expenses to meet. I mean we're not gonna go out and play, uh, living rooms, you know. It's not a nightclub show, I mean. I don't know who said we were gonna play nightclubs, we were never gonna play nightclubs. That wasn't ever intended to be. But we are gonna play small theaters and we have played theaters and we're going to continue to play theaters."

"That Palace Theatre in Waterbury was beautiful, man," Ratso coos, "just like the old Fillmore."

"If you do play the big places," Dylan continues, "like Shea Stadium and all that, you do make a lot of money but you're also gonna cut your head off, 'cause it doesn't leave you anyplace to play. So we're playing theaters."

"Forget about the money," Ratso urges, "I don't want to stress that. I want to stress the music, like what is it about this kind of show that enables you to, I mean you're so loose on stage, you're actually dancing and shit. I never saw you do stuff like that before."

"I used to do that in the old days, you know, when I wasn't popular."

"Really old days," Ratso remembers, "you're talking now about the Carnegie Hall Halloween concert days."

"Right, right," Dylan agrees, "it's just the same old thing."

"It's like that Halloween concert in '64 when you said you got your Bob Dylan mask on and this Halloween you wore a mask, Ginsberg called it a transparent life mask. But it's great to see you so loose."

"Well, what can I tell ya. We're just playing the halls, I don't know where we're booked."

"Forget about that, tell me about the music."

"Well the music is self-evident, it speaks for itself, you know," Dylan pauses, "if it's what you feel, it's what you feel. If not, it's something else."

"How come from that period of time after the abuse you got, about '65 or '66 when people were booing and throwing things on stage until I'd say even this tour, even when I saw you with the Band in '74 you seemed a little uptight on stage. What changed?"

"Well we've got more elements in the show now," Dylan struggles for the right words, "there's much more happening in the show so, uh, it gives you more freedom. You're not compelled to do a few certain types of, uh, songs you know."

"The burden's not all on your shoulders now?"

"No, I'm just part of the show."

"How come you started wearing the Pierrot clown make-up?"

"Are you gonna talk about that." Dylan seems surprised and a bit miffed. "Oh I don't know . . ."

"I got a great quote from Blakley on that."

"What's that?"

"You'll read it," says Ratso coyly. "I'll tell you after you tell me."

"Oh, I don't know," Dylan pauses, "I'm going to get into a lot of things that people are gonna say they just don't understand. There's always people that don't understand, always people that try to make more out of it than what it is."

"I talk about the makeup . . ." Ratso tries to explain.

"Yeah, one reason I put it on is so you can see my face from far away," Dylan coughs.

"Does it really enable people to see your face?" Ratso wonders.

"I think you can see my face from further back, can't you," Dylan says with a trace of anxiety in his voice.

"I think so, yeah." Ratso finds the quote from his article. "Here . . . 'but the effect of Kemp has allowed Dylan the psychic luxury that permits him to perform with the wildest abandon he's ever summoned up. Never a particularly comfortable figure onstage in the past, Dylan now looks as manically relaxed as Sinatra. When he comes out in pancake Pierrot makeup, the geek who you've just handed in your ticket to see, and cups his hands around his lips during the brilliant "Isis," it's not Dylan up there it's a fucking rock 'n roll Jolson.' And here's the quote from Ronee: 'You know why Dylan uses the makeup? Because you're forced to look at the two most expressive areas of his face, his eyes and his beautiful mouth. The rest of his face is blanked out by the clown-white makeup.' That's her quote."

Dylan yawns loudly.

"You tired? Have you been sleeping better?"

"I been trying to get some sleep this morning. I haven't gotten so much."

"What have you been averaging so far on the tour?"

"Sometimes six, sometimes five."

"That's enough," Ratso decides, "I get about four, five, and I'm not getting headaches. . . . I should be there tonight, but the reason I didn't come today was my car was broken into the same day I almost got beat up and I had to stay up all night and wait for the Hertz office to open and I drove back here and got a call from *Rolling Stone* and they wanted another thousand words. But I wouldn't go through all this shit if it wasn't for the music. By the way, how did Joni get on the tour?"

"Joni? Which Joni?" Dylan sounds surprised.

"Mitchell."

"I don't know. Is she on the tour? I don't know if she is or not. I don't know, she just showed up in the last town," Bob yawns, "and she got on the bill."

"Levy told me he programmed the show like that, blank areas where anyone who's in town can just fit in."

"Well, uh, there are points in the show where that can happen."

"That's good, right? You want that shit."

"Sure, I don't care."

"Let me ask you this, do you think it's the new songs that are making you so animated, is it because you're singing new material?"

"Uhhh," Dylan thinks, "I don't know, I mean it's been in me for while, you know. As far as I'm concerned, it's just a natural thing."

"Let's say you didn't have a new album, do you think you'd still be so excited up there singing?"

"You mean without the new stuff?"

"Yeah," Ratso elaborates, "like if you were singing 'Blowing in the Wind' and 'Bob Dylan's 8,000th Dream' or something would you be as excited and running around?"

"I probably wouldn't be so confident," Dylan says cryptically.

"Confident? Why confident?"

"I mean because of the new material."

" 'Cause you think it's good, huh?"

"The new material?" Dylan repeats coyly.

"Yeah," Ratso presses.

"Oh, I don't know if it's good or not, I mean, I just know that it's, uh, it's the right material, uh, uh, it's more true to me. . . . So *Rolling Stone* is bumming you out, huh?" the singer sympathizes.

"They're schmucks," Ratso scoffs.

"Yeah, I know man, all they ever print about me is just gossipy shit."

"You wanna hear this, my fucking New York editor, you know what he asked me: 'Do you know who Dylan's sleeping with?' I said, 'What the fuck?' and he said, 'I know that Dylan's been sleeping with Ronee Blakley.' "

"Oh yeah?" Dylan sounds bored.

"I said 'Oh yeah? how do you know that?' and he said he heard it from someone on the tour. But he couldn't tell who, such bullshit."

"You know," Dylan gets animated, "those people who run that thing, those people who talk like that, they're the same people who got America into Vietnam, you know."

"Yeah, I guess they are. Except they're not as powerful."

"You ever see those Italian troupes that go around in Italy?" Dylan suddenly changes the subject. "Those Italian street theaters? *Commedia dell'arte.* Well, this is just an extension of that, only musically."

"I got a friend who's the articles editor of *National Enquirer* and they want to do a cover story on Bob Dylan's five musical predictions that came true," Ratso recollects.

"Oh really?" Dylan sounds slightly interested.

"But Louie don't want to do that, he thinks it's a gossip mag. But they got a eight million circulation."

"How long do you think you're gonna write about this tour?" Dylan asks. "I mean like we're gonna keep it on the road a while."

"How long?"

"I don't know. I mean like this is a going thing."

"I'll stay on as long as it takes," Ratso decides, "my rent isn't that exorbitant. I share Ochs' old apartment. As long as I can get a magazine to pay the expenses. Oh, *Rolling*

Stone was also pissed off about the pictures of you Regan sent them. Did you approve those *Rolling Stone* photos?"

"I don't approve anything that's written by *Rolling Stone*. I can't get behind that magazine."

"No, I mean did you approve the photos sent for my first article?"

"Yeah, yeah, I think I remember sending, I think we sent them some photos. They're not going to use them?"

"They did. I didn't like the ones they used though. You didn't look good, you looked wasted."

"I don't remember which one it was, maybe Louie picked it out."

"Rolling Stone told me they got shit pictures."

"Well, they always write shit about me," Dylan sneers.

"I don't write shit about you, man," Ratso shouts.

"Well, they do," Dylan pouts.

"I'm not them. Don't take it out on me."

"As far as I know they got good photos. I don't intentionally send anybody bad pictures."

"Anyway, I'll stay on the tour as long as it takes," Ratso finally answers. "Fuck it. What do I have to go back to New York for? To hang out in the Other End with Levy? He's the only person back there. He called me at four in the morning today, I finally got some sleep, I went to sleep at three and he calls me up at four."

"Yeah? What he say?"

"He gave me some good quotes. He told me you weren't making a penny off the tour."

"Well, all the money at this point is going into the film. The film's costing a fortune."

"But nobody talks about that. They just say big arenas, Dylan's making a million bucks. Got a second, let me read you my lead." Ratso reads the first paragraph. "Maureen Orth wrote about that ceremony in *Newsweek* too, she got it all wrong."

"Oh boy, did she," Dylan moans.

"Hey, I'm sorry about that photographer," Ratso apologizes," I really screamed at her for trying to sell the pictures without showing them to you first. She said, 'What if he burns them?' I asked her if she thinks you're a monster or something. I told her you were ,human, you weren't gonna burn no pictures. Anyway, here's the rest of the opener."

Dylan listens then chuckles, "That's good, man, that's

super. I'm looking forward to reading it. I'll see about getting you a badge so you don't get all that bullshit."

"I understand Lou's position. It's a role conflict. But I'm not gonna print gossip. You know that."

"I know that. I'll get a badge for you. Hey, what happened to that guy who was doing Hurricane's defense committee, Richard Solomon? How's he doing?"

"Rubin had a meeting and nicely told him he wants Lois to handle the heavy shit. Oh, by the way, Rubin told me to give you a kiss on the lips but Kemp would freak out. Rubin was bonkers, locked up for weeks after the knifing in the jail. He's feeling good now. The new version of 'Hurricane' knocked him out."

"He liked it, huh?" Dylan's pleased.

"Oh yeah. I told DeVito it was a fucking disco smash."

"It's wild, man. I haven't heard any kind of music like that," Dylan bubbles.

"It's great—it's like weird disco music. The black stations won't go on it though, Lois told me. Because of that fucking George Jackson thing."

"Oh, they didn't dig that?" Dylan seems surprised.

"No, they claimed that George Jackson's mother said she never saw any money from the song. They see this as another rip-off, you ripping off Hurricane this time. They said, 'Well, he wrote a tribute to George Jackson, how come Jackson's mother never got the royalties.' "

"I don't know what kind of rules those are, man," Dylan spits. "We're doing a benefit show and all the money for that is supposed to go to Rubin's family."

"You know Ali's emceeing it. You know what Ali calls you, that big white singer."

"What?" Dylan laughs.

"Yeah, about a year ago when they first approached Ali they told him that you were on Rubin's case and Ali, being cool, went 'Who he?' But now, after the song, Ali told Lois, 'You mean that big white singer?' "

"Who else does Lois got on the show?"

"You."

"Oh, he's got to have some other people too," Dylan protests, "like Marvin Gaye and all those people. I'd like to see some other people come out for Rubin, you know."

"We could get other people, I don't know if we need them," Ratso notes.

"Well, it would be good for them, to show some other faces stepping forth for him, not just a white boy."

"The problem is now you get a lot of people jumping on the bandwagon especially after your song," Ratso cautions.

"Well if you get Aretha and Marvin Gaye, that's enough," Dylan decides. "I don't mind standing up for Rubin but I'd like to see some other people do it too."

Ratso reads two more paragraphs from his aborted *Rolling Stone* story to Dylan and the singer laughs, enjoying the narrative.

"And *Rolling Stone* says it's too general," Ratso complains, "I don't say how much money is brought in."

"Aw, tell em to read the *Wall Street Journal*," Dylan scoffs. "Listen, man, I gotta get some rest, I got an afternoon show to play. See you tonight."

Ratso hangs up smiling. One down and one to go, he thinks as he dials Baez's manager's room. Gelb answers on the first ring.

"Cool your heels," Gelb cautions, "here she comes."

"Ooh, did I tell you I'm getting a badge. Dylan told me—"

"Don't talk the whole time," Bernie chides, "let Joan talk. That's your job. And I want to see you watch the shows."

"I watch the shows, man. I don't sit in one seat, though."

"Ratso," Baez trills.

"Tell him to stop sweating on me," the journalist complains, "I'm getting enough ink for you. I'm getting a badge though, I got beat up by the local gestapo police . . ."

"OK, listen Ratso, my breakfast's in the other room."

"OK, all I want is two paragraphs from you on your reactions to the tour so far, the music."

"I think the music is good. I think Dylan is putting on an extraordinary display of trying to make everyone feel comfortable and sharing time and so forth."

"What's it like singing with him again, not musically, but emotionally?"

"Well, it's very exciting," Baez hedges. "I can't go into great detail. Some nights it's difficult because I don't really know what he's going to do. I mean, I still don't know. That doesn't matter though, it's easy enough to follow.

That's his part of the show, I just do whatever it is to be done, then I have a little more freedom in my part of the show."

"Originally, it was supposed to be small halls, lately you've been doing a lot of large halls, two shows a night." Ratso winces at the mandatory question. Baez just yawns.

"Yeah, I like the little ones," she finally says.

"How do the larger ones affect the music for you?"

"For me it's not the hall so much, Ratso, as it is the people."

"I'm not gonna put that Ratso in," the reporter sounds hurt.

Baez laughs. "I'm sorry, there's nothing else I can ever call you."

"When are you gonna dedicate a song to me," Ratso complains.

"I almost did the other night, I always wave 'Hi' to you," Baez coddles the journalist.

"Yeah, I see you, OK go ahead."

"What was the question? Oh yeah, it's the kind of people there, like in one of these little audiences, the people really didn't know what was happening. Well, if it had been a large hall, full of the same people then it would have been a little more difficult. Sometimes a large hall is cold, sometimes a small hall is cold, it's not the size. New Haven was insane."

"Are you gonna play 'Please Come to Boston' in Boston?"

"Sure, I get a little frustrated 'cause we don't have enough time to rehearse."

"Personally," Ratso froths, "I think that song is the turkey in your set. I don't like it at all."

"You what?" Baez is incredulous.

"I don't like that song. It's a turkey," Ratso repeats.

"I think it's beautiful," Baez says defensively, "now shut up and do your job."

"I can give you a little feedback," Ratso stands firm.

"Sure," Baez says sarcastically, "not now."

"That's right," Ratso remembers, "you want to eat. I need one more paragraph. What can we talk about?" He goes over his question list aloud. "Reactions, hall differences . . ."

"It's a medicine show," Baez volunteers, "you know,

for $7.50 it's an offbeat, weird underground medicine show."

"It's $8.50 now," Ratso corrects, "they raised it."

"Glad everybody tells me," Joan moans.

"How does it work?" Ratso remembers his editor's admonitions, "are you getting a percentage or a salary or what?"

"I'm getting a hunk."

"A salary or a hunk?" Ratso presses.

"A hunk, a set fee," Baez says laconically.

"Oh, a set fee, like a salary," Ratso brightens.

"Well, I settled on and the lawyers carried on and everybody hoosied around and we picked out a number and we settled on it. And I bartered for a few things after the thing got started like I want my own mobile home at the end because my kid's coming . . ."

"Let me ask you this," Ratso picks up the *Variety* story, "I got *Variety* in front of me, you ever read it?"

"No."

"Anyway, there's a big story that says 'Is Dylan Interested in Money—Small Clubs Give Way to Arenas,' and this is what *Rolling Stone* called about yesterday and started sweating on me about. They thought my story was too featurey, they wanted to know stuff like what's the gross, who's the local promoter?"

"Gee, that's fascinating," Baez says acidly.

"That's what I told them," Ratso rails. "Anyway, the charge is that the whole spirit of the thing has been sold out."

"Oh, tell them to shove it," Baez spits.

"Can I quote you?" Ratso nearly shits.

"Yeah," Joan elaborates, "tell them to shove it up their asses. The spirit is, I've never seen such a spirit among that number of people night after night. You've never been on our bus Phydeaux. Well, what happens in Phydeaux some nights after a long day, two shows, a ton of people, the security, the hassle, you get on the bus, out comes a little Kahlua and milk, out come the roast beef sandwiches. Chris O'Dell is up there in her apron passing out food. So one night, Roger McGuinn took the twelve-string and sang every hit we've ever known, so everybody knew them and sang along. Then one night Jack Elliot took it and did every yodel song that ever existed and everybody's yodeling with him, and we all sing and sing and sing and laugh until we pass out. Those people don't know, they should know the spirit of Phydeaux. It's been beautiful. And it makes no difference if we've played to fifteen people or fifteen thousand."

"That's great," Ratso purrs. "Go eat. OK."

"Huh."

"Great quote, go eat."

"Oh, thanks Ratso," Baez seems pleased.

"I'll see you soon. Oh, don't dedicate a song to me to-night," Ratso cautions, "I may not make it to the con-cert."

Ratso hangs up and paces the room. His deadline is 4:30 this afternoon, and he has to transcribe those conversa-tions and whip up fifteen hundred words by then. He sits down to type. Naturally, the phone rings.

"You got it?" It's Flippo in the New York office.

"No, I've been on the phone all morning with Dylan. I got everything you fucking want. Don't sweat on me, I got great stuff from Baez too. Want to hear what I got?" Ratso pauses dramatically. "Tell them they can shove it up their ass!" he exults. "Isn't that terrific?"

"Is that to me or to the public?" Flippo says cynically.

"Don't get so paranoid, Chet," Ratso bubbles.

"I'm tired of fucking around with these people," the editor scowls.

"Who?"

"That whole fucking crew. When is this gonna be ready?"

"What do you want?"

"I want Dylan. A lot of that stuff you sent in initially has got to be wiped out. It's too general, it's not report-ing."

"I stand behind that," Ratso screams, "I read some of that stuff over the phone to Dylan today . . ."

"Don't do that," Flippo nearly bursts a blood vessel. "Goddamn it, I told you that before. He does not have fucking story approval. What about the other stuff Abe talked to you about, reporting on the tour itself?"

"He said he wanted this issue of small versus large halls explored."

"Have all the shows been sold out?"

"Does the Pope shit?" Ratso answers.

"They have not all been sold out," Flippo thunders, "the first show in New Haven wasn't. I know that for a fact and they were still selling tickets for the second show fifteen minutes before showtime."

"Those were obstructed seats," Ratso scoffs. "I've been at the box office. I make believe I'm buying tickets and they're stamped obstructed view."

"But I'm not so sure every show has been a sellout."

"What is this?" Ratso fumes, *"Rolling Stone* or the *Wall Street Journal?"*

"That's news. Part of any tour coverage."

"Oh by the way," Ratso interrupts, "I asked Dylan about sleeping with Blakley."

"What he say?" Flippo's all ears.

"She wouldn't let him. Actually, I'm kidding. Dylan is really sleeping with Peggy."

"Who's that?"

"His dog. By the way, Dylan's not too fond of *Rolling Stone."*

"Well, that's his problem," Flippo gets defensive. "Why doesn't he like it?"

"He says they always print gossip about him."

Flippo just laughs. They hang up and Ratso jumps back to his typewriter, the hours ebbing away. By now, the room is a shambles, two tape recorders, long extension cords, clothes strewn all over the unmade beds, the remains of three days of room service scattered all around. So when the reporter leaps up to go to the bathroom he trips over a wire, tumbles into the night table, and rips it clear out of the wall. Great, he thinks, now maybe Led Zeppelin will hire me as their road manager. Ratso slowly gets up and tries to unplug the broken lamp when the phone rings.

"Hey babes," it's Mel Howard in Niagara Falls, "where are you? Listen, your star is in the ascent." Ratso smiles weakly, from the floor. "Last night, all of us did numbers on Bob about the contribution that you've made and how great it was. He loved the Rolling Thunder songs."

"You missed some great shit in New Haven, man," Ratso moans. "I was gonna take this wino into the show and we were walking and he fell and cracked his head open and the cops came and—"

"Whenever you find something like that just bring it to us," Howard purrs. "Listen we would love for you to work with us seriously."

"Tell Dylan."

"OK, we did last night."

"Hey, Kinky's coming next week, either in Boston or right after that," Ratso screams.

"Great, take care of yourself, babe."

Ratso slowly rises and drags his battered body over to the typewriter.

By five he calls Flippo and reads the inserts.

"You think he's serious about not knowing where he's booked?" Flippo doubts.

"Yeah, that's why he hired people to take care of that shit."

"I just don't like what you filed. Abe doesn't like it. I know Dylan would like it."

"You don't like the lead?" Ratso's amazed.

"It's overwritten, 'lovely, radiant, rotund wife.'"

"Rolling Thunder's wife stands out in a crowd," Ratso defends. "I like alliteration. Don't worry you'll get your fucking *Wall Street Journal* information too. We oughta send you to business school, Chet. Wouldn't you rather work for *Forbes?*"

"It's just that money is a part of any tour," the editor explains.

"Well, I'm an artist, you know," Ratso sulks.

"This is all you got from Dylan?"

"It's a page of fucking quotes, the rest is personal."

"Oh come on, Larry. It ain't much."

"It's a page."

"I'm talking about the quality of the thing. You really haven't asked Bob anything, he's telling you what he wants reported."

"If you think I'm going to ask him about who he's sleeping with, you're mistaken," Ratso huffs.

"I'm not talking about that kind of crap. Business, for one thing. How much is everybody getting? How much is he gonna get out of the thing?"

"I got quotes from Kemp on that, he's not getting a penny. It's all going into the film."

"The film ain't gonna make money?" Flippo chuckles.

"Sure it will. So, he doesn't deserve money? You don't think he deserves money? Did you ever see him sweat on-stage?" Ratso shakes his head in disgust.

"I didn't say he doesn't deserve money. I just said he needs to talk about it."

"He needs to talk about his money. That's none of your goddamn business," Ratso shouts, finding himself very protective of Dylan.

"Well, if he's charging the goddamn public $8.50 it is," Flippo shoots back.

"Why? What does anyone charge? What does Elton John charge?" Ratso finds himself parroting Dylan.

"Well he should answer for it too, man. Look, if someone's putting on a show for $8.50 and the people in the seats can't even hear the goddamn thing. I talked to a lot of people in New Haven who couldn't hear."

"I was in New Haven, I didn't hear anybody ask for their money back after the show. There was a standing ovation."

"What I heard, the night show in New Haven there was no standing ovation," Chet parries.

"Who told you that?"

"People who were there."

"I was on a chair watching," Ratso starts.

"You were the standing ovation," Chet cracks.

"I was standing on a chair in the fourth row facing out with my back to the stage. You got jaded friends who are telling you they didn't like it. Why don't you just come to any one concert? I'm talking from the musician's standpoint, the audience's standpoint, and from other media accounts, they say it's the greatest show they've ever seen. And *Rolling Stone* is getting the inside story."

"We haven't yet, man. I just went over this thing again with Abe and it's not a good story by *Rolling Stone* standards."

"What should we do?" Ratso picks up the challenge. "Forget it, I'll just sell it somewhere else."

"We gotta print something this time."

"You can get something," Ratso jeers. "You got some crack reporters, Dylan'll love them."

"That's the problem. You've gotten too close to Dylan to report the tour."

"So get someone who can get better stuff, more access than me," Ratso challenges.

"Your access is not doing any good."

"What would you have gotten that I haven't gotten?"

"Business."

"I can't. They don't want to talk about that, man. I'm

getting what I possibly can get. You think anybody else could have gotten Joan Baez to say 'shove it up their ass'?" Ratso fumes.

"No. But you wouldn't have gotten it if I hadn't been on your ass to get it."

"So keep on my ass but I can't get business shit. I'm not a fucking accountant."

"Meanwhile you're doing a great thing for the movie and we ain't getting great coverage. Not what you filed with Iris today. It's generalities."

"You're right, it's not a *Wall Street Journal* piece. It's the spirit of the tour. It covers it, the stuff about Lisa. She's a prototype on this tour. I'm a sociologist, I'm not a fucking businessman, and that was a sociological piece. And if it was flowery at times, it was flowery because there's a reason to be flowery, because they're doing something here that's never been done before. I don't know about finances."

"I ain't just talking about the finances," Chet interrupts, "I'm talking about other things. Like what a show is really like, you never talk about the name of the halls."

"I was just trying to get the flavor of the tour and that's the flavor, Kemp's role, Lisa as a fanatic fan, there are at least ten girls like that following the tour like vagabonds, the mask, Dylan on stage, that pins it down. I didn't say he picked his nose in New Haven. How many details can you get in a two-thousand-word article. I thought you wanted to cover the press, Kemp's role, relations with the press, the opening is the guy this tour was named after, nobody else spotted him, when he was onstage, this fucking Indian wanders onstage during the finale, stroking a fucking feather, looking self-confident like he's inheriting the stage. That's a perfect lead."

"Well, there's almost no reporting. Just general impressions. You glossed over Kemp, he's really an asshole."

"No, he ain't," Ratso decides.

"He acts like an asshole at times, locking people up."

"He never locked me in a room. I would have locked up that guy from the *Village Voice* too."

"Why don't you describe some of the things he has done to you? Like kicking you out of the hotel."

"OK, put it in," Ratso relents. "Rough treatment, which included barring all press from hotels, confiscating cameras at doors, put it in, I'm not afraid of Kemp. Is that enough? Want to hit him some more? Say he generally made access to the performers virtually impossible."

"Is he doing this on Dylan's orders?"

"No, off the record, I had told Dylan some of the shit going down. He doesn't know all that stuff. Dylan's not like the head of the Mafia, he doesn't direct Kemp to do shit. Dylan's a crazy artist, like I say in the piece, 'more concerned about those roses shooting out of the waitress' head than who gets backstage passes in Waterbury.' "

"Yeah, what does that mean?" Flippo wonders.

"Artists have different perceptions . . ."

"I know, but what does roses shooting out of a waitress' head mean?"

"It's like a surreal image, artists have different conceptions of reality."

"It doesn't come across that way in print."

"It does to people I read it too."

"We're not putting out *Rolling Stone* for them," Flippo fumes. "When you read that you say, 'What waitress? What roses?' "

"So change it. He's concerned about Rubin. Put that in. More concerned about Rubin in solitary than backstage passes."

"Detail," Chet chides.

"I'm more concerned whether people on the tour thought I captured it, than someone totally removed from it."

"That's what I'm talking about, being too close to it."

"You're too far away from it."

"I know but the readers are far away from it too."

"And this draws them into it," Ratso concludes.

"I don't think it does," Flippo shakes his head, "it doesn't draw me into it."

"Well, then you're a bureaucrat," Ratso shrugs.

"Bullshit, where do you get that crap."

"You're a bureaucrat, you got a *Wall Street Journal* mentality."

"Bullshit, everybody in the fucking country—"

"You're asking me to ask business questions."

"That's part of it."

"But that's not what the kids want to read," Ratso rallies.

"How do you know?"

"I know kids. I ask them. Who talks to more kids and derelicts on the street than me?" Ratso falls silent. "Oh, do you want any stuff on Sara. He's married to her. Not Ronee Blakley, remember?"

"I understand. That was a joke when I asked you that."

"Oh, man," Ratso feigns concern, "I told him that. I didn't know you were joking."

"Oh fuck, I was joking," Flippo's annoyed, "from now on I'll raise a flag."

"I thought you were serious." Ratso suppresses a laugh. "By the way, I got an interview with three groupies the other night, they said they wanted to *schmutz* Dylan."

"What does *schmutz* mean?" Flippo the editor asks.

"I don't know, I guess fuck."

"Put it in, put it in," Flippo yells, "how do you spell *schmutz?*"

10

When Ratso checked out of his Danbury motel on Sunday, after what seemed like a week on the phone, he decided to forego the next night's concerts in Rochester and instead drive straight to Boston, where his friend Pat, who wrote for the *Boston Globe,* would put him up, a timely hospitality since the journalist had already spent most of the expense money *Rolling Stone* had wired him in Danbury. The drive to Cambridge was uneventful, the lodgings there more than adequate, so after unpacking a bit, Ratso jumped back into the Monte Carlo and decided to explore Boston's night life.

After a few hours' sightseeing, he's pretty wired, the few drinks interacting with the amphetamine to produce a restless gnawing angst. Well, if I can't relax I may as well make myself useful, he thinks, and steps into a pay phone to call Mel Howard in Rochester.

"Howard, you fucker, it's Ratso. I feel like Walter Fucking Winchell, I'm speeding, freezing my ass off, standing in a booth in Boston. You got anything for me to do?"

"Rats baby," Howard's soothing voice floats back, "we need a bare room, actually we need an old house, spooky, Edgar Allan Poe-ish."

Ratso hears a muffled conversation then Howard comes back. "Here, Bob wants to talk to you."

"Hey man," Dylan greets Ratso. "Listen, line up all the pool halls and all-night diners you can find."

"How about whores?" Ratso screams. "There's millions here, and transvestites, pimps, all that shit."

"Yeah, yeah, pool halls, whores, and all-night diners."

"I can't make the gig," Ratso apologizes.

"Man, you missed last night. It was super. O. J. Simpson came. O. J. got into a rap with T-Bone." Dylan laughs.

"Hey, where are you staying in Boston?"

"I dunno," Dylan answers.

"C'mon, you can tell me."

"Hey, I'd tell ya, but I don't know," Dylan protests. "Shit, if anybody can find it you can. I don't even know, you'll find it. See you tomorrow."

Ratso bounces back onto Boylston, buoyed by his mission. He strides immediately into The Store, an odd-looking establishment that's open twenty-four hours and takes food stamps, as the large signs boast. The reporter prowls down the aisles, admiring the range of merchandise, everything from food to clothing to magazines to Maalox. He finds the manager, a young guy around thirty, well dressed, and asks about the clientele.

"In this area, we get everything that walks, bums, winos, hookers, street people." In the background, WBCM is blaring *Little Walter's Time Machine*, a bizarre program that seems to have been lifted intact out of the '50s. By now, Ratso has induced the manager to show him where the whores hang out and the two of them walk out and huddle in the fall night chill.

"Not too many whores out tonight," the manager surveys, "maybe 'cause of that scare. There's a guy in a pickup truck driving around in a leather jacket, blue beret, glasses, and jeans and cutting up girl's faces after they suck his dick. But you ought to try Bulkies', the deli down the block. The hookers always hang out there for coffee."

Ratso thanks him and scurries down the block. He enters Bulkies' and slides into a booth. It could be any deli in New York, Ratso thinks, the same glarey orange vinyl decor, the busty, ugly waitresses, the scattered businessmen eating chopped liver, and yes, the chinchilla-wrapped hookers sipping coffee in the rear booth. The journalist decides on corned beef, Dr. Brown's soda, and a side order of derma, and by the time he finishes relaying the order the waitress has already offered him a Compoz.

By the time the food comes, the place has filled up. In the next booth, four gays are discussing football, of all things. Four more hookers have filed in, two of them with a black pimp dressed in green crushed velvet. At the round table to Ratso's right, a half-drunk businessman is busy trying to pick up one of the zaftig waitresses, while a tough small Irish-looking guy cracks up. Ratso finishes his sandwich and joins the table.

"Hi, I'm Phil Dryden, I'm in the shoe business," the tipsy, suited one says, then returns his attention to Arline, the brassy waitress. "I married a well-to-do girl," Phil explains, "but I want to go to bed with her." Arline recoils in mock terror. "Honey if I'm not there, start without me." Ratso turns to Murphy, who's been quiet through all this. "What do you do?" he says to the Cagney look-alike. Murphy whips out his wallet and flashes a gold badge, instantly replacing it in his pocket.

"I'm a night judge in Superior Court. I set bail in Superior Court cases," Murphy lies. Ratso figures him to be a bail bondsman, and asks if he knows any of the prostitutes scattered around the room, explaining that he's looking for people for the Dylan movie.

"Murphy? Ha, ha," Arline booms, "you should see the cast of characters he knows." Murphy smiles. "You want to meet some whores?" he says portentously, his eyes twinkling. "Follow me."

Murphy leads Ratso to a booth in the back occupied by two young white girls. One is wearing a white fur coat, piled-up reddish hair, and a fancy dress, the other's got short hair, one great big earring, a black leather coat, and her boobs spilling out of a black dress. Murphy introduces them as Rega and Kim, and tells them about the movie.

"How much money for the movie," Rega challenges Ratso, "nobody donates anymore. Two thousand dollars and I'll do it." She looks down the aisle. "Get that fucking broad," she motions toward the waitress, "what a dingy creep."

"C'mon," Murphy says soothingly, "she's all right. She's a poet."

"I'm a poet too," Rega snaps, "I'm starving to death."

The waitress, who seems to have a clubfoot, limps up.

"Can I have my water?" Rega asks coolly. "I want my ice to chew on."

The girls' food comes, hamburgers and French fries, and Rega starts to scatter onions over her burger as Kim looks on, horrified. "Oh, it's OK," Rega reassures, "it's after 2 A.M., I'll eat onions. Who cares? I'll just go home and let my dog lick me." She looks toward Ratso and turns serious. "The last time someone tried to film down here the camera got smashed," she says ominously.

"It's slow tonight," Kim breaks the silence.

"Do you know Alison, the fat broad?" Rega asks. "She got cut up. And TC with the big boobs, she got cut up with a rock. Must be the same guy. Nobody'll bust him."

"They got a good description of him," Ratso interjects, "he drives a pickup truck."

"So what," Rega spits. "He'll change cars and come down in a Volkswagen. A girl was stabbed last week in Liberty Mall. I didn't know her, but she had hooker shoes. Sequins on her heels. It was just a slasher. In New York, at least, the cops protect the girls. Here they do shit. I had to fight once to get out of a car that took me out to Chelsea."

Murphy looks bored and he takes out his beeper and flips it on, producing a blast of static. Rega laughs. "I got a beeper too, Murphy," she bats her eyelashes, "I'll show it to you." Ratso offers the girls tickets to the Boston shows, but Rega politely declines. "You can keep the tickets. We won't be able to use them, we'll be working. You know, you remind me of Donald Sutherland. You're better-looking than Sutherland, though, Ratso." He smiles and offers the girls Hurricane T-shirts instead. Rega's eyes light up.

"Yeah, I might want a small. Listen, if you go in to any of the places in the Combat Zone, where the hooker bars are, don't ask too many questions. You don't want your glasses smashed." Rega stares at Ratso, concerned.

"Do you have a pimp?" the reporter wonders.

"No, any girl that has a pimp is just a masochist." Rega frowns. "They hate themselves, they must want to inflict pain on themselves." She looks down at the empty plate. "It's T-shirt time, huh?"

Ratso tries to stall. "How much do you charge?"

"Fifty dollars an hour," Rega shoots back, "but that varies. I like to make it with Chinks. They come quick, in your hand. They're look freaks."

A tall black girl in a long white chinchilla coat lopes by and Murphy stares at the new arrival. Rega slips on her fur coat and they head for the door, passing a white girl accompanied by her black pimp.

"I'm gonna have my own car, someday," Rega dreams, "a Rolls. I'll make five hundred dollars a night."

Murphy frowns. "So what, I'm lying," Rega continues, "I'm better off than that chick we just passed. She better make it or she gets her teeth kicked in. That spade looked like a mean bastard. I'd never give my money away. I don't know, maybe she likes it. Look how many square women stay with a man for fifty years and get beat up every day, fuck 'em three times a week? What's the difference? But with these guys, it's not love taps. I know that broad, she gets cracked bad, but she's out there like rain, snow, sleet, no matter." Rega looks down at her watch. "I'm almost all right for tonight, I came out at ten o'clock, it's three now." She looks down deserted Boylston Street with no tricks in sight. "What am I supposed to do," she shrugs, "manufacture it?"

The four of them walk around the corner to Ratso's car and he opens the trunk and emerges with two T-shirts. "Oh, this is cute, honey," Rega gushes, "I'm wearing it tomorrow night. I'm in a bowling league." They pile into the car, and Ratso starts down Boylston. "I went out with Dustin Hoffman," Rega offers, "four years before he made it big. He was with a theater company in Boston. He looks like Ringo, he's cute." Murphy summons Ratso to a halt and the three get out and head for his car. Ratso drives on to check out the Howard Johnson's, another hangout for the night people in the area.

It's 5:20 A.M. but the adrenalin is still pumping as he swings the Monte Carlo down to the Howard Johnson's and parks behind three Cadillacs in a row. He slumps onto a counter stool, next to a well-dressed man in a trench coat. Shit, he curses silently, no hookers. Only about six burnt-out night people, and a couple of pimps, looking out the window and jiving.

A post-amphetamine gloom begins to descend on our reporter, a gloom intensified by the leering eye of a homosexual on a nearby stool. He's about to pack it in and head back to Cambridge when one of the most beautiful women he's ever seen strolls in. She's a silver blonde, with delicately rouged cheeks, black satin pants, and a red wool jacket. Jesus, Ratso whistles to himself, she looks just like Monroe. I wonder what she charges? Suddenly the reporter decides it's time for some participant-observation.

But just as suddenly she's joined by her friend, who comes in carrying a huge Sterno log, wearing a ratty fur coat, a curly blond wig copped no doubt from an old Three Stooges movie, and red pumps. Ratso's visions of a bacchanal dissolve like the cream in his coffee. But what a pair for the movie, the most beautiful and the tackiest transvestite ever. He picks up his cup and moves down the counter. "Can I join you?" he asks with a smile.

The tacky one looks him over, then shrugs. "Sure," he-she rasps in a low guttural voice. Marilyn, meanwhile, is ordering. "I'll have a cheeseburger," she whispers sexily, "and how much is a salad?"

"Seventy cents," the counterman lisps.

Marilyn sighs the sigh of the world-weary. "All right, I'll have a salad. With blue cheese dressing."

Actually, Ratso learns, Marilyn's name is Lola and the tacky one is named Betty. The scribe mentions the film and the tour and suggests they participate. "Well," Lola purrs hesitantly. "She's a little paranoid," Betty jumps in, "it's just that so many guys hit on us."

"I don't know if I can," Lola says dreamily, staring into her compact as she fixes some makeup. "I do like Warhol movies though. I'd have to be high."

"I'll get you two tickets for the concert, then after the concert, I'll take you backstage," Ratso suggests.

"Give us four tickets so we can bring boyfriends," Betty rasps. "I don't want to go unescorted." She rolls her eyes. "It'll be fun," she prods Lola, who smiles weakly, "we'll dress up very Gatsby, dear, long cigarette holder, makeup, the whole bit. We're not into music that much, I like Baez though, she's about the only female singer I like." Betty frowns. "I don't even like Barbra Streisand."

Ratso points to the Sterno log, imagining new frontiers in decadence. "What's it for?"

"My fireplace." Lola smiles sweetly.

"Do you guys know Murphy, the bail bondsman?" Ratso realizes his mistake too late.

"He bought his motorcycle off me!" Betty shouts. "I used to have a motorcycle and knee-high glitter boots."

"Can I have the catsup?" Lola interrupts demurely.

"I threw the boots out, they were destroying my ankles. They were size eight and I took a ten. I like disco music though," Betty returns to an old subject, "I love the Manhattan Transfer. But personally, I don't like rock."

"We're into R&B," Lola purrs, then signals the counterman. "Can you put some chocolate in the milk for me? I love the Kinks, though, that's where I took my name from."

"I'm the one that named her," Betty boasts. "She won seven trophies, too. See this picture." She fishes in her purse and pulls out an eight-by-ten of Lola. "She looks just like Monroe, doesn't she. Show him."

Lola strikes an exaggerated Monroe pout, and Ratso shakes his head in wonder. "Make me a star," Lola says through clenched teeth, "a fallen star."

"Is there any chance of me going out with Bob Dylan?" Betty growls. "He's a Gemini and I'm a Gemini too. I don't know what I'd talk to him about, though. We're into different things. I'd love to meet him, though."

"Then come to the show, I'll take you back to meet him, and you'll be in the movie," Ratso decides.

"Well," Betty hesitates, "OK, it might be fun. You can wear that queen dress, Lola." Betty laughs and gives Ratso their number.

It's 6 o'clock and Ratso runs from the Howard Johnson's to the car. All the hookers have gone home now, even the pimps are nowhere to be seen. Already, some straights are trooping into the restaurant for coffee before they hit work. Incredible, Ratso says to himself, as he heads back up toward Cambridge, Lola was so ravishing that he still entertains visions of balling her. As the wind blasts into the car, Ratso shivers, pulls up the window, and turns on the radio for company. Roy Orbison shoots out, with that 6 A.M. moan, "Oh, oh, Pretty Woman." Ratso pulls the window tighter and laughs out loud.

The next afternoon, Monday, he decides to drive downtown to the Boston Music Hall, where tickets are to go on sale Tuesday morning for the Friday night shows. Lines had started forming Sunday afternoon, and by the time Ratso drove up at least thirty kids were camping in front of the old ornate theater. The journalist steps over the huddled hordes and knocks on the glass door of the theater.

Owner Al Terbin, a huge, good-natured man with a penchant for chomping on cigars almost as fat as he is, greets the reporter. "C'mon in, c'mon," he blasts, grabbing Ratso by the arm. They walk toward his office in the lobby. "Just look at this place," his beefy arm sweeps an arc in the air, "it's the largest theater in New England, 4,200 seats, 40 years old, plush marble. We get the finest shows here. The Bolshoi was even here." They enter the office and Al directs Ratso to a seat in front of his huge antique wooden desk. "I can't believe these kids," Terbin shakes his head, "they been here since Sunday night and

I don't even have the tickets on the premises. Jerry
Seltzer is coming in tonight at 7, we'll count the tickets,
seal them, give 'em back to him and then he'll come back
tomorrow morning right before the box office opens at
nine. He doesn't even trust us with them." He laughs, and
chomps down on his cigar.

Ratso kibbitzes a bit with Al and then heads outside to
talk to some of the kids. But he no sooner gets out the
door than one skinny student corrals him, pointing to a
Bob Dylan button that the reporter picked up in New
Haven. "Hey man, can I buy that off you? I'd really
like that." Ratso looks at this kid, who seems to be
around twenty-one, well groomed, dressed fairly conserva-
tively in sweater and slacks, but whose conservative de-
meanor is belied by the strange, intense stare that he's
fixing on the reporter right now. "C'mon, man, I'll give
you ten dollars for the button," he pleads, and Ratso,
down to his last five dollars, almost sticks himself taking
off the pin.

Outside it looks like some refugee camp, blankets,
sleeping bags, groups of three and four huddled together,
passing around bottles. The crowd has swelled to about
seventy-five.

All of whom are under the watchful eyes of Chuck
Stern, one of Al's assistants, and his elderly mother who
are peering out through the glass doors. Ratso reenters
and sidles up to Chuck.

"Half these people ain't dealing with a full deck,"
Stern chuckles at the mini-Woodstock outside and fingers
the gun strapped to his hip. "You got a gun?" Ratso marvels. Chuck laughs. "They call this the Combat Zone." His
arm sweeps out covering the streets. "We sit on all this
money, and every degenerate and malcontent around is
after it." Mrs. Stern ambles up, a nice old Jewish mother.
She looks out at the crowd and shakes her head. "I don't
care, I don't care what happens, honey, all I want to do is
get the sale over with tomorrow. My son Chuck and I
stood up and sold Who tickets, we sold three shows in
one day without all this baloney and rigamarole. It went
easy, in eight and a half hours we sold out three shows.
In and out." She smiles and touches her hair. "See my
gray hair? I got that doing rock concerts. But I love these
kids though, without them where would anybody be?
Some call me the Witch, they come up to the window

THE TOUR
PHOTO ALBUM

Above: "This Land Is Your Land"—The Rolling Thunder Revue. BOB GRUEN

Far Left: Blakley inks tour pact. (Left to right) Marty Feldman, Lou Kemp, Ms. Blakley, Barry Imhoff. RONEE BLAKLEY COLLECTION

Left: One of the survivors. Bob Neuwirth in the film <u>Renaldo and Clara</u>. CIRCUIT FILMS

It's hard to keep straight
on the road. (Left to right)
Howie Wyeth, Rob Stoner,
Joni Mitchell, Steve Soles.

Om. (Left to right)
Peter Orlovsky, Allen Ginsberg.
RONEE BLAKLEY COLLECTION

Anyone for tennis?
Mick Ronson in a
hotel drug store.
RONEE BLAKLEY COLLECTION

Right: "Keenky, who's Keenky?" Kinky Friedman (Texas Jewboy) and Ratso.
MARCIA RESNICK

Below: Joan Baez and Mama in The Dreamaway Lounge in the film Renaldo and Clara.
CIRCUIT FILMS

Left: Bob Dylan, Sara
Dylan on the train
heading east.
MICK RONSON ARCHIVES

Below: Sunrise ceremony,
Newport, R.I., Chief Rolling
Thunder (center/rear)
presiding. MARY ALFIERI

Opposite, Top: Three weeks on the road:
Why are these people smiling? (Left to right)
Ronee Blakley, Jeff Raven, Joni Mitchell,
Steve Soles, Bob Neuwirth. RONEE BLAKLEY COLLECTION

Opposite, Bottom: "Rono and Roger!"
(Left to right) Mick Ronson and
Roger McGuinn. MICK RONSON ARCHIVES

Below: Dylan and Helena Kallianiotes
between takes of <u>Renaldo and Clara</u>.
RONEE BLAKLEY COLLECTION

"Mama, you've been on my mind."
Beattie Zimmerman joins her son and
Joan Baez on stage. KEN REGAN

Top: The Revue visits Hurricane Carter
in prison. (Left to right) David Mansfield,
Luther Rix, Ramblin' Jack Elliot, Rubin
Carter, Rob Stoner. MICK RONSON ARCHIVES

Bottom: Sara Dylan, Bob Dylan and
Joan Baez backstage. RONEE BLAKLEY COLLECTION

Opposite: "Touring's in my blood"
—Bob Dylan. KEN REGAN

The Woman in White and Clara confront Renaldo for some straight answers in the film <u>Renaldo and Clara</u>. CIRCUIT FILMS

Ratso. BOB GRUEN

and scream, 'The Witch is here.' But others," Mrs. Stern smiles maternally, "others call me 'Ma.'"

Ratso gets restless and starts on a walking tour of the Combat Zone, keeping one eye open for any potential film discoveries. He steps into a few bars, watching some tired, bored-looking dancers go through their bumps and grinds. Finally, he stumbles into the Two O'Clock, a huge, Las Vegas–style showroom that features three rooms of stripping. Ratso sits down in front of one of the circular stages just as a cute platinum blonde named Monique starts her act. She's got an animal act, rubbing little teddy bears into her crotch, pulling dogs over her curves, culminating when she grabs a monkey with a dildo and inserts it, then pulls it out and squeezes a globe, causing rivulets of what looked to be Jergen's Cream to spew all over her immense breasts. Ratso realizes he's hungry and walks down to the White Tower on the corner.

After dinner, Ratso drives back and enters the theater. In the box office, he sees Seltzer, Jacob Van Cleef, Al Terbin, and Chuck Stern huddled over the tickets. The reporter sneaks in the office then announces loudly, "Stick 'em up."

Chuck Stern whirls and pulls out his gun, training the .38 right at Ratso's heart. Seltzer rolls his eyes heavenward. "Ratso, don't ever do that, don't even fool around when we're counting tickets."

The reporter apologizes and they return to the ticketcounting. Afterward Terbin ambles over to Ratso. "That Jerry's the greatest thing I ever saw." He points a fat finger in Seltzer's direction. "I was talking to him and not for one second does he take his eyes off Mrs. Stern counting the tickets." Terbin shakes his head in awe.

It's about 5 A.M. now, and the Pepper Steak luncheonette across the street has remained open all night to accommodate the few hundred kids who've lined the sidewalk outside the Music Hall. Inside, Ratso sits down to some hot tea and throws a quarter into the jukebox. The place is occupied only by a few kids from the line and a few early-morning workers.

Suddenly Ratso almost chokes on his tea as his eyes follow the strangest-looking person he's ever seen. She's in her sixties, with a weather-beaten craggy face that looks like it was lifted out of Mount Rushmore. And she's wearing all men's clothes, an old squashed fedora, a seedy tweed sports coat, baggy trousers, wing tips, one red and one green sock, and a floppy old white shirt that's having a hard time keeping her pendulous tits covered. She sits down opposite Ratso and immediately goes into a strange ritual, grabbing a napkin and scrubbing the table in a frenzy. Then she starts arranging her clothes, fidgeting with the sleeve buttons, pulling the arms down, then she licks her fingers. She coughs and then repeats the ritual. Jesus, Ratso thinks, an obsessive-compulsive ambulatory schizophrenic dyke. He bolts up and calls the film crew, waking up Howard Alk but eliciting a promise to send a crew right down.

Ratso sits down and asks her her name.

"Amy," she squeaks, through a puff of her cigarette, and resumes cleaning, this time working on the floor with her worn napkin. Then she bolts upright and starts waving her arm. "Get out here, leave me alone, you cocksucker," she screams at the air.

"What's at the Music Hall?" she asks Ratso, then coughs tubercularly into her napkin.

"Bob Dylan." The name draws a blank with Amy. "Joan Baez too."

"In picture or in person?" Amy asks.

"In person," Ratso informs.

"She's OK. She's with the Carpenters," Amy decides, then points to the jukebox. "Do they have anything by the Carpenters there?"

Ratso walks over to the jukebox and drops a quarter in. He plays Billy Swan's "I Can Help" and "Fly Robin Fly." Amy pulls out a wrinkled napkin from her pocket and picks out some change, attempting to pay Ratso for the music, but he refuses and she goes back to picking lint off her jacket, then violently starts wringing her hands. Ratso buys her cake and a coffee.

"Who's Bob Dylan?" she asks. "Who's wonderful an hour from now?" She blows her nose loudly. "Is there a Joan Baez record on the jukebox? Who's Bob Dylan anyway? A singer?"

"Fly Robin Fly" comes up, and Amy starts swaying to the beat. "You got a light, mister," she asks Ratso, then rubs her eyes and starts fixing her gray crew-cut hair. "What is this, fly what?"

Ratso picks out a few more tunes, again declining Amy's pennies, and sits down. "Where you from, Amy?"

"From New York. Manhattan. I had a place in Staten Island, I lived in a church in Staten Island. I was born in England, only very little when my mother came over. My mother was married. I lived seven years in Boston. Hey, play that one again." She likes "Fly Robin Fly."

Amy lights up another cigarette and Springsteen's "Born To Run" comes on, prompting her to leap up and start a weird dance, her arms dangling from her sides like a simian, her fingers snapping, then she starts picking at her nose. Amy finally sits down and fixes her pants, then starts snapping at the air again. "You shut up. Get away from me."

"Relax, Amy," Ratso urges. Amy bursts into tears. "C'mon Amy, stop crying," Dom the owner pipes in. He comes from around the counter and brings her a glass of water. "Can't lose the star," he winks at Ratso, "this is your big break, darling. Fix your pants."

"I gotta go to the bathroom," Amy mumbles. But Dom's is broken so Ratso offers to escort her to the hotel next door. They step out the door, but Amy hesitates, holding the door open for her companion in spirit. At the hotel, Amy pauses a second, then chooses to go into the women's room. Ratso waits a few minutes, then hears screams echoing through the empty bathroom.

"Amy," he yells inside, holding the door ajar, "what are you doing in there? Hurry up, we gotta get back. The film crew's coming."

"OK, Ratso," Amy wafts back chagrined, then orders more softly, "get out of here you cocksucker, leave me alone." A few minutes later, she sheepishly trudges out of the john and they walk back to Dom's.

"All right, we got the stars, Valentino and Greta," Dom laughs as Ratso and Amy come back in. The film crew still hasn't arrived and when he calls Ratso finds they haven't even left the Boxboro hotel yet, a good forty-five-minute drive. It's almost nine now and the tickets are about to be dispensed. Ratso slams the receiver down, tells Dom to keep an eye on Amy, and rushes across the street. He's lined up at least ten people for the shooting, Bob (a weird Jesus freak he met earlier who's convinced the reporter is Dylan), Julien, Debbie, two emergent leaders on the line, Al, Mrs. Stern, and he's running around the line and in and out of the theater like Peckinpah on speed, making sure the cast is prepped.

An orderly line has been formed by now, a line that stretches up the block, around the theater, and almost to the next block. Al is standing in front of the box office, barking out orders like a general. Ratso's watching the Matinee Fox in action when Bob the Jesus freak comes up. He's got the weird smile again, and that hazy look. "You're Bob, right Ratso?" he asks the reporter. "Huh?" Ratso stares. "Are you Bob? You're playing here, aren't you?" "I'm not Bob," Ratso maintains. Bob just smiles. "You're not Ratso, you're Bob," and he disappears back into line.

Satisfied, Ratso marches back to Dom's. But she's gone. He rushes up to Dom. "Where's Amy? Where the fuck is she?"

Dom shrugs. "I tried to keep her in here. She kept asking where you were, kept saying that you lied to her, you weren't coming back. Then she bolted for the door, ran out, stopped, and stuck her head back in and said, 'But tell him, I love him.' " Dom shakes his head and smiles.

With his star gone, Ratso was crestfallen, so when the film crew arrives he perfunctorily rounds up the kids and they shoot a half hour's worth but his heart isn't in it. In fact, the only thing that assuaged the pain was the tall frizzy-haired girl named Sara who went back to Cambridge with him, to help him recover.

But the next day, another blow. Ratso calls *Rolling Stone* for some additional expense money and gets the word from Flippo. It is no longer desirable in their eyes to spend $250 a week to keep the reporter on the road. What they want now is spot coverage, reporting on a few concerts, but not actually traveling with the troupe. Ratso rails at that idea, and slams down the phone in disgust. To clear his mind, he grabs Sara and they drive down to engage in his favorite pastime, scouring the Salvation Army for clothes, all the while scheming how to stay on the road.

That afternoon they drive to Worcester and pull up in front of the Memorial Auditorium. The concert is some four hours away but already the stage door is dotted with ticket-beggars, distant friends of the performers, and various hangers-on. Lisa is back, in her floppy hat with feathers, decked out in a black "Guam" T-shirt. Ratso goes to the door and asks for someone from the film crew. A few minutes later, David Meyers comes out.

"OK, Ratso," he smiles, "this is your big test. Go out and find an old pool hall, we're probably gonna do some shooting right after the concert." Ratso salutes, grabs up Sara, picks up a local kid to act as guide, and spends the next three hours scouring the seamy area of Worcester before finally coming up with one pool hall, two whore hotels, and a great derelict bar. Satisfied, he makes it back to the Auditorium for the concert.

Inside, it's a gorgeous old hall very reminiscent of the first venue in Plymouth, with a beautiful wood balcony, ornate wood carvings, and a nice marble lobby. And the band seems to be up for this the first concert in the Boston area. T-Bone is resplendent in a Merlin outfit, complete with long pointed hat, and Soles looks positively Western in his fringed buckskin jacket, matched by Ronee Blakley in her red cowgirl hat.

In fact, the only sour note seems to be Bobby Neuwirth's voice, which by this juncture resembles a razor blade after a Hare Krishna initiation. And what makes it worse is that the film crew is filming this concert in its entirety and Fedco has brought up a special mobile sound truck to record the affair for a possible live album.

Sara seems undisturbed. "Is that Neuwirth?" she whispers, pointing to the lanky singer. "I wouldn't mind getting into his pants."

"Be careful," Ratso sneers, "you're one step away from the gutter."

Everyone seems to love this smallish hall, especially Dylan, and for the first time that Ratso can recall, he inserts a rollicking version of "From a Buick Six," introducing it as "an autobiographical song for ya." By "Durango," the band is really cooking, four camera crews are positioned at various angles (including the new crew, manned by Michael Wadleigh, who did *Woodstock*) directly in front of Dylan, shooting right up his nose.

The second half is just as torrid as the first, Dylan loose enough to dedicate "Mama You've Been On My Mind" to "my mother and your mother." By the end, he's positively wailing ad-libbing yet another new line to "Knocking on Heaven's Door": "Take these chains offa me, I can't walk so good, An old gypsy told me to stay full length in bed, Feel like I'm looking into Heaven's Door." The kids lap it all up, and at the end, they stand and cheer for five minutes.

Mel Howard has promised to meet with him back in Boxboro, so Ratso and Sara stop for a bite to eat and head straight to the hotel. But at the desk, the reporter runs into some trouble locating any of the guests.

"Where's Mel Howard's room?" he demands.

The night clerk, a young student type, is adamant. "We have orders not to give out rooms. We have to protect our customers."

"Look, I'm supposed to meet these people here, I know they're staying here, I'm working with the film crew of this group. Look, give me Kemp's room. Don't be a fucking asshole." The clerk shrugs and goes back to his paperback.

Ratso fumes, the events of the day having a cumulative effect on him from the ugly phone call with *Rolling Stone* to the wasted effort in Worcester to this ridiculous intransigence. Cursing bureaucracies, he grabs a pen and starts scribbling a note to Kemp.

Dear Lou—
    It's 2:05 and I tried to call your room and the desk told me you would be out for the evening. Mel Howard *asked* me to meet him at the hotel and tell him of any advance work of the past three days. I told Howard that *you* should be at the meeting and that's why I called your room and wrote this note. I'm *not* sneaking into this fucking hotel. I wanted you to be fully aware of my location. I'll be in Howard's room if I can ever find out where the fucker is, they won't give me the room number. Great security! It's better than what Arafat got at the Waldorf.

                                                    Love,
                                                    Ratso

Just as Ratso is completing the missive, Dylan strides into the lobby, accompanied by Joni Mitchell and Roger McGuinn. He's wearing the same outfit as he did on stage, the ever-present hat, dark glasses, black leather jacket, Rolling Thunder Wallace Beery shirt, and worn dungarees. "Hey Ratso, how you doing?" he shouts in greeting.

"I'm fucked," Ratso screams, seizing the opportunity. "C'mere schmuck," he urges Dylan over to the desk.

"What's the matter," Dylan asks.

"I'm fucked," Ratso moans. *"Rolling Stone* just cut me off, they don't want to pay for any more expenses, they only want spot coverage because I wouldn't write that bureaucratic bullshit about how much money you were making and shit like that and I'm cool here in Boston 'cause I got friends to stay with but once we leave Boston I won't be able to afford a hotel room and . . ."

The three superstars just look in wonder at the reporter decomposing before their eyes.

"And this whole fucking tour," Ratso rails on, "I've just been getting jerked off. I'm the fucking nigger on this tour. Look, you fucking invited me that night at the Kettle and since then it's like I'm a fucking groupie trying to fight my way into the rooms. I was speaking to some of the security guys and they said that you were just jerking me off, that if you really wanted me on this tour, you'd get me a room and shit. I don't need this, man, I can write about other things, I don't have to take this abuse and humiliation. Fuck this shit, I'm just gonna go home. . . ."

"Wait a minute," Dylan interrupts, as Joni looks on shocked.

"Do you want a Librium?" McGuinn offers tranquilizer and Ratso scarfs it down.

"Well, what is it you want?" Dylan asks. "Be specific, what do you need?"

By now, Barry Imhoff has been attracted by the racket and he hurries over to calm the reporter down.

"C'mon Ratso, don't take it so hard," Imhoff soothes, "we're only joking. We like you."

"Bullshit," Ratso screams. "You fucking hate me. You make it impossible for me to do my job, every time . . ."

"Hey, what do you need, man?" Dylan interrupts.

"Well," Ratso calms a little, "I got no money for a hotel . . ."

"You need a bed, right? Give him a bed," he orders Imhoff.

"There are no vacancies now," Imhoff remembers, "but he can sleep in the hospitality suite, there's a bed there."

"I need a double bed," Ratso pouts defiantly, nodding toward Sara.

"Is this your sister?" Dylan smiles innocently. "She gonna sleep here too? OK, you got a bed, what else do you need?" His booted heel taps out a rhythm on the tiled floor. "You need per diem, right?"

Ratso readily agrees. "Yeah, per diem. I got no more money, I got cut off from *Rolling Stone* . . ."

"OK, you got it," Dylan flashes. "What else? C'mon man, what else?"

"Well, I don't need no salary," Ratso generously offers, "since I'll make money from articles and stuff. But I need the data, I need the daily newsletter and stuff like that." Ratso searches for the word. His eyes suddenly light up. "I need *access*," he screams at the superstar, "I need access to people on the tour."

Joni looks even more incredulous at this surreal sight, McGuinn is suppressing a smile, and Dylan rolls his eyes in amazement. "You need Ex-Lax?" he shakes his head, "why do you need Ex-Lax? What you been eating?" Everyone breaks up.

"It's not funny," Ratso moans, "I need some credentials or something so I don't get fucked over again."

"Well, we'll get you all that stuff, OK?" Dylan reassures. "You see to it, Barry." Imhoff nods, and Dylan lopes away to get ready for some scenes that will be shot in the lobby. Ratso retreats to a couch as the film crew sets up lights.

Dylan meanwhile is setting up the scene, prepping Joni and Roger who are going to enter and walk over to the desk for their messages. He suddenly turns to the reporter. "Hey Ratso, ya wanna be in the scene?" The journalist jumps up and rushes to Dylan's side. "OK, man, go behind the desk, you're the night clerk in the motel and Roger is coming in and he's gonna ask for his messages."

"What's my motivation?" Ratso smiles.

Dylan rolls his eyes. "I got it," he lights up, "you're a writer, you write songs and you wanna get some of your songs recorded and you know the Rolling Thunder Revue is staying here and you hit on McGuinn. Then after McGuinn can't help, you get really frustrated with your job, throw a pile of papers all over the floor, and stalk out from behind the desk as if you're quitting."

Ratso nods and slides behind the desk. He picks up a phone and pretends to be talking as McGuinn and Joni walk in and the cameras roll. Joni discreetly slinks off to one side of the desk as Roger approaches Ratso.

"Any messages for 521?" he asks.

"Er, yes," Ratso fumbles nervously through some papers. "There's one here from a Mr. Hirsh and one from a Mr. Crosby." He peers over at Joni. "And the lady has a message, also from Mr. Crosby." Ratso smiles efficiently. "Aren't you with the Rolling Thunder Revue, I know you are, you see I'm not really a night clerk, I only do this for a living now, I really write songs, and I have a tape and . . ."

Roger mumbles a short apology, grabs Joni, and retreats to his room. Ratso looks crestfallen, heaves a sigh, and then rushes out from the counter, spilling papers in his wake, almost stumbling right into the camera as he passes Wadleigh. The small crowd that assembled claps heartily.

"Just once more," Dylan yells, "to cover it. We can do better." This time Dylan decides to have Howard Alk, who played Eagle in the Curio Lounge shooting, talking at a pay phone as McGuinn and Mitchell pass by, then whisper something to Ratso, who then does his frustration exit.

They roll and the scene goes off smoothly, Alk coming in on cue, asking Ratso for a dime for the phone, then scurrying away as the reporter makes his dramatic exit. "Bravo" Chesley Milliken, Jack Elliot's road manager, exults, "It's an Oscar, Ratso."

Ratso looks around and notices, for the first time, that Sara Dylan has slipped in and taken a seat on the couch to watch the proceedings. The reporter heard that she had joined the tour in Niagara but this was the first time he has seen Dylan's wife. And she was all he had heard, a stunning, quietly charismatic figure, possessing a fragile beauty, a long slender graceful body, and an enigmatic air. Ratso just gapes for a while, especially when Baez joins her on the couch and starts a conversation. This is fucking history, he thinks, the Sad Eyed Lady of the Lowlands meets Queen Jane.

But Ratso's reverie is interrupted by a grinning Howard Alk. "That was a great take," the burly filmmaker smiles, "you should have seen the look of pure terror that came into your eyes when I asked you for a dime." "It's just my genes," Ratso shrugs, and runs around to the other end of the lobby where Dylan is setting up another shot with McGuinn and Mitchell.

After the take, Mitchell starts toward the front desk but Ratso quickly intercepts the singer.

"So you're Joni," he smiles, "I've been trying to interview you for years but your manager tells me that you hate the press."

"No, no," the frail blond beauty protests, "I don't talk to reporters but I just don't like the interview form. It's the form that I don't like, not the people."

They chat a bit as they walk through the beautiful indoor garden that leads to the front wing. "We got a friend in common," Ratso notes, "Leonard Cohen. Him, Dylan, and Kinky Friedman are my three favorite male songwriters."

"I love Leonard," Joni purrs, "but who's Kinky?"

"You'll meet him," Ratso grins enigmatically, "you'll meet him."

It's about four now, and Ratso decides to pack it in. But when he reaches room 119, the hospitality suite, it's alive with late-night revelers. Buoyed by his new-found status, he joins in the celebration. But things take an additional turn for the worse with the arrival of Louie Kemp, who's not exactly thrilled seeing Ratso hanging out in the hospitality suite.

"What the fuck are you doing here?" he sneers.

"This is my room, Lou," Ratso smiles, "let me explain."

"It better be a good one," Lou fumes.

"Look, I was writing this note to you," Ratso produces the worn document from his back pocket, "just so you wouldn't be pissed and thinking that I was sneaking behind your back and Dylan happened to walk by—"

"Just happened . . ." Kemp mocks.

"Yeah, and I was real upset and he asked me what I needed and I told him and he told Barry to give me a room and per diem."

"Per diem!" Kemp nearly explodes.

"Ask Barry, Lou," Ratso begs. Imhoff nods in assent.

"You're just a *chozzer*," Kemp spits, "you're like a New York cabdriver. Push, push, push. You always want more." Kemp wheels out of the room.

Ratso turns and surveys the room. Ronson and Blakley seem settled in for the night, McGuinn is on the phone to his wife in California, and Neuwirth seems ready to leave. "This is your room," Imhoff says solicitously, "so if you want us to leave . . ." Ratso just shrugs and walks back out to the hall. Sara, the local, has split in the confusion and the hotel is eerily quiet. He wanders into the garden and pool area, and hears the sounds of some late revelers splashing around in the water. By the time he returns to his room, everybody's gone, the sun is almost risen, and after a half hour or so he falls into a fitful sleep.

Interrupted by a loud knocking on the door, Ratso stares vacantly at the clock. Seven-thirty A.M. The knocking continues. He stumbles to the door in his underwear. Joni peeks in. "Hey, I left my bag and glasses in here somewhere." Ratso retrieves them and hands them out to the singer. "Hey, they put you in here, eh. You scored, Ratso!" she smiles and scampers down the hallway. Ratso returns to bed, notes the time and dutifully calls his parents, who are about to go to work, then finally drifts off to dreamland, as the bright rays of the sun splash against the Sheraton curtain.

The next day, Ratso stumbles into the lobby after a few hours' sleep, just in time to catch Dylan, his wife Sara, and Scarlett about to film a scene in the beautiful country surrounding the hotel. Scarlett's manager has pulled his shiny black Rolls in front of the hotel, and the scenario calls for Sara to play a ragamuffin hitchhiker on an old dirt country road picked up by Dylan in the luxury car. But Mel Howard needs some costumes and props.

"I got just the shit," Ratso volunteers and returns a few minutes later with an old beat up trunk-valise and a blue hooded French Navy coat for Sara. While the equipment gets loaded onto the two cars, Dylan strolls up to Ratso.

"Where'd you get that?" He points at the photo button of himself that Ratso had bought outside of New Haven, one of which had netted the reporter ten dollars the other night in Boston.

"I bought it off this kid before the New Haven concert. I got a dozen, want one?"

"Nah," Dylan frowns, "I don't want it."

"C'mon," Ratso smiles, "you must have rooms full of this shit."

"No," Dylan protests, "are you kidding? Give it to him." He drags Imhoff over and Ratso pins it on his corpulent body.

After a while, they start piling into the cars, Jennings and Scarlett and some of the film crew in the Rolls, Dylan, Sara, Gary Shafner, Regan, and Howard in the Caddy. Ratso starts toward the car.

"Eh," Dylan surveys the room situation, "you're not in this scene, Ratso."

"Can't I come?" the reporter entreats.

Dylan doesn't have the heart to say no. "What are you gonna do?"

"Just take notes. Get some color." Dylan seems about to relent. "Shit, man, you can trust me, I ain't gonna burn you."

Dylan smiles and puts his hand on Ratso's shoulders, squeezing them playfully. "All right, c'mon."

They ride for about five minutes down a country lane, until they come upon a beautiful vast stretch of rolling farmland, a perfect backdrop. The cars stop and Mel and Ratso shoo the two cars full of fans that had been following the group. Dylan preps Sara, and then she walks a ways up the road, stops, puts the valise to her side, and sticks out her thumb, a forlorn little waif. They shoot a few scenes of her getting picked up, but then it gets dark and there's a concert tonight in Cambridge, so the two cars swing back to Boxboro.

In the parking lot, Dylan picks the valise out of the Cadillac and hands it back to Ratso. Sara pulls off the French coat. "Hey, do you know Ratso?" Dylan remembers that the reporter wasn't in Niagara when Sara joined the tour.

"No, I don't," Sara smiles wanly, and offers a delicate hand. "Thanks so much for the coat, love."

"Oh, you can have it. It fits you great, much better than me," Ratso marvels at the singsong quality to her voice. Fucking Dylan was right, the reporter thinks, she does have a voice like chimes. "Keep it. I got it at a Salvation Army for fifty cents."

"Oh thanks, love," Sara smiles, "that's very nice of you."

That night the venue is the tiny Harvard Square Theatre, whose 1,850 seats are packed. Once again, the camera crew is shooting in earnest for the concert sequences in the film, and perhaps because of the filming, perhaps because of the cozy ambience, perhaps solely because of the chops that three weeks on the road can give, once again the music is torrid. Especially Joan Baez's set.

This is Baez's turf, after all. She laid down her first musical roots in this area, playing the old Club 47 in the heyday of the folk scene, and tonight Ratso has the feeling that this audience has as much come out to see its Queen as it has to pay homage to its King. And Baez doesn't disappoint them, rollicking through a well-paced forty-minute set, bantering wittily between songs ("I love this town, I lost my virginity on the way to the Harvard dormitory"), frugging with wild abandon during McGuinn's "Eight Miles High" and then delivering the audience right into Dylan's hands with an electrifying "The Night They Drove Old Dixie Down."

By the finale, everyone's standing, screaming, and hooting, there's even a young gypsy girl in complete regalia whirling like a dervish in the orchestra pit. "We'll be in the area a few days," Dylan shouts over the tumult, "see ya," and exits to a thunderous ovation.

The next day, Ratso wakes up at 1 P.M. and after breakfast, rings up Rubin. Thanks to George Lois, Carter has two phones in his cell and the reporter never fails to chuckle when Rubin shouts that there's another call coming in and puts him on hold. He hasn't spoken to the boxer since the transfer and there may be new developments with the Garden show. Rubin's first line is busy, so the reporter tries the other number.

"Is this Rubin Carter Enterprises?" Ratso asks.

"Hey man," the boxer screams, "whatcha doing?"

"It's great to hear you, man."

"It's good to be back in touch. Hey man, I read your piece in *Rolling Stone*. I like it. It's comprehensive and educating."

"You speak to Bob lately, Rubin?"

"I called this morning, around nine." Ratso grimaces. "I think I woke him up, he was probably out late last night."

"Listen, you schmuck," Ratso laughs, "this ain't no prison. All these guys stay up till about nine in the morning."

"I know, I know," Rubin laughs heartily, "Bob says every time I get him I get him when he's fuzzy. I gotta call later from now on. Hold on, I got another call on the other line." A pause.

"Hey I gotta go, take care of yourself, you smuck, you," Rubin shouts and Ratso hangs up, amused that no matter how hard he tries, Rubin still can't manage to pronounce "schmuck."

Ratso goes back into the dining area and joins Sara and Sally Grossman, Albert's wife, who are lingering over their breakfast. Sally and Ratso are both from Bayside, Queens, in fact, they both graduated from Bayside High and that alone is worth a good ten minutes of "Do you remember . . . ?"

"I can't get used to living on the road," Ratso shakes his head, and sips on his breakfast tea. "It's nearly 4 P.M."

"Isn't it weird?" Sara agrees delicately. "I can't believe it. Today I slept the latest that I ever slept in my life. I woke up after 3. At home, I usually get up early in the morning."

"Yeah, it really seems to do something to you. I saw Springsteen in New Haven leaving the concert and it reminded me of Bob's line, looking so fine at first and left looking just like a.ghost."

Sara smiles. "That's a poignant line," she says in her half-raspy and half-silken voice, "I always did relate to that line."

"How do you like touring?" Ratso wonders.

"It's not my thing, love," Sara fluffs her hair, "I really can't take the traveling. And I have no real function here. Back home, I have the kids, and other things, but there's really nothing for me to do here. I'm thinking about going back soon."

The three of them chat on a bit and Ratso takes his leave and wanders in the lobby. The buses have already left for the Boston Music Hall since there's a matinee at four. In fact, the only sign that the tour is staying at the hotel is this shifty-eyed haggard-looking kid who's been sitting in the lobby since one.

Ratso walks by and the intruder beckons him. "Could I speak to you a minute?"

The reporter warily sits down and sizes up the inter-loper. Obviously a sickie, he thinks, staring into those crazed eyes, observing the repressed violence in the halt-ing, soft-spoken pattern mumbled through the tightly clenched teeth. And he's no kid either, he's got to be at least thirty, Ratso realizes as the stranger spins out a tale of tremendous obstacles and intransigent mindguards in his quest to see Dylan and inform him of some land near

his birthplace in Duluth, a birthplace this current Boston-
ian shares.

Ratso decides that he has to act fast. This guy's imagery
is classic textbook paranoia, maybe even paranoid-schizo-
phrenic. And nobody's here, the goddamn security have
all split, and worst of all, Sara's still around, right that
instant sipping tea unawares in the dining room, not five
hundred feet away from this maniac.

"Is Bob around anywhere?" the maniac, who's named
Lenny, asks, shifting his beady eyes around the lobby.

"Look, man, they're all gone, they all went to the
show already. Nobody's here," Ratso stresses.

"I'd just like to see him for a minute. I've spoken to
this guy Kemp, who seems to have a fairly close relationship to Dylan, but he's just giving me the runaround.
See, all I want to do is show him this," and Lenny pulls
out a picture of a beautiful Midwestern lake.

"Look, why don't you write a letter," Ratso suggests
and walks over to the hotel office.

"Can I help you?" a middle-aged woman asks as the
dark-glassed blue-jeaned intruder walks into the carpeted
office of the hotel manager.

"Yes, I'd like some security people to remove someone," the reporter says in urgent, clipped tones, "I'm with
the Rolling Thunder tour and there's a potentially dangerous person who's been out in the lobby furtively looking for Mr. Dylan for hours and everyone's gone except
Mrs. Dylan and he might recognize her and do something
dangerous." Ratso pauses for a breath.

"Well, we don't really have any security people," the
woman apologizes.

"What!" Ratso explodes. "Listen, this guy is dangerous
and we're talking about a potential threat to Bob Dylan's
wife."

The woman scurries into an office and an older gray-
haired man emerges. Ratso explains the gravity of the
situation and the man agrees to the reporter's plan. When
our hero gives the signal, two bellhops will pounce on
the sociopath, pull him into the office, and detain him
while Ratso collects Sara and rushes her to his car.

In the lobby, he calls Sara and tells her of the situation.

"Are you sure this is necessary?" Sara purrs.

"Sara, this is a fucking psychopath we're talking about. Jesus."

"All right, love," she sighs, "I'll be in my room. Anytime you're ready."

Ratso returns to the lobby and sizes up the situation. The letter ruse worked, Lenny's scribbling away on Sheraton stationery. The reporter smiles and walks past the office, lingering long enough to scream "Now!" to the waiting bellhops. As they rush into the lobby, he vaults up the stairs and stops in front of the room. He knocks loudly.

"Who is it?" Sara says softly.

"It's me, schmuck."

She quickly lets the reporter into the room. "I'll be right there," she says, and goes back to the mirror to put on an earring. Ratso wanders around the living room of the suite, peeking under the tin covers of last night's room service. "Aha!" he screams to Sara, in the bedroom, "you don't eat the same cheap shit we peasants get in the hospitality room. And look at this fancy wine, 1964, huh? Good year?"

Sara rushes into the room. "Ratso," she scolds, "Bob'll murder me if he finds out you're looking around here. C'mon."

Ratso frowns. "But I haven't really eaten anything," he whines and picks up a cold chicken cutlet.

"All right, but don't snoop around."

In a minute, Sara is ready, looking beautiful in a long kimono-type dress. Ratso shovels the cutlet into his mouth and slowly opens the door. No one is in sight. They rush out the side door, into the Monte Carlo, and tear out of the parking lot. Success.

"We did it," Ratso exults, after putting a good twenty miles between them and the hotel.

"Are you sure he was dangerous?" Sara wonders.

"Are you kidding?" Ratso looks at her with scorn.

"Well, I don't know, maybe it's just that I'm so used to them." Sara sighs. "I mean we get a Christ every six months coming up to our house. Even the kids are used to it. We even got a John the Baptist last year."

They talk on, Sara periodically checking Ratso's tape recorder to make sure it isn't on.

"I just don't trust journalists," she worries out loud, "they always distort things. One photographer took some pictures of me and one of the kids in my house and promised that she wouldn't use them and one day I open a magazine and boom, they're there. And those movie magazines!" Sara rolls her eyes. "You know, I don't like to fly, so one of my friends brought me a bunch of magazines before I flew out to join this tour, and somewhere between L.A. and New York I picked one up and there's a picture of Bob on the cover, they were saying he was having an affair with Sylvia Miles." She clutches her throat at the memory. "That made me sick, love, I was sick the rest of the flight. I mean, Sylvia Miles! I'd think they would think he'd have better taste than that." She laughs. "I can't believe you're a reporter, though, Ratso, I really like you. I can't believe you're a reporter."

Ratso snickers. "I'm no reporter. I'm a sociohistorian. I've got a masters degree in sociology, studying deviance. That's why I get along so well with musicians."

Ratso enters Cambridge and steers toward Boston and the Music Hall when Sara suddenly shrieks. "Stop!" she yells, and points to an old store that has some antique dresses and old jackets in the window. Ratso circles the block. It's a hippie Salvation Army. "Wanna go in?"

"Sure," she smiles, "I've seen the show already."

And what a used clothes Valhalla this is. There are tons of dresses, scarves, leather jackets, hats, suede cowboy shirts, bowling shirts, Hawaiian shirts, Norwegian Army hats, even boxes and boxes of magical candles. Ratso is going wild, he's running around like a contestant in Supermarket Sweepstakes, piling coat after coat, shirt after shirt after scarf into his arms, racing some imaginary clock. He beats Sara to the cowboy shirts and pulls the first three off the rack. "Hey," Sara fingers the third, "that would be nice for my husband."

"Whaddya mean?" Ratso grabs it back, "he's got enough clothes. Let him buy new ones."

"Well, we have to get him something," Sara lectures.

"I'll consider it," Ratso pouts.

They shop for five more minutes, Sara winding up with two dresses and a handful of candles, Ratso splurging on three cowboy shirts, one warm-up jacket with a huge Indian head on it, a white leather jacket, a suede sport coat, and a huge lamb-fur Norwegian Army hat. Of course, he borrows the money to pay for them from Sara.

By the time they reach the theater, the first show is almost over. But after depositing Sara backstage, Ratso hurries out to catch Dylan's last few songs. And realizes that he's probably missed the hottest concert yet. Tonight, Dylan's phrasing is razor-sharp, the band is tight as a whip, and what's more, Dylan knows it, prowling the stage in total command, gaping while McGuinn sings a verse to "Heaven's Door," mugging with Stoner on the chorus to "Oh Sister," slyly smiling at Baez during the rousing finale. The ovation is tumultuous.

Between shows, Ratso corrals Shepard and gives the Western greenhorn a tour of the Combat Zone. When they return Baez is on finishing a new arrangement of "Wonderful World." "I was at Boston University for four days," she tells the largely student audience, "and the only thing I learned was how to be Jewish when I had to."

"Fucking *goyishe kuppe*," Ratso curses softly then starts boogeying as McGuinn lilts into "Eight Miles High." Suddenly, Gary runs up.

"Lou wants to see you backstage, Ratso," he grabs the reporter.

"What? Bullshit. What is this a trap?"

"I'm serious, I swear to God. Lou wants to see you backstage. C'mon, there's not much time."

Ratso warily allows himself to be led past the burly security guards and down to the subterranean depths of the theater. Kemp is standing there waiting for him along with Regan.

"OK, we got a job for you." Kemp appears conciliatory and businesslike. "We need whores for tonight. A couple of hookers."

"What kind?" Ratso asks without batting an eyelash. "White, black, fancy, street?"

"Fancy hookers, one black and two white. And we also need about ten groupies, good-looking ones, though. We're gonna be shooting tonight at the hotel after the concert."

"No problem, I know every whore in the Combat Zone," Ratso boasts.

"Well, go to work; you don't have much time. And, oh, before you go, Regan wants to take your picture here for your tour badge."

Ratso swells with pride as the photographer positions

him against the brick wall. At last, after taking all that shit, I won't be a nigger anymore, he thinks. In fact, he's still smiling as the icy mist of water squirts out of Regan's false camera and bathes the lens of Ratso's dark glasses, their first cleaning all tour.

Ratso retreats upstairs, a little mortified but still fueled by a sense of mission. He would suffer the petty indignities, he resolves, the trivial abuses that stand in the way of larger triumphs. As soon as he gets back in the audience, he makes a beeline for Lisa, who managed to talk her way in and is hunched now in the first row.

"I hear you're in charge of Peggy now," Lisa smiles, and it was true, one of Ratso's duties, now that he was receiving a room, was to take care of Dylan's not-so-housebroken puppy beagle. The reporter so far had managed to slough that responsibility onto some of the security guards.

"OK, Lisa, we got an official job for you to do." Her eyes open wide with excitement. "You gotta round up ten good-looking groupies, make sure they're good-looking, and bring 'em out to the hotel."

"Are you kidding? Barry and Lou'll kill me."

"Lisa, this is an official mission. It'll be your job. I'll clear it with Barry and Lou."

She nods and starts combing the audience. Ratso smiles and corrals Gary, who's crouching to the left of the stage, watching Bob finish the show. "You got any money, we're gonna have to give the hookers some money upfront." Gary just pulls out a thick wad of bills and starts thumbing through them. Ratso doesn't see anything lower than a Hamilton.

After the show, Ratso and Gary hit the Combat Zone. The reporter runs into Good Time Charlies, ignores the faded stripper swaying over the bar, and scans the room. No luck. He grabs Gary and they drive around the corner and double-park in front of the 663. Ratso rushes inside.

"Rega," he suppresses a shout and hugs the hooker. She smiles, "How ya doing, kid."

"Listen, you wanna do some work. Remember the film I told you about? The Dylan tour. We need three girls out at the hotel tonight?"

"How much upfront?" Rega asks.

Ratso brings in Gary and Gary walks to the corner with

the hooker, discussing finances. Within five minutes, three well-dressed young girls are sitting in the back of the Monte Carlo, barreling toward Boxboro.

Back at the hotel, the groupies are arriving in droves, young ones, ugly ones, fat ones, in fact, Lisa has managed to recruit every conceivable type other than good-looking ones. They're roaming the halls in packs of twos and threes, ogling, pointing, whispering, giggling. Ratso laughs to himself as he escorts Rega and her two friends to the hospitality room.

Tonight, in lieu of the usual modest liquor offering, Imhoff has devised an elaborate spread and rented one of the banquet rooms for the Revue and their guests. Inside, most of the crew, a few of the performers, and guests like Albert Grossman and author Emmet Grogan are seated around tables. Ratso and Gary parade in with their catch and take a table at the rear. After a few minutes, Barry comes in with Peggy and orders Ratso to walk the dog.

The reporter grabs the leash and strolls barefoot around the lobby, a model of sartorial splendor in his white pants, orange Kinky Friedman T-shirt, and huge Norwegian Army hat delicately balanced on his head. And, as luck would have it, he stumbles upon the prettiest little coed Lisa invited, a dark doe-eyed art student. They talk a bit, he tells her to get rid of her friend, runs back to the hospitality room, pawns off the dog to security, grabs a bottle of Jack Daniels, picks up his waiting partner, and sojourns to the deserted game room.

Back in the hospitality suite, the party isn't exactly raging. The hookers are all sitting together at one table, in their furs and slinky dresses feeling as comfortable as war resisters at a VFW convention. In fact, except for a few quickies, their pocketbooks will be the same size when they leave as they were when they came in. And as for the groupies, they keep their patrol up for a few hours, then drive back into town about dawn, with stories to keep their dorm floors enthralled for weeks. But Ratso would miss all this nonaction. He was still in the game room, sprawled across the pool table, clutching the Jack Daniels bottle, passed out cold.

The next afternoon, Ratso wakes up, lurches off the pool table, knocking over the half-empty bottle, and stumbles back to his room. After a shower, he picks up some novelty items he bought the previous night, reluctantly grabs the cowboy shirt, and walks down to Dylan's room. He knocks.

"Who's there?" a groggy voice responds after the third rap.

"It's me, Ratso."

The door slowly opens onto a dark room. Ratso cautiously enters and when his iris adjusts, he makes out the singer standing barefoot in the living room, wearing a huge Mexican poncho and his dark glasses. And nothing else. In the bedroom, he can see Sara huddled under the covers talking to Sally Grossman, who's kneeling alongside the bed.

"Here, we got you a present when we went to the used clothing store yesterday," Ratso proffers the green cowboy shirt.

"Thanks, man," Dylan gushes. "Hey, I'm just getting up . . ."

Ratso gets the message and heads for the door. "Oh, I forgot to tell you, I think I'm gonna sell another feature article to another magazine. Fuck *Rolling Stone.*"

"Great," Dylan yawns.

"Far out, huh," and Ratso puts out his palm. Dylan finally gets the idea and makes a feeble slap, with a herky jerky motion.

"No, schmuck," Ratso screams, "this is the way you do it." And he slaps Dylan's palm with vigor, cracking up Sara and Sally, and then slips out the door.

That afternoon, Ratso visits with friends in Cambridge, and by the time he finds the gym at Brandeis, he's missed the first half of the concert. Just as well, he thinks, as he picks his way across the sardined bodies. Festival seating in another musky gym. Ratso makes it to the sound board in the middle of the floor and grabs a seat next to Bernie Gelb, who tapes every set of Baez's. Joan's wearing basic beachcomber again, rolled-up jeans, barefoot, red tank top, appropriate attire for this sweltering gym. And, like all the other dates so far in the Boston area, she's just about stealing the show from Dylan.

She plows through a searing "Diamonds and Rust" and the crowd goes wild. Ratso leans over to Bernie. "What was that anti-Semitic shit she was saying at last night's concert?"

"C'mon," Bernie smiles, "some of her best friends are Jewish."

She's soaring through "Swing Low" *a cappella* now, ending on a wavering trill that sends these young Jewish students into ecstasy. Gelb cheers lustily. "Stand up Bernie," Ratso tries to drag him to his feet. "Stand up! Then they all will."

"I want to dedicate the next song to the United Farm Workers," Joanie says solemnly and starts into the old Wobbly favorite, "Joe Hill."

Baez cedes the stage to Dylan and he maintains the intensity, ripping through the standard set, peaking to an incredible, "Just Like a Woman." The crowd cheers, but in vain because as usual there would be no encore this night.

After the show, Ratso runs into Faris from Columbia Records. Apparently, Columbia had sent up some very heavy executives to Boston to see the show, since the New York date hadn't been announced yet. And leading the delegation was Irwin Siegelstein, the new president of Columbia Records.

"It was really funny, we went backstage," Faris twinkles, "and there were all these executives in suits and ties, lots of confusion, and Irwin introduced himself to Dylan as the president of Columbia Records. And Dylan grunted. They came out shaking their heads, just couldn't understand. All he did was grunt."

After the show, the partying rages far into the night, with McGuinn, Neuwirth, and Blakley doing guest solos in the hospitality suite, Ronee belting out "New Moon Rising" just as the first rays of the Sunday sun streamed into the small room.

The next morning, Ratso runs barefoot and fur-hatted through the dining area. It was a travel day, the tour going on to Enfield, Connecticut, for a Monday night date in Hartford, but Ratso was driving back to Manhattan to pick up Kinky Friedman, who'd be making his long-awaited appearance on the tour. So the reporter is scrambling around, trying to tie up loose ends, and simultaneously pack for the trip. He spots Dylan, and Sara and Sally eating breakfast and scurries over to the table.

"Remember that article I mentioned yesterday?"

Dylan nods. "Well, I spoke to them today and it might be a cover story." Ratso offers his hand and Dylan wastes no time, resoundingly slapping it. They all laugh.

"Oh yeah," the reporter remembers and hands Sara a

Hurricane T-shirt. "Great," she holds it up, examining the picture, "now I can be a hooker, huh?" Dylan gets up to speak to someone and Ratso sits down. "Sara, Kinky's coming onto the tour."

"Great," Sara purrs, "I love Kinky. I saw him in L.A., he had this great fur guitar strap on."

"Listen," Ratso whispers confidentially, "I want to do a scene in Connecticut or up in Canada with just you and Bob and Kinky in a room listening to some of Kinky's new songs."

"Who knows if I'll be alive," Sara sighs.

"C'mon, don't put me on."

"Look, Ratso, what will happen will happen. I don't want to plan anything." Sara breaks into a slow smile. "But I think Kinky would be great in the film. He should play a priest."

Ratso bids them adieu and rushes up to his room, balances his three valises and a garment bag, and walks out to the car. He loads the baggage, and then saunters over to say good-bye to Dylan who had been talking over by his friend Larry's van. Larry, who's been confined to a wheelchair for years, is an old friend from Minnesota and had come out on the tour for about a week.

Ratso rushes up to the van, in time to see Larry being wheeled into its interior. "Is Bob around?" the reporter asks.

"He just left," Larry smiles.

"Hey, man, if I don't see you, take care."

"You too," Larry responds. "You just missed Bob though. We were just shooting a few scenes for the movie."

"Really?" The tape recorder in Ratso's head clicks on. "What kind of scenes?"

"Oh just fooling around," Larry smiles, as the platform of the specially equipped van lowers. "We did some great scenes with me chasing Bob around the halls in my chair."

Ratso winces, whispers a quick good-bye, and rushes to his car, eager for the sanctuary and sanity of Manhattan and Kinky Friedman; a small, solitary figure wheeling through the night, hurtling from the frying pan to the fire.

11

Ratso picked Kinky up at the Chelsea Hotel on 23rd Street and after a night smoking Kents and drinking tarry coffee at the all-night donut shop at Eighth Avenue, the two voyagers started for Hartford. But first, they stopped to pick up Lynn, a young girl who had caught Ratso's fancy at the Waterbury venue.

By eight, they were almost in Hartford and Kinky began to get finicky. "This may just turn out to be extremely unpleasant," he frowns, and pulls his red-and-blue-sequined cowboy hat over his forehead. "If this whole thing gets too tedious, I'm just gonna bug out for the dugout."

"Don't worry," Ratso smiles, piloting the Monte Carlo through the worsening snowstorm, "everybody's really excited you're coming."

"Well, I just hope it doesn't get too unpleasant," the Texas Jewboy drawls, "I'm in no mood for a tension convention."

They drive the next few minutes in silence, then enter Hartford. Ratso parks outside the modernesque Coliseum, another 10,000 plus date. They start wending their way to the seats, and, as if on cue, Neuwirth steps to the mike to introduce the next song. "Here's a trucker song for Kinky," he barks and the band breaks into a Country Western number.

"I'm gonna bug out for a while, boychick," Kinky announces, "get something to eat, relax for a while." The noise and smoke seem to be fraying Kinky's already frazzled nerves. Rather than lose him, Ratso grabs Lynn and the trio walk across the street to an Italian restaurant.

They come back near the end of Dylan's set, and again, almost magically, Dylan ambles up to the mike for a dedication. "We're gonna send this out to all the people in the house from Texas," and they break into "Durango." Kinky looks a little paler.

But he manages to survive through the show, and afterward, the trio walks backstage, Ratso introducing Kinky to everyone in sight, from the film crew to security.

"Goddamn," Kinky curses Ratso as he buttons his red, white and blue sport coat, "I don't got to meet every single nerd on the goddamn tour. If you introduce me to one more person I'm gonna brody."

"Kinky," Neuwirth rasps a greeting, putting a bear hug onto the Texas Jewboy, "c'mon on the bus with us, hoss." Kinky goes with Neuwirth, and Ratso and Lynn follow Phydeaux in the car.

In the crowded hotel lobby, there's a carnival atmosphere in the air, generated by the well-received show and the arrival of Kinky, and Rick Danko of the Band, who had played a short set during the first half of the concert. The reporter spies Dylan sitting on a bench and tries to drag Kinky over.

"Let's just get a room," Kinky successfully resists, steering Ratso over to the front desk, "let's get registered, get settled, relax a while."

As Kinky starts to sign for the room, Dylan comes charging toward the pair. "Hey Kinky, how ya doing." "Real nice, how you feel, hoss," Kinky smiles, tapping an ash off his long cigar. "How'd you like the show?" Dylan wonders. "I enjoyed myself immensely," Kinky drawls, "I couldn't hear too well, I was sitting all the way in the back of the Coliseum but you looked good up there, waving and stuff." Kinky does a quick imitation of Bob's gyrations during "Isis." "Well, we'll see you later," Bob waves. "Hey, did you get a room? Barry, get Kinky a room."

Kinky gets two keys, passes one to Ratso and they grab their luggage and walk toward the elevators. In the coffee shop, Joni is about to do a scene playing a guitar and a number of people have gathered around to gawk.

As soon as they enter the room Kinky flops onto a bed with, "I'm gonna nod out for a few minutes." Ratso immediately gets to work, running down the hall looking for the film crew. He bursts into the hospitality room, where Rick Danko is singing with Ronson, Stoner, Wyeth, and Soles backing him. No cameramen. The reporter races back into the hall, spies Ramblin' Jack, grabs him and rushes onto the elevator, nearly knocking down Joni Mitchell and Sam Shepard, who are emerging. "Hey, you going to the hospitality suite?" Ratso screams, "I'm bringing Kinky down there soon, we're gonna film him singing some of his new songs."

"What? For a Jewish cowboy?" Shepard, who owns a ranch in California, frowns. "You kidding me?" He grabs Joni, and they hasten down the hall.

"Are you gonna take that Jewish cowboy shit?" Ratso asks Elliot, whose real name is Adonopoz. Ramblin' Jack shrugs and they enter the room.

"Keno, wake up," Ratso yells, "this is Ramblin' Jack."

"Hi, Kinky," Jack doffs his ten-gallon.

"It's good to see you," Kinky squints half-awake eyes.

"I got to tell you a funny story . . ." Jack starts.

"Save it for the film," Ratso interrupts.

"Nah, it's personal." Jack delicately sits at the foot of Kinky's bed.

"We don't want it all over America by tomorrow morning, now do we," Kinky drawls in his peculiar wavering cantorial fashion.

Jack leans over and picks up one of Kinky's snakeskin cowboy boots, admiring the huge metal toeguards. "These toetappers are really good," Jack drawls, "you can kick snakes up the ass."

"I can kick Slocum over there if he gets in the fucking way," Kinky bellows. Ratso shudders involuntarily.

"You know the first time I heard of you was that story that came out in *Newsweek* magazine about all the Jewish folksingers . . . Dylan, you," Jack recollects. "I loved that date we played together in Texas."

"Yeah, that was phenomenal," Kinky remembers.

"They loved it, the audience kept going *whoooo*," Jack hoots. "I wasn't hip to the fact that Texas audiences like to get drunk and yell and I was trying to teach 'em how to be quiet, polite, listening motherfuckers. Houston was one of the first scary towns I've been in, I was shot at the first time I was there, the guy didn't even know me and I didn't know him." Jack looks amazed.

Kinky pulls one of his satin handmade cowboy shirts on, this one emblazoned with all sorts of Hebrew iconography. "That's a great shirt. What do you call that, a menorah?" Jack marvels. "I was supposed to be a Jewish doctor like my dad, but I got so rebellious so early that I never even got bar mitzvahed, I never even got a chance to find out what it was. I was hanging out with cowboys who tolerated me, they said, 'It ain't where you're from, it's where you're going.' "

Kinky lights up his cigar and pulls on his boots. "My brother said that modern popular music was started by two Jewboys, you and Bob Dylan, one on the East Coast and one on the West."

"The only time my dad introduced me to a rabbi he was afraid I was gonna split again and he wanted me to meet this really groovy hip Texas rabbi who was in the Marine Corps and was really tough and he was in Brooklyn but he was raised in Texas . . ." Jack rambles on.

"Texans are just complete assholes, that's all there is to it," Kinky pronounces.

"Well, I used to think that sometimes," Jack scratches his head, "but I met some groovy people there. I'm almost thinking about living there."

"Well, anytime there are that many assholes there are bound to be some good people," Kinky decides with impeccable logic. "Hey, I got a couple of jokes I want to run past you guys. First booger is, What's the recipe for German chocolate cake?" Kinky pauses. "See, the first step is you occupy the kitchen. All right. There you be. The first step is you occupy the kitchen. Pretty funny joke, huh?"

"That's the joke?" Ratso wonders.

"I've heard suicide notes that were funnier than that," Kinky admits.

"What's number two?" Jack drawls.

"Oh, how do Germans tie their shoes? With little nazis. All right! Thank you very much. My jokes have little wheels on them."

"Kinky, why don't you sing a little from 'Asshole from El Paso?' " Ratso tries to rescue the Texan.

"OK," Kinky clears his throat, and begins his parody of "Okie from Muskogee":

> We don't wipe our asses on Old Glory
> God and Lone Star Beer are things we trust
> We keep our women virgins till they're married
> So hosing sheep is good enough for us
> I'm proud to be an asshole from El Paso
> A place where sweet young virgins are deflowered

You walk down the streets knee deep in tacos
Ta Ta Ta Tacos
And Wetbacks still get twenty cents an hour

"That's about it, boychicks, a mere skeletal version of the song."

"Great," everybody choruses.

"C'mon, Kinky, let's go to the hospitality suite, the camera crew should be there by now," Ratso urges, and they all head for the elevator.

They enter the party suite and Ratso quickly scans the room but there's no cameras in sight. Ronee Blakley is sitting at the electric piano, Ronson's jamming along on guitar, Stoner has his bass out, and a circle of about ten people are listening to the proceedings. Kinky walks in about four paces and shyly retreats to a corner, adjusting his candy-cane-frame sunglasses.

McGuinn is singing "Truck Driving Man," and Danko and Kinky settle down to listen, which gives Ratso a chance to run to his room and call up Johnson. "Where the fuck are you, man?" the reporter shrieks, "I got Kinky all primed, he's down in the hospitality suite, ready to play unrecorded songs, and there's no fucking camera crew there."

"Look Ratso, Meyers is sick and Goldsmith is in charge of the other crew, they were down there and nothing was happening so they split to their rooms and went to sleep. Call him, but I doubt if he'll be happy being woken up."

Ratso hangs up disconsolately, goes back to break the news to Kinky, who takes it pretty well, obviously enjoying Danko's company. Gladdened, the reporter goes to bed early. Around 4:30 A.M.

The next morning Ratso and Lynn make their way to the coffee shop.

A few minutes later, Dylan and Sara walk in and find seats at the counter. Ratso waves hello. "You fell asleep last night, huh?"

"Yeah," Dylan's voice is real gruff, "what happened? What did I miss?"

"Not much. The fucking film crew fell asleep before we got a chance to shoot Kinky. Maybe we can do something in Montreal. Sara, you gonna be in Montreal?"

"I don't want to hear about any more scenes," she attempts to head Ratso off.

"Don't you want to hear Kinky's new songs?"

"If they happen, I'll look at them."

Ratso grabs Lynn and drags her over to the counter. "Did you meet Lynn?" he asks them. "Isn't she beautiful? She's a shiksa."

"They're the best kind, Ratso," Dylan laughs. "Don't forget, you met her on the Rolling Thunder." He smiles at Lynn. "You couldn't have met a nicer guy."

Just then, Raven walks in with a megaphone, trying to round people up for the bus.

Chesley joins Ratso and Lynn, and a few minutes later, a harried-looking Joni Mitchell wanders by. Ratso invites her to sit down. "Is there time for something to eat?" Joni frets, obviously upset. She orders an omelette and orange juice.

"Are you staying on?" Ratso asks.

"I can't," Joni mumbles, nervously playing with her silverware, "I was going to, but my house just got burglarized in the city over the weekend, so I got to go back for inventory. It was an inside job, it was like someone who knew where everything was. They were very selective in that they took guitars and a collection of Edward Curtis photographs which are very valuable and don't look valuable. And Indian baskets."

"I can see why you seem so upset," Ratso commiserates.

"I'm not uptight about losing the possessions," Joni says with her soft Canadian accent still rearing up every once in a while, "I'm uptight about everyone calling me like crazy and telling me and inflaming it. Like they're in the middle of it and I'm out here with a toothbrush and I could just keep on going."

"But it's an invasion of privacy," Chesley starts to lecture.

Joni nods agreement, "I said to John that I could dig him being more upset than me because I'm surviving out here with nothing. They were so neat, man. They swept up after themselves, knew where things were in drawers, that's the source of irritation, not the loss of the things but the loss of a friend." Joni sips some orange juice and sinks into gloom.

"Hope you come back, Joni," Ratso says softly. "It'd be nice seeing you in your native environment."

"This is more native to me. Have you ever been ripped off?"

"I certainly have," Chesley pipes in.

"Every place I ever lived . . ." Joni shudders.

Raven rushes in with a last call for the buses and Joni and Chesley hurry out.

So Ratso and Lynn head back up to the room where Kinky is still peacefully sleeping.

"Wake up, Kinky, don't you want to see the scene downstairs?"

"What scene downstairs?" the Kink mumbles.

"The buses are pulling out," Ratso announces dramatically.

Kinky jumps out of bed, his sarong wrapped tightly around his midriff. He pulls his fingers through his curly moss a few times, then scratches the sleep out of his eyes. "Yes the buses are pulling out," he affects the manic tones of a news announcer, "the people are shouting and waving good-bye."

"Seriously, Kinky, what'd you think of the show?"

"Has everybody left yet? No, I had a nice time last night," he burps, pulling on green suede cowboy boots. "I couldn't hear too well at the show, though. Listen, I'll tell you what I don't like. Bringing people in here when I'm sleeping or leaving that goddamn door open when there's some schmuck talking in the hall when I'm trying to nod out. It's not when I'm trying to sleep, it's when I wake up that I wig out. It doesn't bother me when people wake me up, I just don't like to be introduced to people when I'm on the nod. Then you left the door open five times with Negroes walking in here . . ."

"Isn't Ronee Blakley great?" Ratso tries to change the subject.

"In what capacity?" Kinky snaps.

"She's a great lady. We were sitting eating this morning and she picks up the Sweet 'n Low and sings "Sweet and Low, Sweet Chariot." Ratso chuckles again. "I forgot to tell Dylan that I thought he should re-record 'Desire,' the material's great but the versions now are so much hotter."

"You think he'll take your opinion into consideration and change it?" Lynn wonders.

"He'll do one of two things," Kinky puts on his sport coat, "either re-record it or throw you off the tour. He threw Phil Ochs out of a car for that."

"Ah, he's changed," Ratso frowns, "that was in '65."

"He's the same person all the time. Don't excuse a man for being an asshole at times."

"You haven't changed in fifteen years, Kinky?"

"No, I haven't. Basically I haven't, that's my point, and neither have you, you might have matured a little, but you're basically the same cat, a cop is still a cop, the robber's still a robber, the cowboy's still a cowboy."

Kinky finishes dressing and the three make their way toward the coffee shop. But outside, the buses still haven't left and Ratso drags Kinky out for some farewells. "Hey, Kinky," a voice wafts out of the Executive. A hatless, sunglassed Dylan is behind the wheel. "Hey Bob," Kinky salutes. "What's happening guys?" Dylan greets.

"I just woke up," Kinky mumbles, "but I had a great time, it was very pleasant."

"Well, we'll see you in Canada, huh? You guys be careful now," Dylan lectures in a mock-Texas drawl, "you watch out in New Yawk."

Ratso drives Lynn home and returns to Enfield in time for dinner. There's an eerie feeling in the hotel now that everyone has left, a real ghost-town ambience, intensified when Ratso and Kinky find themselves the sole audience in the restaurant for an appallingly loud cocktail-lounge band. In fact, after a brassy "You are the Sunshine of My Life" Kinky is about to bolt, but Ratso restrains him, and a few minutes later, their prime ribs come.

"So, have you changed your opinion about the whole cutthroatedness of this tour?" the reporter asks.

"I didn't say cutthroatedness. My opinion has pretty much stayed the same. I had no firm opinion when I came on the tour."

"You were wary."

"That's not wary," Kinky frowns. "I still dislike the idea of hanging around, waiting for my chance to play in somebody's goddamn shed. It'd be like hanging around outside of Johnny Carson's studio hoping he'll see me."

"The movie'll be big," Ratso ventures.

"Look, Bob Dylan is not the hottest thing happening—"

"But Dylan, Baez, Mitchell . . ." Ratso adds.

"None of them are. No bigger than the Cavett show getting all the old radicals together. No one knew who they were. They fill the stadium but it's not what's happening now."

"You see this as an old folkies' reunion?"

"No I don't see it as that," Kinky snaps, "I just find it repellent to hang around. You got a bit, you're writing a book, I'm not writing a story but I got my own contract, my own life, and my own showdates to play and I got more autonomy than any of these motherfuckers. You're still a reporter on this tour no matter whether Dylan blows you, you're still a reporter and you being around with a tape recorder is something that Roger McGuinn is not doing. I tell you something else." Kinky waves his knife for emphasis. "The minute that you lose that autonomy, you also lose people's respect. Look, boss, you still don't know (1) if it's gonna be made, (2) if your part's gonna be in it or not. It might be great and it might get cut, they might cut it because it upstages somebody."

"Kinky, don't be so paranoid. I thought everybody liked you—"

"I felt extremely well accepted, more than accepted. Many of these people went out of their way to be nice, Ramblin' Jack was nice to me, I thought Danko was a cool cat, McGuinn was nice . . ."

"Dylan loves you, that greeting he gave you when you first checked in."

"Let me ask you something." Kinky puts down his silverware, and leans back, rubbing his eyes. "Can you accept the fact that maybe I would like to accept these people's love and affection and that's it. That I don't want anything else out of them."

"You're always talking about what you want," Ratso eggs.

"But out of these particular people I don't. Do you believe every word I tell you? If I tell you I want to be a wealthy millionaire do you think I really want to be the president of some fucking enormous million-dollar plastics company, that I'll be happy doing that? Do you take me by my word completely? You shouldn't."

They fall silent, Kinky playing with his half-eaten prime ribs as the blaring sound of "Proud Mary" threatens to shatter their water glasses. Kinky considers some action, then realizes they're outnumbered three-to-one by the band.

"You know," he says softly, "that was a nice thing watching Bob play harmonica back there at the show. When he came out with the harp and himself there, it's like under that angry defiance kind of thing, that one man can do a lot, one little guy out there beating his foot on the floor and playing the harp. It brings back a little wave of something. It didn't even matter what words he was saying, it was just a big rush to see it. That audience was so tedious though, so high-pitched. 'Play this, play that, play whatever you want to,' " Kinky shrills.

"How do you deal with it? What's your audience like now?"

"Depends on how I feel. My audience is getting bigger and more All-American. The intelligence of the average fan has decreased dramatically, which is good. Instead of four sociology professors, smoking pipes, asking me about my Jewish background, we got a crowd of people."

Kinky sips on his cold coffee as the band bleats to a halt with "Jazzman." "Once again, I have to say every time we're about to do this next song, we have to fill up this room with about sixty violins, fifteen trumpets, fourteen French horns," the jarring Las Vegas–honed voice of the M.C. washes over the pair. "This is Stevie Wonder's 'All in Love is Fair.' "

"Eiiiiii," Kinky screams and then loudly belches. "Jesus Christ, this is unpleasant." He looks down on his plate, picks up his napkin, and looks frantic. "I lost my mint, goddamn it." Kinky signals the waitress. "Can I get dessert or how about just one of these mint boogers, I lost mine." Ratso sacrifices his, Kinky is placated, and they head back for the room.

Kinky rushes into the room and turns on the TV. "I like watching those movies about giant ants attacking the earth." He pulls off his boots and plops down on the bed. "Hey Rats, I got the limo taking me to the airport at 5:30 A.M. but I could cancel it though."

"What are you gonna do, tennis shoe the bill?" the reporter's known Kinky too long.

"I'm gonna tell them there's somebody else up here. Don't worry about it, then you're just gonna leave. I'm gonna have to leave before you do. Fuck, I'm not gonna tell them anything, just leave."

"There's not supposed to be another party in here," Ratso has visions of holding the bag.

"They don't know that there is."

"They'll wake me up. What if they hassle me?" Ratso frets.

"Look Ratso, I'm sorry you're here but I'm not gonna do it any different than the way I always do it."

"How do you do it?"

Kinky frowns. "Look, I can't explain it. Why don't you ask Abbie Hoffman? You read *Steal This Book,*" Kinky snaps, "you know so much about all that shit. Do what he would do."

"Why don't you tell them to bill it?"

"I'm not telling them a single thing, hoss," Kinky pulls a handkerchief over his eyes, his own version of a Robert Mitchum beautysleep. "I have one of several options: 1) go to jail, 2) pay them cash, 3) pass off some credit card if I can, or 4) try to get them to bill, I always try to get them to bill first."

"I hope they won't wake me up," Ratso worries.

"They're not gonna call you at seven in the morning and wake you up," Kinky shouts indignantly. "If they do, it shows very little class. If they call just say, 'What? You woke me up to tell me this? Of course I'll handle it, I'll handle it later this afternoon, I'm checking out later today.' "

"Then I sneak out," Ratso moans.

"You don't sneak out, man," Kinky lectures. "You leave." He pulls the bandana off his eyes and stares at the now blank TV screen. "Is there another movie on TV?"

Ratso gives up, gets up, and heads for the door. "I'm going down to the coffee shop, want anything?"

"Bring me back a nice waitret," Kinky drawls and goes back to the movie.

Downstairs, Ratso settles into a booth and starts reading a paper. But he suddenly notices that the talking in the booths around him has become muted, and when he sneaks a peek, most of the teenagers at the tables are staring and whispering excitedly. Last night's groupies, Ratso flashes, looking for some thunder. With only Kinky and him to provide it, a shame. He says hello to the blonde in the next booth.

Her name is Eileen, and, Ratso surmises after two minutes of conversation, she's a stone groupie, from her platform shoes to her mood ring to her pseudo-cultivated British whine.

"I had an affair with a nightclub singer, a married man," Eileen is confessing to Ratso after three minutes, "all Mafia. Bodyguards, that scene. We screwed, we got off pretty good. We're both Pisces. He offered me a job."

"Is that Kinky Friedman, the underground artist," a voice floats from the next table over.

"He's with Bob Dylan," Eileen snaps back at the local kid.

"Tell him I want to meet Mick Ronson," the kid screams back.

"Who are these guys?" Ratso asks.

"Douche bags," Eileen spits, "just schmucks. I wouldn't advise talking to them."

Ratso wanders over to their table anyway, and a few minutes later ambles back to Eileen's booth. "I heard you're a cockteaser, from those guys."

"Tell them to screw it because they've never been in my pants," she flares.

"Well, look, me and Kinky are into very kinky sex, Kinky's orthodox and he'll only fuck with a sheet with a hole in it between him and the girl. And I like to make it in linen closets, something about the smell."

"Well, I've made it in cloakrooms, baby," she smiles and they head upstairs.

Ratso bursts into the room with Eileen in tow, finding Kinky engrossed in the movie and not particularly thrilled with the prospect of a strange, young female, with an affected accent at that. Eileen immediately makes a bee-line for Kinky's snakeskin boots, examining them as if they were moon rocks. "What do you have these tips for, to kick people with?" she giggles obnoxiously. Kinky just ignores her. "I think he finds me rude," she says loudly.

"No, just tedious," Kinky sighs, "I don't find anybody rude."

"This dude is obnoxious," she sneers to Ratso.

"No, he's sweet," the reporter smiles.

"Hey baby I've been around," she glares at Kinky, "I know what it's like."

"We are gonna go look for a linen room," Ratso smiles at Kinky, "Eileen likes to fuck in cloakrooms."

"Well, 'bye baby," Kinky sneers.

"I don't give a fuck about you," Eileen snaps back.

"I don't give a fuck about you either, sweetheart. You can come and go. I just find you a little bit tedious." Kinky frowns.

"You are calling me a tease . . ." Eileen's incredulous.

"You're not hearing very well, I said tedious."

"What does tedious mean? I'll call the news service right now and find out what tedious means."

"Good," Kinky dismisses her.

"Why don't you go play in your band and get off on your guitar and screw it up your hole," her accent is beginning to fall apart under pressure.

"What are you doing?" Ratso screams at her. "You alienated my brother. He's very sensitive."

"I'm sorry, I apologize, sweetheart," she says to Ratso.

Kinky gets up and starts packing. "I just want some slack, man."

"You want what?" Eileen prods.

"I'm not talking to you," Kinky rolls his eyes.

"Then who is he talking to?" Eileen asks Ratso.

"Look," Kinky explodes, "you're the most obnoxious slit I've ever met in my life."

"Slut!" Eileen turns white. "Did you call me a slut?"

"Slit!" Kinky screams, "Slit! Slit! SLIT, you're an obnoxious slit." He's roaming the room, waving his hands in the air.

"Hey baby," her accent is back, "you can cram it up your ass sideways and spin it."

"Good line. Good line. I see you been watching Gabe Kaplan on TV tonight too."

"I don't like you," Eileen says with finality.

"I don't like you, I don't like you," Kinky parrots, "I think you're a mean, vacuous little slit."

"That's how you gotta be around here baby if you want to get somewhere." Eileen gives Ratso a knowing stare.

"I'm gonna go get a hamburger," Kinky starts to leave.

"Please leave," Eileen begs.

"It's his room," Ratso yells.

"That's right, it's his room and I'm being rude," Eileen laughs.

"You're not succeeding in being rude, I mean you're not even rude." Kinky pauses, grabs Ratso and pulls him into the bathroom for a conference.

"It's a funny stupid room, why don't you leave? We don't need you," Eileen is screaming from the bedroom. "What are you saying about me? Hey screw you, cowboy. Put it up sideways. I hope you gag on it. I hope you gag on your hamburger. I hope you get the clap. . . . You can kinky it up your rear end." In fact, Eileen's still shouting obscenities as Ratso escorts her to the door and dumps her in the hall, where she stands like yesterday's room service, waiting to be picked up.

It's about 4 A.M. now and Kinky goes back to packing, but Ratso is totally wired from the confrontation. "Look, 86 the limo, I'll take you to the airport, we'll tennis-shoe this together."

So they plot the escape, drawing little maps of the corridors and the exits on the motel stationery, then grab a half-hour's sleep. Promptly at 5:30, Ratso peeks his head out into the hall, and tiptoes to the elevator, followed closely by Kinky, their arms full of luggage and a garment bag. The elevator slides open, and Ratso cautiously peers down toward the front desk, then scoots down the hall. Kinky follows. They screech to a stop at the end of the corridor.

"OK, now we only have to sneak past that one last closed-circuit TV camera that guards the rear door," Ratso whispers to Kinky, pointing to a fire-alarm system on the ceiling. Ratso digs into his bag and emerges with some Gillette Foamy. He tiptoes over to the alarm and sprays it with a solid hunk of shaving cream. "OK, we've neutralized the TV lens. They'll just think it's snowing hard at the desk," he chuckles and they rush out to the Monte Carlo. Five minutes later on the highway they breathe easier.

Ratso drops off Kinky who has to catch a plane to Texas, and then spends the rest of the day driving up to Maine. It's a beautiful day, clear, cold, a light layer of snow coating the countryside, and Ratso is feeling good, despite the lack of sleep. The Monte Carlo hurtles north, toward Fenway, the surroundings getting bleaker and less and less populated, until finally when he falls onto the concrete carpet called Highway 95, Ratso is beginning to think he's in Alaska. It's never looked this dark out before.

He finally pulls into the Fenway Howard Johnson's around 5, picks up his key and newsletter, unpacks, and wanders into the bar. One of the guys from the film crew is there and tells him that everyone's filming across the street at a gas station. Ratso scurries out.

At the station, Dylan and Sara and Sam Shepard are

in the middle of a scene, under a car on racks. Ratso rushes up and pulls Jack Baran the assistant producer, over. "What's going on?" he whispers.

"Just a subplot," Baran answers, and Ratso inches closer to the action. "There's too many people in here," Meyers decides, turning around and surveying the four or five onlookers. Mel Howard hurries out, but Ratso tries to blend into a pile of tires. "There's too many people in here, Sloman, outside! I don't want to see your face."

Ratso and Baran stand outside the station, shivering as a heavy snow begins to fall. "It's snowing hard," Baran notices. "Good. Maybe the snow'll bring this thing to a total halt."

"Then we can sit down and have a Thanksgiving dinner," Ratso hopes.

Baran smirks, "We'll probably get an instant turkey pill."

The mere mention of food sends Ratso into the office of the gas station. He stares at the candy machine, pondering Snickers, Crunch, $1,000,000 Bar, Peanut Chew . . .

"Are you using that machine?" It's Dylan, who's stomped into the office, trailed by the camera. Ratso looks up into the lens.

"You look really familiar. I know you from someplace," Dylan peers at the reporter's face.

"You too," Ratso goes along. "You want some candy?" he asks Dylan.

"You're first," Dylan says.

"No, no, go ahead," Ratso does Alphonse to Dylan's Gaston. They each get some candy. "What are you doing here?" Dylan's eyes narrow. "You trying to steal some thunder?" Ratso shrugs. "I'm going to have to think about that one," he smiles, and Dylan stomps back to the garage area, trailed by the camera. Ratso follows them.

Dylan walks back over to Shepard, who's playing a garage mechanic, and Sara, who's playing Bob's companion. "Where can I get another car?" Dylan asks Shepard. "I'm going to Mexico." Sara tightens the shawl around her shoulders. Shepard asks what Sara does.

"She is a typist, that's her gig," Bob smiles.

"When are you leaving?"

"Tonight, we're going to Tucson." Dylan starts peering at the underside of the car.

"That's a hell of a run," Shepard drawls.

"What happens around here?" Dylan wonders.

"The weather changes," Shepard chuckles.

"Hey, I'll buy the car offa ya," Dylan offers.

Just then, a kid tries to enter the office from outside. Ratso blocks the door. "Hey, let me in. I own the place. I think I got a right to come in." Ratso apologizes and lets the owner in. "You guys are all fucked up," the kid shakes his head. Inside, the scene has petered out and Dylan and Sara walk out into the cold snow-filled air, arm in arm, trailed by the ubiquitous Meyers. He's ahead of them now, backing up, filming all the while, heading straight for the gas pump, when he suddenly trips on the concrete and sprawls on the ice. Ratso catches up to Bob and Sara.

"Hey Ratso," Dylan looks solemn, as Meyers is back on his feet filming, "ask Kemp to tell you what he told me."

"Huh?"

"Just ask Louie to tell you what he told me," Dylan repeats enigmatically.

"Let me ask you one question," Ratso buttonholes Bob, "I've always wanted to know this. When you say in 'Sad Eyed Lady' that 'my warehouse eyes my Arabian drums,' is it two distinct separate images, 'warehouse eyes' and 'Arabian drums' or is it using eye as a verb, you know, 'my warehouse eyes my Arabian drums.' "

Dylan looks befuddled. "Yeah," Sara tugs on his arm and smiles, "I've always been curious about that, too."

"Eh, uh," Dylan's at a loss for words, "oh man, you always catch me at my worst, Ratso." He tugs Sara toward the motel.

Ratso follows into the Howard Johnson's and notices kids running around the lobby, being chased by a silver-haired lady and a middle-aged black woman. They're cute kids, loud, obnoxious, shy, and just generally normal. They're Dylan's kids, the reporter discovers, and that lady is Dylan's mother.

Ratso gets a ride to the gig with Larry Johnson, who's traveling to the Augusta date in his friend's van. Outside, the temperature's approaching zero, as the reporter shivers in the rear of the van.

"Do you know how they named the band?" Johnson asks. Ratso feigns ignorance. "Remember the Cambodia invasion, when Nixon bombed Cambodia? The bombing mission was code-named 'Rolling Thunder.' Scarlett told me that, she's very political. And get this. The planes that attacked Cambodia, the flights originated from the U.S. base in the area, which is Guam." Johnson pauses for dramatic effect. "Heavy, huh?"

"I hear Kemp wants to put you on a boat or something," Johnson leers. Suddenly, Ratso remembers Dylan's cryptic remark. "Yeah, Dylan made a reference to something Louie told him about me."

"I think they're gonna continue to fuck with you forever, until the tour is over," Johnson gleefully relates. "I want to find out, too, so when you get fucked, I can be there to shoot it, I mean you're the fuckee of this tour, Ratso. They all like you; they're just having fun with you."

They pull up in front of a sprawling, concrete oasis in this desert of tundra. Augusta has a beautiful new civic center with a real low-pressure staff, smiling usherettes in uniform. Ratso breathes easily as he scampers in, and finds his seat.

But after three numbers from Guam, he's getting restless, so he wanders around the arena, winding up on the balcony level looking out of a huge plate-glass window facing the rear of the hall. The other camper is parked out there, the one that Baez has appropriated from Imhoff when her kid came on the tour yesterday. Ratso waves at Carlos who's sitting behind the wheel, and Carlos gestures back, waving the reporter to the camper.

Ratso slips out the back door and ambles over to the camper. Carlos opens the door and he hops in, and plops down on a couch opposite Joan. "Hey this is nice, Joan," he peers at the kitchenette, and the rear sleeping compartment.

"Shhh," she puts her finger to her mouth, "talk low because Gabriel just fell asleep. This was Barry's, now it's ours. What's this white pants all about? You're getting spiffed up, Ratso," Baez smiles.

"I'm cleaning up my act," the reporter swells with pride, "I bought a hair blower, I met this nice girl on the tour, I told Dylan she was shiksa and he said that they're the best kind."

"I know," Baez shrugs, "Jewish males can't stand fucking Jewish girls."

"Most Jewish girls I've been with make me feel guilty,

oversexed if I wanted to fuck more than once a week . . ."
Ratso complains. Baez cracks up.

"Who's this new one?" Baez asks.

"Oh, she's great, she's one-quarter Indian, Irish, she
gave me a whole list."

"How old, sixteen?" Joan smiles.

"No," Ratso frowns, "seventeen."

"I was close," Baez rolls her eyes. Ratso raps on, about
Kinky, tennis-shoeing the bill, the groupie, Baez and Carlos taking it all in.

"There goes Ronee with that song," Baez shakes her
head, as "New Sun Rising" resounds from the hall.

"I love that song," Ratso rushes to the defense.

"Oh, so do I," Joan quickly adds, "but she just keeps
adding new choruses to it."

"It's the same chorus," Carlos corrects, "only it was
three times repeat, now it's about seven or eight."

"I love that shit," Ratso reiterates.

"I know she's good," Joan admits.

"Ask her about yesterday," Carlos whispers to Ratso.

"Oh, where'd you go yesterday?" Ratso grills Baez.

"Ever hear of Thomas Merton?" Baez asks.

"Sure, the monk," Ratso nods, "he used to write a lot
of philosophy."

"Well, every year they give an award and they gave me
one." Ratso notices the dove plaque on the table. "It was
an interesting switch out of the rock 'n roll world and into
the other one," Joan adds modestly.

"You got a mood ring," Ratso notices Joan's finger.
"That girl groupie in Connecticut had one of those."

"Bet it got mighty dark, darling," Baez chuckles. "If
it stayed light green you knew you weren't getting anywhere. Was she Jewish?"

"I never had a Jewish girl attack me," Ratso moans.

"Sit on your face and all that." Joan's eyes twinkle.
"Never, huh?"

Ratso looks around the camper. "This looks nice now,
you got flowers and shit."

"Bernie fixed it up to a lady's touch." Joan leans over
and whispers, "It took days to clean it up."

"So where were you yesterday, Joan?" Ratso wants
more details.

"I can't remember, all I know was I left the tour for a
day."

"What was the award about?"

"Her being so wonderful and you noticed, for being cooperative," Carlos smiles.

"Miss Loquacious 1975," Joan smirks. "He was a nice guy, Merton, he died in Bangkok leaning on an electrical wire. . . ."

"Do you know what I heard tonight?" Ratso interrupts.

"See what I mean," Baez tells Carlos, shaking her head at the reporter's insolence.

"Do you know the story of Rolling Thunder?" the reporter asks.

"Which one, the fake old Indian?" Joan snaps.

"No, the Vietnam story."

"Oh Lord," Baez rolls her eyes.

Ratso relates the story that Johnson had told him that night and Regan, who just stepped into the camper, confirms it. "It's true," the photographer says. "Remember the *Time* magazine reporter Jim Woolworth? When he was here the first weekend, he got into a tremendous fight with Ginsberg over this. Ginsberg denied the whole thing and Jim was in Vietnam when this was taking place."

Joan laughs, "Oh and Ginsberg was denying it because of Bobby, right, the same old crap."

"Gabe met Ratso," Joan snickers, "and he said, 'Hello Ratso, how come you don't squeak?'" They all laugh. "Ever see Ratso's place? I'll send you some newspapers for bedding."

"Where do you live?" Ratso snaps back.

"California."

"With all the other space heads? You like that?"

"I live in a secluded little-old-ladies-and-horses kind of place." Joan gets up and goes to the back, checking on Gabriel. She comes back and they decide to watch some of the show. She leads the way to the stage door. "I can't go," Ratso hesitates, "I don't have a pass."

"C'mon, you jerk," Baez grabs his arm, and escorts him in. Joni Mitchell's on now. "My mother will be showing high signs of disinterest at this point 'cause I'm her daughter," Baez whispers to Ratso.

Joni finishes and Ramblin' Jack goes on. Mitchell's in military drag tonight, a pressed uniform and a big badge on her chest. Ratso sidles up to her as soon as she's alone.

"Wanna do an interview?" he leers in his best Groucho Marx.

"With who?" Joni feigns innocence.

"With me."

"Why do I want to do an interview with you?" Joni huffs, "I'm not even third on your list."

"I told you you're first on my list," Ratso protests.

"No, you didn't, you mentioned three people, Bob, Leonard, and Kinky, and you didn't even mention me."

"But . . ." Ratso starts.

"I don't want to do an interview with anybody," Joni declares with finality.

"For two years I've been nudging your manager," Ratso moans.

T-Bone overhears some of this and turns around. "As your lawyer . . ." the deep-voiced Texan starts.

"Talk to my lawyer," Joni coos.

"OK, for two years I've been trying to interview her. But everyone tells me she hates reporters," Ratso laments.

"No, she doesn't," T-Bone decides.

"It's not true," Joni screams from the sidelines.

"She hates reporters." Ratso's adamant.

"No," Joni protests, "you know why . . ."

"I'm your lawyer," T-Bone shuts her up.

"You can't speak for her," Ratso screams.

"She doesn't, you don't hate reporters, right?" T-Bone looks to his client for guidance.

"No, I dislike the form, I dislike the form of the interview."

"What about the content?" Ratso asks.

"I dislike the form and the content," Joni smiles.

"She dislikes the form and the content," T-Bone parrots.

"What do you like?" Ratso wonders.

"I don't like the reviews . . ." she starts.

"She doesn't even like the publicity," T-bone pipes in.

"I don't like reviews either," Ratso agrees. "The only album I ever reviewed was Leonard Cohen's last album, 'cause I was doing a story on him and I wanted to write the review in his own language."

"No," Joni shakes her head, "I'm much jiver than my work and I'd rather have people think that my work is me."

"Right," T-Bone chuckles, "that's true."

Ratso gives up and wanders around backstage. The kids are playing electronic Ping-Pong, and Baez is in the middle of molesting Imhoff, pulling his tie-dyed T-shirt over his massive belly. Neuwirth and Muffin, who's helping with makeup, are twisting to Ramblin' Jack's swing number.

Dylan goes on, and Ratso walks out front to watch. Sara's up on the stage, seated next to Raven. Scarlett, in a long white antique gown, is watching from the side, fiddle in hand, in fact, nearly everyone backstage has filtered out to catch Dylan's set.

And what a set. The band is cracking by now, flowing from "Masterpiece" to a chilling "Hattie Carroll." Then Bob reaches back to *Nashville Skyline* for "Tonight I'll Be Staying Here With You."

Joni walks up. "Want to do an interview?"

"No, I only interview stars," he cracks, as Dylan charges into "Train to Cry," trading incredible guitar licks with Ronson.

"C'mon," Mitchell grabs Ratso by the arm and drags him backstage.

"No, let me go. I wanna watch this," he screams in vain. They walk down the corridor and find two chairs.

"I'm interviewing you, OK?" Joni takes charge.

"You don't have any notes," Ratso notices. "Don't you prepare?"

"I don't even know who you are," Joni gets serious, "to me you're a total stranger. You're just someone who appeared in a funny hat with a button that says 'I'm a Beech Nut,' and initially, had two symbols that may be related to you, one a rhinestone dollar sign and the other a photograph button of Bob Dylan. Are you, like, a fan of Bob Dylan?"

"A fan?" Ratso hedges. "Sure, I'm a fan of his work. I think he's the most important, I told you, he, Leonard Cohen, and Kinky Friedman are the three most important male songwriters. I make that distinction because I really can't compare male and female songwriters, it's a different experience."

"Why do you make a distinction between male and female songwriters?"

"Because I relate to male perspective and as much as I appreciate your songs or Ronee Blakley's songs, which I love, or Joan's songs, to me it's a different perspective, a different way of looking at things, a different slant . . ."

"Aren't you interested in what women think?" Mitchell is doing a slow burn.

"Of course . . ."

"I would think that men would be curious about what women think in the confines of their rooms late at night," Joni snaps.

"I am. All I'm saying is that I can appreciate it but I can't experience it myself and I never can, at least not this time around, I'll always be . . ."

"Don't you think that you have any femininity in your spirit at all?" Joni interrupts.

"Sure."

"Are you comfortable expressing it or are you nervous about it?" Mitchell cross-examines. "You are not afraid to cry?"

"I cry a lot," Ratso smiles.

"Cry a lot?" Mitchell repeats coldly.

"When I have to, I cry. I'm a Cancer and for two and a half years Saturn was in my constellation."

"Right, considering all the water in our systems and the pull of the moon on the tides, that's not illogical," Joni decides.

"But, yeah, I believe I have a lot of female traits, I assign credence to the two archetypes. . . ."

"Do you think there's more similarities between my work and say, Ronee's and Joan's than there is between mine, Leonard's, and Bob's? I want to tell you something. There is . . . I have very little in common as a songwriter with Ronee and Joan Baez. You know, I really think that you have limited your experience by a preconception. We do this all the time. I have to be aware of my preconceptions. I'm speaking in generalities. OK, I'm saying that you have a preconception that there is something that is shared in common between the work of Joan Baez and the work of Ronee Blakley and the work of myself. . . ."

"No, I'm just using you three as examples of—"

"I asked you a question first," Joni says coldly. "I said, 'Do you think there is more in common in the work of us three women . . .' "

"As females," Ratso interrupts, "as prototypical female songwriters."

"I asked you a question and you answered it and I'm confronting you with that question again. I'll ask it again, do you think I have more in common in my work with Ronee and Joan than I do with any of the other men on your list, you said no before."

"What I was talking about before was like women and men—"

"Right, that's a preconception," Joni points an accusatory finger, "it's a limitation, that's what I'm trying to say."

"I'd say out of all those people you probably have the most affinity with Leonard, but I don't know if it's a cultural thing . . ." Ratso decides.

"Up to a certain point, except my work now is much—"

"I haven't heard the new album yet," Ratso admits.

"You haven't listened to the songs I do on the show either," Joni glares.

"I do, I do," Ratso screams, "but I can't get the lyrics from that."

"OK." Mitchell accepts that.

"Gimme a tape, sing them for me," Ratso suggests.

"What I'm saying to you is I'm challenging you to an error of perception in yourself that you're missing the meat of what I do by putting me into a category."

"I'm not putting you in a category. All I'm saying is sometimes I find it difficult, being a male, to completely empathize with a female perspective," Ratso groans.

"Sometimes the songs are coming from a narrative position and they're simply cinematic and they have nothing to do with gender, so you're making a preconception on songs of mine. . . ."

"I'm preconceiving that everything you write is in some way coming from—"

"My own experience," Mitchell guesses, "and also—"

"That you're not projecting," Ratso finishes.

"No, in a lot of my songs I'm a neutral observer, I'm without gender, and those songs pertain to you too. I even write about places that you like to hang out, coffeehouses, bars, like down life, up life, the thing is that I like to describe society as well as the street."

"But you're always looking from your eyes," Ratso adds.

"Well, what other place are you going to look from?" Joni bristles.

"That's what I am saying."

"I can't transport myself into a character."

"And your eyes are always you and my eyes are always me," Ratso sums up with impeccable logic.

"But, don't make the mistake of thinking that what my eyes see hold nothing in common with your own," Joni cautions.

"I never said that."

"Yes, you did, you're saying they don't because I'm a woman." Joni, upset, gets up and starts to leave.

"Wait, no, c'mere," Ratso grabs her.

"That's my last words, there were no questions. I didn't even interview you, I just defended myself. I don't want to talk to you anymore because your vision is too narrow." She stalks away.

Ratso feels bad and grabs Mel Howard. They start discussing what just happened and Joni storms back.

"I'm telling Mel about our discussion," Ratso informs her

"He keeps on trying to put me in this box," Joni complains, "he thinks that my work is too female for him to enjoy."

"I'm not, I'm not . . ." Ratso's flabbergasted, "I didn't say that, Joni."

"So he doesn't even open up his ears," she continues. By now, a crowd has formed around them.

"I didn't say that," Ratso's still protesting, "she's putting me on."

"Play it back, play it back," Joni's screaming and pointing to the tape recorder.

"You sound like a cop today, Joni," Mel smiles.

"I am a cop today, man," she brags, fingering her badge.

"All I said was Dylan, Leonard Cohen, and Kinky were my three favorite male songwriters and Joni, Joan, and Ronee my three favorite females and she said, 'Why do you make those distinctions?' "

T-Bone jumps into the fray. "Is this fucking tape recorder on?" he drawls. "What are you talking about?"

"We are talking about the battle of the sexes," Joni says mischievously. "He's making a distinction between male and female songwriters." Muffin points an accusatory finger at Ratso.

"There's no such distinction," T-Bone says solomonically. "When you get to the third realm, this is the realm of music. Sex becomes like ridiculous there."

"Sex lately has become very ridiculous," Ratso laments.

"But art can transport itself beyond gender and that's the point I think that you're overlooking, Ratso, by categorizing, by making a division between two groups of artists," Joni fumes.

"I'm talking about a finer distinction. You're distorting my position."

"You're distorting my position," Joni shoots back, "you're putting in a section—"

"In a section that's real good," T-Bone drawls.

"You've drawn the line," Joni ignores the joke, "you've compartmentalized me."

"Everybody does that," Ratso protests. "When people listen to your songs they don't say Bob Dylan wrote 'em they say Joni Mitchell did, first categorization."

"That's individuality, man," T-Bone drawls.

"Well, what else do we know about Joni?" Ratso lectures. "One thing is she's female."

"That's a broad statement," T-Bone notes.

"Another thing we see is a beret, she's a beret-wearing songwriter."

"You just don't know Joni well enough," T-Bone is shaking his head. "If you knew her you'd know she isn't a female."

"I stand corrected," Ratso bows.

"So what's your standpoint?" T-Bone presses.

"Well, it's irrelevant anyway, it's all great."

"All right," T-Bone laughs, "whoo. You're easy."

Ratso drifts off to watch the show but Joni intercepts him. "You are distorting my position, Joni," he scores first.

"No, I'm not," she maintains. "You're making a bigger distinction. Obviously you have more in common with Bob Dylan than I do with Ronee Blakley."

"She's got a lot to say," Ratso argues.

"Not to me," Joni shrugs. "She hasn't got anything to say in a melody sense. Wait till I teach you my tunes," Joni flashes.

Dylan's on now and Ratso rushes out into the audience. From behind the sound board, Bob looks like a walking garden, he's got about eighteen flowers in his hat, red, yellow, and white, plus a few peacock feathers. And he looks totally wasted, the voice rough and worn but oh, so sensuous. He reaches back to *Blonde on Blonde* for a compelling "Fourth Time Around," a song about the prostitution of the spirit, and then he waves the band off and does a second acoustic song, "Simple Twist of Fate," a song that reminds Ratso of that all-time great film *Children of Paradise*. And a chill runs down the reporter's spine as Dylan plays with the words like an alchemist plays with quicksilver.

Jack Baran's kneeling next to Ratso and he taps him. "He should do a whole set of acoustic material," Baran whispers. Ratso nods agreement. "What do you make of the hat?" Baran wonders. "You can't ignore it. It means something, he's never taken it off once, every show he's had it on." Just then, Ratso looks up and sees Lisa wander by wide-eyed, drifting toward the stage, wearing a hat with long peacock feathers.

"Look at Blakley," Baran nudges Ratso, "she's mesmerized every time she's on stage with Bob." Just then the lights flash on, and seven thousand people jump to their feet, screaming and clapping along to "This Land is Our Land," sending the two fans scurrying for the safety of backstage.

Ratso manages to bum a ride back to the hotel with Mike Evans, but first Evans has to see the local doctor who's been dispensing advice and prescriptions backstage. He's holding office hours in one of the locker rooms of the gym.

"I gotta get some speed," Evans whispers to Ratso, as they approach the medic. "I've got a problem, Doc," Evans starts.

"Do they have Quaaludes in Maine?" Ratso interrupts breathlessly. Evans glares at him.

"Have 'em but I wouldn't give 'em," the doc drawls in a New England accent.

"Doctor, I drive a lot and I usually get Dexamyl," Evans attempts again.

"You should stay away from those," the M.D. cautions.

"I usually don't get involved and I hate to use street pills. I just need something to help me drive."

"Well, you can't be sleeping driving," the doctor starts writing out a script.

"And I'd appreciate a script for Valium or something to help me sleep. We get so wound up after a concert it's hard to fall asleep."

The doctor complies.

"Could I get some Valium, too?" Ratso barges in.

"Of course," the doctor smiles, thinking that he could be sued for malpractice if he let Ratso go untreated.

The two gleefully run to Evans' car with their booty. "You missed a great card game last night," Evans reports as they barrel toward the hotel. "I was playing poker with five millionaires, Bob, Lou, Barry . . ."

"How does Dylan play poker?" Ratso interrupts. "Does he bluff a lot? He's always bluffing anyway. How's he do? Did he win?"

"I think he walked away minus a few dollars. Mooney won eight hundred dollars," Evans marvels.

At the hotel, Imhoff has prepared a little late-night snack in one of the convention rooms, and Ratso rushes in, grabs some food, and heads for a table. And there right across the table, looking striking in her silver-blonde hair, nice wool pants, and intense blue eyes, the same blue eyes, was none other than Beattie Zimmerman, a/k/a Bob's mom. Ratso introduces himself.

"Oh, you're the one that *Rolling Stone* doesn't like because he's writing too good things about Bob," Beattie gushes in her high-pitched resonant voice. "It's a pleasure to meet you."

Just then, Neuwirth ambles over to the table. "What did you think, Mom?" he says gravel-throated.

"Absolutely fabulous," she raves, pulling her glasses off. "Fabulous. I'll come again." Everybody cracks up.

Ratso starts to say something but Beattie cuts him off. "You sound miserable, dear," she worries. "What's that a cold you've got?"

"I think I've had it for a few weeks on and off," Ratso coughs, "my throat really hurts. What should I take for my throat?"

"Chicken soup," Beattie shoots back without blinking, "chicken soup, or tea and honey. Go get some of the soup," she lectures, pointing at the buffet table.

Ratso dutifully fills a cup and returns. "This is great, just like having my mother here," he smiles at Mrs. Zimmerman.

"I bet your mother took good care of you too," Beattie stands up for Jewish motherhood, "I bet she's a great cook too."

"When I was living at home I was twenty pounds heavier," Ratso admits.

"Oh, you got away from them so you could lose a little weight," Beattie cracks, eyes sparkling.

Just then, Kemp arrives, takes one look at Ratso and Beattie chatting away like they were members of the same ORT chapter, takes one look at Ratso's tape recorder lying there on the table, and freaks. He huddles with Imhoff, and a few seconds later Imhoff calls Ratso aside and suggests he move to another table. But the party is fading, and even though a bunch of musicians drift over to the adjacent ballroom and start a late-night jam, Ratso gets bored and falls out.

Next morning he gets up early and drives into town to find an open pharmacy. It's Thanksgiving Day, but luckily one drugstore is open till noon, and the young bearded pharmacist gets Ratso's script. It's obvious some of the others have found this place, too.

"It's another one of them," the pharmacist whispers to the druggist. "The same prescription as Baez and Sara Dylan." Ratso grabs his Valiums indignantly and heads back. But when he gets back, there's a huddle right in front of the hotel. Mel Howard, Johnson, Meyers, all the film faggots, as the crew calls them, are in troubled discussion.

Ratso pulls up. "That's it," Howard beams as he sees the reporter. "We can use Ratso's car." Meyers agrees. "But wait," Mel cautions, his eyes sparkling mischievously, "Louie might kill us if we let Ratso take Bob." "Fuck 'em," Meyers growls.

Ratso walks over to them. "Hey, Rats baby," Mel croons, "can we use your car for a scene today?"

"For who?"

"Bob," Mel whispers involuntarily.

"Only if I can come, I'm not covered for anyone else driving," the reporter says slyly.

Five minutes later, Howard and Scarlett are in the back seat and Dylan slides in next to Ratso. They follow the film van up a winding country road, finally stopping next to the bare shell of an old farmhouse. The light snow begins to intensify.

The car empties and Dylan leads the way over to the old house. It's an eerie sight, just the wooden beams and floor, a ghost house in the middle of barren winter forest. Perfect for a scene between the wandering hero and the gypsy girl he meets up with after many lifetimes. Meyers directs Scarlett to stand in the middle of the house, and Dylan tells her to start playing. She starts a slow, haunting melody on her violin, her hands numb and shaking from the bitter cold.

While the crew is getting ready, Ratso and Dylan retreat to the car, and its welcome heater. Bob wrings his hands in front of the heat and studies the old worn copy of Dante's *Inferno* in his lap.

"I finally figured it out," Ratso breaks the silence, "I realized why Louie doesn't like me. It's 'cause I'm a New York Jew, I'm pushy, I come from a lower-middle-class family, I'm hungry. But he's from the Midwest, and Midwest Jews are fucking closet cases. They're ashamed they're Jewish, they're just assimilationists. You know?"

Dylan just nods and continues reading.

"Louie thinks I'm just a *chozzer*, that I'm heartless, but I'm not, I'm just hungrier. I have some debts to repay, you see where I'm coming from? You see it from my perspective?" Ratso asks.

"What's that? From an out-of-work writer?" Dylan cracks.

"Fuck you," Ratso feels hurt.

"Well, all your favorite songwriters aren't New York Jews," Dylan argues. "Me, Leonard Cohen, Kinky. None of us are from New York."

"That's true," Ratso admits, and Dylan leans back in the seat.

"Is Pacheco Jewish?" he suddenly asks.

"No, but he's got a Jewish great-grandmother from Odessa," Ratso remembers.

Dylan goes back to his book, then gets called out for the scene. Ratso goes out to look, but the temperature must be near zero, and after a few minutes he rushes back to the car. Five minutes later, Dylan, Howard, Scarlett, and Ken Regan cram in and Ratso starts up, on the way to Bangor, where everyone else must already be enjoying the big Thanksgiving dinner prior to the evening's show.

"We must be late already," Dylan moans in the front seat and Ratso tries to accelerate, nearly careening the car into a skid. "Don't rush, Ratso, just get us there safely," he worries, looking apprehensively out of the window. In the back seat, Regan is snapping away, taking roll after roll of Dylan in the front, who looks like Quinn the Eskimo in a red-green-and-white-checkered coat with a fur collar, and a big Tibetan fur hat.

Mel starts discussing the film. "You know, Ginsberg wants to do a scene with you, Bob, acting out one of his fantasies."

"Which one?" Ratso asks.

"Allen's fantasy is to fuck Bob," Mel reports.

"No, no," Dylan whirls back, "not me. Ronson." He chuckles.

"Anyway," Mel continues after the laughter dies down, "he wants to shoot this scene where you and he are waking up together in the morning, this real tender aftermath scene."

Bob rolls his eyes and retreats into the seat, and in a few minutes he's fast asleep, followed by Scarlett and Mel. Ratso mumbles a silent prayer to Dexamyl, and plows on through the blizzard, on the way to Thanksgiving.

By the time they finally reach the party, most of the other eighty or so people have finished eating, and the kids, Dylan's, Baez's, actress Ruth's, are running rampant. The late arrivals find seats and Mel Howard calls for order. The film crew is about to start filming the proceedings and Howard is about to make a plea for spontaneity, a little like asking for pussy at an orgy. After his warm-up, he looks toward Dylan. "Who can give a little talk? How about you, Bob?"

Dylan looks like the shy one at the orgy. "Let my mother talk," he suggests, pointing toward Beattie, "I'm speechless." Beattie, who's never at a loss for words, promptly stands up and delivers a stirring Jewish-matriarchal-type tribute to all of the revelers, and gets a gusty ovation as she sits down. Ratso claps a few times then buries himself in his delicious turkey and stuffing, polishing off the huge plate in a matter of minutes.

The reporter walks over to where Dylan is standing, talking to Chesley. "How come we didn't do any shooting in Boston?" Ratso's been meaning to ask Dylan this for a while. "I did all that advance work, stayed up for days on end, got to know every hooker, pimp, transvestite in the area, and you never used any of it. What, were you just fucking me over, sending me to do that shit?"

Dylan shrugs. "Why don't you write a song?" he suggests.

"I think I will," Ratso smiles impishly.

"Oh, yeah, what are you gonna call it?" Dylan asks. " 'Jerked Off'?"

"No, I'll call it 'The Combat Zone,'" Ratso shoots back.

"Oh, yeah?" Dylan suddenly gets serious. "I like that. Hey, I'll help you write it."

"OK," Ratso smiles.

It's nearly time for the concert and as Dylan finally sits down and shovels down some cold turkey, most of the others are starting off for the hall, across the street. And what a hall. It was the strangest arrangement Ratso had ever seen. Perfect for a basketball game, with two long sections running high toward the roof facing the court, which was covered with chairs facing the stage. So most of the audience got a great view of the privileged few lucky enough to see the performers who were way off at one end. "This is just like Chicago," Beattie exclaims, craning her neck at the stands. Tonight, Ratso is going to help her babysit, and he dutifully follows her, the kids' granny, and the children to a special row of chairs that have been placed on the balcony in the rear of the hall, which, due to the bizarre dimensions of the place, are actually the best seats in the house.

They settle down and watch Guam's warm-up set. After a few numbers, Beattie leans over to Ratso. "What does Bob Neuwirth do?" she asks the reporter. "Can he do anything?"

Ratso blanches. "Well, he's a songwriter and he's responsible for this first part of the show. . . ."

"I didn't know," Beattie shakes her head, "I don't see him doing anything."

But the conversation is rudely interrupted by the appearance of her son on the stage. Beattie immediately turns back and glues her eyes to the small prancing figure. Dylan sounds a little weak, a little tired as he rushes through the first two numbers, but by "Hard Rain," which he dedicates to D. H. Lawrence, the momentum seems to be building. In fact, by the end of the concert, most of the staff and film crew have filtered up to the balcony. The kids, who'd been running or fighting in their seats, have all fallen asleep, leaving Beattie and Ratso a chance to concentrate on the performance.

Onstage, Bob starts into "Hurricane." "What did they

send him to jail for?" Beattie leans back and asks Ratso. "For defending his people," the reporter answers and Beattie gives a knowing nod and turns back to the music. At the end, the audience rises in a standing ovation and the singer's mother pops up, cheering the protest song. "Isn't it great." Ratso claps along. Beattie just shakes her head and hits a fist against her heart. "It leaves you weak. It leaves you weak," she says in wonder.

"When is 'Sara'?" Beattie suddenly asks. "Do I have enough time to go to the ladies' room? I had too much coffee." The band breaks into "One More Cup of Coffee" and Ratso can't resist the pun. "One more?" Beattie's eyes open wide. "I've already had six or seven!"

She visits the john, and comes back just in time for "Sara," Bob crouching down low, strumming furiously, pouring his heart out. He gets up to the line about writing "Sad Eyed Lady" and Ratso hits Beattie's knee. "Isn't it wonderful?" she shakes her head in awe, "this is the greatest love song ever."

During "Just Like a Woman," they make their move, shepherding the remaining kids backstage, and as the show ends Ratso slumps in the bleachers, taking a well-earned breather.

Everyone's forming a caravan to go directly over the border to Quebec tonight, the two buses, the campers, the Cadillac, the film vans, the support cars, and Ratso has been promised a spot in the procession. But there's a delay, so Ratso chats with Michael Ahern, the stage manager, who acquaints the reporter with the seamier side of the rock 'n roll life, the crew's perspective. It's fascinating talk, Ratso's enthralled, and a half-hour later, he jumps up and runs outside. Nada. "Motherfucker," the reporter screams to the cold Maine night, "they're gone. Like a fucking nightmare."

Ratso storms back inside, gets his things, gets last-minute directions from Ahern, and hops into the Monte Carlo. It's treacherous driving tonight, the soft dewy snow has now frozen into a slick ice layer and it takes him about ten minutes merely to inch down the steeped road leading to the arena. But when he reaches 95 and starts north toward Quebec, he realizes that there is something drastically wrong. The car won't stop, every time it's fed a little gas it lurches forward and continues to accelerate. Shit, the reporter curses to himself. Sabotage? The ultimate dirty trick. And such an old one, tamper a little with the car, make it impossible to drive, wait for the victim to start off, and an hour later he's cleanly eliminated, wrapped around a concrete abutment.

"Jesus, these guys are smart," Ratso says aloud, "pulling this in the most desolate area imaginable, right near the fucking Maine-Canada border. But they're not smart enough," and the reporter swerves into a wild U-turn and heads back to Waterville. After about two and a half hours of creeping down 95 riding the brake all the way, he limps back into the Howard Johnson's and gets his old room back.

By now it's 4 A.M., but with the mixture of the music, the prescribed drugs, the illicit drugs, and the paranoia, Ratso's wide awake. But what to do at four in the morning in Maine? Nothing but call some friends, and since it's only one on the coast, Ratso dials Mike Bloomfield, a great blues guitarist, who backed Dylan up at his first electric appearance in Newport and went on to play searing guitar on the legendary *Highway 61 Revisited* sessions.

"How you doing Larry," Bloomfield booms. "Where are you man?"

"In Maine," Ratso answers disconsolately. "I'm on tour with Dylan and the Rolling Thunder Revue. But it's been real weird. What was it like working with Dylan for you?" the reporter tries to compare notes.

"Well, Larry, the last time was atrocious, atrocious. He came over and there was a whole lot of secrecy involved, there couldn't be anybody in the house. I wanted to tape the songs so I could learn them so I wouldn't fuck 'em up at the sessions . . ."

"What songs?" Ratso shoots in.

"The ones that came out later on *Blood on the Tracks*. Anyway, he saw the tape recorder and he had this horrible look on his face like I was trying to put out a bootleg album or something and my little kid, who is like fantastically interested in anyone who plays music, never came into the room where Dylan was the entire several hours he was in the house. He started playing the goddamn songs from *Blood on the Tracks* and I couldn't play, I couldn't follow them, a friend of mine had come to the house and I had to chase him from the house. I'm telling you, the guy intimidated me, I don't know what it was, it was like he had character armor or something, he was like in a wall, he had a wall around him and I couldn't reach through it. I used to know him a long time ago. He was sort of a normal guy or not a normal guy but knowable, but that last time I couldn't get the knowable part of him out of him, and to try to get that part out of him would have been ass-kissing, it would have been being a sycophant, and it just isn't worth kissing his ass, as a matter of fact, I don't think he would have liked that anyway. It was one of the worst social and musical experiences of my life."

"What was he like?"

"There was this frozen guy there," Bloomfield says. "It was very disconcerting. It leads you to think, if I hadn't spent some time in the last ten or eleven years with Bob that were extremely pleasant, where I got the hippie intuition that this was a very, very special and, in some ways, an extremely warm and perceptive human being, I would now say that this dude is a stone prick. Time has left him to be a shit, but I don't see him that much, two isolated incidents over a period of ten years."

"What do you see as the cause of that?" Ratso wonders.

"Character armor. It's to keep his sanity, to keep away the people who are always wanting something from him. But if a lot of people relate to you as their concept of you, not your concept of you, you're gonna have to do something to keep those people from driving you crazy, but if that is so strong that you can't realize who is trying to fuck with you and who just wants to get along with the business, if you can't tell the difference, it's very difficult."

"How did you relate to him in the early days?"

"When I first saw him he was playing in a nightclub, I had heard his first album, and Grossman got Dylan to play in a club in Chicago called The Bear and I went down there to cut Bob, to take my guitar and cut him, burn him, and he was a great guy, I mean we spent all day talking and jamming and hanging out and he was an incredibly appealing human being and any instincts I may have had to try and cut him and slice him, which is very common in Chicago, it was a thing that almost all musicians did, and it wasn't really a mean thing, and any possible interest I may have had in doing that was immediately stopped, and I was just charmed by the man.

"That night, I saw him perform and if I had been

charmed by just meeting him, me and my old lady were
just bowled over watching him perform. I don't know
what, it was like this Little Richard song, 'I don't know
what you got but it moves me,' man, this cat sang this
song called 'Redwing' about a boys' prison and some funny talking blues about a picnic and he was fucking fantastic, not that it was the greatest playing or singing in the
world, I don't know what he had, man, but I'm telling you
I just loved it, I mean I could have watched it nonstop
forever and ever.

"The next time I saw him was at a party in Chicago and
he was traveling with a bodyguard, a big fucking Arab,
named Victor Maimudes, an Arab, and he was a bodyguard, that's what he was, I didn't know that then, what
did I know? I hung out with the niggers, what did I
know about him and his bodyguard, and he was trying to
get pussy and, believe me, he got a lot of pussy, and we
hung out at that party and we talked, blah blah blah, and
I was watching the bodyguard, the next time, I get a
phone call from him, would I want to play on a record
with him and I said, 'All right.' And I really didn't know
he was a famous guy, I really didn't know, I was so into
the black music scene and AM radio that I didn't know
this guy was famous.

"And I went to Woodstock, and I didn't even have a
guitar case, I just had my Telecaster and Bob picked me
up at the bus station and took me to this house where he
lived, which wasn't so much, and Sara was there I think,
and she made very strange food, tuna fish salad with
peanuts in it, toasted, and he taught me these songs, 'Like
a Rolling Stone,' and all those songs from that album
and he said, 'I don't want you to play any of that B. B.
King shit, none of that fucking blues, I want you to play
something else,' so we fooled around and finally played
something he liked, it was very weird, he was playing in
weird keys which he always does, all on the black keys of
the piano, then he took me over to this big mansion and
there was this old guy walking around and I said, 'Who's
that?' and Bob said, 'That's Albert,' and I said, 'Who's
Albert?' and he said that he was his manager, and I didn't
recognize Albert even though I had met him many times
before. He had short hair before and now he looked like
Ben Franklin, he looked like cumulus nimbus. I didn't

know who he was and I asked Bob if he was a cool guy and Bob said, 'Oh, yeah.'

"We fucked around there for a few days and then we went to New York to cut the record and I started seeing that this guy Dylan was really a famous guy, I mean he was invited to all the Baby Jane Holzer parties, and all these people would be walking around with him, and the Ronettes would come up to him and Phil Spector would be talking to him and I noticed that he and Albert and Neuwirth had this game that they would play and it was the beginning of the character armor, I think, it was intense put-downs of almost every human being that existed but the very few people in their aura that they didn't do this to. It was Bob, Albert, and Neuwirth, they had a whole way of talking, I used to be able to imitate it. David Blue is a very good imitator of it, as a matter of fact I don't even think he knows he's imitating it. It's just like this very intense put-down.

"And he was very heavy into drinking wine, to stay calm and loose I guess. We went to this Chinese restaurant and I started putting Bob down, playing the dozens with him and I did it all night long and he and Albert loved it, they were in hysterics because it wasn't the kind of putting down that they did, it was the dozens, and I talked about his momma and his family and everything, and I had a great time." Bloomfield cracks up at the memory.

"Do you really think . . ." Ratso starts.

"Oh, and then I remember one time Bob wouldn't eat and Albert took him to Ratner's and bought him plates of sturgeon and like mushroom barley soup and he was taking the sturgeon and just piece by little clump putting it in his mouth and saying, 'Eat, sturgeon, good,' I couldn't believe what I was seeing, it was so fucking far out.

"And we cut the album and that was extremely weird because no one knew what they were doing there. They had this producer who was as useless as tits on a pig, he was referred to exclusively out of his presence as Dylan's nigger, this big tall guy, a hillbilly, Johnston, he was a good old boy, no doubt about it. I mean there were chord charts for these songs but no one had any idea what the music was supposed to sound like, what direction it was, the nearest that anyone had an idea was Kooper and he was there as a guitar player, and as soon as I came in and started playing, he picked up the organ, he was a good organ player but it was weird for Bob. We were doing songs like 'Desolation Row' three or four times, takes and takes of that, and that's crazy, it's a long song. I mean the guy had to sing these fifteen-minute songs over and over again, it was really nuts. And the *schwartze* from Paul Butterfield, Sam Lay, was playing the drums, and the bassist was Russ Savakus, I think it was the first time he had ever played electric bass in his life, he had been a studio upright player for years and years, and it all sort of went around Dylan. I mean like he didn't direct the music, he just sang the songs and played piano and guitar and it just sort of went on around him, though I do believe he had a lot to do with mixing the record. But the sound was a matter of pure chance, whatever sound there was on that record was chance, the producer did not tell the people what to play or have a sound in mind, nor did Bob, or if he did he told no one about it, he just didn't have the words to articulate it, so that folk-rock sound, as precedent-setting as it might have been, I was there man, I'm telling you it was a result of Chuckle-fucking, of people stepping on each other's dicks until it came out right."

"You played with him at Newport, didn't you?" Ratso manages to slip a question in.

"Yeah, after that the next thing was Newport, meanwhile I joined the Butterfield Blues Band and Albert managed Bob and me, and I figured he's the manager, he'll tell me what band he wants me to play with best, he'll tell me where it makes the most sense. So my druthers was to play with Butterfield, I mean I had absolutely no interest in playing with Bob 'cause I saw that I would be merely a shadow. First of all, I'm a bluesman and the music would take me in no direction that I wanted to go in and I would be a shadow of this guy that I was finally beginning to see was an immensely popular star, and that held no interest for me at all. So we were in Newport and it sort of came down that I was gonna play with Paul, I was gonna join his band, and I think Bob felt betrayed or pissed, or he assumed I wasn't gonna play with him and I assumed that there was gonna be a business decision made by Grossman, but if I had my choice I was gonna play with Paul and I did.

"So we set up to play, and Barry Goldberg wanted to

play with Bob too, and we were all at Newport, Kooper, me, Barry, and this *schwartze* Jerome from the Butterfield Band playing bass, and he can't play and he's fucking up everything, and we're practicing there in a room and Odetta's staring at us and Mary Travers is there and we're playing and it's sounding horrible and finally it's time for the gig and Barry and me are throwing up in these outhouses, literally outhouses, built like wood shithouses and we're smoking joints and throwing up in there and we get up onstage behind Bob and we play and I think we went over fabulous. I had a fabulous time, I see the lights, the flashbulbs popping, I hear screams and yells. Did I in my wildest dreams, would I have known that we bombed? I thought, hey, rock 'n roll circus, man, heaven, and a year later I found out that we had bombed. I thought we were fabulous. And so Dylan goes up there again after we came down, he's got a yellow shirt on with a tie pin, he's dressed like a fucking Pachuco, some kind of Puerto Rican from the West Side of Chicago. He looked very weird with the black leather coat, the tie pin and the shirt without the tie, real spic clothes, so he goes up there and he sings 'Baby Blue,' or something, some folk song, and Peter Yarrow apologizes for him and I didn't even pay attention, see, I was there with the Butter Band and I was gonna play with Joan Baez, too, I was the only electric guitar player there, I would have played with anybody, did I give a fuck? And I thought we had done real well but apparently we had bombed. The next time—"

"What was Dylan's reaction that day?" Ratso interrupts.

"He was uptight all day. He was uncomfortable, I think he knew that this was a much more serious thing than I did. To play with anyone at a folk festival, I would have plugged my guitar into Pete Seeger's tuchus, really man, and put a fuzz tone on his peter. You know what fucking Pete Seeger was doing? He brought a whole bunch of *schwartzes* from a chain gang to beat on a log and sing *schwartze* songs, chain-gang songs, and he was doing that, can you believe this guy? Here's a white guy, got money, married to a Japanese woman, beating on a log with *schwartzes* singing 'All I hate about lining track, whack, this old chain gwine break my back,' actually saying 'gwine,' whack, and Seeger's doing this and he's pissed off at us for bringing electric guitars to the fucking folk festival. He brings murderers from a *schwartze* prison to beat on a log! Oh, I couldn't believe how fucking crazy it was, man!

"And fucking Theodore Bikel, he's drunk. But Albert was cool, though. He beat up Alan Lomax because Lomax gave the Butter Band this rank introduction and man, they had a stone fucking punchout, rolling on the dirt, Albert was really ballsy, kicked the motherfucker's ass, I loved it. He went to Lomax and said, 'You know, man, you're a dumb fucking prick' and Lomax suckerpunched him and Albert kicked his ass. I was delighted to see that."

"But didn't you get any feedback from Dylan right after?" Ratso tries to focus Bloomfield's narrative.

"No man, we thought we did great. Maybe Bob knew we were booed."

"What about the rumors that Bob was crying when he came offstage?"

"I didn't know, I was with Barry and I said, 'How do you think we did,' and he said, 'Oh, we were fabulous,' and I said, 'Yeah, I thought so too,' and then he's up there playing 'Baby Blue.' And when I saw him afterward, he looked real shook up and I didn't know the nature of what made him all shook up but the next night he was at this party and he's sitting next to this girl and her husband and he's got his hand right up her pussy, right next to her husband, and she's letting him do this and her husband's going crazy, so Dylan seemed quite untouched by it the next day.

"So the next time I saw him, I was playing with Butter in the Café au Go-Go and Dylan comes in with Robbie Robertson and he says, 'I want you to meet the greatest guitar player in the world,' and he introduces Robbie to me, Robbie who I had already known! And I'm looking at him and thinking, Oh, you little prick, you little dork, uh huh, this is where it's at, and oh God, it never got clear to me, if he wanted me to play with him he should have said, 'Man, I want you to get in the band with me.' He was talking about playing with this one and that one. He should have been real clear to me, 'Want a gig?,' 'Fabulous, how's it going down?' But if he had asked me I would have turned him down anyway 'cause I'm a blues player, I wouldn't have done it, who needs the craziness? It would have been crazy for me.

"So after that we like drifted apart, what was there to

drift apart, we weren't that tight, but after that when I'd see him he was a changed guy, honest to God, Larry, he was. There was a time he was one of the most charming human beings I had ever met and I mean charming, not in like the sense of being very nice, but I mean someone who could beguile you, man, with his personality. You just had to say, 'Man, this little fucking guy's got a bit of an angel in him,' God touched him in a certain way. And he changed, like that guy was gone or it must not be gone, any man that has that many kids, he must be relating that way to his children, but I never related to him that way again. Anytime that I would see him, I would see him consciously be that cruel, man, I didn't understand that game they played, that constant insane sort of sadistic put-down game. Who's king of the hill? Who's on top? To me it seemed like much ado about nothing but to Dave Blue and Phil Ochs it was real serious. I don't think Blue's ever escaped that time, in some ways it seems like he's still trying to prove himself to Bob. I know David's one of Bob's biggest champions."

Bloomfield pauses for breath and Ratso wonders how the guitarist evaluated Dylan's music over the years as opposed to the almost Reichian character analysis he was painting.

"Well, I love it man, I love *Blonde on Blonde*, I love *John Wesley Harding*, and I like that album with 'Day of the Locusts' and I love 'Spanish is the Loving Tongue' and I love *Self Portrait*, I even like *Blood on the Tracks*, God knows I couldn't play the fucking songs but when I heard the record I liked it. And yet, you know, none of those records are as good as they could be, none of them. I mean, if you look at his peers and look at what a Randy Newman record sounds like, or any good writer-singer, or a Band record, or a Leo Sayer record, I can't judge, it's like saying Rodgers and Hart, Rodgers and Hammerstein, both fabulous, but as far as producing records, Newman's records are the best-produced."

"Why do you think he pays so relatively little attention to that?" Ratso had been dying to ask that of someone close to Dylan's music, for years.

"Because the song's the thing," Bloomfield booms. "The medium isn't the message, the message is the message and the medium is sort of ignored and I can't understand it, because the nearest thing to a tight record was

Nashville Skyline and *Blonde on Blonde*. As a matter of fact, my favorite Dylan record of all is *The Basement Tapes*, it's got real good music on it, fabulous singing and good songs, good licks. I don't know why he does it though. I mean if I was Bob Dylan and the Beatles were making records like *Sgt. Pepper*, I would want to make a record that was slightly more representative of where rock music was going at that time and maybe he did want to do that but as far as I can see an album has never come out by Bob that was musically equal to the content of the songs or the lyrics. And strangely enough, except for rare occasions, I would rather hear Bob sing his songs than cover versions, but I'd rather hear Bob singing his material better produced.

"I mean even Leon Redbone's albums are better produced than Bob's. Why do you think, Larry? Or why does he have sessions with Eric Clapton there and there's thirty guitarists and that fiddler, she's not the greatest fiddle player that walks, I know fifty better fiddle players than her. What's the story? You must know. A friend of mine played at that session, he played acoustic guitar. He told me it was crazy, insanity reigned, just like that session I played in '65, twenty guitar players playing at once, no one knowing what was supposed to happen, who took what, where and when. Why? What do you think? I mean I'm all for random chance and a Cageian theory that out of randomness, some kind of magic may happen, but fuck, man, he's been in the studio enough times with Nashville guys to see where it's laid down without any randomness, to see what that's like."

"What do you think of 'Hurricane'?" Ratso asked, remembering a previous conversation in which Bloomfield had been very knowledgeable about Rubin's plight.

"I listened to 'Hurricane,' it's a good song, I hope the *schwartze* didn't do it 'cause if he did then it's a terrible song. It's a damned good song though, as a matter of fact, if I was producing that song I would have produced it as a reggae song 'cause that 'Hurricane' chorus always reminded me of something Mexican or Spicish, something reggae or spic. It bothers me. One could make a Dylan album that would be the definitive songwriter's album, the definitive one, the greatest one of all. His singing gets better every year, his voice gets better, more accomplished, his range gets better, and to hear it not utilized is an annoyance. But he must think that as long as he got songs, he got albums, long as he's got songs, he'll go in there and put them down, so he should record by himself, why fuck around? Let him either record by himself or record right."

"How did he contact you for the *Blood on the Tracks* thing?" Ratso backtracks.

"Someone from Columbia phoned and oh, it was so terrible, they told me that no one could come by the house, get everyone away, all the secrecy, who needs this? I've been with Mick Jagger, man, it wasn't like that, it was pretty comfortable, he was a normal old dude, man, I was with him with a bunch of people around and with no one around and he was cool both ways. It was very uncomfortable with Bob and very intimidating, you know how Bob sort of taps his foot, man, like that very hyper foot tapping away, it makes you very uncomfortable, like 'Let's get on with it.' But yet, get on with what? I couldn't correspond, I tried with all my soul, and I read in *Rolling Stone*, I swear if I'm lying I'm dying, how Eric Weissberg and the guys that played on *Blood on the Tracks* couldn't correspond either. They couldn't do it, the same thing happened to them, they couldn't play. Why? Why did he freeze up that way? I can't understand it, all it would take was a little time, not much, enough time to say, 'Hey Bob, listen, one song at a time, let me learn it, and when I know it I know it and it's done.' "

"Well, what was it like that day, I still don't understand."

"He took out his guitar, he tuned to open D tuning and he started playing the songs nonstop! And he just played them all and I just sort of picked along with it, and any attempt I made to say, 'Hey Bob, stop! Do it from the beginning so I could learn it' or 'Let me write a chart up, play it for me just verse and chorus,' but see, he was selling the whole song, and they weren't short songs. He was singing the whole thing and I was saying, 'No man, don't sing the whole thing, just sing one chorus and if it's not gonna change let me write it down so I can play with you.' And he didn't. He just kept on playing he just did one after another and I got lost they all began to sound the same to me they were all in the same key they were all long I don't know, it was one of the strangest experiences of my life. And it really hurt me. I don't mean it hurt my feelings, it hurt me though in some sort of way.

"He was pissed. I mentioned that I had done a session that took these horn players a whole long time to get the thing right and he looked at me and said, 'Uh huh, yeah, I know what you're talking about,' and he gave me a dirty look, he was sort of pissed that I didn't pick it up, but I don't know, maybe I just wasn't a quick enough study or whatever. But if I was gonna teach somebody my tunes, I wouldn't do it in that way, I would sit there slowly until they got it and then I would play it with them and when it was right, we'd know it and if they wouldn't get it after enough time then I would have said, 'Hey man, fuck you' and split. But it made me feel weird, this may have been completely in my mind, but I just felt this big wall, this enormous barrier that was so tangible that there was no way you could say, 'Hey man, how are you? You getting much pussy? Drinking a lot still? How are your kids? What's your scene?' because anything like that would seem like ass-kissing or an invasion of his privacy. It just made me feel very uncomfortable, Larry."

"He doesn't seem like that now," Ratso reflects, "he seems pretty loose, pretty accessible . . ." But suddenly, all the fuckups the reporter's encountered since that brandy-soaked night at the Kettle begin to flash before his eyes like trailers in a movie house.

"I feel the cat's Pavlovized," Bloomfield jumps in, "he's Tofflerized, he's future-shocked. It would take a huge amount of debriefing or something to get him back to normal again, to put that character armor down. But if he's happy, who am I to say? I can't judge if he's happy, this might be his happiness. And God knows I bear no grudges. But I don't know, I should know better. Were there times on the tour when he seemed accessible, stripped of that character armor, or is he just a very private person?"

Ratso flashes a look at the clock, it's after five now, and he remembers being left behind earlier by the caravan, and that long, treacherous drive, and shudders when he thinks about what might have happened an hour into the drive on the way to Quebec, and wonders just who had tampered with the accelerator, and remembers the sabotage in New Haven and the cracked-off ignition in North Falmouth, and for one brief chilling minute thinks that, yes, maybe this was a *Godfather* scene, and remembers Dylan's cherry-red Cadillac, and for one terrifying second

Ratso even thinks that yes, Kemp and Imhoff do look Italian. And he suddenly jerks the cover off the warm snug familiar Howard Johnson's bed, and then sighs. Relieved that there's no Appaloosa head staining the sheets, he slumps back onto the bed, pulls the covers a little tighter around him and answers Bloomfield.

"I don't know," the reporter shakes his head, "I just don't know."

12

Ratso woke up the next morning feeling much better, hopped into the car, and limped towards Quebec, again riding the brakes against a rampant accelerator. Right before the border, he pulled into an Exxon station.

Ten minutes later, the car is repaired, for the exorbitant sum of $7.50, and Ratso barrels toward the border. Miraculously enough, the cover letter from *Rolling Stone* is enough to get him zipped through before the customs agent can delve into his attaché case and find all the benzedrine that's disguised as Elavil. Late that afternoon, the reporter rolls into le vieux Quebec.

The Old World charm of this walled city within a city disarms Ratso and the hotel is the *coup de grâce*. It's built like an old fortress, with turrets, cavernous foyers, a beautiful archway entrance, and a multitude of Continental touches. Ratso unpacks and heads straight for the hospitality suite since tonight is an off night.

But there's little action, just Ronson, McGuinn, a few roadies, and old faithful Lisa.

Ratso grabs a handful of peanuts and scurries down to the lobby, nearly knocking David Meyers' camera out of his hands.

"Hey Ratso, we need a room to shoot a scene," Meyers starts and immediately the reporter dangles his keys in front of the cameraman's nose. "Just don't fuck with my notes and tapes," he cautions and continues down the hall.

By the time he returns to his room, the crew has made it almost unrecognizable. The beds have been moved apart, equipment is all over the room, his clothes are all strewn in one limp heap in the corner, and, indignity of indignities, all the French pornography that Ratso picked up at a little candy store just north of the border is now hanging lasciviously from every available wall, mirror, drape, and painting. Ratso just mumbles to himself, hops on top of a dresser, just below a torrid lesbian dildo scene, and whips out his notebook.

Dylan strides in, followed by Soles, Stoner, Mansfield, Ronson, and Regan, snapping away. Scarlett files in a minute later, just as they start into a torrid jam of "House of the Rising Sun," a musical segment meant to compliment a whorehouse scene that Sara, Joan, and some of the other women will shoot later. They do one quick take and break.

"What do you think?" Dylan asks around, then directs Ronson over to the electric guitar. They start up again and this time it's airier, lighter, with Stoner singing along on the choruses.

"The only thing a gambler needs is a suitcase an' his thumb . . ."

"Hold it, hold it," this distinguished-looking French-speaking man is running into the room, screaming at the top of his lungs, waving his arms.

"What happened?" Dylan, who'd been so involved in the music, suddenly finds himself singing alone.

"That's all, that's all," it's apparently the hotel manager, "we have too much noise in here." He's waving the proceedings to a conclusion, unaware that his entire diatribe is being filmed.

"Well this is my room," Ratso pipes in from his perch, "and these are my friends."

"Well, you stay here and your friends go someplace else," the bureaucrat decides.

"Can they stay if they're quiet," Ratso smiles sweetly, moving from in front of the lesbian centerfold.

"No, no," the manager explodes, gaping at the picture.

"How about if we play poker?"

"Too much people, no, too much people," he's screaming now.

"I have two beds," the reporter gestures toward the ambulatory mattresses.

"Let's do it *a cappella*, man," Stoner suggests.

"We got it," Dylan shrugs, "I think."

"Let's do it *a cappella*," someone repeats.

"Let's go outside and do it," Dylan smiles mischievously.

"Let's do it on the streets, man," Ratso raises a fist.

"Let's do it in Acapulco," one of the sound men cracks.

The manager departs and Ronson goes back to playing, picking out a searing blues line.

"Hey, Ronson's running on batteries," Stoner gleams, "they can't turn him off."

"They wouldn't do this in Maine," Ratso mourns.

"Yeah, they wouldn't do this in the Howard Johnson's," Stoner agrees.

The camera pans over to Ratso. "What's that behind you?" Meyers asks.

"Those are just my friends," the reporter looks embarrassed.

"Slocum, this is a helluva place you got here," Dylan shakes his head, scanning the room.

"Yeah, you invite us to your room and look what happens," Stoner snaps.

Sara, who had been sitting quietly next to a candle, seems bored and picks up one of the porn tabloids. Meyers zooms over and captures her.

Ronson starts noodling on the guitar again and the camera crew starts to break down the set. Dylan and Sara head for the door.

"Nice place you got, Ratso," Dylan shakes his head.

"It's not a bordello but it's all right," Sara offers. Ratso joins them and heads for the elevator.

"Where did you get that scarf?" Sara fingers the silk scarf Ratso picked up at the used clothing store in Boston. Just as he starts to answer, the elevator stops between floors.

"Oh no, I'm claustrophobic," Sara moans. "Breathe deeply," she instructs.

"Let's say 'Om,'" Ratso suggests, "that's what Ginsberg does when he gets mugged."

"I once got stuck in an elevator with a Christian Scientist," Sara shudders at the memory.

The door finally opens at 15, not their floor, but they rush out into the corridor. "You know, Bloomfield told me that he didn't hear anything about Rolling Thunder," Ratso tells Dylan.

"That's it, the Rolling Thunder Revue, nobody knows anything about it," Dylan says with a mixture of glee and despair.

They pass some elegant furniture and Ratso gets hungry eyes. "Let's rip this place off," he whispers to Dylan.

"Man, the place we shoulda ripped off was in Stock-bridge," Dylan gushes. "Were you there? Every piece in that place was an antique."

Sara departs to take a nap, and Dylan and Ratso continue on to the hospitality suite where a party of sorts is raging. Gerber and Zeller, two Quebec singers, are at the piano, belting out French songs for a bevy of listeners, including Joni Mitchell and Bob Neuwirth. Everyone else is lounging around, drinking and ogling Michelle, a statuesque blonde and the girlfriend of Zeller.

Lisa seizes the moment to run over to Ratso. "I don't like Ronee Blakley," she whispers, "she's all over everybody, she's so insecure. I like Roger though," she coos, eying the guitarist.

"What did you do, blow off Dylan?" Ratso looks stunned.

"He doesn't like me," Lisa laments, staring at the singer across the room.

"Well, what do you want from him? A fucking baby." Ratso rolls his eyes.

"I just want to be his friend, now, honestly. I learned my lesson."

"How?"

"When he told me to go back to school, that was a lesson," Lisa smiles, her eyes devouring the room, keeping tabs on Roger. Ratso just shakes his head and leaves the classroom.

The next afternoon, there's some shooting scheduled and Ratso drags himself out of bed, throws on some clothes, and stumbles over to a small cafe. He sits at a table in the rear, along with Joni Mitchell. Baran and Johnson are already there, setting up lights. Joni is sitting underneath a window, practicing a French folk song on her acoustic guitar.

"I love the word *malheureux*," she savors every syllable, "*malheureux. Malheureux.*"

"*Vous êtes malheureuse?*" Ratso asks.

"*Non, le chanson est malheureux,*" Joni responds.

"What's going on here?" Ginsberg ambles over, as friendly as a bear.

"Who knows?" Meyers shrugs. "We're supposed to do Joni's street music scene outside."

"You know that Leonard Cohen song, 'Please Don't Pass Me By'?" Ratso wonders.

"Yeah I know that one," Joni nods, and savors the ham and cheese hero that's just been placed in front of the reporter. "That looks beautiful," she coos.

"Want one?" Ratso inquires.

"Yeah," she drools, like a little kid.

"Could she have the same thing?" Ratso yells to the waiter.

"*Même chose*," Ginsberg adds professorially, then turns to Ratso: "*Même chose* is the same thing."

Joni orders a ginger ale and starts strumming. "Everyone thought you were out of it this morning," Ratso laughs, remembering the vain attempt to rouse the slumbering songstress.

"I was so out of it," she smiles, "I slept with my clothes on."

"We were banging on the door, we thought you obviously weren't in," Ratso laughs.

"I went to bed with my clothes on," Joni marvels. "T-Bone and I sat up and played music all night." Steve Soles joins the table, to confer with Joni about the scene.

"The song you got, Joni, maybe we could start fiddling around on that," Soles suggests.

"It's a great song," Joni's eyes widen, "I got a new verse to it, I just wrote a new verse to it," and she starts strumming frenetically.

I rolled right past a house on fire
In the middle of nowhere in the middle of the night

"No, no wait, let's see . . ."

I looked right at a house on fire
In the middle of nowhere in the middle of the night
And we rolled right past that tragedy
Till we pulled into some roadhouse lights
And a local band was playing
Locals were mincing and shaking on the floor
And the next thing I know it's you, coyote, knocking at my
    door
And you pin me in the corner and you won't take no
And you lead me to the dance floor and we're dancing
    close and slow
You got a woman at home and one for the night and
    another for the day
Why'd you have to get that drunk and lead me on that way,
    ha ha

You just picked up a hitcher, a prisoner of white lines on the freeway

Joni laughs and everyone around is stunned by the power of the new verse.

"Did I tell you I wrote a song?" Ratso asks Joni. "About the hookers in Boston. It's called 'Combat Zone.' "

"Yeah, you told me. Bobby's supposed to look at it or something, work on it with you?"

"That's what he said . . ."

"Yeah, it's hard to pin people down," Joni counsels. "T-Bone and I are supposed to be writing the ultimate armistice song for the war of the sexes."

Dylan still hasn't shown up yet, so everyone orders another round of drinks and settles in to the cozy wood-edged ambience of the cafe. "I had the strangest dream last night," Joni suddenly remembers.

"I dreamt that we were in a helicopter," Joni recalls excitedly, "and we rented a helicopter and we were flying over a reservation and it was dry like Arizona and the river had shrunk away, leaving kind of a sand delta, and behind it a cliff that was about the height of three men, and lined up all along the side of it were really old Indians in sleeping bags. I can remember even the arrangements of their figures, the ones that were standing and also the ones that were sleeping like in a natal posture and some of them had these olive sleeping bags and one of them was half unzipped and then the plane went over and they looked at it, you know, and I looked and one guy was sort of crying and all of a sudden his mood went really angry and behind him at a distance, an atomic bomb thing began to happen and the mushroom slowly unfurled then suddenly became a yellow and pink balloon, like a dirigible. It kept getting bigger and bigger and bigger and suddenly the crown of the explosion became a complete bubble and came drifting toward the helicopter.

"And it changed to blue-greens and it sucked me right out through the glass of the helicopter and I was like this against the bubble and sinking into it like an ameba. I had my legs apart too and all of a sudden I thought, at first I experienced it as pleasant and then I wanted to pop it like you would a bubble, so I took my fingernail and I sliced an opening in it and it began to gush air and take off like a balloon and then it stopped and it was still hanging there and I could see the fish and the Indians down below and I was still holding on to it and it was still like a regular balloon. It was strange." Joni shakes her head as everyone oohs and ahs.

Joni goes back to rehearsing "Coyote" then suddenly stops mid-verse. "When am I gonna sing in the streets?" she moans.

"Look at that," Ratso mocks, "she made it to the top and now she wants to sing in the streets."

"I want to sing my new song, that's all I care about."

"Wanna hear my new song, 'Combat Zone.' It goes:

> Rega just came in from the coast
> She had three kids and a husband that split
> She was looking for some honest work . . .

"Where she didn't have to show her tits," Joni giggles, propelling Ratso into a fit of sulking.

"What did Bob tell you about this scene in the street?" Larry Johnson is over, worrying about the waning available light outside.

Just as Joni runs down her concept of the street-singing scene, Sara and Bob walk in. Sara heads for their table.

"We just passed the Salvation Army, Ratso, and they were just closing, they just turned their lights off."

"Where?" the scavenger screams.

"I don't know, love, one of these blocks." She sits down next to Joni.

"We were just looking for you," Goldsmith, one of the cinematographers, screams at Ratso, "the scene with Bob worked out good, and he wanted you to be a photographer, a paparazzi, sliding down this huge bank."

"Meyers says they're doing my Hunter Thompson flip-out scene tonight," Ratso relishes, "they're gonna get me wired on coke and speed and I'm supposed to do the whole *Rolling Stoned* reporter trip."

"Ratso, you're gonna be a star," Soles smiles, "but keep it clean. This is a family movie."

Dylan has moved into the center of the cafe and he's sitting talking at a table. Meanwhile, Joni busies herself with her sign.

"Let's see . . . 'I am often blind,' no, 'I am sometimes blind,' 'I am blinded by the truth' . . ." she's fretting, pen poised over virginal paper.

"Too Leonardy," Ratso criticizes.

"I'm a prisoner of my passion. A prison of white lines."

"A prisoner of white crosses," Ratso smirks.

"Some women wait for Jesus," Joni starts singing a Cohen song. "Some women wait for Cain . . ." "When I took
mushrooms," Joni suddenly starts a story, "I fell in love
with Jesus, really. It was the first time that I ever understood that. I just kept saying I didn't know he was so attractive, nobody told me that he was so attractive."

She smiles and starts taping the sign which finally reads
"I am a Prisoner of White Lines on the Freeway." Ratso
takes a quick glance and spots Dylan, who's filming his
conversation with André.

"I'm just a prisoner," Joni barks in a gruff voice, "of
white powder." She goes back to tuning her guitar.

"I'm so glad to get out of the hotel," Sara sighs, just as
Joni starts into another run-through of "Coyote."

Larry Johnson walks over. "We lost the lighting," he
breaks it gently, "we'll do it in Montreal." Joni just nods
and plays on, running through all the three verses. She
finishes and the table applauds.

"I'd like to do a scene in blackface with a natural and
sing a sermonette," Joni fantasizes. "Look at all the trouble I've seen."

"Yeah, the Joni Mitchell Dream sequence," Goldsmith
enthuses. "Look, we have to make sure we do this scene,
we have to push to make sure we get it."

Joni nods, and they all get up to leave. Ratso hails a cab
and Joni, Sara, and Soles hop in for a ride back to the hotel. "What am I gonna do about this cold," Joni sniffles.

"Take a sauna," Ratso suggests.

"I don't have time for that. I can't shake this thing."

"She's got to go outside, love, she can't take a sauna,"
Sara gently chides Ratso. "Just borrow somebody's hair
dryer and take a shower."

"I got a hair dryer," Ratso boasts.

"You got one?" Joni and Sara blurt out simultaneously.

"I bought one finally. Joan kept on making fun of my
hair," Ratso smiles.

"What you need, Ratso, are some dreadlocks," Sara grins.
"Just don't bother combing it."

They arrive at the hotel and Soles and Mitchell rush
upstairs to get ready for the show, but Sara and Ratso

decide to shop a bit and go down to the lower promenade.

"So you want a ride to the show?" Ratso asks.

"Call me, love, I got my own name now. Harriet Blaze. Like a stripper." She smiles sweetly as they enter a tobacco shop.

"We need cigarettes," Sara announces, as Ratso paws through the magazine rack.

"What shit!" he screams. *"Hit Parader, Vogue, Beauty and Health Guide.* No porn. Wait a minute, you used to be in *Vogue,* didn't you Sara?"

"Yeah, when I was young," she smiles, and picks out a mild Canadian brand of cigarettes. Ratso rushes to pay. "You're trying to buy me all these lavish gifts, Ratso."

They head back toward the main lobby, small-talking. Suddenly Sara grabs Ratso's tape recorder. "You lied to me about recording my conversations," she says shrilly.

"I didn't lie, I told you I record everything, like a documentarist," the reporter sputters.

"I'm gonna pour Listerine all over your tapes." She feigns shock: "You're gonna put this out as a record."

Ratso points to the cavernous passageway they're walking through. "Yeah, the basement tapes. Then people will know you're the brains behind Pa."

"Well, that's not exactly the case," Sara smiles, as they head for their rooms.

An hour later, Ratso picks her up and after forty-five minutes and ten conversations in broken French, they finally locate the venue of tonight's concert.

And once again, tonight seems to be Baez's show, mainly because of the language barrier that forces the audience to respond to timbre and melody rather than lyrical forcefulness. Dylan tries by dedicating a song to Rimbaud, prefacing the dedication by saying, "I don't speak too much French myself."

Baez, though, connects from the outset with "Diamonds and Rust," which draws lusty cheers that get matched when she plows into "I Can't Help Falling in Love" in French, followed by "Joe Hill" dedicated "how you say, *pour les pauvres du monde."* But Dylan finally scores with the familiar "Just Like a Woman" and the upbeat Guthrie ending rouses the audience into a standing ovation. One that was hard-earned.

After the concert, Ratso gives Dave Meyers a ride back to the hotel. This is Meyers' last concert, the old cameraman was flying back to California tomorrow to start shooting a new Altman film, and the imminent departure was leaving him with the bittersweet taste of nostalgia. "Jesus, am I tired," Meyers slumps into the seat next to Ratso, and for the first time, pulls his black cowboy hat off his head, running a hand through his thinning silver hair.

"We're gonna miss you," Ratso says softly, to the one person who championed the reporter's cause throughout the tour, no matter what the political repercussions were. Ratso remembers Meyers' integrity, his bluntness, his warmth, his wit, his charm, and the reporter feels a lump in his throat.

"It's a weird letdown actually to have to leave the tour." Meyers shakes his head in wonder. "Last night was so great. That whorehouse scene you missed with Sara and Joan. I gotta shift gears now, I gotta do a feature with Altman, *Welcome to L.A.* with Sally Kellerman, Geraldine Chaplin, Keith Carradine . . ."

"It sounds like shit," Ratso sneers.

"No, it's good," Meyers says softly, and peers out of the window at the narrow streets of Quebec City.

"Well, I really owe you a lot," Ratso notes, "you paved the way for the acceptance I've gotten on the tour now. Shit, Mooney came over to me tonight and shook my hand and told me that he respected me for hanging in there. Even Louie's calling me Ratso now, that's a good sign. And fucking Imhoff actually lent me fifty dollars tonight so I could fly to Toronto instead of having to drive five hundred miles."

"Jesus," Meyers grins. "Imhoff doing that, that's the ultimate accolade." They both laugh as Ratso parks. "We'll see you sooner or later," the reporter hugs Meyers.

"Yeah," the filmmaker smiles and heads toward the bar, for one solitary drink before he walks away from the Thunder.

The next day Ratso finds himself on a plane to Toronto, seated next to Greg Mallozi, the sound man.

"One thing I gotta say for Imhoff is this fucking thing is actually being pulled off, to a lot of people's unhappiness, but that's not the point, the point is it's happening. A lot of people are pissed off," Greg relates, "a lot of musicians are pissed off. I had been working for the newsletter but I gave it up because I found that really unpleasant things aren't printed in the newsletter, plus the fact the crew doesn't even get the fucking newsletters."

"Are you guys real niggers?" Ratso's been wondering.

"I get paid well. Better than some of the guys in the band. Nobody makes less than three hundred dollars a week, maybe some new guys, plus per diem. Fuck man, those fucking technicians know what they're doing. You can pick up a bass player in any city, man. I deserve everything I make and more."

The No Smoking sign goes out and Greg pulls out a Marlboro. Ratso declines one. "My guys are coming in from San Francisco tonight, we're going into such a big hall that we get supplementary sound. Eighteen thousand seats, man."

"What happened to the small-hall concept?" Ratso moans.

"Look, my feeling is whatever the fuck is going on on this tour, Imhoff has to make his bread on ticket sales. He's only contracted for the tour part of it. The movie can make lots of money but it's not on the same budget. He's got to make it on the tour itself and the tour was so expensive to produce. That's my interpretation of double fucking shows. Baez is getting lots, most of the band is eating it moneywise, though."

"What?"

"Dig, the whole band except for Ronson is basically unknown so they're all doing it almost for nothing, for the shot to be with Dylan. They're doing it for the résumé. Everybody's eating it on this tour, man, Barry's playing that so well. Doing it cheap, losing money on it, 'cause it's Dylan, man. It's Dylan. Every promoter is eating it, know how that works. Usually there's a guarantee and after 60 percent of the house is sold then the act gets 80 percent of everything. That guarantees the promoter'll make money and then the band gets more if they draw better. This is a flat fee, man, the promoter goes. We even sell the tickets, that's what Seltzer's for. He's the best in the Bay Area, he knocked Ticketron out of the Bay Area. This tour everybody's the best, best lighting designer, best sound man, so there's a certain ego trip behind that. Usually we were the best person in our show, which is why we were brought in, 'cause we're the best. But we're not getting any kind of recognition. I've never seen such poor morale on a tour."

Ratso downs his third martini, as the stewardess announces the landing. They fasten their belts.

"Isn't Elliot great, man?" Greg smiles. "You know, even though we play eighteen-thousand-seat halls, man, there's some element of the concept always there, always there somehow. It's available if people's heads are into it. No one is really being bummed out, on this tour they've created an arena or a forum in which that can happen and if it doesn't happen it ain't because of Barry Imhoff, man, it's 'cause the band isn't into it."

But Ratso was too preoccupied to hear Greg's last remarks. He was leaning against the window, savoring the bright lights of Toronto, thinking about the hotel and thinking about the Gardens and thinking about a whirlpool and the world's largest flea market.

In fact, Ratso remembers little about Toronto. He mainly recollects the amazing Jacuzzi at the Harbour Castle Hotel, a place where he spent hours and hours and hours drying out and letting the sensuous million little jet streams massage him into bliss. And the phones, yes, he remembers the phones. The phones at the Harbour Castle ring in the bathroom, and the bathroom phones are placed so low that they're obviously not meant to be used while one is shaving or combing one's hair. Ratso remembers them so well because he spent almost as much time on the phone in the bathroom as he did stretched out in the whirlpool. But as for anything else, it all remains a haze. An alcohol haze. A Valium haze. A Dexamyl haze. An adrenalin haze. A Quaalude haze. And a marijuana mist. But there were some things worth remembering.

Bobby Neuwirth's freak-out scene wasn't one of them. It happened that first night that Ratso picked up his keys and settled into his opulent room at the Harbour Castle, a towering beautifully modern hotel right on the water. Neuwirth had been drinking, drinking hard, and the legendary Ronnie Hawkins, a fast-talking, hard-drinking, frequently fucking hillbilly singer who had loaned his band, The Hawks, to Bob Dylan back in '66, the rest being, of course, history as the Band established themselves as America's premier group, the Hawk was jiving and joshing up in Neuwirth's hall, and the film crew was sitting around, ready to shoot a few minor scenes, and it seems that Neuwirth decided it was time for some Rolling Thunder psychodrama.

At least, that's the way it looked when he staggers over toward Ronee Blakley's suite, barefoot except for his chicken feet socks, clutching a Southern Comfort bottle. "C'mon Ronee," he's screaming in his hoarse voice, "c'mon out." Suddenly, Neuwirth flings the bottle through the open door, shattering it into a million pieces against the wall of the suite. Blakley comes running out in her nightgown and socks. "C'mon, make your Bette Davis entrance," Neuwirth is goading, as the cameras roll. "Lay off," Ronson is trying to restrain Neuwirth. "Do Tennessee Williams," the inebriated singer shouts.

"Fuck off," Blakley hisses.

"You're the only one who would fuck me," Neuwirth laughs and then stumbles the other way. Dylan, who's been eying this carefully, standing stonefaced in black leather and fur cap, starts to smile as Neuwirth throws his arms around Hawkins, who's resplendent in suspenders that barely span his huge girth and cowboy hat. "Nobody can outdrink you Hawkins," Neuwirth admires.

"Are you kidding?" The Hawk sneers, "Johnny Cash even is afraid of me and he carries two Bibles. I'm a teenage idol, the working girl's favorite."

"He's the only one that can make Robertson play boogie guitar behind his back," Neuwirth compliments The Hawk, "he's the only one that can make Robbie grin."

Ratso sits down in the corridor next to Stoner and Muffin, and watches Neuwirth slowly pass out, sliding down the wall into a graceful semifetal position. But two minutes later, he's up again, prancing down the hall with his arms around Ronson.

"I see you finally found a fag," Stoner cracks, and Neuwirth begins to summon the film crew. "C'mon you assholes," he drops to his knees pretending to go down on Ronson, "film it." He gets bored with that after a few seconds and tries to enter the hospitality suite, but Chuck, one of the security guys, bars him, so Neuwirth wanders over to Ratso and Stoner. "Eat Muffin," he directs Stoner. "I can't eat her, we'd lose our G rating," Stoner smiles. "Then blow me while I eat her," Neuwirth suggests and then disappears down the corridor. Stoner's still laughing when Neuwirth rolls by, stretched out on a dolly. "Jesus," the bass player shakes his head, "this whole scene is right out of Dali."

Suddenly Louie comes down and sizes up the scene. "Where's security?" he asks Ginsberg, who's been fretting to everyone about Neuwirth's behavior. "He's not conscious," the poet worries, "he needs a blackout scene." Just then, Neuwirth grabs a lamp in his room and shatters it against the wall into thousands of pieces.

Ratso also has a very vague memory of a party later that night, a party at Gordon Lightfoot's palatial digs in a suburb of Toronto, a party where Neuwirth fought off three security guards at the hotel, commandeered a cab, stumbled in to Lightfoot's and finding the gathering a little too staid, proceeded to throw his down jacket into the fire, sending billows of ashy smoke all over the house, and sending big Gordon into paroxysms of laughter. But it wasn't a good party, Dylan was shooting a quiet let's-all-sit-down-and-pick-our-favorite-folk-tunes-scene with Gordon upstairs in a sealed room that was guarded by Gary. So Ratso was reduced to nibbling cheese in the kitchen, and hustling this beautiful, dark Jamaican Jewess, who eventually accompanied him back to the hotel and performed some tricks that even in his brainblotted state, he would never forget.

The next day, Ratso stumbles out of bed and falls down to the lobby, where Dylan and Alk and Howard are set to do some shooting during the beautiful, crisp Toronto afternoon. The reporter follows along as Dylan and Howard do a chase scene, running onto buses, down streets, through the bustling downtown avenues, followed throughout by the persevering Paul Goldsmith, and Ken Regan. After a half hour's worth of this zaniness, they walk back to the hotel, the chill cutting right to their bones.

Ratso catches up to Dylan and they walk together in silence for a few minutes. Suddenly Dylan stares at the reporter. "Hey, Ratso, we're counting on you to set the record straight in this book now."

Ratso just smiles and thinks about the thousands and thousands of myths, rumors, gossip, and vicious pieces that have appeared about this little guy walking beside him.

"Don't worry, I tell it like it is," Ratso smiles, "it's all going in, all that shit with *Rolling Stone,* that petty bureaucratic shit about how much money you're making . . ."

"Well, use that before the book," Dylan interrupts. "Why don't you use that in a magazine piece?"

Ratso just smiles and scribbles away in his pad, his hands freezing. Dylan looks concerned. "Hey man," he says peeling off his gloves, "why don't you wear these if you gotta write." Ratso pulls on the gloves, and Dylan stuffs his hands into his pockets.

"Great," Ratso smiles, "I can sell these for one thousand dollars if I get desperate."

"Just remember," Dylan pleads, "we're counting on you with this book. We're counting on you to set those bureaucrats straight." They both chuckle and walk into the hotel.

In the lobby, Sara is waiting with Helena Kallianiotes, a Hollywood actress who, along with Harry Dean Stanton, flew into Quebec to act in the movie. Helena's a hard-edged Greek beauty, reminiscent of a female Brando. Today, she and Sara are going to be filming, but nobody seems to know what.

They stroll out into the street, Sara in a funky brown leather jacket, Helena in denims and a low-cut blouse. "OK," Dylan prompts, "this is gonna be an escape scene. Like from reform school, but you don't have to mention reform school. Just think of it in your head as a reference." The two women nod. "It's great to get out. The guard never fed you right. He never delivered any letters out." Sara and Helena confer among themselves and Dylan sets up the shot, the two girls running down the block to the safety of a boat-restaurant docked next to the street.

They do two takes of the dash, Sara running like a fawn. "OK," Bob announces, pleased, "I think we got it." He walks into the restaurant and freaks. "Jesus, this is fantastic here," he gushes, gaping at the huge side windows that look out over the water. Dylan directs Sara and Helena to a table and peers over Goldsmith's shoulder as they set up the scene. "Man, we couldn't buy this scene," he whispers. "Let's get some shots of them without drinks so we can see that view." But the girls first depart for the ladies' room, to do some last-minute makeup.

"Where'd they go?" Dylan frets a few minutes later, worried about the late-afternoon light disappearing. "We're losing it," Goldsmith shakes his head. "We don't even need dialogue," Dylan marvels at the view. "Can we get those precious girls?" Ratso volunteers to run down to the bathroom. "This shit'll break my heart if we don't get it," Dylan moans.

"Where do I sit?" Sara wonders, as they file back in.

"Just sit," Dylan urges.

"Aren't we gonna talk to each other," Sara seems confused, but Bob just starts the cameras rolling. After a while, they break, and set up the table with the usual settings. Sara demurely grabs a rose and places it in front of her, giving herself a contrast to the hard-edged toughness Helena projects. Dylan crouches down in front of them, and works out a quick improvised scene.

"OK, you know a rock writer in Arizona," Dylan suggests.

"Let's just take it from there," Helena wants to wing it totally.

"How about, 'I know a rock writer in Arizona. Mr. Tambourine Man,' can you get that in there any way?"

"Sure," Helena barks, "his name is Slim Tambourine." She gnaws on her lip, thinking.

They start the scene, apparently one of the girls is going to travel on, leaving the other behind. "I don't know where I'm going," Sara moans.

"I'll see you another time," Helena quickly becomes tender.

"When?" Sara whines. "Maybe never."

"Yes I will," Helena comforts. "You see people."

"You'll see me in Babylon," Dylan whispers from the side.

"It's all a circle," Helena adds.

"It's a spiral," Dylan prompts.

"Just go sit on the rock and put your thumb out," Helena counsels. "That's your weapon, use your mind."

"How do you get there?" Sara shivers.

"OK, CUT!" Dylan shouts. Helena seems miffed. "I can't see the development of character," she fumes, then jumps up and stalks to the other side of the room, shaking her long thick mane. Dylan rushes over to stroke her.

"Let's do it once more," he comes back. "How about this, man. Baran's a truck driver."

Baran who had been sitting at a table, drinking coffee, reluctantly agrees. "You're driving a truck from Nova Scotia to Arizona."

"For Kemp Fisheries," Jack joshes.

"Anything you want," Dylan seems impatient. "You ask the girls if they want a lift. Which goes with you?" Dylan strokes his chin.

"I'll leave Sara," Helena suggests, "then she gets involved with talking to Jack."

"Right," Dylan seems displeased, "I hope it works."

That night Ratso rides to the concert with Sara and Helena, who seems to be a bit bummed out by the scene. Inside the Gardens, he's all over the place, interviewing vendors, talking to ushers, getting the concession office opened up so he can buy some Maple Leaf souvenirs, including a hockey stick that he gets autographed by Leafs' captain Daryll Sittler that he gives to Dylan's son Jesse.

At the finale, Ratso runs up to the front and gapes at an amazing sight. Somehow Beattie has made her way onstage and is up there front and center, leading the troupe through their paces. The reporter marvels at the sight of this display of family unity then joins the troupe for the mad dash to the bus. Tonight there's at least thirty kids waiting at the backstage entrance, all cheering as the musicians file onto the bus. Ratso runs with the pack, and jumps onto the crew bus.

But in the lobby, a surprise was in store. The CBC producer that had been hanging around the hotel earlier that day had evidently gotten permission to go ahead with his parody of a Hollywood opening and the lobby is filled with shills, curious onlookers, Thunder groupies, and hotel patrons who are drawn to the myriad of klieg lights and the fat woman in evening gown who calls herself Sheila Shotton, and who looks like a cross between Kate Smith and Hy Gardner.

"This is Sheila Shotton, covering the Bob Dylan concert. We're waiting breathlessly for Bob Dylan and his revue to arrive here after their concert in the Maple Leaf Gardens and here they come right now . . ." She's almost screaming as the first arrivals stomp off the bus and walk into this surreal scene. Huge cheers arise from the crowd and Sheila starts to grab at the nearest Thunderers, snaring a film crew member who claims to be Bob. After a few seconds, she gives up on him and grabs Ronnie Hawkins, who's also claiming to be Bob and who pulls Ginsberg into the camera. Allen immediately starts an

impromptu song about being in Toronto, to the cheers
of the heterogeneous audience.

Ratso is just now coming off the bus, unaware of the
proceedings, when Howard Alk and Mel Howard come
running up. "Ratso," Howard grabs the reporter, "go in
there and be Bob. Do the whole shtick, it's that BBC
parody and you should be Bob."

Ratso just nods and grabs David Mansfield's violin case.
He pulls his Norwegian hat over his brow, adjusts his
scarf, buttons his long army coat and lopes over to the
waiting interviewer.

"And here he comes now . . ." she starts, and the shills
from the film crew start screaming "Bob," "Bob," "Hey
Dylan." The place is in a frenzy.

"Great to be here, great to be in Toronto," Ratso says
in his best Dylanesque.

"Are you really the real Bob Dylan?" Sheila looks a little
baffled. "Everyone's been giving me such a hard time . . ."

"Well, nobody's the real Bob Dylan," Ratso gets the in-
flection right on the button, "but I've got a Toronto Maple
Leafs shirt on, though." He pulls his coat open to reveal
the T-shirt.

"Well, that's great," Sheila bubbles, "what number are
you?"

"Well, what's your name?" Ratso peers at her, as if
seeing her for the first time, rocking back and forth like
he's seen the singer do countless times.

"My name is Sheila," she coos.

"Sheila, huh, what do you play, Sheila?"

"I play myself."

"Not who do you play . . ." Ratso frowns.

"What I really want to know is what the real you is,"
Sheila gushes.

"*Highway 61*," one shill screams out.

"The inner part, the true Bob Dylan," Sheila continues.

"You're getting a little personal there, Sheila," Ratso/
Dylan blanches.

"Well, what is the first song that you wake up to in
the morning?" the interviewer tries again.

"Uh, 'Early Morning Rain' by Gordon Lightfoot," the
singer shoots back.

"What's the first thing you eat in the morning?" she
continues.

"Hot chili peppers," Ratso smiles, and looks knowingly at Louie Kemp, who's been observing the interview from a vantage point right off camera, "then I have some smoked salmon. Then I'm inspired enough to write."

Sheila starts into another question but Ratso/Dylan is too quick. "Hey we gotta go now, Sheila, it's been great. Take care," and the reporter-cum-singer scurries through the crowd, to a torrent of cheers, whistles, oohs and ahs. Ratso lingers a bit until the final scene is shot, Sheila being carried away by security, and then he wanders back into the crowd. Several of the film crew are in the midst of congratulating him when a small Toronto woman comes up and asks him for an autograph for her son. He complies by signing one of her checks. After a few minutes of this, he scoots upstairs to his room and rings up the real Dylan.

"You shoulda seen this scene we just shot," Ratso screams, "a big Hollywood-opening-type thing in the lobby for CBC. I played you, man, it's on TV tomorrow."

"On TV? Where? They thought it was a real Bob Dylan interview and it's going out all over the world?" the singer moans.

"No, just CBC. It was a parody. But I imitated you great," Ratso boasts.

"Oh yeah," Dylan sounds bored. "Well, what was it like?" His voice seems to be an equal mixture of ennui, weariness, and sarcasm. "What was it like being Bob Dylan? I wish you'd tell me."

The next day Ratso recuperates in the wonderful whirlpool. He just lies there for an hour, joined at times by Chesley who is drying himself out by going from the whirlpool to the pool to the sauna and back out to the Jacuzzi. Ratso just lies there in the whirlpool and mumbles every once in a while to punctuate Chesley's far-ranging anecdotes about life with the Grateful Dead, a group he was associated with before he linked up with Jamblin' Rack, as Chesley liked to call the folksinger.

"Where's Fritz Perls when we need him?" Ratso moans, as he and Chesley paddle around in the whirlpool.

"Are you kidding? This is Fat City baby," Jack's road manager smiles contentedly, "fat fucking city."

Just then, Sara strolls in, wearing a Rolling Thunder T-shirt and looking just like a ghost. "I'm wiped out," she moans and sits down at the desk near the pool. Ratso regales her, Chesley, and Ryan the masseur with his story about the Jamaican Jewess. "That's nothing," Ryan frowns, "the best Jew is a Scottish Jew, then they're wild and tight."

Ryan blows on a while, talking about the massage he gave Baez, the therapeutic value of sex in Jacuzzis, and about the strange living relationship he has with his wife. They both live with other lovers and get together on the weekend. Suddenly he turns to Sara.

"Are you famous?" he asks.

Sara just frowns and turns to Ratso. "Am I famous?" she smirks. Ryan doesn't pursue it and starts talking about her husband without realizing who he's talking to. "I don't like that Dylan. He's got that little adenoidal whine." Ratso finds it hard to suppress a giggle but Mrs. Laundry comes to the rescue. "Yeah," she smiles, "he is kvetchy isn't he?"

Ryan gets up and heads into the locker room and Ratso and Sara start back toward their rooms. "I'm sick of wearing him on my chest," Sara joshes, looking down at her Rolling Thunder T-shirt. "When is he gonna wear me on his chest?" They head up to Sara's room, since Ratso is out of shampoo. She disappears into the bathroom and re-emerges with a bottle of Head, an organic shampoo. "Take this, love, it's all I've got, there's not much left in the bottle."

"Sara," Ratso coos wide-eyed, "can I tell anybody you gave me some Head?" She frowns and he peeks into the bedroom. "Jeez, I wish I had my tape recorder with me," he sighs. "You must have it under your bathing trunks," Sara cracks. "I can't believe you're a reporter. I hate the press." She shakes her head.

Ratso seizes the opportunity to peek under the hot platter at the remains of Bob and Sara's dinner last night. "Ratso," Sara screams. "Bob'll kill you if he finds out."

"I'm just hungry," Ratso whines, "I just want something to eat. These fucking potatoes are cold." He picks up a mushroom, peers at it for a while, then plops it into his mouth. He grabs a bottle of wine.

"Not bad," the reporter whistles, "1971. This shit—"

"Take it, take it," Sara's screaming. "C'mon, Ratso, go take your shower." The reporter dutifully complies, with his wine and Head in tow.

That night, before the concert, Ratso decides to go

shopping on Yonge Street, Toronto's equivalent of Greenwich Village and Times Square combined. He wants to
get some books as presents for the performers for their
train ride to Montreal tomorrow, and he also promised
Dylan he would look for some elk buttons for Bob's winter coat. After a half hour's search he doesn't find them,
but he winds up with a huge furry burnt-sienna vest, and
an authentic raccoon hat complete with tail, making the
reporter look, as Dylan would later describe him, like a
sheep in wolf's clothing.

Ratso grabs a cab, rushes back to the hotel, drops off
the three shopping bags of books, and speeds back to the
Gardens. As he comes in, Roger McGuinn is onstage.

"What'd I miss?" he screams at T-Bone, who looks especially odd tonight.

"Nothing, man."

"How come you're not up there?" Ratso suddenly realizes the guitarist usually plays on this number.

"I took myself out of the show," Bone groans, "I was
too weird." Up onstage, Neuwirth puts his arms around
Baez after McGuinn concludes his number. "Let's show
them some positions," Bob ogles, as Goldsmith and Michael Wadleigh shoot the proceedings from the pit.
Neuwirth's arm goes around Baez forming some weird
sort of position, somewhere between the Kama Sutra and
a hammerlock. Joan blanches. "There goes the ol' Madonna right down the tube."

Neuwirth just chuckles and pats Baez's belly. "I'm not
pregnant," she gets mock-offended, and some people begin to clap their displeasure. "You must be drunk," she
leers at Neuwirth, "they're filming you, that's why you're
so weird."

Neuwirth just continues to pat her belly. "She's hard as a
rock," he notes approvingly.

"Too bad I can't say the same for him," Joan sneers
and brings the house down. "We could have a very interesting meditation at this point," she continues in perfect
guruese, "I think perhaps we could be spiritually, er, I
think that the Western country needs more spiritual
concentration, more spiritual concentration on the material. If everyone would turn to the person next to him
and say something disgusting I think perhaps the spirituality of the entire nation could be raised."

The crowd titters and Baez returns to normalcy and introduces Gordon Lightfoot, who gets an amazing ovation. He lights into his huge hit "Sundown," and everybody starts to clap along. Especially the silver-haired sixtyish-looking woman in the front row, who at the first notes is bouncing up and down on her white go-go boot heels, waving her arms in wild abandon, and shouting at the top of her lungs, "Gordon, Gordon." Lightfoot looks down and smiles at the grotesque near-senile teenybopper. And she's really going at it, dancing on the pit rail, flinging her fur hat off, kicking high like a Rockette in her flaming red outfit. Ratso rushes over and cracks up at her long underwear that gets revealed every time she does a high kick.

But it apparently isn't that funny to the management and after a few minutes of this, an officious young usher goes to escort her back to her seat. And gets met with a solid pocketbook in the head. The documentary crew rushes over and gets a few feet of film, but even they get met with curses and a few roundhouse rights.

Which prompts Gene, the burly security man, to make a headlong dash across the front of the audience, snatch her up as if she were an offside kick, never breaking stride until he crosses the goal line on the other side. At which point he gently deposits her down, right next to Ratso.

"Those fucking bastards," she's screaming incoherently, just as the Stadium security in the form of huge lumbering Royal Canadian Mounted Police come up.

"OK, let's go, you're going with us," they collar her and head for an exit.

Ratso runs along, screaming out a request for an interview, and promptly finds himself booted out along with her.

After a half hour talking to her, and getting booted out of the first restaurant they encountered, Ratso's still puzzled that this obviously notorious public enemy was able to penetrate the defenses of the RCMP elite. "How'd you get into the Gardens in the first place?" he queries the celebrated deviant. Margaret, as she's called, just smiles and slyly looks down at her white go-go boots. "It was easy. They just let me in when I told them I was Bobby Dylan's mother."

Ratso waves farewell to Margaret and starts back to the Gardens. Walking in the rain, he sings to himself and

walks around the corner to where the campers are parked.
The show won't break for about a half hour but already
there are at least twenty people waiting by the stage door.
Mostly young tennyboppers waiting for Ronson, or Mc-
Guinn or Dylan or Lightfoot, but Ratso gravitates to
one neatly dressed guy, around thirty, who's waiting all
alone. The reporter sidles up to him.

"Are you waiting for something here?" Ratso asks
innocently.

"Yeah, Bob Dylan is going to come out this way," the
man says.

"Oh, did you see the concert?"

"I saw it last night," he tells Ratso and the reporter proceeds to recount his experience with the RCMP.

"You got a car?" Ratso asks and the guy nods yes, so
the two repair to a Volkswagen parked across the street.
Roy, a government worker, introduces himself to the
journalist.

"What's your story?" Ratso wonders. "Why are we sitting
here in this fucking Volkswagen, with the heater on, at
the stage, waiting for, waiting for, er what?"

"Well, I just went to the concert last night," Roy explains
in soft, precisely measured tones, "and I like Mr. Dylan's
work a lot. I like Baez too, but I thought the concert
would have been a bit better. Anyway, Bobby does a lot
to instill the emotion of hope and I think he's really important in society today."

"Have you admired his work for long?" Ratso asks.

"I go back to '64, the first time I remember hearing
Dylan was 'Like a Rolling Stone' on the radio." Ratso
laughs to himself at the coincidence. "That was the first
eleven-minute song, back then that was really something
important, but it was the lyrics that kind of got to me."

"What is he saying to you?" Ratso wonders, thinking
of someone who would voluntarily wait in the minus-ten-
degree weather outside of the Gardens.

"A lot of things," Roy muses, peering out of the car
window at the stage-door scene. "Bob's a focal point whether he likes it or not, a focal point for hope, love, that's
part and parcel too. It's more than words though. It's
thoughts and feelings. There's no sense in having thought
on one hand and feeling on the other unless you can
integrate the two in one. I think what Bob does is put

them both together in one point in one place in time and that serves as sort of a catalyst for other people, not that they should project their feelings on him, because he's just human, just an individual, but he acts like kind of a catalyst in that people say, 'Hey, this guy means something, this guy's saying something.' " Roy falls silent.

"I guess he means enough to you to park a block away on a freezing night just to feel some vibe," Ratso smiles.

Roy turns to him. "I think there's a common bond here among people our age. Do you feel that at all?" The reporter nods. "Think it could be possible to feel it all the time?"

"Depends on the circumstances," Ratso says.

"Doesn't it though?" Roy shakes his head and studies his hands. "I think one of Dylan's best songs is 'Talking WW III Blues' where he says some of the people can be half right part of the time, part of the people can be half right some of the time, then he simply says 'I'll let you be in my dream if I can be in yours.' I think that is the proper approach. I'd like to meet Dylan, I really would." Roy peers out the window again. "Just to sit down and talk to him. His music really means something to me. It's sort of like on the cover of *Before the Flood*, where everyone's standing with a match, out there, there's people who sort of glimpse knowledge, not knowledge but they know, they understand. That's what Dylan is to me, a guy that carries certain strains of like thought and knowledge and keeps them alive and that in a sense generates spirit, 'cause that's basically what it's all about, spirit, and Bob's very spiritual."

"What if you met him . . ." Ratso starts.

"I'd talk to him," Roy anticipates, "I've thought about it."

"How would you approach him? He's been hit on so much, he's really wary. Let's say you saw him in the street, not necessarily ten minutes from now in front of the Arena, just on the street, how would you break through that façade?"

"Let me ask you something," Roy says softly. "Do you think it's possible to break through that façade?"

"Not right away. But let's say you saw him, what would you say?"

Roy coughs nervously and looks away. "I'd ask him if he

was looking for a brother and I think if he was interested he might sit down and think about it. He'd probably react."

Ratso smiles. "Yeah, he'd probably say, 'I got a brother.' "

"What's he like, older or younger," Roy asks, and Ratso suddenly finds himself in the middle of a psychodrama.

"He's older and younger," Ratso barks.

"I suppose he would be," Roy nods. "Got any sisters?"

"Now, that's something else there," Ratso chuckles.

"That's true," Roy smiles, "I think it was some cat that said, 'When Ruthie says come see her in her honky-tonk lagoon and I could watch her waltz for free.' I bet there are two types of sisters. What I wonder about the guy who wrote that was how consciously aware he was when he wrote that."

"How aware of what?" Ratso interrupts.

"What it meant to him." Roy suddenly begins to look very spacey. "You're not him."

"No, I'm not him," Ratso feels for the door handle.

"I guess Bob has thought about that too, what it's like being him. I thought about him a lot. Listen," Roy reaches into the glove compartment, "if you see him will you give him this for me?" He hands Ratso a folded piece of paper.

"Sure," Ratso grabs the paper and opens the door. "What should I say to him?" he pokes his head in the car.

"Oh, nothing." Roy glances at the stage door. "Just give him the note."

The crowd has swelled to about fifty now, mostly teenyboppers who are primed to emit a torrent of shrieks as soon as Guam heads out the door and for the buses. Ratso elbows his way to the front and stands there surrounded by thirteen-year-old girls and a guy in his twenties with a dog.

The guy stares at Ratso and his coonskin cap and then meekly asks him who he is. Ratso explains. "I'm a New York Jew stuck in Toronto," the kid smiles, and holds his dog up. "My dog sings with Dylan every time I put on a Dylan album. Whenever Dylan plays the harp my dog goes *grrrr*." All the girls crowd around to get a look. But suddenly they all break rank and tear off after Mick

Ronson, who's fighting his way onto Phydeaux. A few seconds later, they come streaming back.

"I got a kiss, I got a kiss," one nubile twelve-year-old is muttering, walking back slowly in a trance.

"Oooohh," her friend is moaning, rolling her fingers into two fists. "Ohhh, I hate you Gerry. I didn't get one. I'm gonna cry."

But then, Joni Mitchell starts inching her way out. "It's Joni!" Ratso shrieks and he leads the charge, followed by twenty shrieking girls. After Joni successfully negotiates her way to the bus, stopping to give some fans the two bouquets she had emerged from backstage with, Ratso tires of the constant din and heads for the crew bus.

Back at the hotel, he checks out the hospitality suite. It's fairly quiet, only McGuinn, Ronson, Gary Shafner, and Chris O'Dell around. But Sylvia, the Jamaican Jewess that Ratso compared bloodlines with, steps off the elevator and the two walk into the room.

They sit on the couch and immediately Gary starts to harass Ratso. "Do you know the best-looking part of your body is the raccoon tail?" Gary snaps. But before the reporter can respond, Dylan strides in.

"Hey, c'mere," Ratso screams, "I got that Jamaican Jew you wanted to meet." Dylan advances cautiously to the couch.

"Hey Gary, is there any more tequila?" Dylan thirsts, then turns to McGuinn. "You're a trouper, man," he smiles.

"Joan's a trouper, did you dig her tonight?" Ratso remembers the exchange with Neuwirth.

"What happened?" Bob blurts.

"I'll never tell," the reporter turns coy, "I got kicked out of the hall tonight."

"You didn't get hurt did you?" Dylan's mock-serious, the makeup still smeared over his face.

"Nah, I got kicked out with that woman who was dancing in the front row. She got in the hall by saying she was your mother."

"I bet she was," Dylan jokes.

"Man, I love your mother," McGuinn gushes. "Your mother kissed me and said she loved me."

"Stop telling him mother stories," Ratso chides, "you're embarrassing him."

Dylan scans the room. "Is Hawkins still around?"

"No, he left. Hey, this is Sylvia, she's the Jamaican Jew."

"I don't believe it," Bob giggles.

"Prove it to him," Ratso nudges her with an elbow.

"Sit down," he offers Dylan a seat next to her.

"No, I don't want to sit down," the singer shyly refuses.

"C'mon, sit down," Ratso insists.

"OK," Dylan gingerly sits, "but I'm not too good with girls."

"I'll help you," Ratso is generous, "I gave Peter Orlovsky tips."

"Oh, give it a try," Roger pipes in.

"I get too embarrassed," Dylan's rubbing his hands together.

"Oh, just ask her a question," McGuinn suggests.

"A Jamaican Jew, is that right?" Dylan's still shaking his head. "I thought you were getting married to that other girl, Ratso," Roger smiles innocently.

"Hey, don't get him in trouble now," Bob warns, "he's in enough trouble, as it is."

"You know, Linda," Roger suddenly asks Dylan, "Linda? My wife?"

"Yeah," Bob laughs.

"She said she wants to be my friend tonight," Roger announces proudly.

"Instead of your wife?" Bob asks, straight-faced.

"No, better," Roger beams.

"She's finally catching on, huh," Dylan smiles.

Gary bursts in with a tequila report, no bottles to be found, but Ramblin' Jack may be hoarding one.

"Call him, maybe he's got some," Dylan suggests then turns back: "So Linda's gonna be your friend, huh? That's beautiful."

"Yeah, I'm happy," Roger brushes his hair off his collar. "She's even going down to Burt Sugarman's office with a lot of eight-by-ten glossies to let him film them for a tribute to the Byrds."

"So you worked it out so you don't have to bring her eggs and bacon no more," Dylan seems happy for his friend.

"Listen man," Ratso starts to qualify something he had wanted to tell Dylan for weeks, "this is said out of all due respect for your music, but I think you should re-record

Desire, you know, I mean I heard the originals and the band is so much hotter now, the songs all have another life. . . ."

Dylan frowns. "Hey man, a record's a record. I got twenty of them. It's just a record. Gary, how we doing on the tequila?" And with that, the elusive Mr. Dylan gets up and heads out in the lobby.

But a mere minute later, Ronee Blakley stumbles in, wearing a nightgown and two different socks. "I couldn't go to sleep," she moans, "I had to see what was going on."

"Ronee," Ratso shrieks, "that's the same nightgown you've worn three nights in a row."

Blakley fingers the garment. "I'll have you know this is clean," she sniffs and plops down on the couch.

"Rolling Stone fucked me for the fourth time in a row," Ratso moans, remembering the latest article where his byline had been buried after three rewrite men.

"Anybody could fuck you, Ratso," Ronson chuckles.

"Not over, though," Blakley looks for something to drink.

Sylvia meanwhile has been sulking on the couch. "Dylan doesn't like me," she pouts to Ratso, and then heads out to look for her friend, who's roaming the halls somewhere with Ronnie Hawkins. With that Ratso departs, shakes his head all the way back to his room, falls on the bed and passes out.

But luckily the reporter wakes in time to make the bus, which will take the troupe to the train station for a scenic ride to Montreal. Ratso rushes into the lobby, throws his luggage on the rack, and hops aboard, settling into a seat in the rear next to Mel Howard.

Howard has seemed a bit preoccupied of late, and Ratso has just chalked it up to the imminent end of the tour, a prospect that has everyone involved as depressed as a bunch of campers at the end of the summer. In a way this was the ultimate camp, a traveling sleep-away bunk of thirty with a staff of counselors and a crew of fifty. There's been swimming, plenty of recreation, and a canteen that serves liquor until eight in the morning. So to Ratso, Howard just looked like a kid who's on the wrong side in color war.

"I'm bummed out about the film," Mel confides in Ratso as the bus warms up outside the hotel. "What I'm concerned about is that I have an opposing point of view from Meyers and those guys and Alk, even though Howard's a friend of mine."

"What's the dispute?" Ratso perks up.

"Well, let me give you some background," Mel volunteers. "When I first met Louie Kemp, who's an old friend of Dylan's, grew up with him, loves Dylan, thinks Dylan is a special guy and it's kind of if you're someone from the neighborhood and there was a star, a local legend, and somehow if the guy stays connected to that local legend, that's the kind of relationship Dylan has with him. Sometimes the kid, the joker, I mean, he was obviously the energy source of his crowd, and on another level, he's half myth, and they're all a little awed by him and Louie and some of the other guys I met from Minnesota seem to have a relationship similar to the guys I grew up with, a lot of put-down humor, a lot of irony, a certain kind of toughness that city kids get, and I think that Dylan having been a superstar for a number of years is cut off from those kind of roots. People don't talk straight to him, he's always gotta weigh and measure what everyone says because everyone's out to impress him, win him, sell him, whatever, so I think if you do that long enough and have to maintain a public image as a performer, as a poet and as a supersensitive person, I think more and more there's a certain amount of illusion involved in it. Anyway, when Louie and I met what we talked about a lot was what Dylan meant to both of us. In other words, once we got past the formalities of my credentials as a filmmaker and his credentials as a friend who's going to be a producer of the whole tour, in a sense, for Dylan, it then came down to what was my point of view going to be and what was his, 'cause he's never made films and he was trying to ferret that out. Everyone was selling him on making another *Woodstock* with the million cameras, and what we connected on was a few spare things.

"Dylan to me, and of course Louie too, was a kind of icon, a mythological character who represented for us the rebellion that we all went through, searching for newer values, being more independent, trying to find a better way, and when Dylan came back in '74 after having had a public breakdown, which was parallel to so many people I knew having broken down after the kind of enthusiasm and messianic quality of the '60s, like we found the ultimate truth and then suddenly you find that you found nothing, you're still scrambling, and a lot of people got broken by that, and, in a certain way, Dylan seemed broken by that and by degrees crawled his way back. Broken by the motorcycle accident, sure, but some of the albums, some of the music lost the fire, the sense of focus, and in a way, when he came back in '74 he was transformed.

"When I saw him, the halting shy ironic kid was now a very sexual adult male who was taking responsibility. I'm reading a lot into this but by saying I want to play Madison Square Garden to twenty-five thousand fans and acoustically singing 'Like a Rolling Stone' and saying 'How does it feel?' in retrospect is a whole different thing than saying it as a bunch of kids sitting on MacDougal Street and saying 'Let's go out and bop.' Here's a guy saying, 'Well, we all went through shit, stand up and be proud because this is what we opted for, it's a wonderful thing that we've done.' And it was an inspiration.

"And, incidentally, Dylan's Jewish and the rumor was around that he was interested in the JDL, and had gone to Palestine, and this and that. Louie wears a golden chi, the symbol of life, and I'm heavily Jewish, I speak Yiddish, so there's that, the mythology of Dylan as a latter-day Hassid, as a Cabalistic kind of poet, all that, and as a kind of extension of the whole idea of the wandering Jew, wandering poet, the person who is inspired and goes amongst the community to carry the message of inspiration and renewed faith and renewed hope. I mean I'm into that kind of mythology as a filmmaker and part of the malaise that we're all suffering from is that nobody knew what to believe in anymore.

"So here comes Dylan, dumb enough, naive enough, beautiful enough, all of those things to say 'Let's go out and form a caravan and wake up the country,' and in some fluid, unspoken way that seems to be the message that all of us are picking up. In other words, what you pour into it was what it becomes. So what Louie and I talked about is that certainly Dylan had things like that in mind when he was saying 'Let's go to Plymouth,' and it's the bicentennial year, so obviously he had some historical notion in mind, so what we talked about was, wouldn't it be great to kind of shape it into that, in other words to anticipate that, not to be just voyeuristic filmmakers recording the event of everyone's freaking out over Bob Dylan which is frankly, as a filmmaker, very uncreative and boring.

"So we came up with this idea to make an inspirational event out of the film independently of the tour, and to kind of give it all of that dimension and mythological connotation, because it was important to all of us and Louie was hip to that. So Louie said, one of the first things he said, was to buy *Diamonds and Rust* and listen to some of the songs, and they'll give you kind of clues to Dylan and Baez and what it means for them to be coming back together and stuff. And from all this generalized talk we were saying we should filter out some of the best into a movie."

Mel yawns, as the bus finally rolls out, heading for the station downtown. "And with good reason, they hired the best documentary filmmakers and those are guys who are independent, wonderfully spirited cameramen, who have over the years covered every major event and made films about it. And they don't really understand the fictional notion of having a game plan, sitting down and actually having a daily plan and inventing a film. To them, that's somehow dishonest, the thing to do is to discover it as you go along. Now the problem with that, there's long books about *vérité* and what is real and what is truth and it ain't gonna be answered by us, the thing is that if you've been at it long enough, like somebody like Meyers, who's been at it for many years and reputed by everybody to be the best, he makes a story, his energy, his determination and his good humor and all of that, actually takes whatever the situation is and makes an event out of it. So is that more truthful than fiction? In fact, it's not, to me. Because what often comes out of that is people just being grotesque for the camera, trying to be funny, they're on. So to me, a lot of the stuff that we were shooting in New York and at the beginning was stuff that was conventional and worse than that, it was stuff that . . . fuck Dylan as a person, whom I grew to love, but at that point I didn't give a shit, but Dylan as a symbol for something that we all needed, an inspiring man with brains who was able to look at the world and say 'Fuck, man, this is what's happening,' to take the opportunity that rarely comes to any communicator, artist, writer, I mean all of us had this incredible opportunity, in a sense, on his coattails, to say something. To take that opportunity and just parade him around as though he were some lame dick and everybody's gonna freak out over him and we can take funny movies of girls giggling, that to me was lame and a drag."

Howard winces at the memory and stares out the bus window. Ratso is enthralled by this narrative and just waits till Mel resumes his monologue. "So what happened very early on, I became a sourpuss so there was a real rift in the production. The rushes started coming in and everybody was self-congratulatory, 'Oh, they're great, the greatest,' and Bob, who really doesn't know film, I'm saying this with respect, I think he would make a great director but he doesn't yet know film, he wasn't sure what to make of it, so he would respond a lot to people's energy around him. It always happens in films, you want to believe in what's happening, but I thought the stuff was home movies, and I really disliked it and finally it came to a head at some point and I said that and of course by saying that, it was intemperate and it incurred the wrath of the filmmaker cameramen who were saying in effect I was criticizing them, which wasn't the case. It was just an opposition of styles.

"That kind of was a breaking point 'cause when Dylan said if I didn't like it what is it I'm after? There was never any violent disharmony, there was just this rhythm underneath. Every day we'd go out and shoot. But we had a couple of long raps about it and he agreed. I just said, 'Do you want your name, I mean your music and what you represent, do you want to use it to its best intention?' And in that, we had tremendous support and allies in people like Ginsberg. The thing about Allen is he's a wonderful historian, he tends to see things, everything has a historical significance. So Allen saw Dylan rightly connected to the whole tradition of the Beat generation and through that to the earlier poets, Poe, the whole sense of the American vagabond. So Allen was keen to add that element to it, and of course, Dylan is mindful of that, that's why he invited Allen, so that there'd be input from people in the whole area of poetry and Kerouac and what the country was about, because the RTR was coming a lot of people would appear out of the woodwork, old faces from the scene who dropped out, so that there was really the raw material for an inspiring event beyond just a corny film.

"And at some point, Sara comes and Sara is an actress and an old friend of mine and I literally begged her to get involved in the movie because I knew that she would be into certain things. And what the movie has is a conglomeration of some of the most interesting strong women in the world, really. Joan Baez, who is absolutely irrepressible, she's super, a wonderful, enthusiastic, dynamite lady."

"Did she do an incredible scene with Dylan, that almost became psychodrama about their old relationship?" Ratso vaguely remembers muffled rumors about this early on in the tour.

Mel lowers his voice a bit. "Yeah, at Momma's, what happened was, I don't know how much of this we're not supposed to talk about, but basically they had, everybody knows, a really intense relationship years ago and they split up largely I think at Dylan's behest and all those years Baez never resolved that, she carried the torch, 'cause Dylan is very powerful, and she wrote those songs about him. And she and I started to talk and I literally fell in love with her, I had never been a fan of hers particularly, but she's got real spirit, real character, real conviction, and we talked and it was very touching, she talked about how for years she and Dylan had not talked, how there was so much she wanted to say and ask him but that she was afraid to and he was so elusive.

"I said that he is elusive but what's so extraordinary about him is when he's pushed in a situation where it's public and he has to transcend it, he'll bridle for a while but eventually he will transcend it. That's why he's such a great artist. He is a genius. And we talked about the fact that maybe the way to get him pinned was to do it on camera where he wouldn't back down and we both thought that that would be risky but a good idea and she wasn't sure if she was gonna do it and we both said if the opportunity is ripe and by chance one of the scenes we were gonna shoot one day was with this terrific old lady who has a place near Arlo Guthrie's land, a friend of Arlo's, who everybody calls Momma. And she cooks Italian food and sings songs and is kinda a bawdy old lady in her eighties, wonderfully spirited. She saw Joan and just loved her. She took her through the house and sang songs with her and then she gave Joan a dress which was a white sequined wedding dress and told her to try it on and it fit Joan perfectly, it was like one of those magic-charged moments. Everybody was hushed, this wedding dress for Joan, she was touched by it, everybody was high and happy.

"And then Dylan arrives late and somehow or other, all of the conversation that had taken place in the bus that day about pinning him, and Joan in a wedding dress, and Dylan coming up to shoot a scene, and Momma's presence, it all kind of came together and Joan played a scene where she actually played herself, she played a character like herself and in effect, said, 'What happened between us?', and Dylan was stunned but was brilliant and on camera you see him go from . . . I mean, it's this wonderful double-entendre where the two of them are actually having a conversation about their lives, the first one in eight or ten years but done with such wit and high style, it's like a Howard Hawks movie. Dylan is funny and turns what could have been maudlin into something really inspired, a really great sequence, everyone was knocked out by that scene no matter what perspective they had on the movie. And it ended on such good spirits, there was another sequence of hijinks, of real jerkiness where people, including Allen Ginsberg, were climbing through windows. It was Marx Brothers slapstick, it was just great. By the end of the day, everybody who had differing opinions about how we should do the movie, everybody agreed this was clearly gonna be a heavy mythological movie and we weren't just gonna make a documentary and of course with three, four hours of concert to supplement it, we thought it's gotta be the greatest movie in the world.

"There were all these themes running through it. Ginsberg had the idea of Dylan as alchemist, rediscovering America, then the women, Sara is very much into Robert Graves and his notion of the muse, and it suddenly flashed on me, of course, that's probably a big part of their relationship. He's always singing about women that inspire him, because like many creative people his energy can sag unless there's something to bring him out, and the thing about Sara is she always brings him out. I'm sure there have been more beautiful women in his life, whatever, but Sara consistently fascinates him and constantly interests him and that's what kept them together all these years.

"So there was this scene in Niagara Falls where Sara played this kind of witch goddess creature and she set tasks for him to fulfill, and nothing was ever good enough and that was the constant prod to keep him going. So we had a whole subplot, all of the women in the film, black magic and white magic, and the different powers of women and men and the focus of all of this was Dylan himself. Helena came and Harry Dean came and we started to use some of the songs as mythological characters, with horses in Quebec and escape scenes, all sorts of zany hijinks, but the thing that started to evolve as a general theme was Dylan, Sara, and Joan. And Sara and Joan as opposing forces, in different mythological guises, Joan as a certain kind of energy, Sara as a different kind of energy, and Dylan in between, being attracted to both. And Dylan is wise enough not to choose sides, he just lets it play off him, so what we did was devise scenes where those energies would just be revealed and let them play out as kind of psychodrama or improvisational humor.

"And I guess in the last two weeks or so, I guess the tour took hold enough so Dylan was sufficiently secure and the film just possessed him and it took him over, and where before we had to schlep him to come to a scene, he started to get really into it. He has such an incredible eye and an incredible sense of telling stories, something that when he's really on he's really superb. I think he's a great actor, a great actor and when he is up, his smile and his energy, you understand why musicians love to play with him. Because whatever else may be difficult at times because of the entourage and the mystery surrounding him, just playing with him, working with him as a filmmaker and an actor is so inspiring, is so much fun that you just want to work thirty hours a day. If he's displeased, if he's like down or turns off, it's really hard to get him up and it's really hard to work with him, because he's such a heavy presence. But when he got into it, he was really inspired by the film and he started to take these ideas and really shape them."

Mel pauses and rubs his eyes wearily. Ratso sees the station looming up about a block away. "But I'm afraid how the film is gonna turn out. We have an incredible movie: it's all there, if they choose to make it. I think it's important to push Dylan in some way to make the film that's there. That's my real interest. But I don't know how to do that." Mel sighs and grabs his handbag as the bus pulls to a stop. "I'm glad to be going back to New York this Saturday, it's perfect timing. I can't wait to get back. But I'm sorry this thing is over, it's been so intense. Not just fun, it's like you're on all the time, you're on your toes 'cause you're waiting for Dylan." Mel shakes his head and chuckles. "It's like waiting for Godot," he smiles and they hop off the bus and walk into the station.

Even this entrance is being filmed, Goldsmith and a sound man doing the *Eyewitness News* shtick, panning over the Thunderers, as they make their way onto the train. Ratso mugs for the camera and is about to step onto the train when he hears his name called. It's Louie Kemp, barreling down on him. "OK," Louie lectures, "you can go on the train. But low profile. I don't want you to talk to anybody, just relax and enjoy the ride. Otherwise, I'll put you on the baggage car." Ratso just smiles and files onto the car, plopping down next to Beattie. This is the crew train, so the kids are scrambling around, the film crew is ensconced, and seated in the back is Dylan, playing with one of his children.

After the train starts to roll out of the station, Ratso sneaks a look back, sees Dylan alone, and heads back to his seat. "You got a minute to see that song now?" the reporter asks.

"Sure," Dylan grabs the proffered document and begins to read.

"Hey, this is good man," he looks up, "I didn't know you could write such a good song. It reminds me of 'Tom Thumb's Blues.' "

"Why, just 'cause of that first line 'Rega just came in from the Coast'?" Ratso frowns.

"I'd like to hear the melody. You ought to listen to some old Leadbelly records. I kinda hear it as a march," Dylan laughs, and heads for the other car. Ratso's restless though, and walks on to the other car, spotting Sara who's sitting next to Joan.

"Ratso," she greets the reporter. "You know, they should do a cutout book of your outfits." He looks down at his bowling shoes, jeans, Indian head warmup jacket, fur vest, and raccoon hat. "Next to my husband, you're the best-dressed man on the tour, love."

"Who would buy a book of my wardrobes?"

"Sell it to kids or do it underground."

"Do it for underground kids," Baez cracks.

"Yeah," Sara smiles sweetly. "Nobody's doing anything for the troll market."

An hour later, they detrain to the inevitable camera, which records Sara hobbling along the platform missing one boot heel. In the station, Gary is routing everybody to a bus, but Dylan and a few others slip off to do some shooting in the station, and Ratso, two suitcases, a typewriter, and a tape recorder in tow, sneaks past Gary and follows the actor. Neuwirth and Helena start a scene in the middle of the station, attracting a huge, mostly French-speaking crowd who gape at the bizarrely dressed foreigners.

Meanwhile, Dylan, Alk, and Sara sneak down the hall a bit and set up next to a newsstand. Two minutes later, Ratso runs onto the set, carrying what looks to be all his possessions, sort of a highbrow shopping bag person.

"Jesus," Dylan looks at Alk, "this guy could get in to see the Pope!" But then he's down to serious business, prepping Sara on the upcoming scene, shooting some footage of her buying a magazine, checking out the angles for the next shot. Already a small crowd has formed, and a few people surge forward for autographs. Dylan starts to comply, and the crowd buzzes amongst itself. "Sounds like you got a cold," one older fan, a Frenchman in his thirties, worries solicitously.

"Yeah, it's hard to get all them vitamin pills on the road," Dylan answers, then starts to stroll around the station, peeking at the *Playgirl* that Sara bought earlier. And of course, Ratso and about ten other curiosity-seekers follow his every footstep. They walk by Neuwirth's scene and everyone pauses to look, giving Dylan a chance to slip away unnoticed, scampering into the bathroom through the Out door. Unnoticed by everyone except Ratso.

"Are you playing New York?" the older fan pesters the reporter, "Carnegie Hall or just Madison Square Garden?"

"I don't know," Ratso lies.

"Are you going to the concert now?" the fan is beginning to shriek. Ratso nods no.

"Can I have your autograph?" he pulls out a worn book, "I love the rock scene and the artists, that's my life. I like that life, I like it more than just to go see the show. It's my life too, my way of being."

"Running around looking at them?" Ratso stares incredulously. "What do you learn?"

"I find it strange, very fast-paced, going from one place to the other. Especially Dylan, he's so fast. Where did he go? Did you see him? Did he go to the bathroom or the bar?" The fan is nearly frantic.

"Sniff it out," Ratso dismisses him and starts to walk away, "that's your thing."

The autograph hound divines for a moment and then goes scurrying into the bar. Ratso chuckles to himself and heads for a much-needed urination, pulling an alien piece of paper out of his back pocket on the way.

"What the fuck is this," the reporter thinks as he unfolds the paper. It's the note for Dylan from that kid in the Volkswagen outside the Gardens in Toronto. Ratso starts to read the immaculately printed missive.

Cosmic chuckles, Messianic blues
Some are marked for life
Jokers and thieves
Joker and thief
When will we meet again
soon I hope
soon I hope
for I am so weak

Bring the Rolling Thunder Revue to Ottawa for after all Canada is the land God gave to Cain

Ratso stops in his tracks, pockets the letter, and heads back the other way, angling for the bar, deciding that he really didn't have to go to the bathroom that badly after all.

13

In Montreal, Ratso never left the hotel restaurants, except for one night when he ventured out with Joni and Roger to have dinner at Leonard Cohen's house. From Wednesday night till Saturday, he would wake up, rush down for breakfast in one of the coffee shops, hang out, check out the other coffee shop for lunch, hang out, go up to the bar for a drink, then head to the restaurant for dinner. Oh yes, on Thursday night he did manage to leave the hotel to go to see the concert. But it wasn't easy.

The fireworks started when he spied Lisa, sitting like a lost child on one of the massive sofas. Ratso sneaks up.

"Hey, Lisa, did you hear the song Neuwirth and T-Bone wrote about you last night?"

Lisa wheels and a look of disgust crosses her face. "Why? Why do I want to fucking hear that shit?"

"What's the matter?" Ratso's shocked at the rage in the usually unflappable punching bag.

"You upset me so much," Lisa fumes, "you're always down on me at the wrong time."

"I'm nice to you when Bob's around," Ratso smiles.

"What did you do when the guards were spitting on me last night? Nothing."

The pair gets joined by Mike Evans, head of security.

"Neuwirth got down on me last night. He said, 'What are you doing here?' and . . ."

"Now she's got her version and I got mine," Evans interrupts, trying to set the record straight for the journalist. "I think that Neuwirth was more than cool to her. Neuwirth said we were coming down too hard on her, so she ends up giving him the shit." Evans scowls.

"That's not true," Lisa protests.

"He was defending you," Evans glares. "All he wanted

306

was the answer to a simple question: Why do you do what you do?"

"No, he said, 'It's bad enough you come to every show, don't come around here,' and stuff like that," Lisa shouts.

" 'Cause you wouldn't tell him why you do it," Ratso butts in.

"I said I was here because I love Bob," Lisa suddenly goes soft and fuzzy, her huge doe eyes taking on that same familiar vacant stare. "I said, 'I love Bob, I love the music,'" she continues. "He said, 'Bob's not here right now. What are you doing right now?' I was only there because I didn't leave. But I felt I was on trial. I couldn't answer any questions and Ronee, that bitch, was staring at me."

"But you always stare at people," Ratso yells. "Ronee likes you."

"She told Roger she was envious of me," Lisa shrugs.

"Bullshit, she told me she likes you," Ratso chides.

"C'mon," Lisa makes a face, "she just wants to sleep with the whole football team."

"Did Neuwirth tell you to split?" Ratso changes the subject quickly.

"Yeah, he said that one of these days security is gonna break my nose and it won't be their fault." She glares at Evans, who's twice her size. "I said that I would fucking sue. He said that he would go get the police right then." Lisa stalks back to the couch and Evans just shrugs at Ratso.

Ratso turns and hops on the elevator, and goes directly to Beattie's room. No answer. But he remembers there's a nursery where the kids hang out, and Beattie may be babysitting by now, so he checks the newsletter. There are the travel arrangements for tomorrow, a notice about a concert Sunday at the prison that George Lois helped arrange, and a schedule for Monday's concert at the Garden.

Ratso's eyes get drawn to a contribution on page 2.

STRIPERS SPEAK

**LISA HAS OFFENDED THE SENSITIVITIES OF SOME MEMBERS OF THE TOUR. WOULD THE MUSICIANS PLEASE NOT FEED OR ENCOURAGE HER FURTHER.
                              UNSIGNED

He finally locates the nursery and walks in to find Baez, her mother, and Gabe's nurse Gail, with their hands full of little Dylans.

"Beattie's not here, huh? Hey listen, do you want to hear 'Combat Zone' now?" Ratso seizes the time.

"I'm not really ready." Joan really hasn't seemed to relish Ratso's company since he talked nonstop in her bus that snowy day in Maine, instead of interviewing her. "I have no interest."

"I'll never listen to your set again," Ratso threatens.

"OK, OK," Baez rolls her eyes. "Do you need accompaniment?"

"Well, Dylan said it should be a march," Ratso remembers.

"How about if I simulate drums, Ratso," Baez smirks and starts the beat, "Bum bum bum, bum bum bum." Ratso shakes his head and begins to recite it, getting up to the second verse when Baez raises her head.

"Stop, stop," she shrieks. "What was that, 'a certain spark every time she smiles,' we can see who you're copping from."

"I wasn't even aware of the similarity to 'Lily, Rosemary and the Jack of Hearts'," Ratso protests. "Even Dylan said he thought it reminded him of 'Tom Thumb's Blues.'"

"I wasn't suggesting that your writing is coming from your conscious, Ratso," Baez cracks.

Ratso goes back to the reading, getting through about three more verses before Baez interrupts again.

"You're gonna have such an identity crisis after this tour is over, Ratso," she shakes her head.

"Why, I don't think this is particularly Dylanesque. I also like Leonard Cohen, and . . ."

"Yeah, yeah," Joan smirks, "old razor blades and Seconal. I can't believe you came in to sing a song about whores to the children."

"No, Momma," Gabriel blurts something out that Ratso doesn't comprehend.

"What he say?"

"He said that the horses would understand it," Joan smiles.

Ratso goes back to his narrative and in the middle of the climactic verse, Baez starts talking to her mother.

"Jesus Christ," the writer explodes, "the best goddamn verse and she's talking through it."

"Now you know how it feels," Baez smiles sardonically, as Bernie enters the nursery. Ratso hands him the lyric sheet and he scans the song. "Don't use 'Mona,' it's been done. 'Mona says come see me.' Change it to Noma."

"Or Roma," Joan suggests.

"How about Rhonda," Ratso sulks.

"Rama," Joan shouts, "like the God."

"I don't like Rama, I'm leaving it at Mona."

"OK," Baez throws up her hands, "leave it at Mona and just suffer more criticisms and the death of a thousand slashes for imitating Dylan."

"He told me it sounds like 'Tom Thumb's Blues,'" Ratso repeats.

"And he's happy and you're happy so just go on," Baez shrugs.

"OK," Ratso concedes, "forget Mona. Let's call it something else. How about Sally. No. There's a hitch everywhere you turn. Nina?"

Baez chuckles. "All I can say is that you're no longer anal retentive. It all came out in this song. Is the Combat Zone anywhere near Desolation Row? Or are they in different cities?"

"I don't have to take this abuse." Ratso gets up to leave. "Anyway, I'm supposed to interview Beattie now."

"Well you better do it soon, 'cause it'll be a hell of a lot easier now than when she gets all these kids back."

Ratso says good-bye, gets attacked by one of the kids, and finally makes his way down the hall to Beattie's room. He knocks.

"Coming, coming," Beattie's booming voice penetrates the door.

"Come in," she smiles and ushers the reporter into the room, "we just got back from shopping, it was the first time we had a chance to get out of the hotel in this city." Beattie scampers over to the bed and starts unpacking some of the bundles, while Ratso marvels at this tremendously forceful woman, proud, opinionated, solicitous, generous, a bit of a ham, the perfect Jewish mother for Bob.

"I just told Bob I was interviewing you," Ratso settles into an easy chair, "I told him you were the lead of my

article and he said that maybe I should keep Beattie out
of this. But then I told him that I once wrote about my
father so he gave me permission."

"What kind of permission?" Beattie suddenly looks up.

"Just an interview. We can't do anything else, we can't
fool around."

"How about that." Beattie goes back to unpacking.
"We looked for you in the coffee shop. We were waiting
with Helena, she's a lovely person. How do you like
Montreal?"

"I love it, but I haven't been out yet," Ratso moans.
"I've been in the railroad station and the hotel."

"You know, Larry," Beattie suddenly lowers her voice,
"like Bob says, maybe you should keep me out of this.
What can I tell you?"

"Well, I can ask you how you feel about the tour and
being onstage."

"I loved it, I loved it," Beattie gushes. "Are the kids
all right? Are they playing upstairs?"

Ratso nods.

"Oh that's good. Where did you see Bob today in his
room? Did he just wake up? Was Sara there? Was she all
right? Was she sleeping? 'Cause you know she wasn't feeling so good yesterday."

This barrage of questions has given Ratso an incredible
dose of *déjà vu*, plummeting him right back to his
parents' house, reminding him of the good-natured Jewish
third degree he'd get when he came back from school,
or from a night out.

"I gave Sara some vitamin C," Ratso finally answers.
"I told Bob I was putting you in the first paragraph and
he just said to keep Beattie out of it."

"That's right. Keep Beattie out of it." The silver-haired
woman sits down on the bed opposite Ratso. "You know
why? People, they don't care about me, Larry . . ."

"I care about you," Ratso protests.

"But they don't care about me." Beattie makes a
face as if she had swallowed a whole lemon. "What for?
You know what it is, honey, after all, Dylan should be
written about for his music, not for his mother, or his late
father, right? They should write about his music." Beattie
jumps up and straightens out one of the dressers.

"But I think we should clear the air and correct the record of the rumors," Ratso starts to explain.

"Crazy people start rumors," Beattie shrieks, "you can quote that from me. Small thinkers."

"How do you like the tour so far?"

"We love it, we're enjoying it, having a wonderful, marvelous time. The children keep you young, and you keep wanting to help them and do for them and that's about it, Larry. What else can we tell you, honey?" Beattie shrugs the shrug of the content parent.

"You must be so proud," Ratso shakes his head.

"I am proud. Always been proud. It makes me very proud because everybody likes his writings, and that to me makes me feel very, very good, Larry."

"Did you always know he was special?"

"Oh sure," Beattie answers without batting an eye, "he's always been special. His poetry, he wrote when he was young, he wrote for young people then."

"Any idea that someday he'd be this—"

"Noooo," Beattie draws the word out like it was taffy, "uh huh, no idea he'd be this big. No! No!"

"What did you want him to be when he grew up, a doctor?" Ratso remembers his own childhood.

"Noooo," Beattie winces. "Nooo, no, no. I wanted him to be his own self, his own person, to do what he wanted to do. Nooo, we never came from medicine, we never came from dentists, or any of that. We came from a long line of theater. Theater people. We had movie houses."

"You told me once that you came from a long line of philosophers . . ."

"Oh yeah, my father, my late father, he loved music and philosophy. Oh yes, he was a philosopher, sure, years ago." The phone rings and Beattie picks it up. "Hello, yes, dear, did you get to Sara? Sleeping? She is sleeping. Well, this is a California call, we have to get to her. She must be asleep, yes, because she's not felt too good at all. This is Jennifer, a friend of Sara's, she was trying to get her yesterday too but the room doesn't answer over there, they must have the phones off the book. How can I get this over?" Beattie hangs up, and hands Ratso a note. "Can Bob let you in there? Good, give this message for Sara."

"What did your father do for a living?" Ratso wonders.

"He was a merchant. He had a store. He sold men's clothing to the miners. We came from a little mining town in the depressed area."

"How did the Jews get there originally?"

"Well, they came when they were youngsters, they were all little youngsters. Sure, they've been there for eighty years. Eighty years. They went right to Superior, Wisconsin, eighty years ago. Right to Superior."

"Bob once told me he had a little bit of Cossack blood in him," Ratso recollects the conversation they had in the car during the snowstorm in Maine.

"Sure," Beattie shakes her head, "from Russia, Russia. Odessa. But that isn't Cossack now, is it?" She shrugs. "My grandfather owned the theaters, that would be Bob's great-grandfather. His grandfather on his father's side had a shoe store in Duluth. Then we had an appliance store in Hibbing. We moved back because that was my home town. I was born and raised in Hibbing," Beattie says proudly.

She gets up and starts to put some clothes away, the vitality just oozing out of her pores. Ratso just watches her in awe. "Are you a poet too, Beattie?" he gapes.

"Sure, I'm an artist. I can talk a lot. That's an artist. An artist can talk, paint, or write poetry. I don't paint, I talk. So that's my part of the artistry."

"When Bob was growing up did you have an inkling of his gifts?" Ratso repeats.

"No, how can parents know about a genius, really. You can't tell when they're growing up exactly what they're going to do, Larry."

"What was he like as a kid?" Ratso probes.

"Oh, he played the guitar and he liked basketball and baseball. He liked sports, he was always a goer and a doer. He always did everything. He was a joiner, he joined in on everything."

"Was he aggressive and outgoing?"

"Noooo," Beattie shakes her head, "he was more on the retiring end. He didn't get in anybody's way. He wasn't a pusher. He did what he liked to do and he did his own thing. In writing and painting."

"You know that Bob's *Highway 61* album changed my life," Ratso confesses. "I was going to be an accountant, Beattie, and then I heard that and I started hanging out in Greenwich Village. But my parents freaked out. Were you overprotective toward Bob? I mean, were you worried that he was like hanging out with all those *schwartze* musicians?"

"We all worry, Larry," Beattie flashes her ice-melting smile, "but I didn't even think of that. I figured Bob knew his status and Bob knew what he could do and what he couldn't do."

"Were there any restrictions on him?"

"No, no restrictions at all, in our town we didn't need any restrictions."

"What about that scene in Scaduto's book on Bob that has Bob's father seemingly overprotective?" Ratso remembers.

"That's all garbage," Beattie winces, "I never gave Scaduto any information, period. I never gave anybody any information to write in a book, Larry." Beattie's voice is rising and she seems to be getting agitated. She plops down into a chair. "And that you can quote me. I never gave that Toby Thompson, I took him out to lunch, I thought that he was just a fan, I didn't know he was going to go out to capitalize on anything I had to say because I didn't have anything to say about my son, nothing." Beattie's close to screaming now, pounding her fist on the table for emphasis. "Dylan is Dylan, and I am Zimmerman. These people that think that they can just quote me and turn all this stuff around and write garbage, they're badly mistaken because I don't go for it. My son got where he is today not because of his father and me. He was born to us, but then he went away and he did this on his own. And he is the writer, I am no writer, his late father was no writer. Bob Dylan is the writer. Dylan, not Zimmerman."

A stunning soliloquy. Ratso is nearly speechless but manages a question, "Did you feel hurt when he changed his name?"

"No, not at all, he was a writer and he wanted to change his name."

"Did he ask you if he could do it?"

"No, he just said that he couldn't show two cards and that he wanted to have one legal name and that was it. I wasn't hurt, we were never hurt because Bob Dylan never hurt us in any way, there was no way that he could ever hurt us. He protected us, he protected us."

"When was the first time you realized that your son was so gifted?"

"Well," Beattie thinks for a second, "we knew he was gifted when we went to Carnegie Hall, when we heard him in Carnegie Hall then we realized it was a gift, he was only twenty-one or twenty-two maybe. That was in, uh, I don't know the year, it was in Carnegie Hall and he was alone. We flew in for the concert and we stayed for a few days and we knew that he was really enjoying what he was doing and that was important to us."

Ratso talks on, telling Beattie some anecdotes about Bob's influence on both his generation and Beattie's, and then the talk turns to social responsibility. "Beattie, did you feel hurt when people were attacking Bob, claiming that he had abandoned his social conscience, you know, that he didn't write an antiwar song during Vietnam?"

"I'll tell you the truth, Larry," Beattie smiles, "I never paid any attention to any of the gossip." At this, she leaps up and scurries over to her purse, searches a bit, then comes up with a small jar of Vicks Vaporub. She applies some to the ends of her fingers and then rubs the lotion into the insides of her nostrils. "If I don't get any rest I won't be able to go to the show tonight. This congestion is just killing me. Are you sick too, dear? Here, just put a little bit on your pinky, and put it into your nostril and breathe it honey, breathe it dear. I bought it last night in the drugstore because I was sniffling."

Ratso blanches a bit. "Beattie, are you sure you're supposed to sniff this instead of rub it in? Should you really put this into your nostril?"

"Just breathe it, breathe it, dear," Beattie shows Ratso the method again.

The reporter snorts some rub and moves on to a critique of Beattie's performance the other night. "How'd you get onstage in Toronto?"

"I sat right down in the rocking chair," Beattie beams, "I don't ask anybody any questions. I just sat down in the rocking chair."

"Those security guards didn't stop you?"

"No, they knew me. They knew who I was."

"But how'd you get onstage dancing and clapping," Ratso can't suppress a smile.

"I was sitting on the rocking chair when the music was coming to an end, so I just got up and joined them and I clapped along and everybody was in the finale, so I clapped too. I'm not bashful, you can quote me and say that I'm not a bashful woman."

"What was Bob's reaction? Did he say anything to you afterward, like, 'Oh, Ma'?"

"No, uh huh," Beattie shakes her head vigorously, "he was glad, I'm sure, he doesn't care. He knows that I'm not a pusher. I never was a pusher in my whole life. I've always been me. I'm me. I'm just plain old me. I'm glad to help in any place I can." Beattie smiles beatifically.

"You sound like him," Ratso chuckles. "I bet he gets lot of his stuff from you."

"It's the same old me," Beattie continues. "You don't change, you just mature. My quotation is this and I've said it all my life . . ."

"You're a philosopher too, Beattie," Ratso interrupts. "You know that. You're modest but you're a philosopher too."

"I say this: What one likes at fifty," she raises one dramatic finger, "they will detest at sixty. And this is the stage of life. What you like at thirty, you don't do at forty."

"Well, what about you? You're about forty-five?" Ratso compliments her.

"I'm sixty dear, yes, yes, I am, in June. I'm a Gemini. My philosophy is to like people, respect them for what they like to do and not to be that critical because if you can't do it as good as they're doing it, then keep your mouth shut."

"Great, Beattie," Ratso laughs. "Let's end it on that, tomorrow we can talk some more."

"How do you like that quotation?" she beams. "All right, Larry," she ushers the reporter to the door, "I'm depending on you to get that message to Sara . . ."

"Oh, I thought that you were gonna say that you depend on me to write the real story about Bob . . ."

"No, no, no, you will, that I know. That I'm not even telling you about. I know you'll write the real story, you won't let us down. You're not gonna put any garbage in about me because I am not garbage. And you can quote me. I want respect because I give it."

Beattie leaves Ratso at the threshold and runs over to the dresser, returning with a handful of sucking candies. "Do you want some candy, honey? Here take it, it's OK, take it all, I don't want it. Just make sure to get that message to Sara for me, darling. See you tomorrow, OK.

Please put that under the door or give it to Bob to give to her or something. OK, dear?"

Ratso waves and takes the elevator down to the bar, spotting Dylan inside. "Hey Bob," he approaches the singer, "T-Bone, McGuinn, and I made a tape of 'Combat Zone' the other day."

"Great," Dylan grabs a handful of peanuts and wolfs them down, "I'll listen to it later."

"You going to the gig?"

"Yeah," Dylan grabs some more nuts.

"I'm gonna tell Cohen and Jerry Rubin and some other people to come."

"You tell 'em, Fatso," Bob cheers.

"Fatso?" The reporter jumps. "Ratso, not Fatso."

"You're gaining weight, man." Dylan pauses, then wonders, "Can you call Cohen and get him on the phone for me. Can you go do that?"

"Sure, let's go find a phone booth."

They start down the lobby accompanied by Charlie, one of Bob's bodyguards. But after fifteen yards, a young girl comes up and stops Dylan. "Hi," she manages, her hands quivering, "I'm a dancer downstairs and I just wanted to say that we'll dance for you tonight . . ."

"OK." Dylan seems amenable.

". . . Since we can't listen to you sing."

"What kind of dancing is it?" Bob wonders.

"Jazz, jazz dancing."

"Modern dancing?" Bob rocks on his heels.

"Yeah, jazz, lots of things. We think you're fantastic. We're gonna do dances for you tonight."

"What time does your last show end?" The singer seems interested.

"About quarter to one."

"Fuck your concert," Ratso says impishly.

"OK, you stay here, Fatso, and check out the dancing," Bob snaps. "Fatso, isn't it?"

"Ratso."

"Fatso? Fatso Slocum, right?"

"I'm gonna go back and hang out with your mother. She's much nicer."

"Get Leonard please," Dylan gets serious, "I got some people to see."

Ratso walks over to the booth and dials Cohen's house.

After a few rings the poet picks up. "Leonard, this is Larry, how are you?"

"Can't complain," Leonard replies and Ratso remembers his work and laughs at the irony.

"Are you coming to the concert?"

"I guess so," Cohen says in his world-weary monotone.

"You're so coy, Leonard."

"Is it gonna be crowded?" the poet worries.

"You won't have to deal with the crowds, we'll zip in the stage door, Leonard," Ratso reassures him, as Dylan keeps nudging the reporter, trying to grab the phone. "Tell him to come through the back door," Dylan whispers in Ratso's ear. Ratso frowns and hands Dylan the phone.

"Leonard? Yeah, how you doing? Can't complain, huh. Well I could but I won't. You wanna come to the show? Fatso can pick you up."

"Ratso, not Fatso," the reporter pokes Dylan, "but he doesn't know me as Ratso."

"Yeah, Larry'll pick you up. You got four people? Sure, easy, hey, if you wanna play a couple of songs that would be all right too. Pardon? OK, whatever you feel like doing. We're gonna hang around for a few days, we got some film to shoot. We're also making a movie so we're gonna be shooting tomorrow and the next day here. Maybe after the show we can get together if that's OK with you. OK, man, Larry'll pick you up, see you later then." Dylan hangs up and the trio starts back toward the bar. Again they get about twenty yards before an elderly woman approaches Bob. "Can I have your autograph?" the sweet old woman proffers a piece of paper and a pen.

"Do you know who I am?" Dylan seems amazed to be recognized by a geriatric groupie.

"Bob Dylan?" the woman's beginning to hesitate.

"Who told you that?" Dylan's eyes narrow to slits behind his dark glasses.

"Because I think so." The woman is near total confusion, looking over to Ratso and Charlie now for a clue. "My nephew's going to your show."

"Who told you I was Bob Dylan?" Dylan keeps up the game, adjusting his hat.

"I guessed so," the woman points to the hat, "by your flowers."

Dylan cracks up and signs the paper. "Oh, this is for my granddaughter, she'll be so happy."

"What's her name?" Dylan asks.

"Josie."

"Josie," Dylan tries out his best French accent.

"Oui, Josie LaFleur," the grandmother beams.

"LaFleur?" Ratso screams, "is she related to the hockey player?"

"Her father is Guy LaFleur," Grandma smiles proudly, collects her autograph, and hurries on down the lobby. Dylan walks on, then slows down to browse through some of the lobby stores. He walks into one boutique and picks up a necklace. "How much is this?"

"Fifty-five dollars," the saleslady replies.

"Hey Fatso, you got any money?" Dylan asks straight-faced.

"Fifty-five dollars? I think that's a little bit high," Ratso frowns.

"Yeah, I think it's too high too," Dylan agrees loudly.

"How about forty-five dollars and an autograph?" Ratso bargains with the lady.

"Who are you?" the lady peers at Ratso.

Dylan turns to Charlie. "This guys too much," he smiles and heads for the next shop, a clothing emporium. Ratso follows them in. Dylan heads over for a rack and fingers a pair of pants. "That's smart," the unctuous sales-lady rushes over, "those slacks are very smart."

"Are they for a man or a woman?" Ratso asks.

"Oh they could be for both," the lady smiles her saccharine smile.

"Tacky," Ratso advises Dylan, but Bob is already off to the side, looking at a red feathered shawl and a jacket. He carries them both to the counter. "How much is this alone?" he holds up the shawl. "One hundred twenty dollars," the lady assesses. "All right, I'll buy this one too. What is this material?

"That's quiana."

"Quina?" Dylan seems incredulous. "What is it, like plastic or something?"

"It's jersey like. Like silk. It's washable, doesn't shrink. It's synthetic."

Dylan begins to pore through his pockets for cash and he pulls out a roll of bills and starts counting. "I can pay for both of these, if you can trust me for a minute I'll go get some money." He starts to grab the garments but the lady snatches them back.

"Do you have cash now?" Her tone gets a little bitter.

"Sign for it," Ratso urges. "He lives here, we're staying here."

Dylan searches through untapped pockets.

"How much do you need?" Ratso offers.

"It's OK, Ratso, I got it straight," Dylan collects all his cash.

"Here," the reporter offers a twenty-dollar bill, "it's your money anyway."

"It's my money? Huh?"

"Yeah, it's per diem." Ratso holds out his offer.

Dylan ignores Ratso and counts his money out onto the table. "OK, twenty, twenty-five, thirty-five, er, what's the total? Here's $129.60, how much more do I owe you?"

"Ninety-five dollars," the saleslady is sweet again.

"OK," Dylan grabs the two garments, "I'll take these with me and come back with the ninety-five dollars."

"Where are you going?" the woman shrieks." Leave this here." She grabs the partly-paid-for merchandise. "Here, take back your money and come back when you have the complete sum."

"No, I need it," Dylan mopes, "I'm gonna keep this stuff. I'll leave you my coat, it's worth more than the other thing." He starts peeling off his leather jacket.

"Come back," the woman raises her voice, "come back with the money then take it, that's how we do it."

Dylan's about to offer some more collateral, but Charlie comes up with the necessary cash and Bob hands her the bills.

"Nous avons besoin d'un reçu" Ratso suddenly breaks into his strange French facsimile.

"What you say?" Dylan peers at the reporter.

"I said we need a receipt," Ratso snaps.

"Sure," Dylan gives the saleslady a who-is-this-strange-guy-talking-French-with-a-Jewish-accent look, "we need a receipt."

The singer bundles the two garments in his arms and they head for the elevator. Ratso waves good-bye and rushes out at his floor. He takes a quick shower and calls Rubin Carter before leaving for the concert.

"So what you doing, you snake you, you getting any pussy?"

"More than you, you black bastard! I saw that thing in the paper with Hawkins offering Artis clemency to rat on you. What is that shit?"

"Oh man," Rubin moans. "You see, we are dealing with snakes. A political system of corrupt—"

"No speeches now, you fucking *schwartze*, I gotta pick up Sara and go to the concert."

"OK brother, take it easy, I'll see you on Sunday."

Ratso rushes upstairs and Sara lets him in. She goes back to applying the final touches to her eye makeup, which gives the reporter a chance to survey the room, which still hadn't been made up. He sees a slew of mystical iconography on the dresser, including a huge Tarot card of the Empress, the symbol of doom. Over by the bed, Ratso spies a worn copy of *Vogue*. On the nightstand, he peers at some books, one by Gary Snyder, one by Mallory, one by Victor Coleman. "Great books," Ratso shouts.

"We're intelligent people, Ratso," Sara yells over the din of her electric hair dryer. "I'm using all that makeup you got me in Toronto," she smiles. "You look great."

Ratso notices a beautiful necklace dangling on her chest. "What is this?" He grabs the medallion.

"It's Isis," Sara says softly, "I designed it. Should I take the tape recorder? I misplaced all those reggae tapes."

Ratso grabs the recorder and drags her out into the hall. They head for the car. "Now remember, it's our job to get Leonard to play," Ratso lectures. "First we gotta get him drunk, then we gotta make sure that if he gets on stage—"

"He doesn't fall off?" Sara blinks her eyes innocently.

Ratso waits two minutes but the car still hasn't been brought up from the garage so they hop into a cab. "I liked Leonard's last record." Sara settles back as the cabbie heads toward Dominique. "My favorite song was many men have loved the bells that you fasten to the reign."

"That's mine and Leonard's favorite too," Ratso marvels.

"We have similar tastes," Sara smiles, "we both like Bob."

"Yeah," the reporter chuckles, and starts humming, "You angel you, you're as fine as fine can be . . ."

"You're as light as a feather, you're as bright as the moon," Sara sings, "I love the moon. She rides the moon, Ratso." Sara fingers her amulet.

"Who?"

"Isis. All of them."

"Did you read Lawrence's *The Man Who Died?*"

"It's the same thing love, the same trilogy. It's his mother. In the picture I have in my room of Mary, who's the virgin of Guadaloupe, the patron saint of Mexico, she stands on the crescent moon."

They settle back into silence, the cab speeding up a main avenue, lined with expensive shops. Sara stares out the window.

"I'm dying to go shopping. I'm not spending a lot of money. I want to check out the antiques. Was this thing expensive, the thing I got on now?"

"For me it was," Ratso nods, "for him it wasn't."

"I have no idea how much it could be. It's French."

"Guess" Ratso prods.

"Fifty dollars."

"More than double that."

"One-hundred-twenty dollars."

"Exactly," Ratso beams.

"I want to buy a super dress to wear in New York," Sara salivates.

"Wait a minute," Ratso shouts, "you gotta wear a Hurricane T-shirt. It's a benefit."

"Well, if there's a party afterward, I'll change. I want a fancy dress."

"It's nice for Rubin if everyone wears his shirt." Ratso puts his feet up on the front seat.

"Yeah, but I'm not one of those T-shirt chicks. I want to get something elegant." She peers out the window. "I'm excited, there's a whole other world outside the hotel. Today's the first day of my life that I woke up at six o'clock. I'm exhausted."

"Beattie's right," Ratso warns. "You better get some more sleep. Take some vitamins. Did you eat anything today? No, huh? Look at you, you're as skinny as a rail."

"I had eggs benedict," Sara says feebly.

"And you ate them?" Ratso says suspiciously.

"It's really hard, love, I've never been on the road before. You know, you present me with a great problem, Ratso. I don't like reporters. I can't believe you're really a journalist."

"Why don't you say that to the film crew?" Ratso protests.

"It's not the same. I have some kind of character in that context. But here . . ." The driver pulls up to the house and Ratso runs out in mid-sentence.

Cohen's house is a tiny affair, located in the heart of old Montreal, a student, foreigner, bohemian ghetto. Ratso shivers as he walks up the block looking for the address. He finds it, and knocks on the door. Muffled sounds but no answer. A few more knocks. No response. Suddenly the reporter notices the door is slightly ajar and he throws it open.

And steps into a sea of sound, the harmonicas, spoons, kazoos, and spirited voices washing over him like a funky Jacuzzi. Cohen is ringleading, playing the harmonica, stomping his foot on a chair, leading the vocal to a French chanson. "How are you, my friend?" Leonard ushers Ratso in without interrupting the music. "This is Hazel, Suzanne, Armand, and Mort. Pull up a chair."

"We gotta go, Leonard." Ratso remains standing.

"C'mon," the poet urges, "we have time for one more song."

"But Sara's in the cab."

"Bring her in." Cohen gestures expansively and alcoholically. "Here, have a quick sip of wine."

"Leonard, we really have to go," Ratso stresses.

"OK, troops," Cohen calls to the others, "bring your instruments to the car." Cohen pulls a topcoat over his charcoal gray suit, a suit that Ratso has seen him wear for four years.

"Leonard, you're still wearing the same suit."

"It is my suit," he says with dignity, "it's *my* suit."

Suddenly the other four have revolted and start a jig around the living room, whooping and hollering and waving their hands in the air.

"Can you put your coats on while you're dancing," Leonard requests, and a minute later they're all piling into the cab. Introductions are made.

"Leonard," Sara breathes, "are you gonna sing?"

"No, are you?" Leonard shoots back.

"Me? No, they've been asking me to but I refuse." Sara smiles coyly.

"Leonard, you gotta sing one for me and Sara," Ratso implores, "that one 'hungry as an archway.' "

"OK," Leonard whips out his harp, "here we go. Get

your spoons out, Mort." And they break into a cheerful French folk song.

"If anyone asks you, you're all Leonard's backup band," Ratso warns the others, "there's not supposed to be anyone backstage tonight."

"That means Leonard has to go onstage," Sara prompts. Cohen frowns.

They go into a three-part harmony French song. "C'mon Leonard," Ratso whines, "you promised 'Take This Longing' . . . I've been so patient sitting through all these foreign songs."

Cohen whips out his harp and blows some melancholy notes and then he starts to sing, in his low dull-razor voice, "While we're apart, oh please remember me, soon I'll be sailing far across the sea/While we're apart oh please remember me, now is the hour when we must say good-bye, soon I'll be sailing far across the sea." Armand joins in on another harmonica and the two wail away as the cab pulls up to the Forum.

The party scurries inside from the frigid night, Ratso leading them in. Joni, who had just finished her set, comes running up and hugs the poet. "Joni," Leonard sizes up his Canadian counterpart, "Joni, my little Joni."

"I'm glad you're here, I just came off, though."

Cohen looks disappointed. "Well, we just heard the greatest music I've ever heard, the greatest music I ever heard we just played on the way here." By now, Neuwirth and Ronee have come over to pay respects, and Dylan, who's about to follow Ramblin' Jack, trots over.

"Leonard, how you doing?" Bob warmly greets the Canadian. He points over at Ratso. "Hey, do you know this character?"

Leonard rolls his eyes. "This man has plagued me for the last three years." They all laugh.

"Hey, Leonard, you gonna sing," Ratso pleads.

"Let it be known that I alone disdained the obvious support," Cohen chuckles, "I'm going to sit out there and watch."

"Why not sing?" Joni begs.

"No, no, it's too obvious," Leonard brushes off the request and looks to Ratso for guidance. He leads them out to the sound board where some folding chairs have been set up, just in time to see Dylan do his first set.

And what a set. The band is blistering, Dylan has regained the momentum that began to sag during Quebec,
and every song is like a sledgehammer pounding away at
the overflow crowd that has filled every seat, nook, cran-
ny, corner, penalty box, and aisle of the cavernous Forum.

By the time Stoner ends "This Land is Your Land" with
a torrid bass run, everyone—fans, ushers, concession-
aires, even Bob's own security crew—is on their feet, in
a screaming rollicking standing ovation. Ratso rushes back
to Leonard's party and escorts them backstage, worming
their way through the crowds, stepping over the huge rolls
of toilet paper that were thrown from the rafters by the
enthusiastic audience.

Backstage, Leonard greets the troops, and everyone re-
pairs to the hotel for a party in one of the downstairs
banquet rooms.

At the party, Ratso is out of control. He is all over the
place, introducing Jerry Rubin to Emmett Grogan, getting drinks for Sara, bringing the head of hotel security
in to meet Dylan, passing out copies of Joni's just-released
album with the singer pointing out the lucky recipients,
even at one point mooching a bite out of Bob's ham sandwich. So it was a merciful Chesley who dragged the sod-
den scribe to the elevator, fished his keys out of his pocket,
led him into his room, and gently deposited him on his
bed as the first rays of sun shimmered through the sheer
Château Frontenac curtains.

Rays of sun that rudely woke Ratso at midday. And
nursing an incredible hangover he stumbles downstairs to
the coffee shop, peers through half-operative eyes, and
makes out the figure of Ronee Blakley sitting at a table
with Jeff Raven and Denise Mercedes.

"Want to see my Polaroids," Ronee asks Slocum, "I got
a great shot of you you gotta see."

"That's about as tempting an offer as giving Lisa a
withdrawal slip in a celebrity sperm bank," Ratso smiles
and they head upstairs.

Blakley picks up her Polaroids and joins Ratso in his
room. A curious affinity has grown between these two, a
mutual admiration society intensified by the outcast status
each enjoys. Ratso of course is the official film shittee, a
part that sometimes transcends the celluloid and becomes
reality like the time he returned to his car after one of
the Boston Area concerts and found his tires flat.

And Blakley has been in the critical shittee, lambasted by most of the music critics and snickered at by some of the musicians themselves. Her intensely emotional performances are often passed off as histrionic or amaturesh and when she sings backup for Dylan she sometimes leans too far into the mike, propelling her voice like a helicopter over the audience, at times drowning out Bob's lead. But Ratso admires her resilience, her determination to push things to the limit and to accept the consequences of those actions. He remembers both of them being the last assholes left in the hospitality suites and he also recalls late-night sessions when they shone like saints.

"Blakley," he laughs, looking through the surprisingly good Polaroids, "you never quit. That's what I love about you."

Blakley smiles and sips the Coke that Ratso ordered up from room service. "Ronson's the only one who can outlast me. The only thing is that Ronson just always passes out wherever he is, he doesn't bother to go to bed." She cracks up. "When it's time for him he just goes to sleep like a little angel and people just carry him to bed, you know."

"What was it like for you playing in the same arena as Joan and Joni? You being the second wave so to speak."

"Well, Baez is a totally professional genius vocalist. She has presence onstage and presence in her personality. She's so smart, she's like a whip. She's funny, she's nice, she's helpful, she also has an ego. She's very queenly and imperious, after all, she was the first, and it's not just that she was the first, she's still the best. I mean a lot of people said, 'Oh well, Baez sure, but she was the first.' Well, I don't care if she was the first, she could start right now and she'd still be as big as she is. She's that good. She helps people."

"How did the three of you women relate to each other?"

"I don't want to get too much into that," Ronee looks coyly at Ratso's running Sony. "I hope you don't mind. Baez and I related very well, she was the only person, see I was kinda the outsider, the new kid on the block, and I didn't have anybody traveling with me and being the only woman unaccompanied, I didn't have a road manager and there were many times when I was trying to be one of the boys so I could be accepted, yet I couldn't be one of the boys 'cause I wasn't one of the boys. Or, I was in many ways considered a movie actress. A lot of people really didn't know that I had been playing for six or seven years, 'cause they never heard of me because I was so underground that I was below ground."

"You were in a kind of weird position," Ratso sets the pictures down, "really the only girl in Guam, Scarlett was like always on with Bob only."

"True," Ronee nods. "Male musicians are mostly the top musicians, there aren't very many top female lead guitarists for instance. Most of the stars are men. So then when Baez is a star and is a woman, what she gets accused of is acting like a man. It's the masculine identity to be successful and aggressive."

"The guys in the band musta been jealous, in a way, of you, I mean they're onstage the whole time, and you come out and have the same shot. Was there tension?" Ratso wonders.

"Only in the fact that I was a newcomer. As I said, it's a very tight crowd, like anything else, you have to pay your dues and you have to get your stripes. They're not gonna be given to you. There's very few people who will just give you your stripes. I mean, Dylan gave me my stripes. If it weren't for him, I wouldn't have been on that tour for more than two days. 'Cause nobody else would have wanted me around."

"Yeah, I remember when I gave him my first article to read and he sent word out to me in the audience that he was really pissed 'cause I bad-mouthed you until someone showed him that one of the words was in italics."

Ronee smiles. "I appreciate that. It shows the loyalty he feels for his friends, and in a way, it shows some kind of thing that he and I hit off. We hit it off like that. Well, for one thing, you don't sit up and play piano for six hours with somebody and not have any feelings for them. We didn't talk but we played four-handed piano for six hours one night at the Other End and, man, you know after you do that that you don't need to ever talk to him. What have you got left to say?" She laughs heartily.

"So what do you think of him now, six weeks later?" Ratso smiles impishly.

"My impressions of Bob? Oh God, I don't know, my impressions of him, I think he has, you know, the qualities of sainthood. I think he's a total weirdo. I absolutely love him and adore him and I don't care who knows it,

even his wife knows it. He knows it. Everyone knows it."
Ronee smiles again and rolls the Polaroids through her
fingers. "I'd like to think that I'd do anything for him
but I might not, 'cause I want to make sure he's a person."

"Did you get to know him?" Ratso thinks of Bloomfield's anguish over failing to penetrate the "armor."

"I feel that I know him a little bit. The danger is when
you're around people who are really, what can you call
him, a certified genius? What can you call him? What can
you say about Bob Dylan, he's affected all of our lives,
he's affected everybody's life for ten years. I mean what
can you say about the guy, he's not a normal guy. He
can't lead a normal life, he goes to a party, he hides in
the bushes. I mean, you know, 'cause if he comes out of
the bushes everybody gawks. I mean he can't just stand
around and talk to people."

"Yeah," Ratso cuts in excitedly, "even Ginsberg is mesmerized too . . ."

"Sycophancy," Blakley finishes. "Well, I don't think that
I am and I don't have that relationship with Bob. And because I think in a way I fight that, I think that I've been
cruel to him on a couple of occasions and he's never been
cruel to me."

"What kind of stuff do you do in the movie?"

"Bob's? Once, I did a scene where I baptized myself in
the sea, then another scene I played an accused witch in
seventeenth-century puritanical Massachusetts, then I did a
psychosexual scene with Bobby Neuwirth on the bus, then
I did a razor-fight scene with Stevie Soles in the bathroom, and then I did a scene with Dylan where I was
crying in the bar and he came in and acted like he'd been
following us around, like a groupie, he'd been following me around and I said, 'Well, look, I'd do what I can
'cause you seem really nice, I'll see if I can introduce
you to Dylan but I'll have to get through the security
guards. But don't worry, I know a few of them, I think
I can do it.' So then I introduce him to Dylan and it's
Baez dressed up as Dylan, so I bring Dylan in as this kid,
just an unknown nervous kid to meet Bob Dylan, and
it's Baez dressed up as Dylan. Ha. And I did a couple of
scenes in Niagara Falls where we were dressed in black
oilcloth coats. Just the usual, you know," she shrugs
ironically.

"What's your fix on this movie as compared to, say, *Nashville?*"

Blakley downs the Coke. "My fix on the movie is that it's great. It's gonna be a brilliant movie. I would say it's similar to *Nashville* in terms of high quality. It's not gonna be similar in terms of genre, although in the sense that one of the controversies about *Nashville* was, is it or is it not a documentary? I mean, people were criticizing it all of the time saying the country music stinks, that it's really not country music, da da da. Well, it wasn't a documentary, it was fiction, but *Nashville* approached real life so closely that people actually confused it with real life and yet at the same time, it was surrealistic, so there was constant confusion between irony, comedy, tragedy, sincerity, soap opera, humor, and hysteria with no hint and no lead-in or lead-out. It was the creation of one man's vision, and so is this film. And the thing about this that's very similar but goes a step further is that you'll see people singing onstage then you'll probably see cuts into some other scenes where you won't know if they're actually faking it, acting, or whether the scene was actually taking place."

"Was *Nashville* scripted?" Ratso asks.

"*Nashville* was scripted. There's a big difference between improvisation and writing. Some was improvised, some was scripted."

"Well, with this movie it seems everything was improvised," Ratso remembers.

"Never on any of my scenes," Ronee gets indignant. "I wrote some of my scenes and I improvised some of my own scenes. *Nashville* was entirely structured and scripted compared to this Rolling Thunder movie. Altman is not given credit and neither is Joan Tewkesbury for writing scenes within which actors can work. . . . Everybody seems to give Altman some magical credit, which is true, he does have the magical genius to have people appear on the set and something happens, but it just doesn't happen. He discusses things with actors, actors go out shopping for their own props, for their own wigs, their own wardrobes, they go practice in the drugstores, they hang out in the bars, they write and work out their lines, they get everything worked out. They're professionals from the word go, they don't just show up on the set and it's an accident. This whole thing about Altman and improvisation and all his actors not really being actors, you should see the work that his actors put in before they show up on the set. Just because they don't stand in the room and rehearse."

"Did you do research for that character?"

"Lots of research, yeah." Ronee's eyes grow wide. "Oh yeah, I hung around everywhere. I hung around the Opry, I hung around Nashville, I called all the managers of all the stars, and all the record companies, and I went to all the fan club dinners. And I hung out with Dolly, and I hung out with Loretta, and I hung out with Conway. I worked very hard for that part, I studied very hard. I called up Altman every day and told him new little dialogue, new lines I heard, new bits of action, lots of stuff. I studied very hard. See, most people think that I was her," Ronee leans over and confides to Ratso. "You know that? Everyone thinks that I really was Barbara Jean. See, so they don't regard it as acting."

"That's a compliment!" Ratso gushes.

"It's a compliment, except I can't get a job," Blakley frowns. "They think I'm Barbara Jean. If they want Barbara Jean, the girl in the white dress with the Southern accent who falls apart, maybe they would call me, but for any other part, no. What they say is, How did Altman have the genius to find that girl with that ratted hair and that white dress and that crazy neurotic. . . . I was skiing with Miloš Forman for four days, not as lovers but as friends, we were all staying in the same house, Jack Nicholson's house, in Aspen for four days, him and me skiing in our jeans, in our crummy army surplus parkas, fighting our way down Aspen Mountain. Finally, on about the fourth day on a trip up the chair lift, he says to me, 'You know, Ronee, there's somesing I vant to tell you, I saw *Nashville* and I thought it was so brilliant, so very brilliant, but you know, up until this very day it's taken me three days now to be around you but I have to tell you quite honestly that I thought that Bob Altman had just found himself a nut. I thought that Bob Altman had this genius and he had found himself this nut. You know, you're very together. You're a very together person.' I said, 'Well, thanks, Miloš, you know, I'm not that together.'

"He said that I represent the new kind of American actor and I think it's the highest compliment that I could be paid as an actress, he said I represented the new American actor like Jack Nicholson who gives the kind of performance which Miloš called 'You can't see through it.' And it had taken that long and we were staying in the same house and I was wearing jeans, no makeup, and T-shirts, and we were skiing together all day and having dinner and every morning getting up, and it took him four days and he was still seeing that white dress on the ski slopes." Ronee laughs out loud at that surreal image. She gets up and starts for the door, then pauses. "How dare I impersonate Barbara Jean?" she shouts, then shrugs ironically, blows the reporter a kiss, and scampers back to her room.

As soon as Ronee leaves, Ratso remembers he made plans to meet Joni that evening to go to Leonard Cohen's for dinner. So he takes a quick shower, throws on some clothes, and hustles downstairs. At the bar, Joni is waiting with Roger McGuinn, who'll accompany them, and Steve Soles, who'd like to but is on call to Dylan for a movie scene. Ratso pulls up a barstool.

"We're going to a girlfriend of mine's house first, Ratso," Joni explains. "She can't go to Leonard's, her old man just got back from New York, the fire is burning, and there are children. We're going to a real Montreal home."

"These guys are like society," Soles explains.

"Not so much society which implies socialization as it is conservatism. She's just an old girlfriend from Saskatoon. She was the best woman at my wedding."

"Were you married, Joni?" Ratso forgets.

"For two years. I was twenty-one when I first got married."

"I was twenty when I first got married," Roger brags. "It lasted four months. I was attracted to her and I didn't really know. Actually, as it turned out it was a kick we were both on."

"Drink up, Ratso," Joni warns.

"Are we ready to roll?" Ratso gulps his Tom Collins and gobbles some peanuts.

In the cab, Mitchell leans back, sandwiched by Ratso and Roger. "This trip is very addicting, isn't it? I keep on thinking how am I gonna go back to the normality of my situation?"

"You're gonna go back with another level of consciousness," Roger smiles. "You'll never lose that."

"I don't know if my old man will be able to relate to it," Joni frets. "I've already been going through changes. I wish he could go through it too."

Ratso looks out the window at the wet streets of Montreal. The cab begins its steep climb up the mountain and the houses get more and more opulent-looking. They finally locate the address and knock on the thick wood door.

An attractive thirtyish woman named Ruth answers and throws her arm around Joni. The troupe is ushered into the elegant but cozy house and Joni makes the introductions. Ruth leads them to seats on the plush couch and Brook, her husband, takes orders for drinks.

"Doug said everything was so super last night," Ruth bubbles, genuinely pleased to see her old school chum.

"It was so hyper," Joni gushes. "Everyone was playing so fast and talking so fast. It was really exciting. Well, we have one more to go. That fire smells so nice." Ratso settles back with his drink, watching the flames.

"Are you tired?" Ruth worries. "Your voice really sounded bad on the phone."

"I have been sick all the time," Joni grimaces. "I got a flu in Niagara on the second day. Not a flu but a cold that everyone's trying to get rid of and they're canceling it out with someone else's."

"Plus you don't have the sense to go to sleep," Ruthie mothers.

"I spent three days up in a row at one point and I was like a space cadet," Joni giggles. "Wandering around the room and there was music going and I'd still be dancing."

"You couldn't sleep," Ruthie worries.

"I didn't want to miss anything!" Joni smiles.

Ruth kneels down on the thick carpet in front of her friend. "You really drove me mad two years ago," she chides Joni. "We had a mother's helper from London, Ontario, and when she walked in the door, she had a guitar with her and she said, 'How do you do? I'm the mother's helper. I want you to introduce me to Joni Mitchell.' She did not let up for the whole bloody summer," Ruth remembers. "She just idolized you. The whole summer she asked me what you were really like. I said I didn't know, that you chug-a-lug beer . . ."

Joni cracks up at the memory. "She does what?" Ratso wants to get this straight.

"She chug-a-lugs beer," Ruthie grins impishly.

"This is a long time ago." Joni starts to turn red.

"You know," Ruthie demonstrates, "she glops the beer down without closing her throat. Joni was the best. Can you still stick your fist down your throat?" she roars.

"I can't do that anymore," Joni moans, "I lost it."

"She used to do super swan dives off the bed. It just stunned me to have this girl come in and—"

"Idolize this alcoholic," Ratso cracks.

"Then she wanted me to call and get to meet the top models in Canada," Ruthie shakes her head.

"Ruthie and I used to model in department stores," Joni explains, "like we were really heavy in our little town."

"I didn't do so badly here in this little town either, Joni, for about three years," Ruth bristles. "Has she ever told you her favorite song?" she giggles.

"What? 'Bonie Moronie'?" Joni smiles. "I was very skinny at school—when I look back at the pictures I wasn't, but the standard was to be more zaftig then— and 'Bonie Maronie' was my handle. This is some old shit we're digging out," she mock-glares at Ruth.

"What's Chuck doing?" Brook interjects, "if I may ask such a blunt question."

"He's working in small repertory theatrical companies," Joni answers unabashedly. "He still plays in some coffeehouses, doing the same material that he did when we were first married."

"That's ten years ago," Ruthie marvels.

"He hasn't changed a song in his set. He does a lot of Brecht and show tunes. We gotta go," she tells Ruth, "Leonard has kids and . . ."

"Well before you go, finish this wine," Ruthie instructs Ratso and Roger, "and I'll be very selfish and ask Joan all sorts of dumb questions like, are you enjoying your house?"

"My house is like an experiment, Ruthie. When you get the notion in your head that you're an artist you fall subject to artist morality."

"Which is what?" Ruthie asks.

"Which is individualized but there is one sort of common bohemian aspect to it. Which is like that wealth corrupts art or any manifestation of it."

"Say it again." Ruthie holds her hands up. "Wealth corrupts . . ."

"Well, it's a common point of view among artists, while the artist is like struggling for success and recognition, he is also developing an attitude of contempt toward the wealthy and the expression of wealth, so when you find yourself in the position of being an artist and of being wealthy, you have like a lot of moral conflict to deal with. How to express it."

"Joni," Ruth interrupts, "do you like your house or not? Are you doing what you want to do?"

"I'm getting to that," Joni says, distracted. "Initially your feeling is guilt and the point when you feel guilty you find you attract a lot of sycophants. There are people ready there to bleed off everything for like anything, and Picasso, he was lucky in that he was forty when he achieved major success so he had enough sensitivity and sensibility that when he made it, Picasso got little black and white maids, a chauffeur and silk suits, and he attended every social activity and all the artists in his circle said, 'Watch his art go down the tubes.' And for a while he did socialize out but his art never died, he just experienced that, so what I have done at this point is I have gone completely elegant. My house is like completely elegant."

"Like *nouveau?*" Ruthie asks.

"No, it's very tasteful. The best designers in the world did it. I worked with it like I do on my records, in partnership."

"That's why you got ripped off?" Ratso deduces.

"Well, the rip-off doesn't matter. The only thing in that that matters is the violation of my space. I was burglarized five times in Laurel Canyon. It's the nature of the city. I have to have electronic equipment, guitars, and all that."

"I just can't stand that, Joan," Ruthie fumes, "I can't stand that, five times!"

"I can empathize with Joni, it is the nature of our work," Roger is affecting a very clipped, precise tone, the tone of a diplomat. Ratso gives him a strange stare. "It is the nature of our work to have electronic equipment and guitars and a turquoise collection which she had and I also have. It's something to worry about, so I have a perimeter control around my house that has electronic surveillance, closed-circuit television, and dogs."

"I can't live that way," Joni barks, "I can't stand it. So I'm experiencing . . ."

"You just really want to move back to the Chelsea Hotel," Ratso cracks.

"I can live anywhere, Ratso," Joni runs her hand through her long silky hair, "I like to experience everything. I have elegance in me and I have a lot of street in me, but I'm neither street nor elegant. And I'm middle class. I can live anywhere, I've lived in caves, I've lived in shacks, I've lived in mansions. I lived in caves on the island of Crete. I went from the caves to first-class hotels in Paris and bought myself elegant clothing. I like contrast, you know, and I like to experience everything. I'm enjoying my wealth. It's not a symbol of any attainment to me."

"What's it a symbol of?" Ruthie challenges.

"It's something I enjoy the expression of sometimes," Joni seems at a loss for words.

"What does it mean? That you've gotten to the top of the heap? What does the expression of elegance mean to you?"

"I admire Coco Chanel," Joni says by way of example. "I used to design clothes in school, I could have been a fashion designer, Ratso."

"Joni designed something and Judy Lamarche and I got into the worst fight about it if you can recall," Ruthie starts giggling.

"The culottes!" Joni cracks up. "We couldn't wear Bermuda shorts or pants to school. We had to wear skirts, so I designed a skirt, Bermuda shorts with flaps over it. If you stood still you had a box-pleated skirt on but if you went like this," Joni moves her torso, "you had Bermuda shorts on."

"And I actually got her to do one for me," Ruthie laughs, "and wore it to school. And Judy Lamarche was the lovely in our dumb little society and I happened to get that before Judy did and she's never forgiven me."

"One of my interests as a child was to draw cutouts and make clothes and I could have been a fashion designer, Ratso," Joni continues to try to answer the reporter's earlier question. "It's a creative outlet for me, not an expression of status. For example, when I'm really well dressed and I go into Beverly Hills, I have a whole relationship with different shopkeepers in Beverly Hills. I always get there ten minutes before the store is closing and I usually stay an hour after closing and go out to dinner with them and I'm interested in that mercantile aspect and what I have created in L.A. is a small town where I know merchants."

"What you're after is what you just left, a small city like Saskatoon," Ruth concludes.

"But also the larger world," Joni protests. "These are international figures. I'm interested in not being limited by any aspect of experience. I don't want to limit myself, because every time I make a judgment on any particular stratum of society, I find I'm totally wrong so I've set out to break down the barriers in my own life so I can experience people in different aspects of their experience rather than getting sucked into the rock 'n roll thing. One of the reasons my new record is coming up for criticism is because it's a description in some ways of wealth and elegance. It's not about rock 'n roll and Holiday Inns and that's why it's being so well received also. The way I have chosen through experimentation to approach my audience is to maintain the same experimental level that I did in the coffeehouses so I don't go for the big applause."

"Really and truly," Ruthie gushes and hugs her friend, "that's fantastic."

"I can move through my audience, those people, and they'll say, 'Joni come and sit with us,' and they won't even talk to me. I can walk through the streets of Washington or New York and they come up and say, 'Nice show, Joni.' Generally, what I've done is create my own freedom."

"How?" Ratso remains skeptical.

"Because I've gone through my changes publicly, like my weaknesses . . ."

"So has Leonard, so has Bob," Ratso counters.

"Leonard has freedom of movement too," Joni agrees and pauses to think.

"I haven't seen Joni for ten years but I know Joni and you're just about the same as I am in a lot of ways," Ruthie cuddles her friend.

"Even though our situations are like radically different and our experience is too, we have like a lot in common in the expanse of like Ruthie's elegance. In serving tea Ruthie can foster formality and pull it off and go right down to the street level at the same time."

"She's done it tonight," Ratso admires.

"I haven't bared my armpits yet," Ruthie warns. "I think that something is very basic that we get from where we're from and you're asking why is Joni able to do what she's doing without applause. She doesn't need it, she has one thing going for her, and I've got it going for me, it's called loving another guy and making them happy, and you don't need," Ruthie suddenly claps her hands, "that to make them happy, you just need a pure glow. Isn't that fantastic?"

"Yeah," Joni nods thoughtfully, "there have been a couple of moments on this tour when I've had to confront the immaturity of my ego where all of a sudden because I'm in the position in the show of being an opening act and I'm receiving that kind of press attention, whereas in fact, I have attained a much higher . . ."

Ruth waves her arms. "Brook asked me about that by the way. He said why is Joni not No. 1?"

"I'll tell you why," Joni shoots back. "It's experimental. I'm having a good time. It's like a rolling party. Only when I get weak like when Bobby Neuwirth or something . . . when I get a mass of underestimation all of a sudden I get professional and I start thinking career moves. See Elliot, my manager, and Geffen, everybody's against me back there, they say that I shouldn't be doing this being in such a submissive position. I feel that at this point that I have nothing to lose by it, to me this is the most interesting thing. I've felt highly productive, that's another reason why I've stayed. In the slot I have, I have the option, like if I was to go out and do the most popular material the effect would be different. It's much more interesting like winging it."

"You're doing a lot similar thing to what Bob's doing," Ratso says.

"No, his set is much more stable."

"It's stable, but he's doing a lot of new songs. Something that Sinatra doesn't do, that Elton John doesn't do." Ratso smiles.

The cab Roger called for pulls up and the troupe makes their way to the door, accompanied by Ruthie and Brook. Suddenly Joni pauses.

"You know another reason why I stayed. One day I was running away, I even had a plane reservation to New York. I said good-bye to everyone in our dressing room and I went to say good-bye to Bob, rather than just sulk off, it was my intention to say good-bye but I ended up talking to Louie in the dressing room, but when I said good-bye to Wyeth, he looked at me like, I can't describe the look he gave me. He was like hurt, like I was running out and I felt, Jesus Christ, I don't mean to be selfish, like I just want to escape. And I suddenly realized, more than anybody Wyeth's reaction was so heartfelt, his expression of it was so open. Like it's just his soul is so beautiful. So I stayed."

Joni kisses Ruthie good-bye and they depart, piling into the cab for the short ride over to Leonard's. On the way, Joni and Ratso get into a discussion of Castaneda, whom Joni loves and whom Ratso looks upon with disdain.

The cab finds the address and they pile out and enter the Cohen domicile. And what a contrast. If the Mount Royal residence was subtly elegant, Cohen's house in old Montreal is blatantly commonplace. First of all, it's not a house, it's a ramshackle bungalow-type structure, entered through via a door that would be hard put to withstand the ravaging assault of a five-year-old. It boasts exposed beams, slanted floors and ceilings, and a collection of furniture that would do any Goodwill proud. But there's a curious feeling of warm spirituality pervading the home, and the shelves upon shelves of books and the myriad knickknacks and the old, dusty-framed prints and paintings impart a tremendous character to the place. Ratso enters Leonard's house for the second time and feels right at home.

"Leonard," he yells in greeting, smelling the savory aroma of barbequed ribs wafting into the front room, "you're immaculate." The reporter scurries into the back of the long room and plops down at the table. The others follow, exchanging greetings with Leonard and his lovely lady Suzanne.

Cohen has long been a demigod to that brand of musical practitioner that label themselves sensitive singer-songwriters. A fine novelist and a best-selling poet in his native Canada, Cohen turned to the concert hall at the urging of his friends, among them Judy Collins, who put Leonard's song "Suzanne" on the map and the charts. And of course, part of Cohen's attractiveness and his appeal is the graphic description in his songs of the viccisitudes that befall a gentleman in a world of scoundrels. And his documentation of the doings of the scoundrel in the parlors of society. In other words, Cohen just don't fit, he carries around his angst like other people carry chewing gum. And the songs get delivered in that lumbering, world-weary monotone that emanates from that broodingly handsome iconographic wandering Jew face. Ratso loves Leonard's work, it never fails to make him laugh.

"I didn't hear you last night, Joni," Leonard laments, "I'm really sorry. How was your friend tonight?"

"She was my matron of honor when I was married but between that time period there was a long gap since we saw each other and that was only briefly. There must have been five years between that," Joni holds a rib poised over her plate, "so my impressions of her have been romanticized over the years plus her circumstances have limited her experience in certain ways so that we weren't as linked as we were as girls. Like you and Mort have carried your relationship along . . ."

"Yes, Mort is one of these rare creatures," Leonard smiles, "he's really like a completely unrecognized genius."

"You know all those stories you read where the Zen master slapped someone on the back and at that moment he attained. Well, Mort did that one day in New York," Joni says, "he took my problem and in one sentence eliminated it. That's a rare gift, isn't it?"

"He says he wants to give you another lesson," Leonard smiles slyly.

"What was the sentence?" Ratso gets the question out between two mouthfuls of ribs.

" 'Draw me and don't look at the paper,' that's all he said to me and it changed everything, you know? So what you do is actually you trace the lines of highest emotion. It doesn't matter if the person moves, it doesn't matter if the eye overlaps the nose or anything, I've tried to pass that on to a lot of different people and Blakley is like one of the few—"

"She's nice, eh?" Leonard asks.

"Well, nice I wouldn't say," Joni says diplomatically, "we have a relationship that isn't defined by the word nice."

"I enjoyed her last night," Leonard smiles.

"She is like Nico, you know," Joni offers. "She has a strange kind of madness that you would find interesting. My attraction to her is like that too. . . ."

"I like it in you," Leonard grins. "You guys have been pretty close now for how many months?"

"Just weeks," Roger corrects, "but I've been out for two months now."

"It's really interesting," Joni gushes, " 'cause people are always testing each other all the time, you know, misreading you. You know you have to deal with their misreading and you have to like decide whether to allow them to misread you or to clarify it, like I've learned to float like coming from a position where I need always to be sincere and to be understood, I like allowed myself to float through situations, that's what I was trying to tell you, it's so exciting to me, it's not giving a shit. It's not consistent. It really is an interesting thing because it's a traveling commune."

Suzanne interrupts the monologue with a soda break. Joni sips at her Coke and continues, "I've come to deal with my multiphrenia, they're all realities. There are so many ways to look at the thing, you know that as a writer, cutting through the layers of personality to get to the one who is the most honest, you know."

"I don't know how honest I am," Leonard smiles sheepishly. "I'm unstable."

"Maybe I'm more unstable than you," Joni boasts. "You have a more consistent character than you play out."

"Oh yeah," Cohen smiles sardonically, "I'm as constant as the North Star."

"But I find that different people will manifest different aspects," Joni goes on. "You know, some people will bring out the sage, some people will bring out the child, some people will bring out the rebel, some people will bring out the conservative."

"I find everyone too revolutionary these days," Leonard comments as he grabs another rib.

"You are wearing a suit in your own funky old house," Roger notes.

"But that's the only clothes he has," Ratso explains.

"This seeming cattiness was one aspect of tour that I had to adjust to after I came in late," Joni picks up her thought and starts to address Leonard. "I got on the bus and I thought, God that's cruel, they're cruel people being cruel to each other. Next thing that I noticed was that everybody was quite strong and the manifestation of multiple personalities was almost a necessity."

"There's a definite pecking order," Ratso says, from the bottom.

"There is a strange pecking order," Joni agrees, near the top.

"Baez has this amazing George Harrisonesque dressing room with rugs on the walls and incense and food spreads and you guys got this funky closet for a dressing room," the reporter reports.

Leonard interrupts with cups of hot sake.

"You're quite a host, Leonard," Roger marvels, "I'd like to reciprocate sometime."

"Roger and I did a scene," Joni remembers, "and we were great in the scene except I quoted from pure Nietzsche and Bob wouldn't let me give him credit. I said, 'C'mon, Bobby, I got to say like *Thus Spake Zarathustra*, I can't be like an intellectual quoting from Nietzsche, with no originality, give me a break. He's got a mean streak, he gets mean.'"

"You're talking about Bobby Neuwirth?" Leonard misunderstands.

"Oh Neuwirth is different," Joni smiles. "It's much more open, he just tells you you're cold and you're a cunt and you're an asshole." She giggles. "With Dylan, he just like strikes you out of a scene or puts you in the scene where he wants you to manifest parts of your self, it's different. He's got the power, he's got the hammer and Neuwirth just attacks and he can really hurt. Neuwirth really hurt me and then he said, 'There's no fear allowed on Rolling Thunder.' He just keeps whittling away at you and whittling away at you until he finds the place of you which you're most afraid of and then, whew, he just like presses on it till he gets you, then he says, 'No fear.' It's an excellent exercise." She giggles again.

"He's been unable to pin me," Roger smiles, "and he always rolls away in frustration."

"That's 'cause you always say 'I'm sorry,' all the time," Joni cracks. "How can you pin someone that's always apologizing?"

"Gee, I'm sorry," Roger gushes, "I didn't mean to offend you last night, I'm really sorry."

Ratso gulps down his sake and accepts Suzanne's invitation to a guided tour of the place. They tramp up the rickety stairs and view the small cubiculed bedrooms and, in one room, come upon Leonard's two children. "Jesus, they're so cute," Ratso marvels at the two small figures.

"Yes, they're angels, aren't they?" Suzanne says in her delicate voice, a voice that oozes grace and charm and patience, an avalanche of patience. When they return downstairs, Joni is enmeshed in a long story about her marijuana bust a few years ago in L.A.

"I really started to feel like a fool, I felt so frustrated because I was really on the verge of a song," Joni remembers, "and they didn't give me a pencil or paper and I asked them for my guitar, and this one guy was like a guitar player and understood, and I felt like Huddie Ledbetter, 'Give me my guitar,' and they wouldn't do anything. So finally the narcs called me out which was good because I could smoke and at that point I was like three hours without a cigarette. So they called me in and the Man said this was off the record, it didn't have to do with what I was up for and in the meantime they were analyzing my vitamin pills and had changed it from marijuana to like narcotics because I had this whole mixture of different kinds of vitamin pills that they were putting through the lab or something. So the guy asked me what my drug experience was because his kid was being hit on the playground for reds and he was only eight, and I asked them if they had experienced any drugs themselves because in this room I was in there were pictures of marijuana leafs of different shapes, pills and their titles underneath, all the way around the room.

"I said, 'Do you know what these things do to your chemistry? Have you tried anything?' And he told me he wanted to be a professional baseball player but he couldn't make it so he became a cop, and he was like half tough and half soft and we just talked for a long time. I said, 'Ask me anything you want as long as I can keep smoking, this is the worst, you got all the leaves and pills up here but this,' and I pointed to my cigarette, 'is the really serious villain, this is the socially accepted drug.'"

"They used tobacco as a tool against you," Roger smiles, "they used it to get you to talk."

"But there was supposed to be a release to the press, they always do that, like they did with Steven Stills, and I said, 'Well, you're talking 'bout your kid, eight years old, and people hitting on him on the playground for reds, if you put that I was arrested for dangerous drugs, by nature of the people who listen to the things that I have to say, do you know how many people you'd turn on. Why don't you try a little preventive crime?' So the captain said, 'No, we have to release everything to the press,' and they didn't release it! They didn't put anything out. Sometimes the laws are very insensible and he was a man that went beyond the law to his own sensibility."

"Horse sense," Roger cracks.

"Then I went back to my cell," Joni relates, "and they threw this girl in in the middle of the night, about three o'clock in the morning and I had already meditated three times, I'd done every dance step I know, and I was really starting to die of boredom. I'm fading," Joni yawns, "we should go home pretty soon. I wish I had a guitar, I'd like you to hear the new song."

"I'd like to play myself," Roger adds, a little tipsy from the sake, "but mine's all packed away. We gotta fly tomorrow."

"We all want to serenade you guys," Joni giggles, while Roger breaks into a spontaneous "One More Cup of Sake for the Road."

"Did I ever tell you I loved your live album, Leonard?" Ratso asks.

"You and twelve thousand other people liked it," Leonard sighs.

The songwriter and the reporter walk into the front room as the others exchange good-byes.

"Sing me some of your new shit, Leonard," Ratso says eagerly, "the stuff you told me you were working on when I was following you around doing that story for *Rolling Stone*."

"OK," Leonard assents and begins to recite the song in his haunting voice.

> A lady found me calmly boasting in the Guerrero
> When I was running smoke across the line
> She let me love her till I was a failure
> Her beauty on my bruise like iodine
> When I was weak enough to learn her method
> I said 'Will I be punished for my crime?'
> She said 'There is a table set in heaven
> But I don't like to eat there all the time'
> She pulled away the mask of her madonna
> She pulled away the valley of her thighs
> She bid me find herself in other women
> Until I should exhaust her last disguise

And I was with her when there was no ocean
When there was no moon to spill the tide
Oh long before the wild imagination
Could lay us in Guerrero side by side.

"Jesus, Leonard," Ratso kvells, "that's great. But you told me you were gonna write some top-forty stuff. That ain't no Tommy James and the Shondells."

"Here's another," Leonard glances back and deduces there's time for one more.

It's time I let you go
I've never seen your eyes so wide
Your appetite is occupied with someone else
As if I didn't know
It ain't my style to hold this tight
So let's be married one more night.
I guess it's time I finally let you go
A while ago the scenery started fading
I held you 'til you learned to walk on air
But don't look down, it's gone, it's faded baby
The smoky life is practiced everywhere.

Joni walks up just as Leonard comes to an end. "We should go," she hugs the poet good-bye, "I need a week's sleep."

They say good-byes and the troupe hops into the waiting cab and starts back to the motel.

"Who was that guy?" McGuinn mysteriously whispers.

"The Lone Ranger?" Ratso guesses.

"No, it wasn't Tonto either," Roger grins.

"I'm a stone Cohenite," Joni brags. "Dylan, ehhh," she jokingly dismisses the singer with a flap of the wrist.

"Let's call Dylan," Roger starts to unpack his attaché-case phone.

"I love Cohen," Joni continues, "I'm promiscuous with my love. I love a lot of people. Who I can live with, that's another question," she laughs. "I can make it through, but I'm feeling like the mother of a large family."

"I've come around to a new way of thinking about everyone in the world." Roger puts the phone away. "I'm serious."

"What new way?" Joni's curious.

"It's called acceptance," Ratso says cynically.

"Small-town acceptance," Joni smiles.

"I love the people I love and I ignore the people I can't tolerate if I can," Roger says with impeccable logic, "and try not to loathe anyone."

"I don't loathe anyone," Joni agrees. "I try not to feel superior, like a jiveass superior chick, but I keep myself in check 'cause there are other perspectives I'm able to appreciate; the beauty of people on different levels until I get pushed in a corner."

"I'm against possessiveness and monogamy," Roger interrupts.

"I did it for two years, Roger," Joni confesses.

"I did it for five," Roger three-ups.

"Really?" Joni seems incredulous. "You didn't cheat on the road?"

"Not once," Roger moans.

"I sure broke down in a hurry," Joni shakes her blond head.

"I'm not talking about this trip," Roger is quick to qualify.

"Yeah," Joni laughs, "we all know about this trip. It's very difficult and it's very limiting and very indulgent at the same time, none of us are mature enough to be able to accept the fact that other people can love other people. We all want to be the conqueror, the one and only in every relationship that we begin." Joni pauses for the right words. "There's a duality that I can't make out, I don't mean to be a victimizer but sometimes I find I am by my own spontaneous nature, you know, like gravitating to people who interest me in a room and neglecting the one who is like hurting by my interest in other people."

"Yeah," Roger leans forward in his seat, "like if I don't give a fuck if you come around and say hello to me, you're probably more likely to come over than if someone said, 'Oh please, oh please, come over here and pay attention to me.' I'm the same way with people, if they're craving my attention."

"But Dylan makes mistakes because of his inconsistency," Joni suddenly invokes the songwriter. "There are people that he lets in to a certain degree, he's let me in pretty close in certain ways, and yet he will," Joni goes into a perfect Dylan drawl, "act like we never have met the next day. I don't trust him. He like put me on the spot in the film. I have preferred parts of my personality and part of my personality that I regret because of what it creates and he like wouldn't cop, he copped to perfection, to being able to deal with all his personality and that's bullshit. He must pinch. If he doesn't pinch then I accuse him of inhumanity because he turns left so many times on people."

"What the fuck are you talking about?" Ratso is finding it very difficult to follow Joni's drift.

"I'm speaking English." Joni has a trace of irritation in her voice as the cab pulls up to the hotel. "I find his humanity is all on a very ambitious level. He goes for the big causes and neglects the people who could be potentially friends. He may be king artist, that's an accomplishment, but he won't be one of my favorite people."

"Yeah, well how come he enjoys people who don't take shit from him," Ratso remember's Bob's almost awe of Kinky, and Roger's conversation in Vermont, and even the brassy woman in the lobby of the hotel who melted him till he eagerly signed an autograph.

"Well, of course," Joni stumbles a few seconds looking for an out, "he does it because what he says and what he is is a hypocrisy."

The next day is getaway day but since Ratso is driving back to New York he can afford to sleep late, and it's four in the afternoon before he starts rolling. He locates Dylan and the film crew over at novelist Emmett Grogan's house. Ratso arrives just as the shooting ends and he joins Bob, Sara, Emmett and his lovely wife Louise, a nationally known actress. The reporter does a quick survey of the wonderfully restored old house and heads straight for the kitchen where a buffet of roast beef and cheeses is set up. He makes a sandwich and sits down next to Dylan.

"I heard that you were worried about the press tomorrow at the concert in jail," Ratso mentions.

"Yeah," Bob nods, "Louis told me that there was a lot of press gonna be there."

"Well, Lois told me that he had rounded up AP, Reuters, UPI, *Time, Newsweek,* CBS, NBC . . ."

"Fuck it," Dylan dismisses the list. "It don't matter. I'll go out some other time to see Rubin. I don't have to see him with all that press around."

"What?" Ratso's mouth falls open.

"Really," Bob says straight-faced, "I'd rather see him man to man, without the press."

"We need the press for Rubin," Ratso shouts.

"Naw, they'll be enough people there doing it. No, the show is covered. I'll just go out there to see Rubin, man. I don't go to see the press. The press can come to the Garden."

"Maybe we can arrange for the press to split before the concert in the prison," Ratso thinks.

"I just won't do it," Dylan decides.

"OK, let's just not do it," Ratso plays the same game.

"OK, cancel it then," Dylan waves cavalierly. "Call Lois and tell him it's cancelled."

"And you'll come back alone and play for the prisoners without press?" Ratso prods.

"No problem," Dylan shrugs. "Give Lois a call. Just tell him I canceled and that the rest of the people will be there though."

Emmett strolls by and notes Ratso's pad. "In Boxboro I'm wondering who this guy is wandering around. I go into the bathroom and he's writing down stuff. I thought he was writing down the life of my schlong or something."

Ratso goes to the refrigerator for a beer and returns to Grogan and Dylan talking about Montreal.

"I didn't get a chance to get out at all," Bob complains.

"The people here, all they ever do is smile," the expatriate Brooklyner says in his raspy voice. "They never hit on you."

"It's civilized here," Dylan says with longing.

"It's also only three generations of people here," Emmett reminds.

"All I know is that when we cross that border," Bob shakes his head. "We spent about six weeks in New England, that was great, real Old Town America. But it was still America, you know? Then we crossed that border into Quebec City . . ."

"How was Quebec City?" Emmett asks.

"It was heavy," the songwriter whistles, "it was fantastic."

"How was it for the Revue?"

"They didn't understand a word but they loved it." Bob

smiles. "They loved it, they didn't understand anything. I could tell, anybody could tell. Quebec City was the nicest place I've seen, I can't figure it out."

Meanwhile, Ratso during this discussion has called Rubin in prison and, in an attempt to get Dylan to commit himself to playing tomorrow pulls the cord its full eight feet and offers the phone to the singer.

"Wanna speak to Rubin?" Ratso smiles.

"This guy is something else," Dylan shakes his head, pointing to the scribe. "You got your own ideas, man," he frowns and dutifully heads for the waiting phone.

"Rubin. How are you doing, man? OK, we've been doing the film. No, it isn't a porno one, close but not quite. We're planning to come down tomorrow, yeah. Uh huh, OK, good, pretty smooth. We're wrapping it up and we're up here. It's pretty cold. Yeah, we're heading back down to never-never land, right. Well, see you soon, OK Rubin, OK man."

Dylan gives Ratso a stern look and sits down at the dining-room table again.

"Did you hear about Dylan Thomas yesterday?" Emmett asks.

"What happened?" Bob perks up.

"His wife went to an auctioneer yesterday and she brought all the love letters he wrote to her. She brought them and nobody would bid and she had to wrap them up and leave."

"Really? All the love letters?"

"And nobody would make a bid," Emmett laughs. "So if you're interested they're up there."

"How much did she want for them?" Bob asks with mild interest.

"I don't know, there wasn't even a bid."

Dylan picks at a piece of cheese. "Sounds like she's trying to exploit him there a little bit," he smirks.

"I think she might be in trouble," Emmett explains. "She's had them but I think that she went to the wrong room because usually they pick that stuff up."

"They're buying Jack's stuff and all that," Dylan points out.

"I think she went to the wrong room, engineers or something, people looking for Chinese vases or something," Emmett laughs heartily.

"Lawrence's letters went for a lot of money though,"

Bob leans back in the chair. "I'd like to leave from here. I don't want to go back to the hotel. I'm gonna leave from here."

"You gotta get your stuff from the hotel," Ratso reminds him.

"I don't have any stuff. Gary can wrap up all Sara's shit, or I don't know, all our shit. Rolling Thunder shit."

"I'll go back and tell him, I have to get my own shit," Ratso volunteers.

"Would you? That would be great. I haven't been in a place like this in three months." Dylan surveys the room. "I like houses, old houses."

Emmett starts to tell Bob about his child, Max, as Ratso prepares to go back to the hotel. "Max'll love it here," Emmett smiles.

"How could he not?" Bob says, wide-eyed. "This is a great place to grow up in."

"Leonard's got kids his age," Ratso relates.

"Leonard does?" Bob seems surprised. "By his first wife?"

"No, Suzanne, she's not his wife." Ratso smiles.

"What?" Bob feigns shock. "Comment!"

"*Elle n'est pas femme* from the song," Ratso fractures both languages, "she's not the one from the song. Leonard claims the song conjured her up, *elle est conjurée par le chanson.*"

"He's got us confused now." Bob nudges Grogan. "This guy met a black Jamaican Jew."

"She wasn't black," Ratso protests.

"She looked black to me," Bob joshes.

"She was Sephardic," Emmett compromises.

"Whatever, she was great in bed," Ratso remembers fondly. "She said . . ."

"I love you very much," Bob pimps the reporter.

"I love you, Ratso," Emmett continues, "I'll give you anything if you just fuck me again."

"No, schmucks," Ratso fumes, "she gave me this bracelet, this sterling silver—"

"Looks like a slave bracelet to me," Emmett examines.

"I traded her for one of those cheap ten-cent Dylan pins," Ratso laughs.

"I wouldn't repeat that if I were you, Ratso," Bob warns, "especially with that dollar sign on your left shoulder."

Ratso starts for the door and then pauses, "Hey, did you ever get a telegram from Kinky?"

"No." Bob looks puzzled.

"You did get a telegram from Kinky, love," Sara, who had just come down from changing, reports.

"I did?" Bob stammers. "What did it say?"

"I know," Ratso smiles. "It says, 'Made Hartford, Missed Montreal, Move Over Malibu. Stop.'"

"Move over Malibu?" Dylan's really puzzled now. "He's moving to Malibu?"

"Maybe," Ratso shrugs, "he's in L.A. now."

"Wait a minute," Dylan stops, "how did you know what it said?"

"We wrote it together on the phone," Ratso chuckles.

"Which part did you write?" Dylan's curious. "Move over Malibu?"

"No, actually he just read it to me." The reporter heads for the door.

"OK, you'll get Gary to get that stuff, right Ratso," Bob reaffirms.

"Sure." The reporter heads out.

Dylan leans back, and taps out a rhythm on the wood floor with his boot heel. "Man, I love this place," he gushes.

"Robbie told me he wanted to come up here and spend a year," Louise reports.

"I can dig it," Bob smiles.

"Most Americans say that after a while if you hang around here, the people start asking you what you do." Emmett smiles mischievously.

"They ask you that here?" Bob seems crestfallen.

"They say that everywhere." Louise shrugs.

"They don't ask it in Brooklyn or Chicago," Emmett growls.

"Well, I like the vibes in this place." Dylan peers around the house again, and gets up and restlessly starts pacing the dining room. "You could just come up here and disappear," he says longingly, and sits back down, patiently, to await Gary and the stuff and the camper and the kids and the long drive back down across the border.

14

Ratso went back to the hotel, alerted Gary, and then had a great idea. He dumped the Hertz Granada, left the keys with the manager, loaded all his stuff into Bob's red Eldorado and drove over the border with Andy, one of the security guys, and Jesse, Bob's oldest son, who slept through most of the late-night drive in the rear seat.

They drove straight to the Hotel Westbury, on Manhattan's fashionable upper East Side, a good hideaway to sequester the troops till Monday's show in the Garden. But even as Ratso perused the room list as soon as they pulled in that early Sunday morning, he could sense that the magic had been left north of the border.

For one thing, a lot of the musicians lived in New York, so, as an economy move, Imhoff had decreed that they should stay at home, resulting in an instantaneous division in the *esprit de corps* that the assemblage had generated.

Furthermore, this was the Apple, and everyone but everyone, down to the last equipment man, knows people in New York, and even if you don't, there's always the instant camaraderie of the Village, the amusing tackiness of Times Square, the all-night gastronomical lures of Chinatown. Whereas on the road, the troupe had played, for the most part, relatively small towns, towns and cities where the encapsulated world of hotel to gig to hotel to hospitality suite to room was an attractive option. So after ten minutes in the stately shabbiness of the Westbury lobby, Ratso could feel that the vibe was dissipating.

And those feelings were intensified four hours later, when the buses were loading for the trip out to New Jersey and the special concert for Rubin and his friends in the slammer. It started when Ratso was thrown off the performers' bus by Louie, apparently because Bob had decided to ride with his fellow Thunderers rather than take the camper out. The reporter was shuffled over to the other camper, which was being driven out by Mike Evans and Andy Bielanski. And the feeling grew stronger yet when Chesley was told by Imhoff that there was no room at the prison and he would be better off staying back.

So when the camper finally rolled out behind the rented Greyhound, Slocum was seething.

Evans pilots the vehicle through the heavy Sunday Ninth Avenue traffic. "Breaker one, breaker one," a voice crackles over the CB. "Does anybody know what the score is at Shea Stadium?"

"Six-nothing," Evans barks into the mike.

"The only way the Giants could win that game," the disembodied voice groans, "is if the other team doesn't show up."

"Turn that shit off," Andy grimaces, just as Evans slams on the brakes, hurtling Ratso against the front seat. "Jesus," Evans shakes his head, "that poor dog."

"You're a real humanitarian," Ratso smirks, dusting himself off.

"I could easily kill you before I kill the dog." Evans half-smiles. "I'm one of those crazy people that if someone said to me that the city of Paris would be leveled to the ground and everyone killed and I could stop it by sacrificing my dog, I'd go out and buy my dog another can of Alpo. My dog is my best friend." Evans swerves around a corner almost swiping two shoppers. "I don't generally like people. They're too materialistic, they lose a brush and they go crazy. They're ruled by their possessions."

"Look at Dylan," Andy looks up from his paperback, "he's got two pairs of pants, four shirts, a leather coat, and a hat, but if he ever lost one of those, watch out! I wouldn't want to be around." The bodyguard shudders.

Evans pulls into the tunnel to Jersey. "Bob doesn't read, does he?"

The bodyguard laughs. "Are you shitting me? He reads tons. You ought to see the camper in the back there, he's got bookmarks in about ten books. He reads mythology, poetry. When he writes he doesn't have that much time but when he doesn't, he reads everything."

Ratso has been taking this all in, but the wear and tear

of the all-night drive is getting to him, so he stretches out on one of the couches in the rear. When he wakes up, the security is gone, the camper is parked in a parking lot, and the beautiful wintry day has turned pitch black.

"Those fuckers," the scribe screams to himself, "they left me behind." He curses and runs through the frigid evening air to the cold brick building. A guard opens the door and he scurries into what seems to be a gym, outfitted with folding chairs facing the stage, and bleachers on the side. Complete with about a hundred humans with tape recorders, cameras, Portapacks, notebooks, all roaming around this chilly gym, so hungry for copy that it seems likely that if the concert, which has been delayed already for over an hour, doesn't start soon, they'll set on each other.

In fact, the only person really available for interviews is Bob's nine-year-old son Jesse, who's roaming unaccompanied through the milling reporters and entourage. And one sharp young blond reporter is snuggling over to the youngster, patting him on the head, smiling her sweet copy-crazed smile. Ratso spies this and rushes over. "What's your name?" the girl is asking, pen poised over pad, as Slocum swoops in. "Hey Freddy," he grabs Jesse's hand, "your mother was looking for you." He drags the youngster about forty yards, out of ear range. "Jesse, why the hell were you talking to that reporter?"

"Reporter?" the kid squeezes the word out, just like his old man, "I didn't know she was a reporter, I thought she was a woman." He's still scratching his head as Ratso deposits him with Sara. But the few hours' sleep coupled with the excitement of being in this setting, added on to the adrenalin rush New York City invariably gives, is propelling Ratso all over the gym. He's instructing reporters and cameramen and herding them to one side, talking to the guards, jiving with the convicts, who are slowly streaming in and filling the folding chairs, generally scurrying around like a furry ball of white heat, heat a bit too hot for the tastes of Imhoff.

With a straight face, the fat mandarin calmly points out the reporter to a prison security guard. "He's not with us," Imhoff decrees, and seconds later Ratso finds himself, shivering and banging on the locked gym door, shades of Maple Leaf Gardens.

"You cocksucker, let me in, this is my turf," Ratso

rants, and then has a brilliant idea. He runs around the building to the far wing, stopping under the last window. With a Herculean effort, he leaps into the air and smashes his fist against the pane.

"What the fuck is that?" Lois yells, as he and Hurricane and the others rush to the window. "It's Ratso, you crazy motherfucker!" Lois grins broadly.

"Ratso, what you doin' out there?" Hurricane laughs.

"That prick Imhoff had me kicked out," the reporter's voice seeps through the thick glass pane. "Get me in, you schmucks, I'm gonna get double pneumonia."

Lois grabs a chair and fakes throwing it through the window, and Hurricane laughs some more. "C'mon you smuck, come around to the door on the other side, they'll let you in."

Ratso gains entry there and joins them in the library. "I can't believe this place," Lois is looking around the building, "I didn't know it was this open. I can't find any fucking bars? Where are the bars, Rubin?"

"There ain't none," Carter shrugs.

"What a fucking image," the adman shakes his head, "this joint looks like a country club."

They start to stroll down the lobby when Lois suddenly stops short. "What's that?" he points to a grill hanging out of the ceiling.

"It's a gate, sir," one of the unctuous guards smiles.

"What does it look like when it's down? Does it look like bars?" Lois screams.

"I suppose," the guard agrees.

"Pull it down, pull it down," Lois is screaming and the guard complies, separating Ratso from the rest of the party, by the steel grill gate that looks fairly ominous. "We got our bars," Lois shouts. "Hey Ratso, go get Dylan. Tell him Rubin wants to talk to him."

The reporter rushes down the hall and returns with Bob. In the meantime Regan has been sent for, and he arrives with his ever-present Nikon. "Hey Rube, how you doing man," a hatted, multiscarfed Dylan pokes his fingers through the grill to meet the boxer's. Lois whispers to Regan and points to the pair, and Regan fires away, capturing the singer on one side of the gate and the boxer on the other, huge stubby fingers curled around steel latticework, a picture that a few weeks later will grace two full pages of *People* magazine, with a caption that reads,

"Bridging a prison gate in New Jersey, Rubin 'Hurricane' Carter, inside, and Bob Dylan, out, rap before showtime." Ratso laughs to himself as Regan shoots away and a few feet out of the frame Lois just smiles like a Cheshire cat.

Back in the gym, the inmates have crowded into the floor chairs, most dressed much classier than the mediaoids who have been herded into one corner and are bleating to each other about their misfortune and the delay and their deadlines and their drinking problems. Ratso wanders around and finally spots Robbie Robertson, the guitar player from the Band and longtime friend of Bob's and Sally Grossman. A few seconds later, Joni Mitchell ambles up.

"Joni, you made it." Ratso feared that she might be talked into honoring her quasi-commitment to play at a fund-raising Jerry Brown—William Buckley debate that night in California.

"I got a replacement," Joni beams, "James Taylor. James is like a really good cover. I couldn't be happier. I tried to get some different people to do it but nobody would. Bobby was talking about that today, like he tried to get Aretha to come today and they talked to different people and they hemmed and hawed and Roberta Flack just said 'Yes,' and you don't forget that."

"She's gonna play, great," Ratso enthuses, remembering Dylan's wish that it didn't look like only a white boy was supporting Rubin.

"I was interested in the debate though," Joni continues. "I like Jerry. I'm not political myself and I don't like to get involved . . ."

"Especially since you're a foreigner," Robbie, who's also a Canuck expatriate, reminds her.

"That's true," Joni nods, "the choosing of the flag and the changing of the money, that was all I ever remembered about politics."

"People have been trying to get me together with Tom Hayden, man," Robbie marvels, and straightens the sleeve of his impeccably tailored dark-blue suit. "It's incredible, for the last couple of months they've been trying that, and I'm a foreigner."

"I don't like the guy." Joni frowns. "I say that because in a comparative way, which I shouldn't do, I like Jerry Brown because he admits he's in a power game and he's curious to play with it and Hayden won't cop to it. He's too self-righteous and he's also very condescending to the artist. Where with Jerry, he'll like call me up and he puts it on the line, like if I'm gonna be working for someone and they're gonna be using me, I like them to know that I know that they know and it's all on that level. That's what I like about Jerry Brown, he understands that 'cause he allows his people to manipulate him. He goes to parties and shakes hands and does that whole thing and is aware of what he's doing. He's very intelligent."

"Yeah, and he's said right-wing things," Ratso the eternal cynic spits.

"Hasn't everyone though?" Joni shrugs. "So does Trudeau. I think Trudeau would be a very good dictator. The best moves he did politically were dictatorial."

"It's incredible how much more well appreciated he is outside of Canada than inside." Robbie shakes his head.

"Well, he's got a pretty wife," Ratso notes.

"That's right," Robbie smiles his rare toothy grin, "his wife is pretty, that's his biggest problem. His old lady is young and says 'What's this shit?' "

Neuwirth kicks off the set by introducing Stevie Soles to do "Don't Blame Me" and from the onset, Ratso gets a strange vibe. First of all, the acoustics are horrid, making everything sound like musical mush. But more important, the audience is about 95 percent black and they really don't seem to be spoken to by these first few opening numbers. Even Stoner's funky "Catfish" fails to elicit a good response.

And when the quintessential honky, blond, blue-eyed Joni steps up, Ratso cringes in anticipation. "I wanted to be a painter," she starts out by way of introduction, "and I was told this was the age of the camera so I put it into songs. Some of these are of me, of those on the tour, maybe some of you can relate to them." But halfway through "Coyote" it's clear these ain't no *Court and Spark* fans, and some people in the front row start screaming for Joni to sit down. "Wait," she yells over the music, "I got one more verse, it's the best one too!"

After Joni, Elliot rambles on, remarkably composed despite the fact that his mother had died just the day before and he had arrived at the prison in a limousine provided by George Lois, the same limousine that had taken him to his mother's funeral earlier that morning. And, in an odd way, the audience relates to this bizarre-looking

Brooklyn cowboy playing a funky '50s rock 'n roll song. Ratso leans over and looks at Rubin who's yacking away into Lois' ear. "Hey George," Ratso screams, "tell him to relax and dig the music." But the boxer goes right on ignoring the performances, a move that does not go unnoticed by Ratso and some of the singers. Even as Dylan starts into an incredibly moving version of "Hattie Carroll," singing the tale of racial and legal injustice to an audience of blacks who one way or another got screwed and are sitting in this audience tonight as proof, Rubin chats on. And the moment reaches Dylan, he's straining, squeezing out the words like some kind of Turkish taffy, with Ronson wailing a chorus of sighs in the background. Ratso is stunned, he's never seen a more moving performance, the chills are cascading down his back like water over a fall, and at the conclusion, the reporter leaps up in his chair for a standing ovation of one.

However, the gesture isn't lost on Dylan. "We play for all kinds of different people," the dark-glassed singer leans into the mike, "and if we can get through to just one person out there we feel our mission is accomplished." Incredible, Ratso laughs, Kinky's old line, and marvels at Bob's laser-quick wit as Dylan plows into "Hard Rain." And everyone seems to be getting off on this one, even the all-night girls from the D train, encamped in the first few rows.

Then a surprise, as Dylan yields the stage to "Mr. Allen Ginsberg, an American poet from Paterson, New Jersey." And Ginsberg is great here, sing-screaming his poems of rebellion, getting a huge rise out of the convict section with a line about butt-fucking. Then Baez races on, joining Dylan for two duets and inheriting the stage from the singer.

"We'd like to thank the authorities for making it so easy for us to get in," Baez grimaces sarcastically, no stranger to these places, "I wish they'd make it easier for you to get out." The crowd goes wild, and the fever pitch grows with a soulful *a cappella* rendition of "Do Right Woman."

Roberta Flack is up next and the place goes bonkers, cons start dancing in the aisles, standing on their chairs, whooping and clapping along. After the commotion dies down, Joan grabs the mike. "We're gonna end this more or less like we've been ending this. Bob Dylan is gonna sing a song which he'll just say a couple of words about and I think you'll relate to it." A bit of scattered applause and Dylan steps to the mike. And without any words of introduction the band kicks into "Hurricane," and in the audience, the bald former boxer shakes his head to the beat, a sly smile slowly creeping across his face as CBS, NBC, ABC get the shots they've been waiting for all night.

After the inmates are shepherded back to their cells, a makeshift press conference starts. Ratso elbows his way into the crowd of about seventy journalists and winds up at the lip of the stage, right below Rubin.

"How can you say that the current Congressional investigation that Gov. Byrne's empaneled is trying to reframe you?" one journalist asks.

"Now they're saying that John Artis and I, who were convicted in 1967 of being the actual gunmen in the tavern, the only two ones, now Hawkins and his agents or his masters are saying that we didn't kill the people but we were outside." Hurricane pauses and fiddles with his sport coat button. "What they're trying to say is that we were innocent but they want to prove us half guilty."

"Has Hawkins said this to you personally?" the same reporter follows up, "has he asked you to plead to anything other than murder?"

Rubin's face cracks into a broad grin. "No, he didn't but he asked my co-defendant John Artis to sign a statement against me, implicating me, and then John Artis would be home by Christmas."

"Right now you would accept clemency but not a pardon," someone shouts.

"Absolutely," Rubin nods.

"Rubin," one older woman who writes for a wire service chimes in, "what's your personal deep-down feeling about the fact that Bob Dylan and the group came down here to perform at the prison?"

Carter pauses a minute, adjusts his wire-rimmed glasses, and peers out of his one good eye. "My personal feeling?" His hands, disproportionately big for so diminutive a frame, slap against his turtleneck shirt. "My feeling is that nine years ago when the country was rampant with racism, when the country was rampant with other social ills, I knew that if I just kept myself alive, if I just kept strong, just kept well, I knew that my brothers and sisters all over, black, white, blue, green, yellow, rich, poor, I knew that if they keep thinking, they keep moving, that finally they'll start respecting themselves and finally they'll start loving themselves and finally they'll start to respect me and they'll start to love me and I knew that was going to happen and here they come. Look at you, look at all of you, even if you're news media you're comin' too." Rubin drops his Billy Graham hands and Ratso half expects to see wheelchairs and supplicants making their way to the stage.

"If you get a new trial," another newsperson asks, "if they declare you innocent, how then are you gonna feel about America and the American system of justice?"

"I love America, you know. It's not a system that works, a system never works. It's the people who are in control of those systems that make those systems what they are. So if we have people who love other people, people who help other people, people who respect other people in control of those systems, then those systems will respect other people, those systems will love other people and I think that way we'll be able to do something."

Ratso's getting a little bored, both by the questions and by Rubin's gnawing habit of repeating phrases two, three, even four times, so he waves a pen at Rubin. "You were moved from a high-security prison in Trenton to what appears to be a country club. Do you see that as a move to co-opt you?"

"No, no, no," Rubin repeats, "I relate to being here because of the people, because of the people caring about me, other people power. Because of people loving other people power." Ratso winces. "Because the people are coming, they can no longer do what they want to do with Rubin Carter or John Artis."

"So this is like a halfway house, then," Ratso chuckles.

"That's right," Rubin slams his fist into his palm, "the next step is out. This is just R&R, just getting me ready. And I'm ready."

One college newspaperman raises a finger. "How did you get connected to Bob Dylan? I understand he visited you in jail?"

The Sixteenth Round, the book I wrote, I sent it to Bob Dylan as I sent it to many people before anyone was aware of this case, and I sent it to him hoping that he would read that and stir his emotions and stir his intellect and it did. And he came from France on a special trip one day to visit with me. He knew and I knew that because he was white and I was black neither one of us had any choice in that but two men can always meet no matter what their political persuasion or philosophy, men always meet but that's why Muhammed had to go to the mountain, you see, because two mountains never do and a man is a man, that's how we met and . . ." Suddenly, Ratso realizes Carter's answer is almost identical to his response to his own query three months earlier.

"Speaking of Muhammed," Ratso mercifully cuts in and derails Rubin's train of thought, "how did Ali get on the case?"

"Muhammed Ali has been fighting for us for two years now and he's a champion amongst champions. People say he's the champion of the world, no, no, no, he's the champion of the universe. . . ." Ratso feels a wave of nausea.

"I heard an interesting story about how he got onto your case, though," Ratso to the rescue once again, "how a white policeman approached him."

"That's right," Rubin grabs the bait, "there was Ronald Lipkin, a white police officer who knew that this had been a frame and he went to Ali and told him that his brother was in prison and he had been framed and so when Muhammed Ali received this information from a police officer," Rubin pauses dramatically, "and then a white police officer at that, because this is a racist-type crime, Muhammed Ali felt he would not be the man if he didn't come here and help a black brother when there's a white brother helping the black brother."

Rubin finishes and for a few seconds there's a lull in the gym, some people scribbling, some people thinking up questions, some aching to start the drive back to Manhattan, some aching to attack the boxer. Attempting to salvage the situation with humor but without really knowing why by now, Ratso leaps into the void.

"One last question, Rubin. Is there anything to the rumor that George Lois right now is working on a campaign for your gubernatorial race when you get out?"

Rubin grins briefly then turns cold-serious: "I'll tell you one thing, some news media have attacked the people that have come together to help Rubin Carter and I think that's diabolical, because what it shows is that the powers-that-be know that if people get together we can solve problems and in these committees, rich, poor, black, white, actor, dancer, singer, have all come together and these criminals who have covered this up, who are now cringing in their wormy corners, they know that if people stay together that means power. And they also know that as long as we stay together, they can't outfight us. Which one of these politicians is gonna get in the ring with a Muhammed Ali or a Joe Frazier? Are you? No. Which one of these politicians can outsing a Bob Dylan or a Joan Baez or a Joni Mitchell? Or which one of these politicians can outact a Dyan Cannon or an Ellen Burstyn? You see, so the politicians can't outfight us, they can't outsing us, they can't outdance us, so what makes us think they can somehow outthink us either?"

Rubin gives the media people below him a chastising smirk. "So when we start thinking and thinking very intelligently, that scares them, so that's why they attack people like Ellen Burstyn, it's criminal, because if the Constitution of the United States says if the people can find something wrong in the society then the people can get together and change it and that's what the people are doing."

"What's the next step now?" someone yells from the rear. "We know there's a new trial coming up, it looks that way and—"

"There is no such thing as we know that there is almost a new trial," Rubin snaps bitterly, "there's no such thing. We're talking about right and wrong here. Two men in prison illegally for nine years for being framed for committing a crime that there's no evidence anywhere that even suggests that they did anything, so we are talking about right and wrong, talking about in jail or out of jail. We're not talking about almost in jail. So I am in jail, so until we are out of jail then we can start talking about a new trial. But until that time there's no such thing, because the very people who created this monster in 1966 are still in power today."

Rubin pauses dramatically, then goes on: "Gov. Byrne, he has something to do with this crime, he went to the judge in his county to give Bello and Bradley leniency. Now we at the Chief Justice Hughes of the State Supreme Court. He was the governor of New Jersey in 1966, he appointed a lawyer, Lerner, made him a judge and shipped him to Passaic County, so all of our reviews have always been in the same hands of the people who created this. . . ."

To Ratso's right, Lois is listening to this and getting paler by the minute. Sensing Rubin's about to talk his way up the river. "Shut up, Rubin," he's whispering under his breath, "talk about Muhammed and mountains again, for Chrissakes."

"What we want to do is have an unbiased, impartial arbitrator of the facts and just let it all hang out from there. We're willing to accept that."

"Do you think that's possible in the state of New Jersey now?" a journalist yells.

"No," Rubin screams, and Lois blanches a bit more, "in the state of New Jersey absolutely not. We need to get into Federal Court before we can ever get a fair trial or a fair hearing. . . ."

This is getting too much for even Ratso and simultaneously the reporter and the adman lunge for the microphone in Rubin's hands.

"They want to put you to bed, Rube." Regan, who's been shooting stills, picks up the cue, leading the boxer away.

"They're gonna tuck him in," Lois cracks, and grabs the mike.

Ratso just smiles at the absurdity and peers back at the mass of reporters, none of whom apparently has sniffed out what's going on. "Thank you, Mr. President," Slocum cracks bitterly and waits for Lois' limousine and the ride back to Manhattan.

Which was a glum ride indeed. Lois keeps asking Ratso to replay the tape of the press conference and with each answer by Carter, the adman moans and slumps back into the seat. Answers which seemed brilliant and courageous to Ratso just a few months ago now reek of rhetoric.

And Ratso realizes, as the limo glides to a halt, that no, Rubin was still no murderer, but he sure as hell might be a damn good con artist, and that realization wreaked havoc with Ratso's sleep and drove storm clouds over tomorrow's Night of the Hurricane.

Clouds which intensified at the preconcert press conference called by the New Jersey Carter Defense Committee. It was a shoddy affair, the highlight of which came when a slightly tipsy Rep. John Conyers got into a shouting match with Saponakis who threw his drink, glass and ice cubes and all, at the Congressman's august body. Ali, who was the star of the show, arrived an hour late, enabling Conyers and himself to make complete fools out of themselves with their lack of knowledge about the boxer's case that they were so fervently defending. So Ratso fled to the Garden, hoping that at least the music would save the night.

Backstage, Imhoff had borrowed one of Bill Graham's old tricks, and had set up free hot dog, pretzel, and beer stands. The Garden had been sold out the day the event was announced, and most of the patrons had no idea that Roberta Flack had been added to the bill and that Joni Mitchell was still on the tour, plugged into her guest spot, and that Ali would act as an M.C. of sorts. And there would be other surprises too, like Baez running out in the middle of Jack Elliot's set disguised as a blond, white-go-go-booted teenybopper and being hauled off by security after about thirty seconds of the Hustle. Or that the audience would get a chance to hear Rubin live from prison on a phone hook-up thanking them and Bob, and the Revue, and Ali and Roberta.

Which was why Richie Kahn, a member of Rubin's New York Defense Committee was sitting stage right, behind a bank of amplifiers, with a phone glued to his ear. In order to take no chances they called Rubin before the concert began, establishing a hook up, enabling Rubin to listen to the music, and then speak to the multitudes at the appointed time.

Which wasn't quite yet. The crowds are still filing in and getting seated as Ratso storms into the Garden and heads backstage. And right at the foot of the stairs, Dylan's huddling with Robbie Robertson and Joni.

"What are you guys gonna do?" Ratso wonders, thrilled at the prospect of seeing Bob and Robbie perform together for the first time since the 1974 tour.

"I don't know," Bob shrugs.

"Do 'Dirge,' " the reporter pleads.

"Yeah, but I don't know if I know all the words." Bob shakes his head.

Joni buttonholes Ratso. "I think that Rubin is a jive nigger," she frowns, "after what happened yesterday at the prison."

"You turning fascist?" Ratso inquires, pulling on her policeman's coat.

"Yeah," Joni laughs, fingering the police memorabilia that she has been collecting all tour. "The more I get the more I think I turn Nazi."

Just then Neuwirth and Guam take the stage and Ratso watches from backstage. And sure enough, perhaps because of the tension of playing in the Garden, perhaps because of the feeling that the concert is really a postscript to the tour, whatever, the edge is gone. Everyone seems to be plodding, so when Ali inherits the stage, along with four or five people from his enormous entourage, Ratso is grateful for the respite.

Grateful for about three seconds, because for some bizarre reason Ali, instead of pleading Rubin's case, is delivering an unsolicited political announcement promoting some Southern businessman who's been flying the fighter around the country in his huge jet plane, promoting this total unknown as "the next President of the United States." Perhaps for the first time in his long career, an avalanche of boos descend on the champ.

"Maybe he can get away with that shit at the Apollo but he can't tell white people who to vote for," one cop says.

"Yeah," one of the equipment men puts in, "just fly him around the country and he'll endorse anything."

Ratso glances behind him and Dylan who had come out early to watch Ali seems to be puzzled by the speech. "I got called about this concert," Ali continues, "and they say Bob Dylan is playing. I never heard of no Bob Dylan." Another chorus of boos descend. Ali throws his hands up, half in fright and half in laughter. "All you pretty girls came to see Bob Dylan and not me!" Dylan cracks up.

Ali finishes and fields a phone call from Rubin, chattering away and changing the subject every time Rubin starts into his rap about oppression. After a few more boring speeches, the music in the form of Jack Elliot finally returns, and a few minutes later, Dylan strides onto the Garden stage.

He's greeted with a standing ovation and, once again, drives a lagging band into a frenzied renewal, scorching through "Masterpiece" then "It Ain't Me Babe" and "Hattie Carroll" in succession. Then after the new augmented version of "Tonight I'll Be Staying Here with You," Robbie Robertson, looking dapper as ever in a slick blue denim suit, steps onstage and picks up his electric guitar.

"We're going to do a song for Mr. Albert Grossman," Dylan, whose hat by now is completely encircled by different colored flowers, laughs, "who won't be our next President." And it's back to *Highway 61*, and "It Takes a Lot to Laugh, It Takes a Train to Cry," a torrid rocker that Robbie is lacing with amazing razor-sharp riffs. "Durango" is next, Dylan's pulling out all stops, moving, singing, even breathing like the trapped gunfighter in the West. "Here's another song about the marriage ceremony between man and woman," Dylan pronounces and it's into "Isis."

But at some time during Bob's dynamic set, Richie Kahn, who was still sitting on stage, holding the phone toward the amplifiers so Rubin could take it all in back at the prison, at some time Kahn sensed that something was wrong. He heard a faint muffled noise coming out of the receiver, a noise that intensified as he brought the phone closer to his ear. It was Rubin, screaming his black ass off.

"I'm gettin' out, I'm gettin' out," Rubin's yelling.

"Rubin, I can't hear you, wait until the end of the set," Kahn yells back.

"I'm getting out," the prisoner yelps, "I'll be home by Christmas. I just saw it on Channel 5 News."

"You're kidding," Kahn breaks into a big smile, "that's great."

"Rich," Rubin continues, "this is what I want you to do. Let Bob announce it."

"Are you sure, Rubin?" Richie, who handled press and media for Rubin, remains skeptical. "We should make sure it's accurate."

"Richie," Rubin's voice gets ominous, "I want to talk to Bob."

"He's playing right now," Kahn looks over the stage at the singer, who's miming his way through "Isis."

"I want to talk to him," Carter pouts.

"OK," Kahn concedes, "at intermission."

The song winds to an end, the audience starts a standing ovation, and Dylan wends his way off his stage. Suddenly a stranger jumps in front of him.

"Bob," Kahn points toward the receiver, "Rubin wants to talk to you."

Dylan ambles over and picks up the phone. They talk for a few minutes. "OK, Rubin," Dylan smiles, "I'm gonna announce it and you're gonna hear a roar like you never heard before."

Dylan puts the phone down and starts offstage. "Bob," it's Kahn again, "you gotta wait on this thing. We gotta check it out." Dylan nods.

By now, word of this has reached George Lois, who's rushed from his seat with Paul Saponakis and Leo Stevens, and is backstage attempting to verify the rumor Channel 5 had broadcast. Dylan steps down from the stage.

"Bobby," Lois runs up, "don't announce a fucking thing until we check it out." Dylan gives Lois a nonchalant shrug and heads backstage. The adman grabs his two compatriots and they start to look for a phone, assisted by Herb Jaffee, the New Jersey newspaperman. They rush down the corridor and stop at the first room.

"We have to use the phones in there," Lois tells the two uniformed guards, "we have to call the Governor of New Jersey."

"Get the fuck out of here," the cop sneers.

"Look, man," Lois raises his voice, "Dylan's about to announce something to twenty thousand people and we've got to confirm it first and we got to use these phones."

The cops stay adamant and Lois and Saponakis' Greek tempers get the best of them. The adman throws a wild right, the restaurateur a cross body block, and one cop starts to go for his gun when a Garden official rushes up.

"We gotta use a phone," Lois explains to the bureaucrat, who leads them to another office. George tries the governor, then his aide, and then finally reaches a press officer in Byrne's office. The adman looks grim as he hangs up the phone. "Not a chance," Lois shakes his head, "the guy just said 'not a chance.'"

Meanwhile, Rubin has been ranting on the phone to Kahn, screaming about Dylan making the announcement. And just as Dylan starts up for the second half, Lois comes barreling out from backstage. "Don't announce anything," George manages to yell up at Bob as he starts toward the front of the stage.

Meanwhile Kahn has been waiting in ambush and as the singer passes by, he jumps in front of him and almost gets speared by a Martin as a result. "Bob, you can't do this," Kahn throws his arms out like a left tackle, unaware that Lois had just delivered the word.

Dylan stops short in his tracks. "I ain't doing anything

until I hear from you," he barks at Kahn, and then walks out to open the second half.

And what a start, Dylan resplendent in a white Wallace Beery shirt, black vest, flowered hat, and makeup, and he's followed by Baez as Dylan in white Wallace Beery shirt, black vest, flowered hat and makeup. Ratso finds a seat next to Beattie out front as the two Dylans break into "Times They Are A Changing." The reporter sings along in his seat.

"If Dylan goes broke, he can always play New York," Beattie smiles at the reporter; "you'll buy the first ticket."

The Dylans finish that and launch into the good-timey "Mama You've Been on My Mind," prompting Ratso to elbow Beattie.

"See," Beattie laughs, "I'm always on his mind."

Suddenly Ratso develops an intense headache, compounded by the blaring speakers no more than twenty yards away. "Beattie," he moans, "you got any aspirin?"

She makes a quick check of her purse and comes up empty-handed. She shakes her head.

"What?" Slocum spits, "what kind of Jewish mother are you? No aspirin!"

"I never had a headache in my life," Beattie brags, "Bob and his band were singing like this for ten years in my garage and I never got a headache."

"Anybody remember Johnny Ace?" Bob asks from the stage. "I hope so."

"I don't know him," Beattie shrugs, "who is he?"

Dylan and Baez soar into the old '50s song and Beattie watches enthralled. Then she turns to Ratso. "He should wear his glasses more often," Bob's mother worries, "he'll hurt his eyes this way."

"Doesn't he wear contacts?" Ratso stabs.

"No, no," Beattie shakes her head with relish.

"We're gonna send this next one out to Mr. Herman Melville," Bob dedicates.

"What label is he on?" Ratso screams out.

"I don't know the guy," Beattie shrugs.

Ratso turns back to the show and starts to watch, when a familiar figure wanders in front of him. It's Mike Porco, the owner of Gerdes Folk City.

"Porco," Ratso screams and grabs the club owner, steering him to an empty seat in the row ahead, "what do you think of this?"

"Issa great," Mike smiles, "issa great but my taste . . . I enjoyed the other concert in '74 with the Band more, when he was alone. He sanga lot of songs I was more familiar with then. I went back ten years with that concert." Porco smiles. "I been seeing him now for fifteen years, Ratso. And it's funny, in the beginning, I didn't get much impression of him. I didn't say, 'Oh this guy's gonna be a star.' It was just another person that came in and performed. Then he started to come in every Monday, I don't think he missed a Monday, and a few people liked him. They started to call my attention to him, they said, 'That kid is pretty good.' And as he kept coming in, I paid more attention to him and I noticed that he wasn't a really great singer but his songs used to penetrate.

"People said they thought I should give him a break, then some people like Gil Turner started coming in and singing his songs, and I thought that they sounded pretty good even though other people were singing them, and I started paying more attention to his words, and they were great. He musta been at the hoot night twenty times or more, when I spoke to him and said, 'Bobby, I know you will like to work here. Maybe we can get you a job.' And his eyes almosta pop out of his head, and he said, 'Oh yes, man, anytime.'

"So I made arrangements and I gave him a date in April 1961, a couple of weeks after Judy Collins performed there," Porco continues, straining to be heard over the enchanting din of Roberta Flack and her ensemble. "I knew Bob didn't have a cabaret card or belong to the union, so I put him into the union. I took him up there and I pay for the card, I think it was $80 or something. At the union, they ask how old he was and he said twenty and the guy says if he was only twenty he gotta bring somebody from his family to sign the contract, to come back tomorrow with the contract. So Bob said, 'I ain't got no mother,' so the guy says, 'OK come back with your father.' And Bobby says, 'I ain't got no father either.' So the guy looked at me and said, 'What are we gonna do? I can't put him in the union unless, Mike, you want to sign for him.' So I asked Bob and he said he'd appreciate it, so I had to sign as his guardian. Then we went downtown and he was all happy, he kept saying how glad he was and we stopped at a picture machine to get some pictures for his cabaret card and his hair was all bushed up at the time. So I gave him a comb but he wouldn't comb his hair. I said, 'Tell me the truth, how come you no comb your hair?' And he says, 'Wanna know the truth, I'm a little superstitious. The last time I combed my hair something bad happened to me, so I don't like to comb it.' And then I gave him $2 for a haircut, and he came back the next day with the hair a little bit cut, and it didn't look like a barber's cut. I think some woman did it."

"What was he like then?" Ratso wonders. "This was in what, 1962?"

"He would take a glass of wine once in a while. When he wasn't working I used to give him a sandwich with a glass of wine and he was happy. He used to come in every night, he was very conservative and quiet. Not a wise guy. Before he went on that first day, I spoke to my wife and got some of my kids' clothing that they overgrew. I gave him some shirts, not rags, they wassa still in good shape, pants and shirts so he would look more nice. The woman that cut his hair, I think she gave him some shoes. He looks very good, I called a photographer in and took pictures, I still got those hanging up outside the club."

"Didn't he ask you to be his manager?" Ratso recalls an old rumor.

"I used to use the kitchen as my private room, office, and he'd come and I'd see he didn't eat. So I'd ask, 'You feel like a sandwich?' and he'd say, 'I'd appreciate it,' I knew he'd say roast beef if I asked him what he wanted, he used to love roast beef. And I told the people working in the kitchen if he wants a sandwich to give it to him, that the kid isn't working but he's honest, he's not a wise guy. When he see that, he'd come in and put his arm around me and say, 'Mike, why don't you manage me? One of these days I'm gonna be big. I'm gonna be somebody.' I used to laugh and don't answer but he asked me a lot of times. One day I told him I'd love to do it, I feel he's gonna go places but I couldn't devote enough time to him and the club, it wouldn't be fair to him. He says, 'That's right, Mike. You're honest.' "

"Did he change after he got famous?" the reporter hollers above Roger McGuinn's solo spot.

"Not with me," Mike shakes his head vigorously, "I never noticed any difference. Even today he puts his arms around me, asks me how my wife is, even today it feels like years ago."

"What's he like?"

"You mean his character? Very warm all the time, very friendly. Even when he had the last show in the Garden with the Band, I was one of the first to receive four tickets. His disposition is wonderful, when I went to see him in France he was on tour and Bobby Neuwirth answered the door after I had seen Albert Grossman in the lobby and Neuwirth told me Bobby wasn't in and I told him that I heard Bob's voice inside and he should go in and tell him that Mike Porco from New York was here. And Bobby came out and opened the door with one hand and pushed Neuwirth aside with the other and said, 'Get out of here, thassa my father.' So he hugged me and my wife, put me and her under each arm and took us into this room where about thirty people were sitting around. He took us in and started at one end of the room and introduced us to everyone saying, 'This is my father from New York.' Then he called the bellhop and ordered some champagne and told us, 'Get anything you want. You make me so happy, Mike.'

"Then they set up a table with stuff to eat and the first thing he said to me was, 'Mike, you been great to me. Remember when I said that someday I'm gonna be big?' I said, 'Yeah, I remember,' and he said, 'I told you to manage me,' and I said, 'Yeah, I recall that. Well good luck. But you're not any bigger, you're the same size.' " The same mischievous smile spreads across Porco's face, even now ten years later.

" 'I'm big now, Mike,' he says, 'but I never did nothing for you and you're the one that's helped me more than anybody else.' He says, 'Anytime you need me, don't call Grossman, don't call the office, if you want it and your business is not too good, pick any theater you want, outside of New York City, and I'll give you one day of my life anytime you want.' "

Porco smiles and his eyes grow wet. "I was very surprised at my birthday party this year, I didn't expect nothing like that. I just thought it was Channel 13 and the lights and stuff like that had attracted a big crowd. I didn't see Bob when they came in, I was mixing drinks, so my wife calls me and says somebody wants to see me a minute. I told her I'm busy and I spoke to her even rougher. So I collected for a couple of drinks and to make her happy I go, and there's this guy there with a round hat and he turns around and hugs me and it's Bob. And I look around and see Jack Elliot, Joan Baez, Bette Midler, fifteen at least well-known people, and I felt like I coulda cried then. I felt anybody who was in the area and knew me came in, Eric Anderson, Patti Smith. Patti, she brought me a little horse as a gift and she broke a leg on the way and held the leg in the other hand. And when they went onstage to sing "Happy Birthday," that made me feel more great."

Baez is finishing her solo set now with "Dixie," Dylan waiting in the wings to close the show. Porco peers up at Baez then turns around again and leans toward Ratso. "I'll never forget that in France. Bobby kept telling me how big he was and how he had told me that would happen. He grabbed me and brought me over to the window and we looked down and there on the sidewalk and the street was at least two hundred people, all with the cameras. And Bob kept pointing down and saying, 'See how big I am now, Mike? They think I'm going to go out now but I'm not gonna leave until it's time for the show.' They was all press, newspapers or writers or television and Bob just kept repeating, 'I told you I'd be this big.' And he was right."

And he was. And he was about to demonstrate why, too, as he climbs the short steps and inherits center stage, just him and his Martin. And once again the magic of the man was enough to overcome all the traumas, the travesties, all the trivialities. "Simple Twist of Fate" gets cheers on each new line, and then the band trots out and they do a sensitive "Oh Sister" followed by a torrid "Hurricane." Then the tear-jerkers, "One More Cup," followed by a tender "Sara," topped by the highpoint of *Pat Garrett*, "Knocking on Heaven's Door."

And this is it, the confusion and ecstasy and depression and joy and tumult and fury and love and rage and boredom and transcendence of six weeks on the road, six weeks as a traveling karass, a musical medicine show on wheels, the real magical mystery tour, it's all boiled down to this last three minutes, this last salute to Ol' Woody, and to the audience and to themselves. "This Land is Your

Land" of course, and this stage is your stage, too, at least it looks that way, with friends, sound men, stagehands, old ladies, kids, and managers streaming out, singing along beside the musicians. Ratso and Porco are standing stage left as Joni Mitchell and Richie Havens scamper by to join the throng.

"Joni," Ratso stops her and grabs Porco, "this is Mike, he owns Folk City, bring him up there with you."

"No, no," Mike starts to retreat but Mitchell laughs and grabs one arm, Havens the other and the old man gets pulled onto the stage.

"Lots of people make it up," Bob shouts over the din, "and most people who make it up you don't see." He pauses and throws a paternal arm over the assemblage onstage. "We are the Rolling Thunder Revue and we shall return," and with that, he slings his guitar off his shoulder, wheels around and starts offstage.

Only to bump smack into Porco who was shyly singing along behind the front lines. "Mike," Bob yells, and grabs his New York father, giving him a buss on the cheek. And, in the process, smearing most of his white-face all over the club owner's jacket. Dylan starts to wipe the coat off. "Hey don't shake it off," Porco laughs, "I'll just senda youa bill." And the father dismisses the son with a slap on the back.

At the party afterward all is chaos. A long table filled with hors d'oeuvres, Chinese food, barbequed ribs and the like has been set up in the Felt Forum, and the guests, performers, and crashers fill only about one-third of the vast auditorium, leaving two thousand or so seats empty as silent witnesses to this surreal event. Made all the more sur-real as Ratso shepherds his parents around, introducing them to everyone in sight. He's like a whirlwind, intro-ducing Mel Howard, then lining up Ronee Blakley as Howard and his folks finish their pleasantries. In fact, he's worked about half the room when there looming in front of him is the big catch. Dylan had sneaked in amid the confusion a few seconds earlier. He's loose, aided by a few previous drinks and the cup that he's twirling in his fingers right now. The reporter comes up from behind.

"Hey Bob," he shouts, and the singer whirls around, his face still caked with makeup and sweat, "I want you to meet my parents."

"C'mon, Ratso," the singer scoffs, "you don't have any parents."

The reporter drags Dylan the few feet and deposits him in front of the Slomans. And after all these years since that wintry night in White Plains, the old man is finally getting a chance to shake the hand of that kid with the guitar who looked like a shipping clerk.

"Glad to meet you folks," Dylan smiles and points toward their beaming son. "You should be real proud of him. Your son is going to make his mark on the world some day."

Oh, what an accolade! The perfect thing to say to two Jewish mothers. The Slomans start to swoon, the kvell just gushing out of every pore, thrilled at the ultimate substantiation of all these years of silent prayer, private collaboration, and public display. Their son was going to be something, he was going to make his mark on the world. What a phrase! And coming out of the mouth of such a big star, he should know too, shouldn't he. And he didn't have to be an accountant after all, he could still be somebody! Mr. Sloman smiles, convinced that all those years of pasting the son's artifacts in those scrapbooks, all those years were not in vain. It was a happy couple that would float back to Queens that night.

But Ratso lingers on, pressed into service helping Gary escort the by now very loose superstar around the party. And what a job, everyone is streaming over, surrounding Dylan, following his progress around the room like a daisy chain. There are those who want autographs, those who want a slice of the fame, even those who want a slice of the flesh. Ratso and Gary are filtering the assholes out, keeping the ones with land schemes and plant shows and film offers away. And in the middle of this madness, Bob Dylan is wandering around, more than happy to talk to anyone with land schemes and plant shows and film offers.

"Can I shake your hand, brother?" a black street kid who snuck in thrusts his fist through the entourage, "you were great, man."

"Everyone was great," Dylan gushes, then turns to Ratso. "Where's Jann Wenner? I thought you were gonna do a thing with him. You're all talk Ratso, all fucking talk."

"Are you kidding?" the reporter shoots back, "Wenner was afraid to show his face back here after the job Neuwirth and Raven did on him last night. Supposedly, he came to the hotel with a bottle of wine and Neuwirth just sliced him apart for the shitty way he hacked my second *Rolling Stone* piece into an attack on the tour. Raven told me that the young *Citizen Kane* looked near tears, but was holding it back."

They parade around a little more, Dylan balancing a drink on one hand and a plate of refried beans in the other. And from the seats, it looks like a bizarre march with Dylan as Pied Piper. Dylan veers left, the tail of about twenty people turns left, he moseys right, the body follows right. In the middle of it, Ratso feels like he's in some hippie Mummer's Parade.

The parade passes George Lois and his family, who have been standing quietly to the side with some other members of the Hurricane Fund. Ratso drags the compliant Dylan over.

"Lois," Ratso yelps, "where's my limo?"

"I will never get you a limo, you motherfucker," the adman explodes, "I just found out that you were Jewish."

Dylan leans forward and grabs George's hand. "Hey man, I loved your book, Ratso gave it to me the other night. I love your sister and your parents," and Lois is amazed as Dylan reels off the long, unpronounceable Greek names with photographic precision from one reading of the book.

The two men talk a bit and George introduces his teenage son to Bob. "Hey man," Bob smiles at the kid, "you got great parents."

"All right, all right," Ratso cuts in. "Jesus, Lois, do you have to hit on him for ten minutes?" He throws a protective arm around Dylan.

"You been giving him propaganda," Lois screams, "my book!"

"Hey Bob," George grabs the singer, "you really know this guy Ratso. All the time he's been telling us he's tight with you but we just thought it was bullshit."

"Are you kidding?" Dylan throws his arm around the reporter, "I love this guy. He's my brother."

Just then a black kid barrels his way through the crowd.

"Where's the revue going next?" he screams.

"Get him out of here," Andy points to Bob, and Ratso leads the singer toward the exit, with thirty people on their trail.

"This way Bob, this way," Andy is the advance man, trying to grab his attention.

"Thanks for the concert," one kid screams.

"Bobby, Bobby," another girl is near tears.

"Hey man," the black kid has caught up, "do you know where the Revue's going next?"

Dylan pauses. "The next one's in St. Augustine."

"St. Augustine, Florida," the kid repeats excited, "that's my home town! I'll sign up twenty million people to be in the Rolling Thunder Revue."

Dylan just nods distractedly and tries to eat a spoonful of cold beans off his paper plate, as they lead him to the elevator and the garage where the camper is parked.

Ratso starts to head back into the party but nearly gets bowled over by a frantic Joni Mitchell. "All my gear is gone," Joni frets, "I'm so confused. We put it in one room but I don't know what floor it was on or nothing." Without waiting for an answer, she speeds toward the elevator.

"There's something that's so evident here," Greg, the sound man, corrals Ratso as he walks back into the party. "Look at this," he sweeps a hand over the party panorama, "you have to really understand the relationship between this year and Hollywood in the '30s. The same magnitude and production that was involved then is involved now. It's the same concept of stardom." Ratso chuckles and looks out at the scene, a scene that could very well have come out of *The Day of the Locust*. A feeling reinforced as an almost comatose Roger McGuinn limps by, followed by Gary carrying Bob's son Jesse over his shoulders, who's followed by an even less conscious Phil Ochs.

But, as incredible as it seems, this party is only a warm-up, a dress rehearsal for a more exclusive shindig that's about to start uptown at a restaurant near the hotel. This late party is the real one, the farewell to the tour and everyone, from the sound men to the performers to security. Even Ratso has been invited.

But by now, around 2 A.M., everyone seems to be partied out. Oh, they're all going through the motions, some dancing, some drinking, some eating the tasty Italian fare, but without conviction.

Outside on the street, a slew of crashers and would-be invitees are battling to get in, led by Phil Ochs, who eventually receives the OK nod. Which leaves Lisa, leaning up on her old reliable Chevy, as the Queen of the Shutouts. Ratso and Larry Johnson peer out at the street scene. "Look at Lisa," Ratso marvels, "she's still out there, still waiting, still hoping. Winner of the Rolling Thunder Persistence Award!" Both men lift their glasses and toast perseverance in the face of futility.

But inside, things have picked up since Bob and Sara are walking around and presenting beautiful handmade Rolling Thunder medallions to the band members. The reporter passes by on the way to his table. "Love," Sara puts a hand on Bob's shoulder, "did you give Ratso his yet?"

"What?" Slocum stops dead in his tracks.

"Hey Ratso." Dylan digs into a small bag and comes up with a velour pouch with a nameplate on it. "This is for you, man."

"I picked it out especially for you," Sara smiles.

The reporter digs into the pouch and pulls out a beautiful silver medal, inscribed on one side with "Rolling Thunder Revue" and boasting an eagle on the other side, with three gemstones embedded on it. "Far out," Ratso whistles and slips the medallion over his head, adjusts it on his neck, smiles, and for the first time on the tour, feels like a white man.

The party drags on for a while, with the hangers-on and guests departing early, leaving the hardcorers to last it out till the bitter end. And slowly but surely it begins to resemble the endless hospitality suites. Why there's Neuwirth over there talking to Ronson, Soles, and T-Bone. And Stoner and Wyeth drinking at the bar, Blakley chatting with McGuinn, Mitchell and Shepard tête-a-têteing in the corner, Dylan mysteriously slipping in and out.

Ratso heads for another drink, and, at the bar, overhears two crew members deep in conversation.

"You know, after all the stuff about brotherhood, and playing for the people, and spreading the word, and all that, I finally realized what the sound of Rolling Thunder is."

"What is it?" the other picks up the bait.

"Just look," he sweeps his arm over the room, "there's Stoner, who was an unknown bass player, Wyeth, a journeyman drummer, T-Bone, an obscure Texas song-writer, Soles, an L.A. sessionman, Mansfield, a Quacky Ducker, Scarlett, fronting for a Latin band. Dylan takes 'em, they gig around for six weeks, maybe they do another tour, right, then they ride out those Rolling Thunder coat-tails. For them, the sound of Rolling Thunder is a ringing cash register, man." And the two roadies crack up and order another round.

15

Ratso stays up that whole night, hanging around the Westbury lobby, making long-distance calls, accompanying Gary for some corned beef sandwiches from the Star Deli at 8, then opening the Westbury coffee shop at 10. Later that afternoon, he calls on Robbie Robertson. Robertson has always been an intriguing figure for him, both because of his long association with Dylan as Bob's guitarist in the mid-'60s, and his own tremendous work both musically and lyrically with the Band. So the first question that occurred to Ratso was how Robertson would compare this tour with Tour '74, the last outing where the Band accompanied Dylan.

"It was looser, it wasn't done with as much seriousness," Robbie says in sober measured tones. "The other thing we were trying to have a good time too but we were also doing a real tour and this thing has been a thing that Bob's been talking about for years. I'm sure he would have liked to have taken it all the way and done it by train, he's always wanted to have that kind of gypsy caravan situation happening where it was loose and different people could get up and do different things at different times and nothing would be out of place."

"How would you compare this to the '66 period? That was the first time you guys went out with Bob and you got such abuse from the folk purists," Ratso remembers.

" 'Sixty-six was just off the wall to all of us." Robbie rolls his eyes slightly behind his tinted glasses. "The guys in the Band, they didn't know what the fuck that was about. We were just doing what we said we would do and whatever happened when we got there was beyond our control. It happened, it seemed really silly and bizarre at the time but I guess for the people who were really feeling it, it wasn't silly at all. They meant it."

377

"What was Dylan's reaction?"

"I don't know, normal reactions. Sometimes he thought it was funny, sometimes it made him angry, sometimes it was a little scary, sometimes it didn't make a shit. It was just the usual, just like anybody would react to it. But the amazing thing about the whole thing was that he persisted. I mean everybody was running around in his ear saying, 'Listen, it's this group, they're terrible, get rid of these fucking guys.' Everybody was telling him that and the amazing thing was that he never went for it. I mean because we were playing so out of this world, we didn't even know what the fuck we were doing, because he didn't want to learn any of the songs. It was just play them."

"That's what Bloomfield told me too," Ratso blurts, "he told me that those *Highway 61* sessions were just total chaos."

"Bob has always made records like that and the best thing you can do is get the most competent studio people so they're flexible and fast. That's his best for recording and always has been in that technique of just getting them down on tape. That's the idea, so they feel good and you can hear all the words."

"Is that the way *Planet Waves* was done? How did that collaboration come about?"

Robbie cracks a smile for the first time. "There was no collaboration. He just had a few songs and we were rehearsing for the tour."

"The tour idea came first?"

"Oh yeah, the album had nothing to do with it. Bob had a few songs so we just went into the studio for a couple of days and recorded them all. But that's a different thing. That's after the fact, that's after the *Basement Tape* period and the other tours we had done with him. We already knew the game. We knew how to do it and it was just a matter of the songs after that, but that was effortless, we just went in and put them down on tape and that was that."

"What was that whole Woodstock period like?" The questions are literally pouring out of Ratso. "It seemed to me to be a reaction to the whole insanity of the '66 tour, a retrenchment, a retreat . . ."

"I don't know what that was, the only thing I know about it was that Albert Grossman had a house up there, then

Bob got this house and the first reason I went to Woodstock was that he was working on *Eat the Document* and he asked me to help on the film, and that's what I did, I went up and lived at his house and worked on the film for a while, and Bobby Neuwirth was kind of in and out, he was one of the sound people on the film, and it seemed like a nice scene. We had been living in New York and there was nothing really happening outside of it being more of a pain in the ass than anything else, so Woodstock was a nice relief and we went up there and fooled around and it was kind of a fun thing and we ended up making it our base for a while. When the festival came along then it became a different thing, it was actually kind of a charming little place, then it became a haven for wayward dopesters and it kind of lost its littleness, its quaintness, it became a little bit of a cult number. It just became less and less interesting."

"Were *The Basement Tapes* originally demos or what?"

"It was more fun than anything," Robbie recalls, "it was done for no reason whatsoever and then as we got going it seemed that it might have some obscure use, and just as we went along once in a while, there'd be a real song come out of the batch, but most of it was for fun. We just sat there and laughed all day and all night. It was really a fun time in our growing up, that *Basement Tape* period, and we learned a lot from it, too."

"What was the impact of Dylan on you and vice versa. Was there an artistic ruboff?"

"I think the basic thing is we just opened up some new worlds for one another and we both were very good at our own particular thing. We were just coming from two different worlds altogether and he was no more familiar with ours than we were with his. I mean we had listened to a minimal amount of folk music, and although he had listened to quite a bit of rock 'n roll, because it was closer to the surface than folk music was, he probably knew more about rock 'n roll and blues and what not than what we knew about folk, but we didn't just know about it we knew how to really do it and we knew all of it, so we were both really well seasoned in our own bags and we just basically and accidentally showed one another a lot of things about different kinds of music and education.

"You know, I think that although Bob's initial impact

on the whole music scene was lyrically, that's what every-body really remembers the strongest, it wasn't necessarily that way for the Band, 'cause the Band was a musical group and I don't mean instrumental, I mean it was the musical hit that was either gonna get it or not get it for the Band and it wouldn't matter whether someone was re-citing the fucking Bible while they were doing it, the thing for us was that if it didn't connect musically, it just didn't matter what anybody was saying, saving the world just wouldn't matter. The fact is Bob's phrasing and his melod-ic connections were really extraordinary and it all had to do with the other thing, it just wasn't some guy up there saying a bunch of lines that were kind of poetically enhancing. There was a lot more to it than that, but any-way people preferred to receive it on whatever level that they can and it seems like most people received it on an intellectual word level where we didn't receive it that way at all so we weren't nearly as impressed with that thing as everybody else was.

"And, I'm sure that Bob was very aware of that too because we never remarked, 'Oh, that third line in at fourth verse is such a whammy," I mean nobody cared about the third line in the fourth verse, we cared about how it phrased and connected and slid into that fourth line much more. If it said anything really incredible at the same time, terrific, that was a bonus. We came at it from the other side and that's the level that we were im-pressed on. So it was just an education all the way around and we didn't even probably realize it from the beginning, but after a while when I could actually think about it for a second, that's the way it affected me."

"But your lyrics are great," Ratso protests, "they're not throwaways at all, they have real literary value."

"No," Robbie smiles shyly, "but I don't narrow that down. I think if you took those lyrics and isolated it with some music that didn't make it, they wouldn't make it. But I think you could have taken the same music and changed the lyrics to three or four different things and still made it work, that's the emphasis where we were coming from. But from Bob the emphasis was always on the other side and it was even more so from the people that were listening to him. So when we played with him the people couldn't hear the lyrics too well anymore, they were offended by us. They thought we were interrupting their lyrics." Robbie lets out a hearty laugh, the first from the taciturn guitarist. "So it was all very simple when it came down to it but at the time it seemed confusing and silly."

"But from the other view, people also criticize Dylan for that musical spontaneity, they talk about it as sloppy musicianship," Ratso turns around.

"It is, it is, I mean people can criticize it all they want but the thing is whether it works or not. Whether you get the feeling from it, in the long run, whether it has the essence, that's the whole thing and whether somebody makes a mistake or doesn't know that the ending is coming, whatever it is, that's beside the point if the essence is there, if it really feels good and it sounds right and you get the effect of it, then it's OK. But if somebody criticizes it and says it's sloppy, it is sloppy, but that's not necessarily anything to get nervous about, there are incredible classic blues records that're just sloppy but do you listen to it and say, 'Ah, that's sloppy, turn it off?' " Robbie laughs again, a warm, infectious laugh. "That's not the point of the thing, the point still remains it's some kind of tradition, the thing that Bob is into. And, also, it's just really his lack of patience, I don't think that there's really any merit to the spontaneous thing. I don't think it gets worse, I think it gets better, the music gets better. I think if you play the song twice and you learn it, that isn't the best it's gonna be to me, but Bob doesn't want to mess with it anymore and if it's got the essence there, then it's fine. I agree with him."

"The Band's stuff seems much more crafted."

"Our stuff," Robbie pauses, searching for the phrase, "there's a thing going on there, there's a fine line we're playing off of. You know, Bob's music is ad-lib music except for the chords and the words, so that's terrific, it's all terrific as long as it comes out in the end."

Ratso senses Robertson is getting restless so he starts to wrap up the interview. "How do you relate to Bob's new sound, with the violin . . . compared to the Sixties thing?"

"I'm not even sure what that was." Robbie sounds incredulous even today. "I don't know. Anyway, with the violin thing, it's fine, it's all part of the picture, the gypsy caravan. It all has its place in the thing, it sounds great to me. A lot of the stuff at the Garden the other night sounded extraordinary to me."

"Yeah, the tour really built up a momentum . . ."

"Yeah, there was no question, that's what I mean that it gets better. I don't think it gets worse, I don't think you lose it, I think it gets better. People get to digest it and understand what they're doing and they're not just running on some nervous anticipation. That's what the *Basement Tapes* are, just very spontaneous but without that nervous anxiety of 'Oh, what's gonna happen next?' If you're playing with that feeling it prevents you from just relaxing, you know, you're not relaxed when you do it, you're on your toes so much that it's tight. *The Basement Tapes* are the loosest thing I've ever heard in my life, including any blues records or anything. That, to me, is the epitome of what looseness is."

Before he'd let Robbie go, Ratso had to interrogate him about *Planet Waves,* one of his favorite Dylan LPs and one that was woefully underrated by critics and public alike. Again, it's the essence of Dylan's art, some songs hastily written, some just fragments of songs, done up in a three-day period before the '74 tour. And, to Ratso's ears, one of the finest rock albums ever made.

"It went by so quick," Robbie smiles, recalling those sessions, "I mean, *Planet Waves* was as good as we could make it in the situation. Under the circumstances, Bob was not, I mean he really didn't have a bag of songs there so it was just kind of a last-minute thing and it came off to me, under those circumstances, I thought that it was extraordinary. But if we had been doing the same thing, since then he's written such songs of a lot more depth and zing to them. There were a lot of simple songs on that album, and people don't necessarily want to hear very simple songs from him. I mean, every once in a while they take a 'Knocking on Heaven's Door' just to kind of get on with it, but basically what they want is a very complex song. . . ."

"Something in the 'Idiot Wind' arena," Ratso interrupts.

"Right, and it wasn't that kind of album at all, just songs like 'Hazel'; they couldn't be more simple."

"I thought 'Hazel' could have been a top-forty hit covered by somebody like Neil Diamond or Sinatra," Ratso offers.

"I like that song," Robbie agrees. "I like a lot of them very much and I thought we played them very good and we got off some unusual stuff."

"Yeah, like that interplay on 'Dirge,' that was fantastic."

"But that's just, we . . ." Robbie stammers. "I never heard that song before, and we sat down and we played it once and that's it. But I know Bob's thing by now, I don't have to deal with that nervous anxiety of what's gonna happen next. I know how to fake and slip to the left and slip to the right and it all sounds how it was supposed to be. I just learned it over the years, I guess, but I really enjoyed that album, we had a lot of fun doing it. Anything you do that fast is really rewarding, I guess. But it wasn't an appropriate Bob Dylan album, that's what the problem was, and it wasn't superunusual so it got a different kind of credit. People put so much weight on the words that it really limited that album, all those songs, 'Going Going Gone,' 'Hazel,' 'Forever Young,' very very simple, as simple as he's ever done and people just thought that it wasn't a real effort and the whole thing went onto him. I listened to that album in somebody's house last week and there's some extraordinary playing on it."

"Incredible ensemble playing," Ratso gushes, "like on 'Never Say Goodbye' . . ."

"But if it doesn't have the complex lyrics then it doesn't even get to the point where it's worth acknowledging, it's like that on Bob's records and I can see why he doesn't want to go to a lot of trouble. It wouldn't matter if he had Booker T and the MG's and the New York Symphony Orchestra playing, people still wouldn't hardly notice it, they'd be concerned whether they can hear that line and they're not interested in accepting him on a musical level, his phrasing, his singing, his effect, his drama."

"Do you think that the Rolling Thunder Revue was a reaction to Tour '74?" Ratso has saved this question for last. "It seemed that Bob was so uptight . . ."

"Oh, I don't know if they had anything to do with one another," Robbie shoots back, a bit defensively. "And if they did . . ."

"C'mon," Ratso again, "he seemed stilted on that tour. I almost felt that this tour was like a response to the impersonality of that thing."

"On Tour '74?" Robbie's incredulous. "I don't think he

was particularly uptight, other than the fact that he hadn't done a tour in eight years! There was a kind of pressure to the thing. . . ."

"Right," Ratso jumps in, "and the Rolling Thunder thing in some respects seems to have taken that pressure off him, the whole revue format. It's not like DYLAN/BAND with all the burdens on his shoulders."

"Yeah, but that's what a tour is," Robbie laughs. "I mean, when the Rolling Stones go on tour that's what it is. You can either accept it as being a very nerve-racking operation or you can say that I've done this a lot of times before and we're just gonna make the best of it. Tour '74 was hard work, just the intensity of the music was so high that it was really straining. Whenever Bob sings with the Band he wants to get an energy level out of it, or I don't know, not necessarily wants to but he does, end up singing things and it's like Thunder and Mountains," Robbie makes some expansive gestures, "you know, screaming at the gods in the sky and everything is so high-pitched, such intensity and energy. I mean, we can certainly do that but we can do a bunch of other things too, and we didn't get to that. I think that his anticipation and nervousness on that tour didn't allow for any laid-back stuff and we do lots of that. We didn't do any of that on Tour '74, it was really like a train going by and I missed that, all those different moods. On the Rolling Thunder I heard more of that and I like that. So that's what the relaxation allows you to do. Rolling Thunder was extraordinary, everyone told me they had a really good time and it was loose and it was fun and it was nice to do something without having a gun at the back of your head."

Ratso thanks Robbie and scoots back downstairs, goes home, and puts on *Planet Waves* for three hours. The next day he cabs it back uptown to the hotel. The crew, the film crew, the security men, most of the tour has gone but the performers are finding it difficult to leave. Only Baez has escaped without much trouble, but Mitchell, Neuwirth, Elliot, Blakley, Soles, T-Bone, even Dylan himself, they all seem to want to linger around and keep the thing going, if only in spirit.

So in the spirit of Plymouth or New Haven or Montreal, Ratso meets Soles up in Joni's room. Today finally is getaway day but they seem to be having trouble packing.

Steven is sitting on the floor noodling on an acoustic guitar, while Joni sprawls across the unmade bed, engrossed in a review of her new album in the *Village Voice.* "Ooh," she says, "this is a great line, '*The Hissing of Summer Lawns* sounds to me like a towering igloo of artistic conceit,' that's a good line." Joni cracks up, as the phone interrupts.

After the call, the reporter plays social director, running down a list of favorite cheap restaurants, of every conceivable ethnic stripe, proposing music clubs, after-hours clubs, in short a full night of entertainment if the performers should decide to linger one more day.

"This is really your town, huh?" Soles admires.

"I think everywhere is Slocum's town," Joni laughs. "He's got every phone number down of every hotel. It's like that joke, picture this, there's a huge crowd, two million people in front of the Vatican, and I'm in the audience with Steve and Steve says, 'Look!' and points up to the balcony. And I say, 'Yeah, but who's that guy up there with Slocum.'"

"I just got Lisa's poem," Joni yawns, searching through the paper debris on her bed for the poem in question. "I skimmed through it and I don't know what her trip is, whether she's a terrible masochist or if she gets something out of it, but it's like very disturbed."

Just then the phone rings and it's a call for Ratso, this one from George Lois. They do a postmortem on the concert and reviews, Lois particularly thrilled that the *Daily News,* "the enemy," gave the center spread to the concert. In the background, Joni borrows Soles' guitar just before he leaves and starts into "Coyote."

"Joni, sing," Ratso holds the receiver aloft, "sing so Lois knows it's you."

She shakes her head.

"She won't sing," Ratso reports, then holds the receiver near the guitar again. "You're his wife's favorite singer. While you were playing at the Garden, George was talking and she told him to shut up."

"There's something in there for him too," Joni snaps. "Look Ratso, I'm starting to get angry now."

"He's a sincere guy," the reporter pleads, "he spent his own fucking money on Rubin. There's no guile in him."

Joni starts singing in a low, hauntingly beautiful voice

and Ratso gives Lois a hurried good-bye and listens to the words.

Every picture has its shadows
And it has some source of light
I'm talking about blindness and sight
The perils of benefactors
And the blessings of parasites
That's what I'm talking about, Ratso's blindness and sight
Threatened by all things
By the devil of cruelty
And we're drawn to all things
By the devil of delight

Mythical devil of the ever-present laws
Pertaining to everyone's blindness and sight

Joni pauses, then breaks into a long introduction, finally starting into "In France They Kiss on Main Street," the opening song on the *Hissing of Summer Lawns* album. Ratso sits enthralled, really hearing the songs for the first time, unfettered by the large halls, the noisy crowds, and the temptations of the arenas.

"Great," he whistles at the end. "Next time in Boston, I'll take you to the Combat Zone, they're great people down there."

"Here's one they'd like." Joni smiles and does "Edith and the Kingpin," Ratso marveling at the lyric, which he was never able to discern during the tour.

"That's a nice one," he admits. "Do 'Coyote.' I want to hear the whole song."

"I only had two verses then in that cafe in Quebec," Joni smiles sheepishly, "that's why I kept repeating it. I was writing it still, so every time I played it I changed it."

"Is it done?"

"No, not yet."

"You're still gonna add shit to it, huh, there are more coyotes on the road, in different cities . . ."

". . . and I collect their pelts," Joni picks up the line and runs with it, "the coyotes in different cities I sing in, and nail 'em up in my shack in Canada on the wall."

"And I bring 'em when I come to the hall," Ratso sings.

"I show them and exhibit them when I come to the hall," Joni embellishes, "shameless hussy that I am." They both laugh, and Joni starts strumming the hypnotic, driving beat of the song, then she starts to sing.

I'll collect their pelts
And I'll tack them upon the wall
In my cabin in Canada
And I bring 'em to exhibit 'em in the hall
Shameless hussy that I am
The most shameless of them all

"That's the end of the song," Ratso screams just as Joni starts:

No regrets coyote
We just come from such different sets of circumstances
I'm up all night in the studios and you're up early on the ranch
You'll be brushing out a brood mare's tail
While the sun is ascending and I'll just be getting home
There's no comprehending just how close to the bone and the skin
And the eyes and the lips and still feel so alone
Still remain related like stations in some relay
You just picked up a hitchhiker
A prisoner of white lines on the freeway

I saw a farmhouse burning down in the middle of nowhere
In the middle of the night
And pulled right past that tragedy
Till we pulled into some roadhouse lights
And a local band was playing there
And the locals were up shaking and kicking on the floor
And the next thing I know the coyote's at my door
He pins me in the corner and he won't take no
He drags me out on the dance floor and we're dancing close and slow
He's got a woman at home, he's got a woman for the night
Now he wants one for the day, why did you have to lead me on that way?
Just picked up a hitchhiker
A prisoner of white lines on the freeway

I looked a coyote right in the face
On the road to Baljennie near my old home town
He went running through the whisker wheat
Chasing some prize down
And a hawk was playing with him, coyote was jumping up and making passes

He has those same eyes just like yours under your dark
    glasses
Privately probing the public halls
Peeking through the keyholes in numbered doors
Where the players lick their wounds and take their
    temporary lovers
And their pills and their powders to get them through this
    passion play

No regrets Coyote
I'll just get off up the way
You just picked up a hitchhiker
A prisoner of white lines on the freeway

Coyotes in the coffee shop and he's staring a hole in his
    scrambled eggs,
He picks up my scent on his fingers while he's watching
    the waitresses' legs
He's too far from the Bay of Thunder, from Appaloosas
    and Eagles and the ten-mile tide
The air-conditioned cubicles and the carbon ribbon rides
Spelling it out so clearly, either he's gonna have to stand
    and fight
Or take off outa here
I tried to run away myself,
I tried to run and hide the trouble with my ego and with
    my playing
Just picked up a hitchhiker
A prisoner of white lines of the highway

I'm gonna take your pelt coyote
Nail it on the wall of my house in Canada
Drag it into the arena, tell them all about you
'Cause I'm a shameless hussy
I'm the most shameless of them all
But I can live, I can really love
And I don't need applause but I do need love

A huge smile sweeps across Ratso's face as Joni starts to
improvise on the spot.

I'm way out in the front lines
And they said I wasn't too electrifying
They said I was kinda ordinary
And they didn't hear one line
Except for a few sensitives
Straining to hear it through the tacky sound
But I'll be around
'Cause I'm fucking good

Joni's screaming now, Ratso's encouraging her with whoops and yelps of his own:

I'm fucking good
I'm not just a writer for woman, oh no!
I'm a writer of common human feelings
Subtle human feelings
Complicated human feelings.

"And you're number five with a bullet," Ratso shouts.

I'm number five with a bullet!
I'm the champion of this song.

Joni collapses the song with laughter. "You knew what I was saying that day," Ratso smiles, "you just blew it all out of proportion. I was just saying that I got different eyes."

"And I was saying don't come around me until you widen your scope a little," Joni bites her lip, " 'cause I can tell now as you hear the lines there's more than one good song here and you really didn't know that. . . . I'm getting so low energy all of a sudden." Joni holds her hand to her head, and collapses on the bed. "I feel like I've absorbed so much, being in the middle of a human experiment, and I've absorbed so much information, I haven't had time to sort it out yet."

"We oughta get Roger in here to sing," Ratso says cheerily.

"C'mon," Joni frowns, "let's not have a party. What did you notice about the prison show?" Joni turns reporter.

"That Dylan sang like he never sang before," Ratso shoots back. "He never sang 'Hattie Carroll' like that to honkies. That song's like a prototype for the Rubin song. You know, I told him to recut the album, and he said it was a question of time. I told him to add Robbie, Ronson, even Ginsberg for karma. Did you hear the new words he added to 'Simple Twist of Fate'?"

"What are the new words?" Joni sits up on the bed.

"I don't know, he made it more Levyesque, more narrative. He changed 'that emptiness inside' line to 'picked up a note.' I hate that change."

"I heard that change, it's superficial," Joni agrees.

"Did you ever hear the change he made in 'If You See

Her Say Hello'? He changed 'if you're making love to her' to 'if you get close to her,' " Ratso shakes his head.

"He's gutless a lot of times," Joni chides.

"C'mon," Ratso yells, "in 'Sara' he comes out with that Chelsea Hotel stanza, that's not gutless, that's the guts pouring out of him. 'Hurricane' isn't gutless. You know that whole story, he came back from France, where he was hiding out from all the assholes that hit on him here. He can't speak a fucking word of French, you saw that in Quebec. He couldn't talk to the audience. They hated him there."

"They didn't hate him," Joni calls out Ratso's exaggeration.

"Yeah, but it was lukewarm in Quebec," he backtracks.

"But that's a provincial town," Joni flashes, "what did you expect? You have to take that into consideration, that's the subtlety of performing and of life and if you get hurt because you don't get enough applause like in a certain situation—"

"How'd you feel at the prison?" Ratso jumps in, "the audience booing, and screaming and catcalling at you and shit."

"I loved it," Joni leaps up and starts to pace the room, "I loved the prison, I loved the confrontation in the third verse of 'Coyote.' I said to that chick who told me to get off, I said, 'You want me to get off? Well, I'm not getting off because my best verse is coming. We came here to give you pleasure, if you can't take it from us that's your problem not ours.' I enjoyed getting feisty and I enjoyed the people at the end. At the end, that guy said, 'C'mon down and dance with me,' and he was in for like seven years on a homicide charge. He had like an eighteen-year sentence. He was a good cat. He didn't have nearly as much jive as Hurricane."

Joni retreats to a chair and curls up, her face turning sour. "Hurricane was so jive. He was like shaking hands with one person and looking toward the next one that was coming to greet him like David Geffen or some-one and the only song he listened to the whole show was the song for him. He talked through that whole show. I got no respect for that cat. He's a phony, he comes on like a spiritually enlightened cat and he's not. That's bullshit. And I told that cat Wayne, his friend, I saw him at the party that last night and he asked if I wanted to send word back to Hurricane. So I told him, 'Yeah, tell him I think he's really an egomaniac, man, if he can't give respect to other performers. Let him use some of his karmic pseudospirituality to cool the audience out if he's so powerful. He's not; he's a fake. He's an innocent man but he's a fake. I got no respect for him.' "

Ratso falls silent, half agreeing with the singer.

"And that whole political thing at the Garden show," Joni flares, "I hated that show, that whole show was bullshit. Even that line, that man in that hell, that's no hell, he may have had trouble but you carry your own hell around with you. You can be in hell in a mansion, in the streets or anywhere. I talked to kids that were in there that were in better shape for their experience, so it was like romantic politics. The whole thing makes me puke."

"Ali was bullshit," Ratso admits. "He left the minute he was through, with his contingent."

"What's the difference between a singer standing up and talking about the prison that people are all in as they walk through the streets and so-called freedom," Joni gropes for the phrase, "the prisoners of spirit . . ."

"Yeah I know, I know," Ratso pooh-poohs, "are the birds free from the chains of the skyway?"

"Let's not get poetic about it," Joni shoots back, "but what about that? To me that's just as heavy, but politics always . . . Nietzsche said something in *Thus Spake Zarathustra,* something like 'around the great actors, circulate the people. What do they know of subtlety with their forty-two thoughts and none of them original?' Today I feel contemptuous. That's one of the feelings that I intend to experience, my contempt."

"No one is saying you shouldn't do that," Ratso returns the service from left field.

"No, I'm not saying I shouldn't either, that's why I stayed in New York for three days to re-examine my attitudes in different spaces of consciousness, away from people consciousness, hyper consciousness, lampshade consciousness . . ."

"Coyote consciousness," Ratso can't resist.

"Out of control consciousness," Joni hits back.

"Let me finish that first story about Dylan and Rubin hooking up," Ratso backtracks a half hour.

"I see there's a certain amount of genuine human motivation and a whole lot of like political bullshit . . ."

"Of course there's gonna be political bullshit involved in getting him out of jail," Ratso screams. "It's gotta be done."

"I mean even in performing, like the inflammation-of-the-crowd psychology . . ."

"Sure, they turn the lights up, boom up the sound . . ."

"The ways the press reviews it. They're impressed with the roars." Joni sinks into thought. "There's so many subtleties to it, but three times I've had to curb my bitterness."

"Sure," Ratso picks up the ball, "what if you came on first? Here's a special guest star, Joni Mitchell."

"It has a lot to do with the position on the bill to the press," Joni admits.

"And that whole thing was supposed to be negated on this tour."

"What," Joni almost shrieks, "billing? Do you know how much politicking there was? Do you know how many times when I started to get too hot in my spot, how like I let people cut my power off? Let me talk to you a moment about the fallacy of power. It depends on what your ideas about power are and how stable you are emotionally, from a point of view of clarity and emotional stability, this is like a philosophical cliché but to the wise man the victor and the loser are both fools. You know, the victor puffed up in his celebration of victory and the fool depressed from losing. Now that's a concept I understand from time to time, unless I get emotionally insecure. It's related to applause and feedback too, and as a result you can be invulnerable to that as a measure of your worth as an artist. But people have different priorities depending on the subtleties of the life experience that they're interested in, so some people find it's hard to follow a roar, maybe it's really harder for them to follow a silence. It's bad if somebody bombs out there; it's hard to go on like if people have been put in a pensive mood. Like it's hard to change moods and everything, like my main reason for coming out on this tour initially was to see the show. Then I was going up to Toronto to visit some folks; then I was going to Vancouver to see my parents. It was like a cycle, I had my ticket and everything, then I got sucked into it and the magic happened for me at Niagara Falls."

Joni's cigarette is all ash by now and she absentmindedly

flicks it onto the carpet. "I couldn't get off it and I got sick then too, and I had no pipes or anything and I didn't sing any familiar material and I was going on as a front runner. Now OK, dig the odds for making a splash, going on in that position in the show, and also having it manipulated so that even your exit offstage is controlled in a way. I allowed it to be controlled for a while . . ."

"Who controlled it?" Ratso cuts in.

"The people involved. The musicians in the show. Like three times I had this ego battle and it was emotional immaturity, knowing that it really didn't make a difference in that my longevity as an artist is not affected in any way by what position I'm in in this thing or whether they say Joni Mitchell was ineffective or whether they don't even mention my name in the article, but from time to time when you get emotionally low I begin to say, 'Like wait a minute, I'm a sophisticated musician in a naive kind of way. I'm a sophisticated observer . . ."

"You know what," Ratso leans in toward Joni and whispers conspiratorially, "you're as good a songwriter as anybody on the tour."

"You're right," Joni blurts, "see! Remember when we talked and you put me in a bag with women and I said that you should come around me when you widen your horizons and stop limiting me to gender, you know. Because really, I have a lot of anima-animus, a lot of male perspective. I'm talking about roles; it has nothing to do with gender."

A minute later, Soles comes in and he and Joni start frantically packing, as the singer has a plane to catch in about an hour. Ratso just sits back and watches the frenetic activity.

"I have this terrible itch in my throat," Joni complains. "Maybe it's hotel ear rot. This room is too classy. I really wanted to skid it before I left town." She shrugs.

"You should have stayed at my place," Ratso laughs, "you could have crashed on my couch."

"My voice is gone," Joni rasps, "I sound like an old spade. I lost like ten notes on this tour. They are just gone forever. I'm just a prisoner of notes. I guess I'll have to do more with the four I have left."

Joni's almost finished packing when Soles lugs out the huge framed plaque that Imhoff has presented to all the performers, a plaque made up of all the backstage buttons, ticket stubs, and ID cards from the tour. Joni frowns at the sight of this.

"Want this, Ratso?" she suddenly brightens.

"Jesus, I'd love it." The reporter laughs at the irony of getting thirty-five backstage buttons at once at the end of the tour when he couldn't cop one during the whole trip.

"It's yours," Joni smiles, "there's no way I can get it back."

Slocum is truly touched and as they start down the hall, lugging the suitcases, he realizes how fond he's grown of the singer, and how much more appreciative he is of her work. And as he hails the Checker and copes with getting all her luggage together and getting her frazzled self together, and when she pecks him a good-bye kiss and climbs into the cab, and heads off toward LaGuardia, with just her blond mane visible as the cab disappears slowly into the late-afternoon Madison Avenue traffic, and as he turns and walks back into the hotel, the reporter feels a strange emptiness inside.

An emptiness that's assuaged a bit when he immediately inherits her room and starts making a battery of calls. He calls Lois, he tries Dylan, he calls Kinky, and then he calls Rubin in jail, greeting him with "Carter, you motherfucker."

"Hey Larry, you son of a rascal you, what's doing?" the boxer laughs.

"I need to get a quote from you, a reaction to the concert, a quote."

"Dylan is a fantastic human being . . ." Rubin trails off.

"Keep going, keep going," Ratso chants.

"That's it," Rubin stops, "that's it."

"You gotta give me some copy, schmuck," Slocum screams.

"You write it," Carter yells. "You write it, you smuck, say I said it. Just don't say nothing bad about Bob."

"But Rubin . . ." Ratso starts to protest.

"You do it. You're a writer, you know what to do. Listen, smuck, I gotta go, speak to you soon."

Ratso shakes his head and decides to call Phil Ochs. Phil had deteriorated since the last time Ratso had seen him, at Porco's birthday party. He was more ragged, deeper into the depressive cycle of the manic-depressive syndrome that ravaged his soul. He had taken to drinking again, and mutual friends had reported to Ratso during the tour that Phil had been found sleeping in alleyways, and flop hotels, and one night, even in the bathroom of the Chelsea Hotel. But Ochs had attended the Garden concert and he had seemed a bit better to Ratso, at least as well as he was when the reporter lived with him the previous year. And, at the urging of some friends, Phil had left the city and was living in the Rockaways in Queens, crashing at his sister's place. It was there that Ratso reached him.

"Phil, how are you doing?"

"I'm hanging in," the meek, gentle voice fights its way out of his body.

"What did you think of the show?"

"I loved Dylan." Phil perks up a bit, as he did whenever he discussed Bob with Ratso. "I thought it was the best I'd ever seen him."

"Really." Ratso, unaccountably enough, seems pleased.

"Absolutely, absolutely, because of the new material. And the band was incredible, especially the violin. I loved the new material. It's classic. I loved 'Durango.' The whole thing was just incredible."

The reporter tries to draw Phil out but the folksinger was really not in the mood to talk and Ratso, being no stranger to the terrors of the dampening of the spirit, respects the emotional state that he found Phil in. Slocum wishes Phil well and hangs up, totally unaware that this would be one of the last times that he would ever hear that sometimes soft, sometimes vibrant voice.

Ratso gets restless again so he wanders down to the lobby for a breather, and five minutes later, Kemp comes out of the elevator, suitcases in hand. A curious bond had begun to grow between these two adversaries, an admission that beneath the built-in role conflict that set them at each other's throats, beneath that automatic hostility, these two men still managed to share certain things. A deep admiration for Dylan, of course. And a love of lox and salmon, although Ratso could never stomach the other fishes Lou thrived on. And, a common respect for the merits of individual entrepreneurship whether it be supplying Sunday brunch to the multitudes or providing the copy in the newspaper that the masses read with their brunch. It seemed that they both instinctively realized that the next day that newspaper would hold only the bones from the fish of the previous day's meal.

So it was a gesture of camaraderie when Ratso leaps out into Madison Avenue and waits five minutes, in the shivering cold, finally flagging down a Checker for the fish peddler. He opens the door.

"Well, Lou, this is it," Ratso smiles.

"Yeah, well you behave yourself and don't bother Bob."

"You know, I think I'm going to miss you," Ratso smiles again.

"Too bad I can't say the same," Louie cracks and starts into the cab.

"C'mon, don't I even get a handshake?" Slocum pouts.

Louie pauses and grudgingly grabs Ratso's fingertips giving them a short, firm squeeze with his own. "Take care, Ratso," Louie half-smiles.

"Bye, bye," Ratso waves as the cab pulls out and then he quickly runs back into the hotel, to prepare the bait and think about the biggest catch of them all, waiting up there in that room with the fishing season only seconds old.

But Dylan was no easy catch. For days Ratso tried to snare him for an interview, calling his room at all hours, hanging out by the hotel, hanging out with him at parties, at a film screening, even bringing Sara some chicken soup direct from the Lower East Side when she was bedridden with a cold. Then finally, Ratso got a bite.

It happened late one morning. Ratso woke Dylan up and the singer told him to call him back in an hour and they could do the interview then. Ratso took that to mean over the phone, and an hour later, with his equipment set up, he dialed the hotel and coolly requested Dylan's room. Two rings go by.

"Ratso," a bleary but cheerful voice floats downtown.

"Yeah, how'd you know it was me," the reporter wonders.

"Listen, I'm talking with my beloved . . ."

"Oh, no," Ratso curses.

"You just interrupted me again," Dylan jokes, "every time I'm talking to her the phone rings and it's you, or there's a knock on the door and it's you, every time I'm trying to talk to her and get some really serious discussion out of the way, the fucking phone rings and it's you or the doorbell."

"Hey, man," Ratso gets indignant, "I haven't been sucking on your soul today and I don't want to get in between you and her at all."

Dylan chuckles. "All right, so what do you want? What do you need right now?"

"Well, I have a list of questions."

"OK," Dylan says amiably enough, "give 'em to me."

"All right, it's the end of the tour, right . . ."

"What do you mean?" Dylan objects, "end of what tour?"

"Well, what is it?" Ratso probes, "a hiatus?"

"Hiatus? You mean Hyannis?"

"Oh, you're starting in Hyannis again?" Two can play the game. "Playing for the hoi polloi? Is this is a resting point now?"

"What resting point?" Dylan laughs. "We never rest."

"I know, man," Ratso testifies. "Do you ever sleep? What are you doing now?"

"What am I doing right now?" Dylan pimps.

"No, not right now, I mean in terms of your public persona."

"Public persona, huh?" Dylan spits the words out warily.

"In other words, you just completed a tour . . ."

"No!" the singer shouts. "Yeah, well we're regrouping."

"OK, a regrouping. And then what?" Ratso pries.

"Then we're gonna hit it again," Bob oozes enthusiasm, "we'll be out there again."

"People should be looking for you?" Ratso asks and Dylan laughs. "Where are you gonna be next?"

"Well, lookit, there's no way of knowing that at this point, there's no way of knowing nothing. I mean we just play, we don't do the paperwork."

"Right, I agree with you," Ratso approves. "Talk a little bit about the spirit of the tour, because I've never seen such a great, I mean I've been on the road with a couple of groups and I've never seen such a close camaraderie and brotherhood and feeling of . . ."

"Well, that's because we're all brothers and sisters," Dylan says half-reverently and half-caustically.

"I've seen that closeness before but all I'm saying is that I've seen less ego clashes on this tour than on any tour I've seen."

"OK," Dylan's getting impatient, "what's the next one?"

"That's it? That's the answer?" Ratso feigns shock.

"Yeah, what's the next question," Dylan grabs the offensive.

"How do you respond to the one tack that people take to attack the tour, namely that it's the same old shit, that the original concept of playing for the people has been subverted and it's the same crass commercialism?"

"Is this a question, Ratso?" Dylan sounds like he could fall asleep before the question is articulated. "Is this a question?"

"Yeah, what was the original guiding philosophy behind what you were doing?"

Bob whispers to someone in the room for a few seconds then comes back to the phone. "What's the philosophy behind anything, Ratso? When a bricklayer goes to work every morning, what's his philosophy?"

"Well, he's probably got a pretty well-defined philosophy even though it may not be articulated," the reporter remembers his sociology courses.

"All right," Dylan yields, "lemme sleep on that one."

"All right, sleep on that one," Ratso allows, "because what I was leading up to, was, hello, are you still there?"

"Yeah," Dylan yawns.

"The question was that people have attacked this tour—"

"They've attacked it?" Dylan sounds perfectly incredulous.

"Yeah, I've read attacks on it," Ratso barks.

"Who?"

"*Rolling Stone*, for example, after they ripped up my article and wrote their own bureaucratic garbage . . ."

"You know why they attacked the tour, Ratso?" Dylan leaps in, a mile a minute. "Because they hadn't seen it. They sit in their offices on their asses and can only fantasize about it. They are the establishment. OK, so you can't be responsible for people that haven't seen the tour, that's like somebody who doesn't know you."

"What about that early publicity that it was only gonna be in small clubs?"

"I don't know how that got started. I didn't start any of that stuff."

"Did you read the Paul Simon attack on you in *Newsweek* yet?" Ratso casually slips one in.

"No," Dylan yelps, "read it to me."

"OK, basically it says, 'But Simon the cerebral and careful craftsman of some of pop's most memorable melodies, "Bridge over Troubled Waters," "Mrs. Robinson" ' . . .'"

"Who remembers those?" Dylan jumps in. "What meaning have these songs in anybody's life?"

"Wait, wait," and Ratso continues to quote, " ' "Pop music is in a terrible state right now," he says. "It stinks. Only a handful of people are doing something good . . . Dylan comparisons make me emotional," says Simon. "There's hardly a point of comparison except we're the same age. He writes a lot of words. I write few words. In the 1960's Dylan for the first time used the folk tradition of Woody Guthrie and sang a grown-up lyric. He single-handedly took the folkie emphasis on words and made it the predominant style of music in the '70's. But what he spawned is boring." Pensive and soft voiced, Simon gazes out of his picture window overlooking New York's Central Park. "When I listen to Dylan I think, Oh no, not the same three or four chord melody again . . ." ' "

"Hey lookit, Ratso," Bob bursts, "you can play a song with one chord."

Ratso laughs. " 'Simon goes on, "The staple of American popular music is all three- or four-chord, country- or rock-oriented now. There's nothing that goes back to the richest, most original form of American popular music—Broadway and Tin Pan Alley—in which sophisticated lyrics are matched with sophisticated melodies." ' "

"Hey, Ratso," Dylan in again, "you can play a song with one note."

" 'Simon says, "When I started writing I didn't think there was any space for me between Dylan and the Beatles—they had it covered. I was writing little psychological tunes based on wandering melodies. Now I'm trying to get closer to Broadway and Tin Pan Alley." ' "

"Well, I hope he gets where he wants to go," Dylan laughs.

"But he's not the only one. There are lots of people who say that you're a great lyricist but you just don't understand music."

"Oh really," Bob spits. "Well I don't understand music, you know. I understand Lightning Hopkins. I understand Leadbelly, John Lee Hooker, Woody Guthrie, Kinky Friedman. I never claimed to understand music, Ratso, if you ever heard me play the guitar you'd know that." The singer laughs. "I'm an artist," he adds.

"I like your guitar playing, man," Ratso steps to his defense, "I love your harmonica playing too. George Lois' secretary, Blanche, says you're the greatest harmonica player she's ever heard."

"She's probably right then," Dylan giggles.

"Maybe. I think you're a great harmonica player and—"

"You've seen the show, Ratso, how many times? Thirty? Forty?" Dylan interrupts. "Have I ever let you down onstage?"

"Never, man, never," Ratso knows without having to think.

"OK, so why don't you tell them that," Dylan shouts.

"I will man, I will," the writer promises.

"You saw the show," Dylan continues. "Well, it goes without saying, we'll follow anybody."

"What do you think of that charge, though, that Simon is making? That your music is boring . . ."

"Well, maybe he's just bored, you know. I really can't tell ya, I don't know the man."

"Like you're making a new kind of music now I think . . ." Ratso says.

"Well, I'm always changing, always moving around, forging new paths. I'm blazing a trail. I don't know what Paul Simon's doing."

"What are you listening to nowadays?"

"What am I listening to?" Dylan pauses. "Uhhh, you know who's really good? Oum Kalsoum."

"Who's that?" the reporter wonders.

"C'mon, Ratso," Dylan mocks.

"I'm not hip to him, man," Ratso confesses.

"All right," Dylan laughs. "First of all, it's not a him."

"Who is it?"

"Well, you asked me and I told ya. Otherwise I don't listen to nothing. I play my own music and I listen to that."

"I don't believe you."

"I like 'Earth Angel,' " Dylan says impishly.

"I know you loved 'No Woman, No Cry' by Marley when I played it. You loved that, you asked me for the fucking lyrics."

"Well, I like that the same way that I like 'When A Man Loves a Woman.' Same thing."

"Jerry Wexler says your music is—"

"My music is pagan," Dylan interrupts.

"He didn't say that at all," Ratso resents the interruption, "he said it was cantorial."

"Well, I don't know what that means but you're getting it right here from the horse's mouth."

"Cantorial means possessing the qualities of a cantor in the Jewish religion," the scribe turns Webster.

"No, no," Dylan disagrees, "cantorial means that which has to do with food and banquet ceremonies."

"No, that's not cantorial. That's gustatorial. Anyway, what kind of direction is your music taking?"

"Well, you'll see. We're gonna keep it a surprise and everybody's gonna be surprised because everybody thinks the music boom is all over. They don't know, they just don't know where it's gonna come from next. That's all, they're all looking to find somebody in some little folkie town that's gonna bring it to 'em, be the new Paul Simon. They're all looking for a new Paul Simon. Or a new Bruce Springfield, you know."

"What do you think of Springfield, by the way?"

"I met him and I liked him. I played 'Born to Run' on a jukebox and he's a great singer and he's got a great band. But I haven't heard his music so much recently."

"Haven't you heard the *Born to Run* LP?"

"No, but I been meaning to play the whole LP. I mean how many hours in the day is there, Ratso? There aren't that many hours for me to sit around listening to record albums."

"What about when you're home, you listen then don't you?"

"Nah, I don't," Dylan drawls.

"What do you do?"

"I'm working all the time, man, just doing what I'm doing. You been seeing me for the past six weeks. You know."

"Oh, man, I hardly see anything," Ratso whines, "I see such a small segment of your life. I see a very public segment of your life. I don't know what goes on behind closed doors, that's a good song by the way, and the first time I was on the camper was last night."

"So what?" Dylan snaps impatiently.

"So I learned a little more about you."

"OK, keep going," Dylan interrupts, "what else you got?

I think we're doing pretty good. I think it's almost wrapped up, right?"

"Almost," Ratso lies, "I got a couple more. You're doing new songs and a lot of people in the audience are expecting the old ones . . ." Ratso hears a muffled sound of conversation at the other end. "Is this boring you, man," the reporter screams, annoyed, " 'cause if it is . . ."

"Hey, you never get what you expect, Ratso," Dylan is back, "ultimately you're let down. That's one of the first rules, basic rules, expectations you know. If you have big expectations you're gonna be let down. You can't have any expectations, you know. You stay on the borderline and then you move when the space unfolds."

"But people do have expectations . . ."

"Well, that's their problem, Ratso, that's their own problem. We can't account for everybody who's walking around having expectations. I mean who gives a shit."

"Were you pleased with the reception to the new songs . . . seriously," Ratso adds a caveat.

"Yeah," Dylan admits.

"Why do you think people cheer so much at the beginning of 'Oh, Sister'?"

"I think, uh, Jacques Levy asked me that, too. What do you think?"

"I think it's 'cause it sounds like another song," Ratso admits.

"I think they just think it's another song, right," Dylan agrees, "I don't know what song they think it is, but whatever, it's all right."

"Well a lot of your songs sound alike. 'Hurricane' sounds like 'All Along the Watchtower' at the beginning, right?"

"Right, sometimes that happens," Dylan laughs, "sometimes I influence myself."

"I wouldn't be embarrassed in the least by that, man, I'd be proud to have written another song from one of your other songs, man."

"Well, you have," Dylan chuckles, " 'Combat Zone.' "

"C'mon," Ratso scoffs, "what was it like playing in jail for you?"

"Look, man, an audience is an audience . . ."

"Oh come on, that wasn't a paying audience, that was a captive audience."

"They were a good audience. Hey, we got it wrapped up now, right?" Dylan is itching.

"Well, no, a couple more. I want to talk about fame now."

"What?" Dylan wants him to rewind.

"Fame. F-A-M-E. I think what's most interesting about this tour is your accessibility, you going out again and doing the things that you did when you were younger . . ."

"Yeah, yeah," Dylan agrees.

"Was 'Idiot Wind' like getting all those feelings about fame out, exorcising them, and now you're able to deal with—"

"I don't want to answer them kinds of direct questions," Dylan starts to bristle, "I mean what can I say? Give you an answer of yes or no?"

"Well, then, give me an answer of what's it like coping with being a public figure," Ratso redirects.

"A public figure, well, it can be something that walks on you. I just decided that it ain't gonna walk on me. It can be the horse, riding on you, sooner or later, but you just gotta realize that you can ride it and drive it into the ground, if necessary. But either you've gotta use it or it's gonna use you, one or the other."

"Well, for a while there, what was happening? You were letting it use you?"

"For a while there, yeah, it was quite a surprise for me when it happened and I didn't know how to deal with it. I mean who knows how to deal with that stuff."

"Why did you go out on tour with the Band in '74?"

"It seemed like the righteous thing to do."

"Were you happy with that tour?"

Dylan clears his throat. "No, no man, I wasn't happy with that tour like I was with this one."

"Oh man, there was such a difference," Ratso gushes. "You looked stilted on that tour, you didn't look comfortable, you didn't look happy."

"No," Bob admits, "I wasn't comfortable and I wasn't happy."

"And you were singing . . ." Ratso jumps in.

"I wasn't comfortable and I wasn't happy but that's got nothing to do with the tour. I don't think any of the guys were comfortable and happy but that's got nothing to do with it."

"Well, it does. Because people who relate to you not as a friend but as an image, a media person . . ."

"Look, they can see me in person," Dylan jumps in, "I'll be available. People can see me in person all over the fucking world, they can see me in person. It's just gonna take some time to get around to everybody but they can't get it all in one shot like they think they can. They can feel it firsthand, right up close, and they'll be given that opportunity."

"That's great, you mean the tour is gonna roll all around the world," Ratso enthuses.

"Yeah, this tour ain't gonna stop."

"That's great, that's really righteous. The thing with the last tour was that it was just—"

"A timekiller," Dylan finishes the question. "Something to do for a period of time. It was good, though. I been on tours that were worse than that."

"Hey man, *Planet Waves* had just come out then, right? Now *Planet Waves* is a great fucking LP, one of my favorites, but the album itself seems to be very ambivalent. That LP seems to spread the kind of feeling I got when I saw you on that tour, which was like you didn't seem to know if you really wanted to be there or wanted to be watching the river flow."

"Yeah, I got kind of held up on that tour, you know. I mean, I wasn't really in control of the situation. Nobody was in control. We were just shuffled around from airport to limo to hotel lobby to hockey rinks. I felt like Willis Reed. And in order for me to do whatever it is that I do, I have to have control and I didn't have too much control on that specific tour. Look, that Bob Dylan and the Band tour was a valid tour, no question about that."

"Well, it was valid but people who saw it and listened to it on the LP musta—"

"Well, you see, they had bad expectations. They shouldn't have expected anything."

"Wait a minute, man," Ratso yells, "I know a lot of people who paid a lotta money, and they didn't necessarily have it, and they save up money to go to your concerts and they expect, uh, I don't know what they expect."

"They expect to be turned on," Dylan finishes it.

"Exactly, they expect to really feel a vibe. But on that Band tour in '74, a lot of people didn't feel that vibe."

"Right, well, but that's all in the past," Bob says cheerfully. "People tell me who've seen some of these recent shows that they'll remember them as the ultimate, whatever that means."

"Also what excited me about this tour was that you were doing two different things. You were singing and you were doing the film. That really excited me. I'd seen your movies but I never had seen you directing a film and that was exciting because I felt you stole the whole *Pat Garrett* film with that cameo role, you were like Chaplin up there on the screen. Why did you decide to direct the film?"

"Well, after a certain period of time, somebody just had to take charge of the shooting," Dylan laughs. "You'll see that when the film comes out. There's no way that I could explain that."

"Well, when are we gonna see the film?"

"Uh, uh, you're really low, Ratso," Bob laughs. "When are we gonna see the film? Well, when do you want to see the film?"

"Well, I haven't even seen *Eat the Fucking Document* yet," the reporter growls.

"Eat the Fucking Document?" Dylan laughs at the added adjective. "You know it's called *Fuck the Document* now."

"I want to see that fucking film," Ratso rants. "Arrange a screening for me."

"Listen, I'll talk to you tomorrow," Dylan decides to bail out before Ratso gets too much further out of control.

"No, wait!" he yelps, "I have two more questions only. By the way, do you have a name for the film yet?"

"Not yet."

"OK, Hurricane was a big influence, I mean, in prison, framed, losing an eye and all that shit. Was that a big influence on you deciding to go out on tour again?"

"No, it was a coincidence that I met Hurricane. I wanted to go out and play again. I had already made my mind up last spring."

"Before France or after?" Ratso probes.

"I was in Corsica."

"What made you decide it? Describe the scene, what it was like when you first said, 'I want to do this again, it's in my blood.'"

"Yeah, right," Dylan pauses, collecting his thoughts, "I was just sitting in a field overlooking some vineyards, the sky was pink, the sun was going down and the moon was sapphire, and I recall getting a ride into town with a man with a donkey cart and I was sitting on this donkey cart, bouncing around on the road there, and that's when it flashed on me that I was gonna go back to America and get serious and do what it is that I do, because by that time people didn't know what it was that I did. All kinds of people, most people don't know what I do, only the people that see our show know what it is that I do, the rest of the people just have to imagine it."

"Well, what's your concept of what you do, verbally?"

"A picture's worth a thousand words, Ratso," Dylan smiles at his end.

"What is it you do? Is it like psychodrama?"

"Yeah, you could say that," Dylan hedges.

"How would you describe it?" Ratso presses.

"I don't know, it's all I do. It drives me crazy to think about it. That's your job, to describe it, I just do it." Dylan turns serious: "It's all I've ever done. I don't know anything else."

"You know a lot, man. You know film. Howard Alk tells me you're a natural film genius."

"I'm gonna know film, man," Dylan bubbles, "we're gonna make some movies that are gonna blow Hollywood apart. Remember how we blew the music scene apart?"

"When was that?" Ratso plays coy.

"Remember in the '60s? All the music you're listening to is a product of all that stuff that went down in the '60s. Phil Ochs, Tom Paxton, the Fugs, the Byrds, Joan Baez, Buffy, it can go on forever."

"I agree with you, man," Ratso smiles.

"There is nothing that really strikes me as being really new or really old although that's not to say I'm bored with it, because I'm not bored with it."

"Well, what is in your blood, man? Making movies or touring . . ."

"Making love and making music is in my blood."

"Which has the priority?"

"Uhhhh, that's hard to tell, sometimes I wonder about that myself."

"Well, most of the time I would much rather listen to you sing 'Sooner or Later One of Us Must Know,' than get a blow job."

"I'd rather sing it than get a blow job," Dylan chuckles.

"Last question. Have you been writing on this tour?"

"I been writing some letters, that's about all, yeah, personal letters."

"Any songs?" Ratso hopes.

"I have some things on scraps of paper."

"Gonna put them together?"

"I might, yeah."

"Anything you wanna—"

"Anything I want to sing right now?" Dylan anticipates. "No."

"No fragments, no exclusives?"

"No, not really, Ratso. You'll get it though, you'll get it."

Ratso hangs up and starts to work on something else when the phone rings. It's Dylan.

"Hey Ratso, I've been thinking, maybe we should take out that stuff about the blow jobs?"

"OK man, OK, what do you want to say?"

"What's the question again?"

"Uh, 'What's in your blood, making music or making movies?' " Ratso repeats.

Dylan hesitates. "Uh, uh, making music, making movies, making love, it's all in my blood. Look, I'm just outgrowing, er, settling my old accounts but the restoration of honor is also still in my blood."

16

And that was pretty much it for Ratso and the Rolling Thunder Revue. At least the Rolling Thunder Revue, take one. Everyone had left for home, everyone except for Dylan and McGuinn, who was hanging around the city to do some writing with Jacques Levy. And, of course, the musicians like Stoner, Wyeth, Ronson, and Mansfield who call New York home.

So that meant a generous dose of more sleepless nights, all-night jams, 4 A.M. tequila sans sunrises. More rock 'n roll time. There were things like Ronson's demo sessions, a boring party at Norman Mailer's flat in Brooklyn Heights, and a better party at Mel Howard's loft where the New Yorrican poets read their insurrectionist verse and Ratso later dragged Dylan over to a phonograph and made him listen to *Planet Waves*.

The reporter cues up "Tough Mama," a pile driver of a hard rock song, the poet howling his ode to his resilient muse over the fervid torrid flagellations of the Band.

"This is fucking brilliant," Ratso is shouting in Dylan's ear as the song screeches to an end.

"Hey, that is good," Dylan bubbles, "that is good. Play that again, play that one again, Ratso."

And, of course, there were those nights at the Other End, just like before the six weeks of sheer insanity. And that's where the camper stopped that night of the Mailer party, unloading its cargo into the Bleecker Street bar.

Dylan strode briskly if soddenly into the dimly lit club and immediately checked out the jukebox. Imhoff bounced into the kitchen, which was already closed and started cooking hamburgers for a 4 A.M. snack.

Ratso moseyed over and sat down next to McGuinn and Dylan who were cached behind a post at a small table. Everyone was pretty well blitzed so the talk was sparse, the trio content to listen to the jukebox in relative silence. Until three old Byrds songs came up, in a row.

"Hey McGuinn," Dylan gave the ex-Byrd a fuzzy stare, "you didn't do your best songs on this tour, man."

Roger shrugged and mumbled something.

Dylan turned and focused his stare on Ratso. "Hey, the press never picked up on the tour, man." A sly smile creeped across the artist's face. "But the people, man. They know, they know what Rolling Thunder is."

And Ratso suddenly flashed that Dylan was right. And he realized that after being in close proximity to the songwriter, after being on and off and on the tour, after seeing the concerts and the parties, the film scenes and the breakfast-table scenes, the interviews and the outerviews, Ratso realized that his respect and admiration for the poet had grown immeasurably. Simple gestures, like the glove exchange that frigid day in Toronto, or the rabid defense of Blakley in that misunderstanding over the first *Rolling Stone* article, or the touching way Bob cooled out Phil up there on Gerdes stage when the troubled troubador mistakenly thought his long-time colleague and friend was walking out on his tortured performance, it was these small things that convinced the reporter that Dylan was back on dry land, back out in the unfrozen traffic, unfettered by the armor Bloomfield had perceived.

Ratso thought about the other persons he had encountered who had been blessed or cursed by FAME, senators, movie stars, sports idols, other musicians and artists, and he realized that if Dylan was protected by armor from human interchange, then these others were walking around in masoleums. And Ratso smiled to himself, and then a chill ran down his spine as he remembered the public performances of this man fame had grappled with. He remembered Plymouth Rock, and the Halloween show when Dylan tried to sing with his mask on, and the big halls, and Waterbury, how could he ever forget that night, when the singer dedicated one of his favorite songs to him.

And he recalled Burlington and that furnace of a gym and the makeup streaming over Dylan's sweat-soaked face. The list could go on and on, but in the end Ratso knew that Dylan was right. He had never let the reporter down onstage, never. And Ratso peered out through his dark glasses at that little genius, who was downing tequila after tequila, alone in a crowd, celebrating privately in public, and he thought about all the great songs over the years, the songs that shook empires, the songs that made men weep, the songs that turned around so many people's visions and ideals and aspirations, the reporter himself being one of the many who were rescued by "Like a Rolling Stone."

And then, as if by magic, that song started playing, the majestic Bloomfield guitar filling the stale bar air, and then that voice, that icon of pride and rage and torment and despair and, yes, hope. "How does it feeellll?" it asked, and Ratso looked to the creator for an answer. Dylan just slumped down a bit more in his chair, pulled his hat over his face, and downed another shot.

"Hey, schmuck," the would-be accountant leaned over to the superstar, "listen to this. You didn't do your best songs on this tour either."

Dylan shot up and peered at Ratso. "Well, what about you? You didn't do nothing on this tour, man. I didn't read one article you wrote. Why don't you go home and write, man? Produce something. Do it, man, go home and write."

And with that, Dylan and the Thunder stragglers moved out to the camper and piled in. And Mooney took the wheel and headed up Bleecker Street, toward Lexington Avenue and the Westbury, hitting every pothole for spite, the real rolling thunder, on their way home.

And Ratso just stood there out on Bleecker Street and watched as the Executive slowly passed from his early-morning sight and then the reporter slowly made his way home. To write.

Postscript

And Larry wrote, and gradually began settling back into his old routine. Until he picked up his mail at his post-office box a week after they had all gone. He spied a letter from Lisa, postmarked West Dover, Vermont. He pulled the ruled paper out of the envelope and started reading the handwritten letter.

12/10/75

Larry,

It's over. It went by so fast. I don't regret one minute of being hustled or shit on though. It was definitely worth it.

I just got home today. I'm speeding. I'm sitting on my bed and I feel the wind coming in through the uninsulated walls.

I'm writing because I want to know if you're going to come up here or if you want to see me in N.Y. to interview me for the book. It would probably be better if you came here just because it's very mellow. I don't care, though. If you want to come tell me and I'll tell you how to get here. Would you also send me the address of the office Ava works at. She told it to me real fast and I forgot it. I need it because no one ever gave me a release to sign for the film. I gave her my address but she was pretty high when I gave it to her the other night so she might have lost it.

You know, you should be very grateful to God. You are very lucky or maybe fortunate is a better word to have gotten so close with Bob. He really trusts you. At first I didn't think he really did because Evans and Larry (film guy) and a lot of people were telling me you were the joke of the tour. People were calling you things like a sleazy prick. You can be adjetating often (excuse my spelling).

Well, anyway, Gary told me Bob thinks I'm okay.

I'm very blissed out, he wrote love, Bobby on the picture, you wouldn't believe. I miss him already and it's only 2 days.

Allan gave me some good criticisms on my poetry. Do you know his address? I have to send him my address so he can send back my manuscript. That's what he wants to do. So if you know both Ava's and his it would be far out.

What do you think of Bob Weir? I love him. I'm going to have to come see Kingfish. He said he'd remember me next time we meet.

Well, I'm really fucked up and I'm just writing the first things that come into my head so if I keep on it'll be a 10 page letter about nothing. Write to me and tell me what's happening. Oh, I asked T-Bone about the song they wrote about me and he said if I didn't hear it in the future, I'd hear it in the pasture. That's a good line. Take care.

Love,
Lisa

P.S. I'm sorry the letter is so sloppy. I'm too fucked up now to write it over. You should take me along with you on the next tour. Bob approves.

I was particularly interested when Gurdjieff said that the same performers would have to act and dance in the "White Magician" scene and in the "Black Magician" scene; and that they themselves and their movements had to be attractive and beautiful in the first scene and ugly and discordant in the second.

"You understand that in this way they will see and study all sides of themselves; consequently the ballet will be of immense importance for self-study," said G.

I understood this far from clearly at the time, but I was struck by a certain discrepancy.

"In the notice I saw in the paper it was said that your 'ballet' would be staged in Moscow and that certain well-known ballet dancers would take part in it. How do you reconcile this with the idea of self-study?" I asked. "They will not play and dance in order to study themselves."

"All this is far from being decided," said G. "And the author of the notice you read was not fully informed. All this may be quite different. Although, on the other hand, those taking part in the ballet will see themselves whether they like it or not."

"And who is writing the music?" I asked.

"That also is not decided," said G. He did not say anything more, and I only came across the "ballet" again five years later.

—P. D. Ouspensky
In Search of the Miraculous

ABOUT THE AUTHOR

LARRY SLOMAN was born in New York City and graduated Phi Beta Kappa from Queens College. He received a Master's Degree in Sociology from the University of Wisconsin. He has written extensively for *Rolling Stone, Crawdaddy, High Times,* and was articles editor for *Avant-Garde.* He is currently working on a book on marijuana. In his spare time, he collaborates on rock songs.